As it is Written

BOOK ONE:
A Study of Last Things

Christopher A. Clanton

This book is a work of non-fiction. Unless otherwise noted, the author and the publisher make no explicit guarantees as to the accuracy of the information contained in this book and in some cases, names of people and places have been altered to protect their privacy.

LifeRich Publishing is a registered trademark of The Reader's Digest Association, Inc.

LifeRich Publishing books may be ordered through booksellers or by contacting:

LifeRich Publishing
1663 Liberty Drive
Bloomington, IN 47403
www.liferichpublishing.com
844-686-9607

Because of the dynamic nature of the Internet, any web addresses or links contained in this book may have changed since publication and may no longer be valid. The views expressed in this work are solely those of the author and do not necessarily reflect the views of the publisher, and the publisher hereby disclaims any responsibility for them.

Any people depicted in stock imagery provided by Getty Images are models, and such images are being used for illustrative purposes only. Certain stock imagery © Getty Images.

Authorized (King James) Version (AKJV)
KJV reproduced by permission of Cambridge University Press, the Crown's patentee in the UK.

ISBN: 978-1-4897-4232-2 (sc)
ISBN: 978-1-4897-4231-5 (e)

Print information available on the last page.

LifeRich Publishing rev. date: 07/06/2022

Contents

To the Reader

To the reader; to my fellow soldiers in the trenches; to the watchmen on the walls; to the weary pilgrims the beloved saints of the Most High God, grace, truth, and peace be unto you from God the Father, and our Lord Jesus Christ.

I have often sat and wrote and rewrote this opening discourse to my fellow pilgrims, with both a bit of frustration and trembling. I find myself an unworthy man whose been tasked with the daunting duty of slaying a two-headed giant. Thank God, he can make the unworthy worthy, may he alone be glorified and he alone attains the victory.

There is a great sickness in the "Christian West," particularly in her Churches. Most of us feel it if not see it. It's as if its light has begun to dim, its salt has begun to lose its savor, and we are in danger of being trampled by the unbelieving world. For those that can see, it is evident that there is a swirling spiral of corruption everywhere we turn. It is an infected wound that festers in the heart and blinds the eyes. The Church seems to have entered into a slumber in the middle of the battlefield. Some blame the world, some the Devil, others a lack of discipleship and holiness. Even others will claim that things are playing out the way they were always meant to, that all these things are just a sign that the end is near.

What if none of those things are the main cause? What if we are just witnessing symptoms of a giant in our midst? What if we are seeing the beginning and not the ending? What if this giant has just wooed us to sleep, and our wound could be healed if we would seek the Great Physician?

I serve a mighty and true King. His is a kingdom of great power, glory, and victory. No giant is too large that he is not able to defeat, no wound too grievous that he is unable to heal. Like dead tissue in an infected wound, we must let the great surgeon cut it out. Like a true king, we must let him lead us upon the great battlefield.

This book is meant for the edification of the Church, but sometimes that means tearing down so that something can be built up in its place. I seek to tear down this giant's fortress and erect the strong tower of almighty God in its place. If the Lord wills, this little book will be like the stone slung from David's sling. Too long has this giant taken captive many saints, too long has its touch tormented hearts, deprived the saints of inheritance, and been a stumbling block to the spreading of the kingdom. Let us tear down this great giant and set the captives free. May the saints of God awaken to righteousness and take their arms to the battlefield.

This two-headed giant is the source of the infection. It spreads from the wound into everything it touches. One head is a theology, the other is an eschatology. Few would consider that such a giant would be the source of our troubles. Of course, this giant isn't the only one of its kind pillaging the Church, but it tore down a segment of the walls of sound doctrine and allowed many others of its kind to swarm into the gap. It is our job to slay this giant, rebuild the wall, and hunt down the other giants that have run freely among us. We must cut off the retreat of these giants and their ability to call in backup, and thus this two-headed giant must be slain first for it is a most venomous creature always seeking to weaken the saints.

Eschatology is the study of the last things. Theology is the study of the nature of God and religion. There have been many two-headed giants in the history of the Church. Some have been more deadly than others, but I would consider this ugly beast to be a very deadly giant indeed.

This two-headed giant called others into the kingdom of the Church, to distract, divide, and spoil the saints. Some of these giants are called thus: New Age, Double-minded, Carnal Vanity, Prosperity, Social Justice, Critical Race Theory, Liberalism, Evolution, Zionism, Abortion, and Modernism. These are but a few giants we face.

But it is the two-headed giant that strengthens these, it brings them through the gap he placed in the wall of the kingdom. The two-headed giant disarms the saints and encourages them to let the pillaging of the Church take place by offering them false hope.

The reasons why this giant has such an effect on the Church are two-fold: First, our view of the events related to the end of the world will affect how we view the world, the Church, the Kingdom, and our role in it. This ultimately shapes our view of God and thus its second head, theology, must also be considered. One could not exist without the other. One will prop up the other. If one is slain, it will keep on living through the second head, so both must be destroyed before this giant can be removed.

The name of the giant is False-hope, the name of it's first head is Dispensationalism, and the name of it's second head is Premillennialism. Many pilgrims may be unfamiliar with the terms Dispensational Premillennialism as these are theological terms used in seminary schools that list a broad range of interpretations concerning end times events. Though there are variations within this theology they are minor, and most key points will remain consistent. All variations are a great source of trouble in the Church and all have a single source. To put it simply dear friends, in the last 150 years, in the average Evangelical Church, this theology, or some variation of it, has been the primary source of all teachings about the end times and the second coming of Christ.

Even though this has become the primary interpretation concerning such topics today, the teachings of this giant were not believed for the vast majority of the Church's history, and far more importantly many of the things said by this giant go against many of the clear bible passages concerning these events. This will be the heart and purpose behind this work. Not only do I have a heart to expose such errors if they exist, but also a desire to bring to the attention of my fellow pilgrims the great dread of danger that we now face because of this giant.

I name this beast not to condemn those that have fallen into its snares, but to condemn the beast itself and hopefully set the captives free from the snares of this giant. False-hope is unlike many who came before it. It began to take up its residency in the Church less than 200 years ago, but it has done more harm than nearly all other giants of the sort.

The heart of this book is to address the teachings of this giant and compare them to the teachings of the word of God. It is my great hope that in so doing, the eyes of the sleeping Church will wake up and see the giant as it is: our enemy sleeping amidst the strong tower of True-hope.

I must state clearly here my fellow pilgrims that those that have fallen into this giant's snares are not our enemy. Deception is the tool of False-hope and our arrows must fly straight at the giant itself lest we lose them and slay our fellow pilgrims. Our enemy is cunning and tries to lure us to fight one another, or a different giant so that we will forget about it, for it is a coward.

Like all enemies of the Church, False-hope will fall at the double edge sword of the word of God and our savior shall set the captives free.

To slay any giant the simplest course of action is to cut off its head. So it is on these that I will focus this book on.

The first head we will focus on is its eschatology, that is Premillennialism, as once this head is chopped off the second will be much easier to handle. We will do this without prophecy charts, complex diagrams, or going back to the original languages. We will simply take the bible and compare the declarations of False-hope to the testimony of our Lord and his Apostles. May the Lord rebuke this Giant.

Though we tackle False-hope, this work seeks to compile a list of many of the words that our Lord speaks so that we can easily defeat other giants that try and take False-hope's place. Think of them as weapons in our arsenal by which we can keep giants from taking the tower of True-hope.

Let us better define the heads of False-hope so that all may understand.

Premillennialism speaks about the 1,000-year reign mentioned in Revelation 20. This chapter speaks about a most curious event. It speaks about Christ and his saints and a rule for 1,000 years upon the earth. All such giants argue over what this 1,000-year reign means. Yet it is not giants we should listen to but the Word. Pre, speaks of before, and millennium speaks of 1,000. So when this head speaks it says that Jesus will return before this 1,000 years.

It speaks of many great things happening before this time can come. The head says that first, the Church will fall into great apostasy (corruption, a falling away from the truth), that the Jews must come back to their land and rebuild the temple, and then there must come a rapture of the Church, a 7-year tribulation by a man called Antichrist, and many other terrible judgments must happen on the earth.

Few men ever heard such things before False-hope came, and many Mighty Men of God fought hard against False-hope's lies, but many would not hear. Young pilgrims thought False-hope's words were so beautiful and grand.

Then came the second head, Dispensationalism, which began to speak, so that it could explain how all that the first head had declared could be true. It argued against the Mighty Men of God and after they had died to few took up the banner of truth and soon the second head's words prevailed. Dispensationalism cried out declaring, "Thus says the Lord, 7 dispensations are declared upon the world, yet 8 shall be for sake of rebellion."

Dispensationalism would explain that these dispensations, or ages, were unique periods, both in the bible and in human history. They began in the Garden of Eden and are thus: Innocence, Conscience, Human Government, Promise, Law, Millennial Kingdom, and the Eternal State. These were the original 7, but because of rebellion by the Jews an 8th was added parenthetically between the Law and Kingdom known as Grace, or more commonly as the "Church Age."

Dispensationalism declared that during each of these ages, God dealt uniquely with his people, but each age ended in corruption and rebellion, so God had to create a new plan of salvation and a new age to go along with it. Dispensationalism has a forked tongue as sometimes he says that people were always saved by Grace alone, and at other times he says that only during the Church Age are people saved by grace alone, and in all other ages men are saved by grace and works.

Our current age, say Dispensationalism, will end in corruption and rebellion, as all ages will end, and so God will rapture his Church and judge the world during the 7-year tribulation of Antichrist. This 7 year period is the transition between Grace and the Millennial Kingdom. During these 7 years, God will return to the Jews who were put on time out by God during the Age of Grace and it is through this tribulation period that the Jews will return to God. Christ will come with all of his saints to destroy Antichrist and he will then bodily rule from Jerusalem with his saints for 1,000 years of peace after which the Kingdom Age will end in rebellion and corruption before the final judgment.

God then resurrects all the dead and destroys the world and creates a new heaven and earth and all shall be in the Eternal State either of salvation with God or damnation in the Lake of Fire. Because these ages exist, certain portions of the bible are only authoritative to specific ages. All scripture is to you, but not all scripture is for you. Therefore the Bible itself was divided into 8 parts; a section for every age. The Church Age is the age of the Gentiles and thus only Paul's writing is the main authority during this age for he was the Apostle of the Gentiles.

So declared the two-headed giant of False-hope.

This giant has spoken for generations now and most of us have become so used to his words that we hardly notice he is a giant at all. Over time, denominations would rise in the Church that would take certain aspects of what False-hope taught and change things here and there or reject certain aspects and keep others. They all argued that they had a better understanding of truth, however, most failed to see that it mattered not to False-hope what lies were taken and changed for the source was foul and corrupt and the result would all end the same: in blindness and bondage.

If an issue arose, False-hope would change something slightly and do wonders and signs to make sure no one is the wiser. We have grown to trust him as a friend and true preacher, but consider this my fellow pilgrims:

The Church is the body of Christ (1 Corinthians 12:27). Jesus is the head of the Church (Ephesians 1:21-22). The Church is the temple of God (1 Corinthians 3:16-23). If the Church and the Gospel fail in corruption, as False-hope claims must happen, then Christ is a failure. Think long and hard about this statement. If the Church ends in corruption and the

Gospel fails then we must admit that the Holy Spirit is powerless and Christ is a terrible king, and the Father is a liar.

Blasphemy you will say, and I will agree, yet every statement is so if False-hope is true.

For it is written:

Psalms 110:1-2: A Psalm of David. The LORD (God the Father) said unto my Lord (God the Son), Sit thou at my right hand, <u>until I make thine enemies thy footstool</u>. 2. The LORD (God the Father) shall send the rod of thy strength (the Son's strength) out of Zion: <u>rule thou in the midst of thine enemies.</u>

This, my dear pilgrims, is the most quoted Old Testament verse in the New Testament. It is the promise of the glorious and victorious reign of the Messiah. The writer of Hebrews adds to this:

Hebrews 1:8: But unto the Son *he* (the Father) *saith,* Thy throne, O God (the Son), *is* <u>for ever and ever: a sceptre of righteousness *is* the sceptre of thy kingdom.</u>

Peter declared when this Kingdom reign began. It wasn't in our future but began on Pentecost:

Act 2:29-33: Men *and* brethren, let me freely speak unto you of the patriarch David, that he is both dead and buried, and his sepulchre (tomb) is with us unto this day. 30. Therefore being a prophet, and knowing that God had sworn with an oath to him, that of the fruit of his loins, according to the flesh (meaning from a physical direct descendant), he would raise up <u>Christ to sit on his </u>(David's)<u>throne</u>

31. He (David) seeing this before <u>spake of the resurrection of Christ,</u> (Peter just said that the resurrection of Christ was the fulfillment of the prophetic promise and vision David had of one of his descendants sitting on the throne) that his soul was not left in hell, neither his flesh did see corruption. 32. This Jesus hath God raised up, whereof we all are witnesses.

33. Therefore being by the right hand of God exalted (We know from the above passage this is upon the throne of David at the Father's right hand.), and having received of the Father the promise of the Holy Ghost, he hath shed forth this, which ye now see and hear (meaning the Holy Spirit falling on the Church was a proof that Christ had received his

throne). 34. For David is not ascended into the heavens: but he (David) saith himself, The LORD (God the Father) said unto my Lord (God the Son), <u>Sit thou on my right hand, 35. Until I make thy foes thy footstool.</u>

Isaiah proclaimed:

Isaiah 9:7: Of the increase of *his* (Christ's) government and peace *there shall be* <u>no end</u> (meaning his kingdom is always growing and producing more and more peace), upon the throne of David (The very throne Peter just proclaimed he sat upon after he ascended), and upon his kingdom, to order it, and to establish it with judgment and with justice from henceforth (from this point on) even for ever. The zeal of the LORD of hosts (God the Father) will perform this.

Paul explained this reign:

1 Corinthians 15:25-28: 25. For he (Jesus) <u>must reign, till</u> he (God the Father) hath put <u>all enemies</u> under his (Jesus') feet. 26. The <u>last enemy *that* shall be destroyed *is* death.</u> 27. For he (God the Father) hath put all things under his feet (God the Son). But when he (the Father) saith all things are put under *him* (the Son), *it is* manifest (declared/revealed) that he (the Father) is excepted, which did put all things under him (the Son). 28. And when all things shall be <u>subdued unto him</u> (the Son), <u>then</u> shall the Son also himself be subject unto him (the Father) that put all things under him (the Son), that God may be all in all.

The Father declares it, the Son creates it, and the Spirit gives it life. If Jesus must sit at the Father's right hand and rule until all of his enemies are put under his feet, as the Father declared, and if the Church is his body, then the feet are in the Church. Christ is not to come back to defeat any enemy but Death, which shall be the last. This is the resurrection.

The promise is of a victorious and everlasting Gospel and Church. Christ our king is the fountain of True-hope for the world and the Church, his promised victory is the True-hope of the Church. If False-hope is right then all the verses we just saw concerning his victorious rule are wrong. God the Father is a liar, Christ is a failed king, and the Holy Spirit was not powerful enough to enable the will of God.

What is worse, is that if we agree with False-hope that the kingdom is not yet, but will be after the rapture, we see an even greater failure. For

Christ, himself will be physically on earth with resurrected saints ruling over the whole world, and they too will fail! For False-hope claims that the 1,000 years of the physical reign of Christ and his saints will end in rebellion and failure before the final resurrection and judgment of the world. In this way, a double failure of Christ is promised by False-hope.

This is an example of what we shall do in this small work. This is the pattern of blows of which I shall cast upon this two-headed beast. We shall primarily focus on the bible and compare it to the words of false teachers who work for False-hope and let the Holy Spirit open the eyes of the people of God. I may out of necessity quote from well-respected pastors to add clarity to a period or passage, but I do this rarely wanting rather to stick with the clear word of God. May God alone be glorified, and honored for victory is his.

I do not seek fame or wealth from this work. If I did not have to put my name on this book for the sake of publication I wouldn't use it. I do not believe that pen names are honest and so my name is attached. I say this not out of fear or shame of what I will present, but out of a deep desire that this work is not about me but Christ and his word. As for wealth, I intend to donate 100% of the money made from this book, beyond the cost of publication and marketing, to the Church and ministries.

Please note dear pilgrims, that I will only use a few verses from the book of Revelation in this book along with an occasional reference, except for chapter 20 of the Revelation which we will look at in great detail. Some may criticize me for this. I understand said feelings, however, by its very nature, the book of Revelation is written in visions and prophetic language that must be interpreted by what the rest of the bible is teaching. False-hope loves to go straight into the Revelation and uses its apocalyptic language by itself to enchant the soul and cast darkness over the truth.

The term "apocalypse" originally meant a revealing or unveiling of something that had been previously hidden, not its destruction. The term usually incorporated colorful or pictorial language that tried to teach a truth that was meant to be hidden from common eyes but plain for those that would seek out its meaning. That is why the Apocalypse of John is more commonly translated as the Revelation of John in our English bibles as the Greek word behind both English words is the same.

As I stated, I have little desire to go back to the Greek, a language very few who read this book would know, so I will not. However, one can easily conclude that the words apocalypse and revelation hold the same meaning when one looks back at their original meaning in a dictionary, or use a simple google search.

The colorful language of the Revelation is not unique to the New Testament as many of the Old Testament prophets also spoke with similar terms that we can look back on having now seen how they were fulfilled. By doing so, we can gather the proper meaning of these terms as they were meant in the bible. When we do this, we find these terms are very consistent and once understood very plain.

This language, though mostly lost on us today, was very common in the first century when Revelation was written. More importantly, the early Church was made up of many Jews and Gentiles who were familiar with the language of the prophets in the bible and would have been very familiar with this type of language. By and large, the first-century Church relied on the Old Testament for the bible as the new was still being written during this time. We also know that the prophets were emphasized by these early churches as we see the apostles and Jesus quote them more than most other Old Testament books.

We shall delve into this to a lesser degree in this book to help our understanding when the needs arise. I daresay that an understanding of the apocalyptic language of the prophets is critical to properly understand the Revelation which was written in the same fashion. This should also be done with a clear understanding of these events built by the non-apocalyptic sayings of Christ and the Apostles to be a guide against errors in the interpretation of apocalyptic writing.

I say all this to reveal an issue we have in our modern society. Today, we think apocalypse means the end of the world, but that is not what this word means when dealing with the bible. The Revelation was meant to be a revealing of truth related to specific events that I believe have been shrouded by False-hope and other giants throughout Church History. These revelations were meant to glorify truths laid out in the bible by the Apostles, Prophets, and Christ himself, and were never meant to cloud the truth. This is exactly what is declared by the opening verse of Revelation:

Revelation 1:1: The <u>Revelation</u> (This is the same word as apocalypse. Revelation is a revealing of something. The subject of which is very clearly laid out in the following words) <u>of Jesus Christ</u>, which God (The Father) gave unto him (Jesus), to shew (the old way of spelling show) unto his servants (So the purpose of this revealing was to teach his Church something. The question is what? It is immediately answered) <u>things which must shortly come to pass</u> (So the revealing of the truth about Christ was given to Jesus for the first-century Church to declare things to them that would shortly come to pass. What was going to come to pass is directly linked to a truth about Jesus, a truth given to Jesus by the Father. This should be our first clue among many of what the focus of this book was meant for and it has little to do with our future but much to do about theirs. This is what is plainly declared. The verse ends with how this was to be declared to the first-century churches), and he (Jesus) sent and signified *it* (To signify something means to set it as an example) by his angel unto his servant John:

The above is just a simple example and is not the primary focus of this book. If we just took this opening line for what it says we should all immediately know the context and purpose of the Revelation. All that will follow in the Revelation all hinges on some events that the first-century Church was going to go through, and that these events were directly tied to a truth about Christ given to him by the Father of which the Father desired the son to reveal to his servants so that they would know beforehand what was about to happen. All the events happened because of the truth about the Son given to him by the Father. This seems straightforward enough and is the key to understanding the Revelation, unfortunately, giants like False-hope make everything shrouded in uncertainty. I imagine that just from this little example some pilgrims reading this will already have a different perspective on the Revelation that they have never seen before.

I would propose that the Revelation has been misinterpreted because of False-hope twisting and misinterpretation of passages in the old and new testaments, thus we must start in the old and new before we go into the Revelation. Many examples of this will be dealt with in this book. If the Lord wills, this book will act as a foundation for a second more thoughtful book delving into the Revelation.

I also take the stance that the Revelation was written before 70 A.D. and not the more popular stance that it was written in 90 A.D. or later. It is also my belief that the misdating of the Revelation has helped cast great confusion about events described in it, a point that will become much clearer as you work through this book. Many internal and external pieces of evidence support this. I will not make dating the Revelation the focus of this particular book, but I will make mention of this stance occasionally when analyzing certain passages that also play out in Revelation, so my stance should be plainly known now to avoid confusion.

I would point anyone interested in the date of Revelation to the book titled, "Before Jerusalem Fell," by Dr. Kenneth L. Gentry, Jr. who wrote an amazing book breaking down and examining all the internal and external evidence for both dates and from it, you will see overwhelming evidence for the earlier date. He is not the only man who has written books on this, but I have found his book to be the best on the topic.

For those pilgrims that fear that by not using the Revelation I will in some way miss the truth please consider this: The Revelation *may* shed more light on His coming, but what is revealed will not contradict nor go against the testimony of what came before.

If such appears to be so in the Revelation, it is not Jesus or his Apostles that are wrong, but our interpretation that is in error. We must use clear scripture to interpret unclear scripture, so by looking at clear scripture about the end times, we can build foundations of truth by which we can interpret all the scriptures about the end times. Such has always been the nature of every truth of the bible for all bible truth agrees with, and builds upon one another.

This is why False-hope tries to divide and distort the bible. He fears the chief cornerstone upon which all foundations of truth are built.

Let me give a brief example of this concept with Paul and the Berean Jews in Acts 17:10-12. During Paul's ministry, he constantly came up against Jews who believed he was teaching brand new doctrines contrary to the rest of the word of God. In this account, Paul commended (praised) the Bereans for daily searching in the scriptures to see if what Paul taught was true. For the younger pilgrims, at the time that Acts was taking place, the only scriptures the people had was the Old Testament. This means everything that Paul taught was also true in the Old Testament.

The truths of God may have been less clear in the Old Testament, but when the clarity came in the new, it glorified the truth of the old and agreed with all that came before. It is built upon the old as a master builder builds upon a foundation stone. For the foundation of truth is Jesus Christ and all truth comes from and is built upon Him.

With great love, I dedicate this book to the beloved Church of God

May our great God and Father bless all who read this little book. May He unite our hearts together in a Spirit of wisdom and understanding that we might all see and understand the glorious truth of his word. Teach us to fight giants O Lord. Remove the eye scales from our eyes, that you might be glorified and magnified. Blow the trumpet of battle O Lord may your saints arise and slay the giants of your Vineyard that we may rebuild the walls and strong tower of True-hope. O, mighty God, may thy Kingdom come thy will be done in earth as it is in heaven.

In Jesus' mighty name Amen

About the Author

Before we get into the heart of this little book I think it is just fair that you know a bit about my testimony and what led me to want to write this book. I am a simple man, the son of a simple man. I am not a pastor of a church, nor have I ever attended a seminary school, or studied under a scholar (beyond reading a great many books written by them), rather I am a man who loves the bible. At the time of writing this book, I am 30 years old and currently working in the Housekeeping Department of my local hospital. I also have the privilege and honor of teaching adult Sunday School at my local church.

I was raised in church attending from the time of my birth until my teen years in the Church of Christ (Not the Mormon Cult). When I was about 12, my parents decided to take my siblings and me out of the public school system and home school us.

At the time, a church in the area we lived in opened its doors and allowed all the home-schooled children in our valley to meet together in a school-like environment run by parents. This allowed us to have sports, drama classes, music classes, and even field trips. Because this church also had a large youth group, my parents decided to start bringing us to this church.

To say that there was a major change going from the Church of Christ to a more modern non-denominational Charismatic styled church is an understatement. As the years went on, my siblings and I became more involved in the church. I began teaching Sunday School for the youth and helping with many youth activities. My two brothers and I even got baptized on the same day. In the eyes of many, we were young zealous Christian men.

I cannot speak on behalf of my siblings, but I had a huge problem. Although I knew my bible relatively well, I could quote doctrinal statements, "speak in tongues," and give prophetic words, I'd went to nearly every prayer meeting, taught children's ministry, went to revival meetings, raised my hands and voice in worship, and even on occasion taught the main Sunday service, yet I wasn't saved.

It was as if the words of the Apostle were written just for me:

1 Corinthians 13:2: And though I have *the gift of* prophecy, and understand all mysteries, and all knowledge; and though I have all faith, so that I could remove mountains, and have not charity, I am nothing.

I didn't want to admit it, but I was as lost as any sinner heading to hell. I struggled constantly with fears and uncertainties and hidden sins that sought to consume me. I had a head knowledge of God and a form of godliness, but inwardly I was dead man's bones filled with all unrighteousness.

For I was caught up with a great vain need to appear as the perfect Christian that others could look up to. All the while I fell further and further into a pit of darkness. I tried desperately not to let anyone know my wretched state. I could easily get caught up in the emotionalism and the music, the air of godliness, but my heart was so very far from God. Worse, I didn't even know how to reach God, part of me wanted desperately to, but my pride refused to let me.

After a series of events in my late teens that tore apart my family, I finally had enough. I said to myself, "If this is Christianity (both what I had seen and what I experienced) then I wanted nothing to do with it." I wandered away for nearly 7 years.

During that time I could not get the thought of God out of my mind. I knew there had to be a God. Atheism made no sense, one look at the stars and the intricacies of Creation was enough to convince me there had to be a God. Evolution then appeared as a wicked falsehood that had no evidence to back it up, yet my experience in "Christianity" had left a foul taste in my mouth.

So I began to study most of the world religions knowing that one of them had to be right, but none of them held up to the truth except Christianity, but this was a truth I could not reconcile with. Eventually,

I got married to my wonderful wife Amber, and we began to settle down in our lives, religion being a far and distant thing in our marriage. She too had gone through some bad experiences in churches, and as the years went by, I more or less gave up on my pursuit of God and truth.

But thank God, who is ever rich in mercy, that He never stopped pursuing me. Eventually, God orchestrated a series of events that led me to Him. I heard the Gospel clearly for the first time in my life and I believed it. At that very moment, God saved me and gave me a new heart. I can truly say I understand what it means to be born again for I had a very new nature, new desires, and a new life hammering in my soul against the flesh of that old carnal man. My wife can testify that God gave me a ravenous hunger for the word of God and the pursuit of true religion, to the point that she had thought I lost my mind.

I wanted to, no I needed to, study and learn all that I could. I didn't want to believe certain teachings in Christianity unless I could see them in the bible. I was fed up with dead religious formality that taught doctrines of men and devils for their own lust's sake. I was fed up with the emotionalism and will worship that pleased the flesh and offended God. I wanted true Christianity pure and undefiled from this world.

In my first year after being saved, I read the bible cover to cover 4 times (Once in the NKJV, once in the ESV, and twice in the KJV). I also found a deep love for great works of literature written by men like Martin Luther, John Calvin, John Bunyan, George Whitefield, Charles Spurgeon, Johnathan Edwards, John Owen, C.S. Lewis, John Wesley, Leonard Ravenhill, A.W. Tozer, David Brainerd, and so many others. I say this not to brag but to demonstrate the great burden of desire that was laid upon my heart to learn and study. This was something that I never had any desire to do at any point in my early life. All this I solely praise God for, as it was a work that he alone did in my heart and I can take no credit for it.

For I can glory in nothing save my wretchedness apart from Christ. Without him, any good that I could do is as filthy rags. I can do nothing but sin apart from Christ, and before Christ, all I did was sin. Such is the nature of man's fallen heart. So I glory in him for any good thing I have comes from him, and I can claim nothing as my own but my sin.

For everything I have apart from that sin has been given to me by him. I deserve nothing but hell, yet he offers an abundance of pardon, life, and above all he offers himself!

Such a free gift he offers that wretched creature he calls man! To be received by faith, for we have nothing we could give to purchase such a marvelous love. May no flesh glory in their own eyes. Therefore may I decrease that he might increase.

I went from one church denomination to another looking and seeking and testing what it taught against the bible. After a year-long search, I found a place to call home. It isn't perfect, but it was a place I could in good conscience call a temporary resting place on this pilgrimage called life. As of the writing of this book, I have spent the last few years serving my church as faithfully as I know-how. All the while God has continued to push me to study.

So what am I today? Usually, when people ask that question they are looking to place you into a box that perfectly describes what you are. I dare say I am a peculiar soul and such boxes wouldn't fit me. Some might say that makes me a nonconformist, I say amen.

In truth, as much as I understand denominational divides, I also deplore them. Do not misunderstand me when I say this. I am also greatly opposed to the ecumenical movement trying to unite all religions and false denominations together. I firmly believe in the importance of ecclesiastical (Church) and personal separation concerning gross error (save to minister the truth to these groups). However, I desire a purifying ecumenical movement to happen that does not breed compromise but brings unity to Christianity.

As it stands our division often confuses and harms the Christian testimony for the unbelieving world. I would that we would be one body with many members (Churches) speaking all the same doctrines as we are commanded to be. Oh that God would answer the prayer of his son that we would be one as he and the father were one. That we would learn to love one another as he loved the Church. Dare we pray such prayers with our savior and mean it?

As it stands now, one could go to one church that will profess this and that, and another that says no it's that and this, and yet another that says this way and that way, and the last will say no it is that way and this way. Add to this that each often makes war with the other claiming their views are the only true views, yet all claim to worship the same God and read the very same book. They often hate their brothers and demand that they submit to their personal views as being the final authority.

This in fact reveals hypocrisy among Protestants who proclaim that it is not the church that is the final authority on the truth, but the Bible alone is the final authority. Yet often a denomination will promote its own doctrines and interpretations of the bible over the word and refuse to even consider they may have it wrong.

This attitude is an echo of the fall of man, "Ye shall be as gods... knowing good from evil." Each of these divides highlights this fall for we put ourselves as God determining right from wrong. The whole point is not for men or denominations to be God determining what is right or wrong, but for God to be God and tell us what is truth. That is the purpose of the Word. Thus great confusion plagues many concerning the simplicity of Christ. Of course, our enemy uses this to his great advantage.

The reality is we cannot all be right in our views. The first phase of healing such divides is charity and open and heartfelt conversation about what divides us. I have found that there is a lot more than unites us than divides us and we should use these principles as a foundation for open dialogue. I praise God that we are seeing this more and more.

So, in reality, what I am, is simply a Follower of the Way. What was later called a Christian. A child of God who follows Jesus Christ that happens to go to a Baptist Church.

I confess that I am a wretched sinner that deserves a devil's hell and has no power or good works by which I can save myself. I believe with all my heart that Jesus is the only begotten son of God, that he was born of the virgin Mary, that he died on the cross for my sins, that he was buried and rose on the third day for our justification. That salvation is a free gift from God through grace alone by faith alone in Christ alone apart from all works. I believe that the bible is the perfect, inspired, inerrant word of God preserved as a testimony to all generations. I believe that Christ sits at the right hand of the Father and will come to judge the quick and the dead on the last day. Having professed this I was baptized in the name of the Father, Son, and Holy Spirit.

I have no issue affirming the Apostles, Athanasian, and Nicene Creeds. I also have a reformed view of the bible and believe in Covenant Theology. I long to see the Church at large shine in this lost world as a beacon of truth again. United we stand divided we fall or as the teacher says: "a threefold cord is not quickly broken…and a house divided against itself shall not stand." Alas, the only cure for such errors and divisions is to return to the doctrines delivered once to the saints: the very word of God and not to the doctrines and traditions of man.

This was the heart of what led me to the desire to write this book. As I began to delve into the bible I had a great heart to learn not what my denomination or favored teacher said about a topic, but what the Bible itself said about a topic. I knew something was wrong with Christianity and I wanted to know what it was and I knew it had to do in some way with the bible. The bible is the source of our religion, in all matters of faith and practice, and if it was the Word of God, meaning it was God's testimony to Man about all things he felt we needed to know about Truth, then it alone is the only sure true thing. If the bible was false then our hope was in vain. If it was the Truth then it was not at fault for the issues I had experienced in Christianity or churches. I knew the error must lie in us; in our lack of faith, in our lack of obedience, or our twisting of what the bible said.

The question then came down to this, how would I know what the bible said about a subject? How would I know if I had learned the truth or if I was simply twisting it to match my desires? Many people are convinced that they know what the bible says, every church is sure and argues its views with conviction, but they cannot all be right. I could be wrong as easily as any of them. But I knew one thing was for certain: God if he was all he claimed to be could never be wrong. If he said something it was the truth. I also took verses like these to heart:

Malachi 3:6: For I *am* the LORD, <u>I change not</u>; therefore ye sons of Jacob are not consumed.

Hebrews 13:8: <u>Jesus Christ the same yesterday, and to day, and for ever.</u>

From such verses, I realized how I could determine a matter. If men wrote the Bible under the inspiration of the Holy Spirit as it is claimed to be (2 Timothy 3:16-17, 2 Peter 1:21, etc), and as I had proved in my search to have very little doubt that it was, then God penned this book using men much as we might a pencil or computer. Meaning it alone was the truth. If Truth wrote the bible then the bible would not and could not contradict itself. If God determined to write a book for humanity and he promised to preserve it for all generations then he would do so with clarity and consistency so that men might learn Truth. This was of course the whole purpose behind the word in the first place.

Psalms 12:6-7: The words of the LORD *are* pure words: *as* silver tried in a furnace of earth, purified seven times. 7. <u>Thou shalt keep them</u>, O LORD, <u>thou shalt preserve them from this generation for ever.</u>

Matthew 24:35: Heaven and earth shall pass away, but <u>my words shall not pass away</u>.

John 12:48: He that rejecteth me, and receiveth not my words, hath one that judgeth him: <u>the word that I have spoken, the same shall judge him in the last day.</u>

Psalms 138:2: I will worship toward thy holy temple, and praise thy name for thy lovingkindness and for thy truth: <u>for thou hast magnified thy word above all thy name.</u>

I realized then that because God changes not, his views on principles that he teaches in his word do not change either. He may grant men more and more understanding, but such new understandings would always be consistent from the very start. That is the nature of Truth it cannot change, however, our clarity on a matter can improve. Even the changes that happened to the Law were not changed for the sake of change, but changes based on their fulfillment by Christ. Thus they were done away with or transfigured, as their purpose and lessons were fulfilled, but the reality and the lesson meant in the law were still the same as they had always had been.

Let me give you an example, the sacrifices of animals in the Old Testament did not and never did save anyone from their sins as their purpose was to demonstrate a picture of the sacrifice and shedding of the blood of Christ. Once Christ came these sacrifices were no longer necessary to teach this as now we look upon Him whom all animal sacrifices were just a picture of. Here are a few verses showing this, the first was given by king David who understood this concept even in the Old Testament:

Psalm 51:16-17: For thou (speaking of God) <u>desirest not sacrifice</u>; else would I give *it*: thou <u>delightest not in burnt offering.</u> 17. The sacrifices of God *are* a broken spirit: a broken and a contrite heart, O God, thou wilt not despise.

Paul, whom I believe wrote Hebrews, declares plainly why this is true:

Hebrews 10:4: For *it is* not possible that the blood of bulls and of goats should take away sins.

Hebrews 10:11-13: And every priest standeth daily ministering and offering oftentimes the same sacrifices, <u>which can never take away sins</u>: 12. But this man (Jesus), after he had offered one sacrifice for sins for ever (himself), sat down on the right hand of God; 13. From henceforth (From now on) expecting (What is Christ expecting? The expectation is declared in the following) <u>till his enemies be made his footstool</u>.

Once again this verse is quoted (Psalms 110:1) at the end of this passage. This is one we will see often in this book. Jesus having satisfied the payment of sin, something the animal sacrifices were pointing to, sat down in rule and victory at his Father's right hand until his enemies are made his footstool. Christ is sitting and ruling in the expectation that the Father will perform this as we already saw in other passages. The Father is the one who will subject all enemies under Christ's feet. Christ is waiting for the day that this will be so that he can conquer death and deliver the fullness of the kingdom unto the Father. This is an important theme throughout the New Testament as we will see in this book and it directly relates to the Second Coming.

Because of this, if I wanted to learn a topic I would not focus on a single passage or verse but I would look at all the verses on that topic and by so doing I knew exactly what God had to say about a topic. By letting the word of God speak and interpret itself by itself, <u>in context</u>, one could see the truth in its purest form for it was written by a perfect being. Over the last several years, I would take topics like sin, salvation, redemption, justification, holiness, repentance, etc, and see how the truths were revealed and built upon one another and perfected in Christ. This helped me not only know what the bible said on a topic, but what the truth of a topic was according to God, his word is his testimony to mankind of all manners of life and truth.

Therefore, if a doctrine/teaching/topic was not clearly and consistently in the bible the way it was being taught, in a church or by a pastor, no matter how large and great, I'd either dismiss said doctrine or I'd alter it to match what the bible taught.

The Reformation's declaration of, "Sola Scriptura" which means, "the bible alone," is a concept near and dear to my heart; dearer than any theology or doctrine of man. This has been my guide and is a lifelong process of discovery for as long as we are in this flesh we see the truth only in part and only as much as the Holy Spirit will teach us. Without the Holy Spirit no matter how much of the bible we could claim to know we would be blind to the truth unless he opens our hearts to it. This was the lesson Jesus taught us all and beautifully displayed in his dealings with the Pharisees and Sadducees, for them, of all men, knew the word but they were blind to its truth.

I believe, by and large, the main issue with Evangelical Christianity today is a chronic lack of bible knowledge that has been replaced with theological ideals, programs, worldly carnality, and religious formalities and traditions that have been twisted by our culture and carnal natures. I believe if we are to see national revivals as in the days of the Great Awakenings of America, or the Reformation itself, then we need to get back to the heart of truth and seek God with pure hearts uncorrupted by the world.

In every sense of the word, the Church needs another Reformation.

All of this has led to the burden to write this book. As I turned through the same process of testing other doctrines, I turned my attention to eschatology, the study of last things.

In nearly every church I have been to, regardless of denomination, the ideas concerning the end times were mostly very consistent. More or less, the concept behind films like "Left Behind" or "A Thief in the Night," though works of fiction, seemed to be the general idea of what most

Christians believed about the end times. Also, nearly every Christian talk show, podcast, and literary work I read or heard declared these ideas over and over again. This has shaped people both inside and out of the Church with a general idea of how the last events of the world will unfold.

I too held to this general idea behind the films, media, and books. I knew people who made short films for those "left behind" by the rapture in the hopes that the films would lead these "left behind people" to the Lord after they were gone.

I do not mock where their hearts were in this, but it paints a picture of just how much our view of eschatology affects our lives. It also shows how pervasive these views have been ingrained in our culture. As a small challenge, when next you find an opportunity, ask even an unsaved person what they think the end times will be like if the bible were true and most of them could name something taught by this way of interpreting the bible.

Just because the majority believes something, however, doesn't make it the truth. The majority do not believe a virgin can give birth or that a man can be raised from the dead, yet we as Christians know these things to be true despite the majority who claim it's impossible.

Because of how ingrained we have been as a culture by modern teachings, very few have ever challenged them. I was guilty of never questioning this narrative, that was until the last few years of studying this topic. It was then that the giant of False-hope began to become very clear in my mind.

I realized quickly that the concepts that I had taken as fact were not so clearly defined in the bible. Once I removed the prophecy charts, books, podcasts, and teachers that promoted the common beliefs, and stuck rather to the bible I found that I could not see the modern concepts at all in the word. At times some of the concepts seemed opposite of what the Lord Jesus said clearly would happen.

Having discussed certain aspects of this with close friends and family, I found that the vast majority of people had never actually sat down and studied what the bible said by itself concerning the end times. That means setting aside all preconceived notions of what was being taught and taking the bible as its own testimony for such events.

I found that most people, rather, would sit down, usually without their bibles, and they would pick up a book, listen to a podcast, or other such work on the topic. They may perhaps use their bibles only to reference the occasional verses mentioned in said book or work, though few did even this. Ultimately, they would take what was said in the book or work as fact because it matched what they had always been taught about the subject. Or they would sit under or listen to preaching on the topic, and in the same way, take what was being said as fact because it sounded exactly as they had always heard it.

A common thread of consistency with many of these outlets was taking scriptures that seemed to agree with what was being declared by themselves without looking at the bible as a whole on this topic. Usually, all such works focused only on a select few verses pulling them into whatever context they wanted them to be about and constructing them in such a way that they appear as the truth. They ignore any passages that might give greater clarity or clear passages that might completely contradict what it was they were saying. Most importantly they usually didn't keep the verse in its direct context something you will find, as we go forward in this book, drastically changes the meaning of verses.

It would be difficult for any work to easily compile all such verses in a single easy-to-digest and relatively short book. That is not to say that the effort should not be made. As I approached this book I desired it to be small so as not to intimidate anyone who read it. I also desired it to be focused on things most relevant to the issues without falling into the same snare described above.

So, for the sake of this book, I will narrow the focus as it relates to our topic and focus primarily on what Jesus, whose words should have the greatest of all authority on this topic, and what the apostles all claimed and compile them together to have clarity. However, God declared the end from the beginning, and one could start in Genesis and go to Revelation building truth on this topic and you will find a very clear and beautiful picture laid out when you do this. If demand is high enough, I would love to write a longer book compiling this truth.

I pray that as you go forward in this book the truth will become clearer and clearer. This work is but a glimpse at this topic and I hope it will provide a stepping stone for any wishing to delve into the Word. May the Lord be the judge of what is presented.

The above-described snare is not an issue linked to the topic on the end times alone. The sad truth is that rather than have the Holy Spirit and the word teach us, we tend to heap up teachers that say what we want to hear. Would this not accurately match what Paul said:

2 Timothy 4:3: For the time will come when they <u>will not endure sound doctrine; but after their own lusts shall they heap to themselves teachers, having itching ears;</u>

Because very few people are students of the bible today, they have no reason to doubt what their preacher or the writer of the work is saying. They blindly trust that these teachers are being honest and that what they say is in the bible. These teachers tend to use enough scriptures to make it seem as if their views are supported by the bible and, due to ignorance, most are none the wiser whether a matter is a truth or an error. Blindly following a teacher like this with any doctrine is dangerous and has been the source of almost all heresy being propagated in churches today. A minister no matter how large of a church or how good of a reputation they have in Christianity, is no substitute for the teaching of the Holy Ghost and the authority of the bible.

Do not get me wrong, I do not think that the vast majority of preachers purposefully mislead people on these topics, rather it is done out of ignorance if done at all. They have been raised in the prison of False-hope or other giants that all seek to lay the Church in darkness. If you tell a child from the time they begin to learn that red is green and green is red, it will take a lot to convince the child that such thinking is wrong or backward. In the same way, these pastors are taught from the moment they enter bible college that False-hope or whatever giant is correct, and as young students, they do not question what they are being taught. After all, they are just a lowly student, and standing before them is a great scholar or professor who has studied the word for years, surely they wouldn't be wrong.

Ignorance does not excuse an error, however, it does help us have understanding and compassion when trying to sort it out. I would never encourage anyone to go out and attack their pastor or loved ones because they got twisted up by the snares of giants. Rather in love, go to them with the word and ask the Holy Spirit to lead you both into the truth.

God will hold you personally responsible for your lack of discernment (testing) of any biblical truth if you own a bible, and you fail to read it. You are responsible to study and learn the word of God. Your pastor and teachers are gifts from God that should lead and teach you the word of God faithfully, but they *are not* responsible for your personal reading of the word of God. They are to watch over your souls and keep you from falling into error, but that will only work if they themselves are not in error.

It is my opinion that the responsibility of the mature members of the church is to hold their pastor and teachers accountable to the word of God. They are to oppose what is being taught with love if he is in error or to be willing and joyful receivers of the truth if he is not. The Laymen (common Church members) as well can do so if they are grounded in the word and filled with the Holy Spirit, but their primary job is to learn and receive from the teacher and faithfully apply what is said to their lives. That is the whole point of God's people saying Amen to the end of a prayer or sermon. It is decreeing, "I agree, or "It is so." This should all be done with Charity, Wisdom, and for the edification of the Body.

God will hold the laymen responsible for who they follow and who they listen to. Each one of us will be accountable to God for how we receive the message of God from a true man of God. We should know the "why" behind the reason for receiving any truth before we receive it. It shouldn't be based on the popularity of the preacher or the size of the church or ministry he may lead, rather it should be based on clear scriptures.

If you do not have a Bible reason for why you believe something then God calls you to study his word and find out preferably under the careful supervision of a faithful Elder lest the devil takes advantage of your ignorance. This of course is the heart of the nearly lost art of discipleship. Not only that, but once a truth is received, God will want to know what you did with it. Do not think I jest, there is coming a day when we must all stand before God and give an account. On that day you will not be "standing" beside your pastor, but you will be standing on your own before Almighty God. (2 Corinthians 5:10)

With all that said, I desire just to go to the bible with a general understanding of commonly accepted "facts" concerning the teachings of False-hope and see if they agree with the bible. I challenge all those who would read this book to do the same. That means putting away the various books on the topic, all the prophecy charts, shutting off what pastors are preaching about it, and putting aside all preconceived notions about this topic. That also means ignoring the notes in study bibles which by and large only propagate the modern understanding of False-hope. Study bibles may be good tools, but the notes are just the opinions of men and not a substitute for the word itself.

If the bible doesn't agree with what you are taught, then what you have been taught is unclean and should be done away with.

This is the attitude we should all have with all matters of doctrines that we profess to believe. We should know why we believe them and be able to give an account of why we believe what we do when people ask. Can you say you believe whatever you do because you read it clearly in the bible? Can you show me a verse for everything you believe, or do you believe them just because that's what you were told to believe? The Bible contains wisdom and guidance for all matters of life, faith, truth, and religion. It is relevant to all ages including our own. It is not an old-fashioned book it is a true book.

All sorts of materials concerning modern eschatology are in a great glut online and in the world today as people are seemingly obsessed with the topic. False-hope has worked very hard to drown out all voices of opposition to what he teaches.

Men and women have made great profits off this topic. Do not let them make merchandise of you anymore if they are indeed teaching this topic falsely (2 Peter 2:3).

That means I don't even want you to take my word for anything on this topic either. Do the research, read the passages, and make sure I am not leading you around by the nose. It is not my desire to do so. Rather I want you to be confident that you can stand before God with His word in your hand and say Father I believe this because you said it and this is where you said it.

That is the heart of what I wanted to do with this book. If you are willing to take a step back and just read what is presented I think you may be surprised and it may shock you. It certainly did me to the point that I didn't want to even conceive of it when I first began to learn. But in the end, either I believe the Lord and what he says, or I believe what man says. As for me, I prefer to serve the Lord.

Lastly, I only preach and teach out of the Authorized Version of the bible more commonly called the King James Bible, as I believe that in the English language, it is the word of God faithfully translated from the inspired and preserved word of God as passed down in the original languages. I believe it to be the best translation of the bible in English. As such, all of the scriptures used in this book will come from the King James Bible. That is not to say you cannot follow along with whatever version you prefer.

I say this because often I will reference verses with the intention that you will have your bible readily at hand and will be able to look up that verse as I reference them—and please do look them up. This was done with the King James scriptures in mind.

I only say this now because you may be surprised at the differences between what is presented and what your version may say. The difference in bible translation is a whole topic in itself. I believe it has played a huge role in the great confusion of what God's word says today. As Satan taking advantage of the great glut of translations, has made it so that many things are no longer certain that once were.

May God bless anyone who reads this little book, may I teach clearly and simply the word of God without my own thoughts or desires. May God alone be glorified and honored by what is written. In Jesus' name Amen.

CHAPTER ONE

False-hope Considered

"If you tell a lie often enough and loud enough the people will believe it. People are more willing to believe a big lie than a little lie"

JOSEPH GOEBELS ON BEHALF OF ADOLF HITLER

I f you are reading this book first I want to say I am honored. Many who pick up this work will not read it, and of those who begin it few, I fear, will finish it. My heart is not to stir up controversy but to edify. I pray my words and lessons are full of charity and salt. Many may wonder why I start this book with such a strange declaration.

You may look at the quote at the beginning of this chapter and wonder why such an evil man like Hitler is quoted in a book looking at the bible. To the first point, I'd answer because far too few are willing to challenge and grow in their knowledge of God, therefore the word of God often offends those who do not study it. This book will challenge most people who read it. To the second point, I dare say that Hitler's words are proven true all through history.

When people first began to teach that man Evolved through millions of years from a single-celled organism, and that the universe created itself from nothing without the need of God, the people mocked (Both saved and unsaved). Yet today, despite no evidence to prove these ideas, this theory is believed by millions, even among those who call themselves Christians.

When the fundamentals of the Christian faith and the authority of God's word were being challenged by human concepts of higher criticism that denied the miracles and authenticity of the bible, the people of God mocked that such an idea would ever last. Yet today, entire denominations deny the virgin birth, the miracles of Christ, and the historical accounts of the bible.

Instead, they prefer to teach a watered-down book that promotes loose morality and is accepting of all religious views and immoral lifestyles. Truth is subjective, and God is love and doesn't judge or criticize. Tolerance has become the proof of a born-again life for many modern Christian.

I could go on with examples of this quote proven true time and again throughout human history. This is nothing new, for from the beginning the father of such lies said,

"Ye shall not die: for God doth know that in the day ye eat thereof, then shall your eyes be opened, and ye shall be as gods, knowing good and evil." (Genesis 3:4-5)

The fall of man was a temptation to live our lives without God. It promised that we did not have to have God rule over us or tell us what was right and what was wrong. This lie implies that God is hindering your life and preventing you from living life to its full potential because of his rules and authority. It played on man's own desire to determine their own truth and live life as they pleased, to, in essence, be their own god.

This was the heart of the first temptation and is the very heart of the fallen nature of man. People despise truth that does not fit their lusts. The very heart of man rebels against such authority especially the authority of God's word. The reason for this is simple, man's fallen heart is exceedingly wicked (Jeremiah 17:9, John 3:19)

It should not be any great marvel then when we see the rise and fall of heresy and error even in the Church. For all such things come from the flesh (Galatians 5:19-20) which is tainted by the rebellion that is in man's hearts. Heresy is a perversion of truth. A perversion is usually one that has enough truth in it to be seductive and deadly. This is why the people of God are told to study his words (Matthew 4:4, 2 Timothy 2:15,

3:16-17, etc). Such heresies and errors are a result of the enemy taking advantage of our ignorance and lusts. It is from this lack of knowledge and wisdom that the people perish (Hosea 4:6).

When the children of God rebel against the truth, it is such a woefully sad thing to see. One does not need to be a student of the bible long to see that often even God's children, rebelled against him more than they obeyed him.

For this cause, God has given us his word to be a testimony against us. (Deuteronomy 31:26) His word is the cure to all heresy. It shall slay the flesh and rebellion in man if we present our bodies as living sacrifices unto the Lord, which is our reasonable service. (Romans 12:1)

This truth was not unknown to the apostles as we are warned that such heresies would come in these last days.

2 Peter 2:1-2: "But there were false prophets also among the people (referencing the Old Testament saints), even as there shall be false teachers among you, who privily (privately/in secret) shall bring in damnable heresies, even denying the Lord that bought them, and bring upon themselves swift destruction. 2. And many shall follow their pernicious (destructive) ways; by reason of whom the way of truth shall be evil spoken of." (Note that the way of truth is spoken evil of, meaning Christianity is mocked, hated, and thought false because of what these false teachers/prophets are doing/saying.)

This is not the only such verse referencing this. Jesus himself warned against false teachers, and to be wary of wolves in sheep's clothing hiding among the flock. The word of God shall be a light unto our feet and guide us during these times keeping us from such snares.

This brings us to why we are here today.

There was a lie that started in the 1830s by the prophet of False-hope that prepared the way for his arrival. This individual was a disgruntled Anglican pastor who left the Anglican Church and joined/started a cult. This man's name was John Nelson Darby. His lies slowly grew to infest most of the Evangelical Church today. At the beginning of this book, I called this lie a giant, for it has become such, and named it False-hope. This giant was able to infiltrate the Church because we failed to heed the warning mentioned above by Peter.

False-hope didn't come in violence, such would have alerted the Church. Rather he sent false teachers and false prophets in the hire of his lord Satan. These came as wolves in sheep's clothing coming into the Church in secret and spreading lies and compromises concerning truth. Slowly over a few generations, these lies were accepted as truth. When False-hope finally came and inhabited the tower of True-hope very few resisted him. Such a process of deception echoes another warning given by Paul:

2 Thessalonians 2:10-12: "And with all deceivableness of unrighteousness in them that perish; because they received not the love of the truth, that they might be saved. 11. And for this cause God shall send them strong delusion, that they should believe a lie: 12. That they all might be damned who believed not the truth, but had pleasure in unrighteousness."

This passage, in context, is speaking about unbelievers and the nature of the Man of Sin, and those that follow him. Some might think that this doesn't apply to what we are discussing. However, if you notice in this passage it says that men were deceived because they loved not the truth of God and that it was God who gave them over to the delusions of the lie so that they would think the lie was the truth.

This is a concept that is not exclusive to the Man of Sin or unbelievers. We have many examples in the old and new testaments of people, both saved and unsaved, who were so deluded by the lies taught to them or believed by them that even when the truth stood right in front of them they couldn't believe it. This was because they loved not the truth. This was the task of the false prophets and teachers. They were to infiltrate the Church and make the truth of God sour in the ears and get the people to hate the truth. Some might immediately say that this could never happen to saved people. Let me give a few examples of when this very thing did happen:

John 5:46-47: For had ye (ye is an Old English word that is a plural singular word meaning it was personal to all who he was addressing and he was addressing all equally. In this passage, Jesus is speaking to all the religious leaders and Jews who had come to him. The closest modern "word" would be y'all) believed (meaning they didn't believe) Moses, ye would have believed me (Jesus is speaking): for he (Moses) wrote of me. 47. But if ye believe not his writings, how shall ye believe my words?"

For context, in the above verse, Jesus is contending with the religious leaders of the day. They did not want to believe that Jesus was the messiah because he did not match the teachings of, nor did he match the preconceived notions of, the elders concerning the Messiah. They were looking for a conquering king that would overthrow their oppressors (Rome at the time) and reestablish the physical kingdom of Israel that would be a golden age for the Jewish people that would last for a thousand years. (Sound familiar? This is the same thing many modern teachers say will happen when Christ returns and rules on earth for 1,000 years). They believed these lies so earnestly that they put more value in them than they did in the bible. Therefore they rejected Christ, the truth made flesh, who came to establish a spiritual kingdom.

These were the false teachers and prophets when Jesus walked the earth. They tried very hard to make the truth sound sour in the ears of the Jews. This battle is one Jesus often fought with the religious leaders, especially their concepts of him as the Messiah and what they taught about this thousand-year golden age of the Messiah's Kingdom. That is why Christ said:

Luke 17:20-21: And when he (Jesus) was demanded of the Pharisees (Jewish religious leaders) when the <u>kingdom of God should come</u> (they believed and taught that when the Messiah came he would establish a physical kingdom of God on earth—which he did do but they couldn't see it. They are asking Jesus this question because he claimed to be the Messiah), he answered them and said, The kingdom of God cometh <u>not with observation</u>: 21. Neither shall they say, Lo here! or, lo there! for, <u>behold, the kingdom of God is within you.</u>

First Jesus said you don't believe me because you don't believe the bible (Moses). Then he overturns their idea of the kingdom of God being brought physically by telling them the kingdom isn't physical at all but it is spiritual (it's inside of you). The above statements by Jesus would have been very offensive to these elders. Many of them studied and memorized the bible from a very early age, but this just added to their blindness because they did not believe what it was they knew. Which is the very definition of not loving the truth. <u>May this be a warning to all of us!</u>

If we reject the truth we show that we love not the truth; our god then becomes our own lusts, and thus we fall into the first lie of sin, "Ye shall be as gods..." Meaning we put ourselves in the seat of God and declare the truth we want to hear rather than the Truth that God tells us. This is the reality when we overthrow God in our hearts by rejecting the truth.

This brings us to the example of deception that I told you about. All of the Apostles grew up under the teachings of the religious leaders. The false teachings of these men perverted their understanding of the truth and Jesus is always trying to correct it. It wasn't until the Holy Spirit came that the blinders were fully removed from the Apostles. That was how ingrained their giants of false doctrine were. The following is how this deception caused Peter to fall:

Mark 8:31-33: And he (Jesus) began to teach them, that the Son of man must suffer many things, and be rejected of the elders, and *of* the chief priests, and scribes, and be killed, and after three days rise again. 32. And he (Jesus) <u>spake that saying openly.</u> (Jesus knew he would be rejected, killed, and resurrected long before the events happened. Many of his sermons contained these very truths a fact many of us do not always consider. These same truths were foretold of Christ in the Old Testament by the Prophets starting back in Genesis 3:15) And Peter took him (Jesus), and began to rebuke him. 33. But when he (Jesus) had turned about and looked on his disciples, he rebuked Peter, saying, <u>Get thee behind me, Satan</u>: for <u>thou savourest</u> (Love/delight) <u>not the things that be of God, but the things that be of men.</u>

In this account the very idea that the Messiah was going to suffer, and die devastated Peter because it went against all of his ideas about the Messiah. Peter knew that Jesus was the Messiah, yet Jesus contradicted everything he knew the Messiah to be.

This is an issue that all the Apostles had any time Jesus spoke about his death they couldn't understand him. They also didn't understand the kingdom being inside them as they often asked if Christ would now restore the kingdom to Israel. Even though Christ often mentioned such things throughout his ministry. No doubt Peter also loved Christ and did not want to see such horrible things happen to his friend, but Christ had to suffer and die to be the Messiah which was one of his purposes in becoming incarnate. (Luke 24:44-47)

The truths about the kingdom and the need for the Messiah to die were things Jesus began to teach his disciples long before the events took place, yet all of them remained blind to this truth. The bible goes out of its way to say they understood not until Christ was glorified (Luke 9:44-45, Luke 18:31-34, Mark 9:32, John 12:16).

This blindness came because they loved not the truth of the words being spoken to them, loving rather the man-made doctrines they preferred to the words that Jesus spoke. That is why Jesus said Peter loved the things of man rather than the things of God. By rejecting the word, Peter became blind to the truth and was used by Satan to try and attack Christ and confuse the other disciples. This is also why Mark records that Christ looked over his disciples before he rebuked Peter as this was not something that just Peter struggled with, and Peter was looked to as a leader among the disciples.

Thus we have a pattern of blindness even among God's people. When one rejects clear truth in God's word for the sake of their own interpretation of the truth or traditions and theologies passed on by men, God as a punishment, will give us over to strong delusions so that we believe the lie. This is one of the main reasons why God has left us his word as a witness to us of all things. It is by embracing that witness and believing it that our blindness is removed.

This very concept is what launched the Reformation of the Church. The word had been hidden and kept from the common man, but once the truth became freely available the lies of popery could no longer hold sway over the hearts of God's elect. Men like John Wycliffe, and Luther were able to overcome the strong delusion of falsehood by embracing the word. By it, they were able to slay the giant of popery.

In the same way, I hope to help us all slay the giant False-hope if the Lord will aid me.

The result of these sorts of lies and perversions is to take people away from the truth of God and bring them into bondage. False-hope holds many in bondage causing Christians to fall into idolatry idolizing national Israel, the rapture, and their own doctrines of man concerning the end times above that of the bible. To idolize something means to praise, reverence (respect), and greatly and excessively love something. This causes them to believe in a defeated apostate church, a short-sighted gospel, and a doomed world. Their false hope is in the rapture which will help them escape from the world.

Essentially the lies of False-hope are: "The World belongs to satan. History is heading to the Antichrist. Nothing the Church can do can help save this world, Christ himself will come and rescue you out of it while Jesus rains wrath upon the earth. Let the world and the Church continue to fall into sin, just focus on getting as many as you can ready for the rapture. The world is supposed to be falling into greater sins and the Church is supposed to fall into apostasy and lukewarmness. Take these things as signs that the rapture is at hand..."

Rather than turn the world upside down with the power and authority of the gospel and the kingdom, something Christ told his Church to do (Matthew 28:16-20), the church that embraces False-hope has lapsed into a spirit of sloth. Rather than understanding that the earth is the inheritance of the Lord and his saints (Psalms 2. Romans 8:17, Matthew 5:5, Pslams 24:1, etc) they see the world as Satan's. It wants to believe that the world will not be won by their preaching and that no matter what they do the enemy is going to win until Christ comes. They expect the Church to be lukewarm and apathetic, taking it as a sign of Christ's imminent return. They see the world getting darker as proof that their false hope is near, but really it allows them to avoid their own responsibility to this world and keeps them from seeing their sin of hating their call to the Great Commission. It keeps them from their inheritance. The world is falling into darkness because the Church has forgotten its purpose. All of this is due to False-hope.

These statements might seem harsh or untrue to you dear pilgrim, but I pray you will change your mind by the time we end this book. I must use blunt terms as cold water splashed in the face of a sleeping man. The tune of False-hope has made our ears heavy and hearts bitter to the truth. So to clarify fully what this tune is let us look at the most basic things that are commonly taught by all churches that embrace False-hope. If you have ever heard anything taught on this topic you should recognize this list:

- The world will continue to grow worse and worse, and churches will fall into greater and greater apostasy (a fancy way of saying they will fall away from the truth of God's word).
- **The establishment of the modern State of Israel in 1948, was a fulfillment of bible prophecy.
- **God has to reestablish Israel to fulfill all the promises to Abraham that God has yet to fulfill.
- *Jesus can return bodily at any moment like a thief in the night.
- **At some point, a figure will appear on the world stage. He will unite the entire world, possibly after a world calamity or war, under a one-world government and religion. This will be a rebirth of the Roman Beast/empire. This man is commonly referred to as the Antichrist, the Son of Perdition, and/or the Man of Sin. He will rule over the entire world for 7 years commonly called the time of the Great Tribulation.
- *The False prophet will help deceive the religious world into following this Antichrist and give the Antichrist great power by which he can do miracles.
- *Depending on your church's particular views, either right before or right after this Antichrist and False Prophet comes into view, Jesus will secretly and suddenly come for his church. The Church, meaning all saved believers alive and who had died previously, will be raptured into heaven and all unsaved people will be left behind. (Some churches also say that this event happens halfway through or at the very end of the Antichrist's 7-year reign).
- *The battle of Gog and Magog also called Ezekiel's War or the war of Armageddon, will take place either right before or right after the Church is raptured and will begin this period known as the Great Tribulation.

- *During this 7-year tribulation, the raptured saints will be partaking in the marriage supper of the Lamb in heaven.
- * Either right before or right after the rapture the Antichrist will make a treaty with the modern state of Israel for 7 years. This treaty he will violate 3 ½ years later.
- *At some point either just before the treaty is signed or as a result of the treaty being signed, the third Jewish temple in Jerusalem is built.
- *Animal sacrifices will once again be performed at the temple.
- **At some point the Antichrist will sit in this temple and declare himself to be God. He will force all the people to worship him and take a mark in their right hand or in their foreheads otherwise they will be unable to buy or sell. They will be beheaded for not obeying. This is where we get the famous 666 from.
- *The Antichrist will either be killed or be given a death blow to the head around this time and will miraculously survive and be healed. He will be able to perform miracles to deceive the nations.
- *During the reign of the Antichrist, God will send 144,000 Jews and his two witnesses to preach the gospel to the world. People who get saved during this time are called the Tribulation Saints.
- *At some point, the two witnesses are killed in Jerusalem and are raptured into heaven.
- *During this 7-year reign of the Antichrist, God will once again be dealing with his favored people the Jews. God will also be pouring out wrath on the earth destroying most of the human population.
- **At the end of the 7-year tribulation, Jesus and his Church will come back and defeat the Antichrist. Babylon is Destroyed.
- *The Tribulation Saints will be transformed into immortal bodies like the saints that were raptured and like Jesus himself, but the unsaved are not yet resurrected/changed.
- **Jesus will establish a physical kingdom on the earth for 1,000 years. He will bind Satan and throw the antichrist and the false prophet into hell. Jesus will rule from Jerusalem upon the throne

of David with his saints during a time of great peace on the earth. During this time the unsaved people that did not perish will rebuild nations and have children and live in harmony under Christ and his saints.

- *All nations will be required to live once again under the laws of Moses and perform the temple rituals. Christ will enforce this with a "rod of iron." Animal sacrifices may or may not be a part of these rituals.
- *Some teach that the bottomless pit will be opened so people can see the false prophet and the beast as a testimony for Christ, during the 1,000 years.
- **After the 1,000-year reign is over, Satan will be allowed to go free, most likely to test the nation's faith. He will gather out of all the nations of those that did not truly believe to make war against Jesus and his saints one final time. This army of Satan will be very great, described as being more than the number of the sand of the sea. (Meaning tons of people born under Christ's physical reign on earth will not be saved).
- God rains fire down from heaven and consumes Satan and his vast army for their rebellion.
- God then resurrects all the dead who ever lived and the whole world is judged. This judgment will take place after the 1,000 years are over.
- God then consumes the entire creation with fire and casts the unsaved and the devil into the lake of fire. God then creates a new heaven and a new earth where the saints will live with him forever in the New Jerusalem.

Depending on the books you have read or what your pastor may have taught you, or what you've heard on radio or podcast, you may also believe:

- *That Israel and the Church are two separate things. That the Church was not in God's original plan for salvation, but he allowed the Church to exist for a time because of the rejection of the Jews to provoke them into jealousy. This time of the Church is often called the Church Age. It will end at the rapture at which point God will return to dealing with Israel.

- *The Great Tribulation is the time of Jacobs Trouble and is also the fulfillment of Daniels's 70th-week prophecy.
- *Jesus came to establish a physical kingdom and rule over Israel but the people did not want him as their king and thus Jesus was rejected. In this way, Jesus was a failed Messiah because the Messiah was not only supposed to save his people but also create a physical Jewish kingdom. (This last point is very popular among extreme Christian Zionists and may not be well known outside of these groups).

The above is the main themes taught by False-hope and all churches that follow his tune will teach much of the above. I would imagine that most reading this book will have heard a lot of the things on this list. These are the main things False-hope declares though sometimes he has slight variations in certain details, remember he has a forked tongue. Please take a moment and look over this list again and note the * next to many of the points.

All the points listed with * in front of them were never taught or believed by any denomination before the 1830s. I'll let that sink in.

As for the points with **, this was believed by some, but they did not believe that the tribulation would be 7 years, or that Christ's 1,000-year reign was literal or a physical thing. Rather, many believed that the 1,000 years were figurative of Christ's current reign from heaven and that these events would happen after or during an unspecified time of tribulation that the Church would go through.

Though most of our forefathers were long gone before the modern State of Israel was established, most of them would agree that if such a thing would happen as a fulfillment of prophecy it would mean a mass conversion of the Jews to Christianity and not be a secular movement that still rejects Christ. With that said, there is absolutely no reason to claim or think that the modern state has anything to do with any fulfillment of bible prophecy. This is a touchy statement but there is good reason to make it. We touch on this concept later in this book.

Our forefather's also understood that God has already fulfilled all the promises made to the fathers concerning Israel, therefore God is not obligated to bring them back to fulfill them. That is not to say they will never be given their land back, but if they were given it back it would be the result of them returning to God by faith in Christ and coming into the New Covenant. This is something we dive into in chapter 11.

Many of our forefathers also all believed that the Gog and Magog War was not a war of our future but was speaking about the war of Antiochus Epiphanes that happened in 175 B.C. The modern idea of it being a future war that starts the 7-year tribulation wasn't even taught until the 1900s, as far as I am aware.

Our forefathers understood the message that Peter preached in Acts 2 and thus they did not teach that Christ had to return physically to rule from the throne of David. They understood that the kingdom was primarily a spiritual thing and not a literal physical one.

There was a small group of people who believed that this 1,000 years would be literal, but these thought that the Revelation had to do with the Church going through suffering by the Man of Sin (this was another beast who was father to False-hope named Deceived-hope. His two heads were called Historic Premillennialism) and they did not believe in the rapture as it is commonly taught today just that there would be a resurrection before the Millenium for just the saints.

Many taught that there would be an "Antichrist" that would force a mark on people but none thought his rule would be confined to 7 years, or necessarily be a singular figure. Also, the very idea of being raptured away from the persecution of this Man of Sin wasn't even in the imaginations of believers, rather they thought the book of Revelation was about the suffering of the Church by the Son of Perdition and his beastly system.

The concept of the rapture was not even understood or considered by any denomination before the 1830s. Rather, they believed in the resurrection of the dead, of both the saved and unsaved, on the final day of human history when Jesus returned to judge the world. All scriptures that most people think today refer to the rapture were understood to be speaking about the resurrection of the dead. There is a very big difference between the concept and teaching of the rapture and the resurrection this also is a concept we will see very plainly as we move through this book.

As for national Israel being separate from the Church, this would have been considered heresy before the 1900s by nearly every denomination. They saw the Church as Israel made up of both believing Jews and Gentiles, from Adam to the last soul saved before Christ returns. They also never thought that this tribulation period of Antichrist was Daniel's 70th week or that it was a time for Jacob's Trouble.

We will be looking at much of this as we go on in this book. The reason why our forefathers believed that the Revelation was focused on the Church and not the Jews is that they believed that in the New Testament the Church was Israel. We will look at that at length in the next chapter. This is sometimes called Replacement Theology. I do not agree with this term. The Church is the fulfillment of the promises of what Israel would be in Christ as promised to Abraham and many others (Romans 15 explains this very well). The only thing the Church replaced, in my opinion, was the Bride. The Old Testament called Jerusalem (representing the Old Covenant whose religious seat was Jerusalem) the Bride of God, the Church is now the Bride of Christ (God) in the New Covenant. This becomes very important later on.

Semantics aside, to help understand this better I am going to quote from one of the Mighty Men of God that I mentioned in the beginning discourse. He is considered in Evangelical America today, as the Prince of Preachers and is highly respected. Ironically he would most likely be kicked out of every Evangelical Church in America if he was alive today. This man is Pastor Charles H. Spurgeon.

Charles H. Spurgeon, for those of you who are unfamiliar with him, was renowned around the world for his preaching in the mid-1800s. Spurgeon was a reformed baptist preacher who pastored the Tabernacle, a large church in England, but his messages went around the world in newspapers/magazines, many of which are still read today. When these modern ideas of False-hope began to be taught, Spurgeon spoke and wrote openly against the prophet of False-hope. I will quote him briefly as he was a contemporary of Darby, and ironically many who have fallen snare to False-hope's lies have great respect for Spurgeon, although I would assume many have not ever read his writings against False-hope's prophet:

"I nor any other {pastor} have ever heard it asserted that those who lived before the coming of Christ <u>did not</u> belong to the church of God! We shall never know what we shall hear next {from the Dabyites}. Perhaps it is a mercy that these absurdities are revealed one at a time, in order that we may be able to endure their stupidity without dying of amazmnt" (From the Sword and Trowel 1869, Spurgeon responding to the teachings of John Nelson Darby that separated national Israel from the Church. {} Added for clarity/context)

This was written in response by Mr. Spurgeon to the brand new doctrine that the Church and national Israel were two different things under the New Covenant, and that the Old Testament saints were not a part of the body of the Church. Darby taught that God had a separate covenant still with the Jews that was different from the Church's covenant, and that the Jews, even though they rejected Christ, were still the covenant people of God. This Zionistic False-hope approach to bible prophecy was just beginning to find footing in the Church around this time. This idea was completely foreign before the 1830s.

How in the world do I know these things? Well, that's because these modern concepts were invented by the prophet of False-hope: John Nelson Darby in the 1830s. His views were later made popular by C.I. Scofield, D.L. Moody, and Clarence Larkin. In the modern era, writers like Hal Lindsay and his book "The Late Great Planet Earth," the films "A Thief in the Night," and "Left Behind" (films and novels), and the many prophecy conferences that constantly try and tie current events to fulfillments of the bible all brought these ideas to the forefront of modern eschatology.

However, it was Mr. Darby that initially came up with the ideas. He believed that God had given him "Divine Knowledge" (his words) about the end times that the rest of the churches had never known or had completely lost in their apostasy for 1800 years. He developed his views by taking the Historic Premillennial view, which had long fallen out of acceptance in the Church, and twisting it and adding his new views of Zionism, the rapture, and Dispensationalism to it. This became an unrecognizable blend of doctrines that had never been heard or seen until that time.

Interestingly, these statements of, "Divine Knowledge," and, "fixing 1800 years of apostasy in the Church," were also the same statements used by another false teacher Joseph Smith, founder of the Morman Cult in 1830. This was also claimed by another cult headed by the Watchtower Society in 1881, and to top it all off this was the same period that Charles Darwin began to develop his theories of evolution. Seems to me that Satan's attacks were in high gear during this period and there is a reason for this as America and the world had gone through many great national revivals just before this time.

Darby's views would eventually be called Dispensational Premillennialism also known simply as Dispensationalism, or as Spurgeon called it Darbyism. I have called it False-hope.

A simple google search of this man will show you that he lived from 1800-1882 and that he was the inventor of this doctrine. Simple math will tell you that his teachings are less than 200 years old. You will also see that this is the man who invented this theology, and many of the above end-times concepts are based on his interpretation of the bible. He claimed fully to be the first person to articulate these things and was given "divine inspiration" from the Holy Spirit to do so. He was also criticized by nearly every church of every denomination that had anything to do with him.

If that wasn't enough to give you pause, John Nelson Darby was considered to be a heartless cult-like leader by his contemporaries. The name of his cult was the Plymouth Brethren. He did not create the Brethren but once he joined up with the group it quickly split into two groups; the Open Brethren and the Exclusive Brethren under two different leaders.

Darby was the leader of the Exclusive Brethren and his group was also called the Darbyites (as referenced in Spurgeon's previous quote), and this group was the very definition of a cult. At its height, it reached about 20,000 members in both England and America, mostly among young men and women.

I'm not just saying these things about Darby, these claims were said by, Mr. Charles H. Spurgeon and many other Mighty Men who were contemporaries with Darby.

Spurgeon wrote extensively against this group in his magazine (newsletter) called the "Sword and Trowel," which I have already quoted previously. Not only did he openly preach and denounce this group and their heretical teachings, but Spurgeon also deplored Darby's views of bible doctrine calling them dangerous. His words echoed the feelings of nearly every pastor of every denomination both in England and in America that had any dealings with this man or his followers. The only exception that I am aware of was D.L. Moody who was openly mocked by Darby because Moody refused to follow all of Darby's teachings.

D.L. Moody latched onto the "rapture" doctrine and realized it could be a good motivator for people to be saved. People were compelled to convert out of fear of the coming destruction, and terror of the Antichrist and not out of faith. As with modern preachers, Moody began to attribute many world events as fulfillments of prophecy and proofs of Christ's imminent return, and if people didn't want to be "left behind" and suffer tribulation they needed to come to the alter.

I do not think Moody meant harm by this, I truly think he meant it for good, and many were saved despite the false doctrine not because of it. However, this began to become the staple of evangelical theology which has only grown worse and worse over the decades. Salvation is now more focused on fear and a promised escape from tribulation and suffering and less on Christ and the Kingdom.

As a result, they see no hope for this fallen world and the inescapable corruption of the Church which will ultimately end in failure. Their only hope is the rapture and getting as many people as they can before it's too late. This has bred a sort of apathy when it comes to spiritual affairs and their impact on world events as no matter how much tribulation people go through, or how bad the world gets, they think it doesn't matter and it's not their responsibility as its, "God's will," because Christ will be coming back soon.

This has caused the light of the Church to begin to wane, and its salt to begin to lose its savor. The warning of Christ should bring us to our knees in repentance as we are now beginning to see its fulfillment. (Matthew 5:13)

This is why we are seeing a boldness among the heathen who have begun to trample the Church underfoot. The reason why the world seems so dark is that the Church has lost its savor, its hope, and its purpose. The trampling has only begun, only if we repent will this judgment be reversed, otherwise, we will go into captivity for a time.

Entire books have been written by "prophets" in the pay of False-hope declaring, that the generation that saw Israel become a nation again will be the last generation of the Church. This inevitably impacted the shift in Evangelical Churches that has led to our current crisis. This has also resulted in literally hundreds of end of the world cults and countless books predicting the end of the world and the coming of God that have all proven false and destroyed the faith of many both inside and outside of the Church. Remember Peter said the purpose of these false teachers and prophets was to do this very thing! (2 Peter 2:1-2)

This has done great harm to the Christian testimony among the unbelieving world. This book will soon show how everything that False-hope says is a lie, and why this must be exposed for what it is.

To end this chapter, I would like to give a few more quotes from Spurgeon's "Sword and Trowel" about Darby and his followers to help show how dangerous and evil Spurgeon saw them. There are dozens if not hundreds of more articles online and they can be found at archive. spurgeon.org just search for the articles.

"Plymouth Brethren have no feeling wherever their principles are concerned. I know indeed of no sect or denomination so utterly devoid of kindness of heart. It is the most selfish religious system which I am acquainted with. It is entirely wrapped up in itself. It recognizes no other denomination, whether the Church of England, or either of the Nonconformist denominations, as a church of Christ. Mr. Darby has again and again said in print {public}, as well as in writing in private, that those who belong to his party in the metropolis {that is the Plymouth Brethren}, constitute {or are the only} church of Christ in London...

The Brethren look upon all other denominations, however evangelical in sentiment, and however high their standard of religion, as so largely infected with error in doctrine, as well as wrong relation to church government, that they believe it would be sinful to associate with them for the promotion of religious ends...Believing <u>they alone</u> of all religious bodies have <u>attained the knowledge of the truth</u>..." (Sword and Trowel, June 1869 {} added for clarity)

Pretty harsh coming from a man known as the Prince of Preachers. Here is one more example:

"We have been requested to reply to a small tract which has been given away at the door of the Tabernacle {Spurgeon's church}, by one of the "Plymouth Brethren," <u>but it is so devoid of all sense, Scripture and reason, that it needs no reply.</u> We have not learned the art of beating the air, or replying to nonsense. The only meaning we could gather from the rambling writer's remarks was a confirmation of our accusation, and a wonderful discovery that a long controverted {debated} point is now settled; *the unpardonable sin is declared to be speaking against the Darbyites.*" (Spurgeon, Sword and Trowel, February 1867 {} added for clarity)

Not only did Darby create Dispensationalism but he also believed:

- Ecclesiastical positions of authority in a Church were sin: Meaning he did not believe a biblical church had pastors, deacons, elders, or church members (these used to be called bishops, presbyters, and laymen). Thus he opposed all historic ideas of Church authority, structure, or discipline be they Roman Catholic, or Protestant in nature.
- Ironically, despite believing the above statement, the only authority concerning scripture interpretation that Darby allowed were his own views. This led to the split in the Brethern I mentioned earlier. Darby even wrote his own version of the bible propagating his views.
- He rejected the idea of imputed righteousness through faith alone. This is the idea that once we accept Christ by faith his righteousness is placed on us, meaning our sins are forgiven based solely on the work of Christ and depend only on Christ

received freely grace through faith alone. This also means his perfect life is imputed, meaning accounted on my behalf. In essence, he took my nature and failing and sin upon himself and was punished in my place and his perfect holy life was placed on me. Darby rather, taught infused righteousness meaning that Christians were given righteousness by grace as long as their works and faith remained. Meaning works were required to merit (deserve) and keep salvation.

- Darby said that communion must be taken weekly and if it was not you were not saved. Darby famously denied anyone communion who did not bow down to his teaching and join the Brethern.

- Darby would seek out young single women to indoctrinate into his ranks. He would then teach these young disciples to infiltrate churches and seduce others to their cause and in the process cause as much harm to the church as they could. This was considered a good work for God because they were dismantling false religion in the eyes of the Darbyites.

This is pretty crazy stuff. I am not exaggerating on any of these points. Please research and see these facts for yourself. The logical question then is if False-hope was invented by this radical cult leader, how on earth did his views become the most accepted view by mainstream Christianity today? How did False-hope take the tower of True-hope?

Great questions and I dedicate an entire chapter in this book to how this happened, but first I have a far more important question: Were Darby's interpretations correct? Could False-hope really be True-hope?

I ask this because it is entirely possible, as some claim, that God used Darby to correct an error and that when men of God stand up for truth they are often criticized by the mainstream religious people. This assertion is sadly often correct. Perhaps Spurgeon's writings were just propaganda by a larger-than-life preacher that was trying to hold onto his theologies?

So how do we know what is correct? Did our forefathers have a better understanding of these things, or did Darby muddy the waters? Well, that leads us into the heart of this book and the close of this chapter. I would like you my dear readers to please go back and review the list of points that most people believe will be the events surrounding the Second Coming. Perhaps you may want to put a bookmark in these pages and refer to them as we go on and let us see if these points are true.

If Darby was indeed inspired by God to create Dispensationalism to correct a gross error in the Church, then his ideas should line up with the bible? Sounds reasonable enough right? Well, let's see what our Lord says about all this.

CHAPTER TWO

Five Pillars of Truth

"The Truth is like a lion. You don't have to defend it.
Simply let it loose and it will defend itself."

St. Augustine Bishop of Hippo 354 A.D.-430 A.D.

S o far I have made several bold claims in this book. Some who have read them have perhaps already put this work down. For those that remain, know that I have not said these things without cause and trembling. In this chapter, I would like to explore five pillars of truth. These were things that, as I began to study the bible, began to stick out in my mind. These truths were very clear, yet when considered they went against everything I had ever been taught about the end times. It was for these five pillars that I began to study this topic in earnest.

For this reason, I felt it is necessary to start in the same place I did when exploring this topic. These pillars will act as the foundations of truth that will be helpful as we go forward in this study. At first, these will seem improbable as they are contrary to what most people are taught, but I would ask that readers would take them and as we go through this book see if they indeed hold up to the bible.

Pillar One: Jesus and the Apostles spoke of two distinct comings of Christ

At first glance, the most common reaction that people will have to this statement is most likely to reject the very notion. Or they may think, "Of course it does, he came once as a child and then will come again from heaven." What I intend from the statement is one most may struggle with. I am saying that Christ spoke of two distinct comings from heaven, once to judge, and once in victory.

I propose one coming was a type/picture of the other. This is important as the events that happened in one declare light upon the other, and thus they will share a similar language but not fulfillment. It was declared that the first would happen within the generation that rejected him. This coming would be a coming in the clouds of judgment against Jerusalem through the Roman armies and was spiritual. These types of coming judgments happened often in the Old Testament and were figurative of God's sovereign judgment against nations.

Each time one of these judgments was declared, they often spoke of God coming in/with the clouds. During these, God sends the armies of other nations to judge his enemies. Often he did so in colorful and apocalyptic language through his prophets. Both Jesus and the Apostles used identical language describing a soon coming fiery judgment at the hand of Christ against Jerusalem.

I propose that this event took place in 70 A.D. and was often called the Day of the Lord, the Great and Terrible Day of the Lord, the Great and Glorious Day of the Lord, the Notable Day of the Lord, and the Day of Christ in both the old and new testaments. If this assertion is true many of the passages used by False-hope to prove the Second Coming of Christ are actually about an entirely different event. Many are taught that all of these titles belong to Christ's physical second coming, but I hope to show that this is not true.

A day of the Lord is in truth, a day of coming judgment from God of which there have been many. We will dive into this much more as we work through the scriptures, and the distinction of these two comings will become very plain to see as we go. For now, I will briefly explain for clarity and then give a few examples.

On the Day of the Lord as it relates to Christ, I propose that Jesus came sovereignly/spiritually to judge Jerusalem and destroy the Levitical Priesthood, and the Jewish Economy—meaning spiritual system, which is the Old Covenant. Jerusalem and the current priesthood at the time had fallen into complete apostasy becoming spiritually Sodom and Egypt (Revelation 11:8-9). Many of the Old Testament prophets called her the harlot (Ezekiel 16:14-16, Jeremiah 3:8, etc).

Because of this, it was done away with. This event is spoken of throughout the old and new testaments. Even to this day, those that claim to follow Judaism do not follow a biblical Judaism but a Babylonian Talmudic Judaism or an Orthodox Judaism only loosely based on the bible. They do not follow the Judaism of the Old Testament (no animal sacrifices, no Levitical priesthood, no tabernacle or temple, circumcision is not always necessary, etc).

This judgment was to affirm the authority of the New Covenant and establish with great power the Melchizedek Priesthood (priesthood of Christ), the kingship of Christ, and to avenge the blood of Christ and all the prophets slain by the Israel of old. This was meant to be a sign to all nations of the validity of the Christian Economy—spiritual system and the kingdom of Christ. It was Christ's marriage celebration to his Church. As such it was also the declaration of the divorce of Israel as the covenant people and the declaration of the Church as the Bride of Christ the New Covenant people made up of both believing Jews and Gentiles.

This entire concept is most likely abhorrent to most readers, I simply ask that for now, you hold off on crucifying me and wait and see if this is true. I am not speaking such judgment against the modern state of Israel or the Jewish people, I am simply referring to the historic significance of the destruction of Jerusalem as it relates to bible prophecy. This was a truth held by most before the 1800s and lost nearly entirely in the mid-1900s due to False-hope.

For nearly 1800 years, the Destruction of Jerusalem was one of the key historical facts that validated the ministry of Christ, the accuracy of bible prophecy, and the divine origin of Christianity. All of this we will go into in great detail in chapter ten of this book.

The actual second bodily coming that Christ and the Apostles spoke about was of the final judgment of the whole world in which Christ would come back bodily in full power and glory to raise the dead and judge the entire world. This is when the bodily resurrection of the just and the unjust (saved and unsaved) takes place and Death is defeated.

This is when the consummation of all things happens (when heaven and earth become one as in the days of Eden). This is also a day of the Lord in the sense that he comes in judgment, but it is not the "Great and Terrible Day of the Lord" as stated above. To help make things less complicated I will be referring to the bodily return of Christ as the Second Coming, and the coming judgment of Christ as the Day of the Lord.

Because most people today are taught that there is only one such "Day of the Lord" and it's when Christ returns bodily, I would like to give a few examples of how this is wrong. It was these things that stood out to me and once considered should make these things plain. As I stated before, the prophets often spoke in apocalyptic language that foretold days of the Lord and truths concerning God. By going back and looking at these we can understand the language of the prophets and understand this pillar.

Key features of the days of the Lord by the prophets are the pronouncement of judgment and usually contain within them is the statement: "The sun and moon shall be darkened," or the "Lord shall come in/with the clouds." Looking back on these events, we can see that God did not literally blot out the sun and stars nor did he bodily come in the past, these are but metaphors of God's sovereign judgment of nations through other nations. He declared such things against Egypt (Ezekiel 30), Edom (Isaiah 34), Babylon (Isaiah 13), and multiple times against Israel, Judah, and many other nations in the Old Testaments. This is especially prevalent in Isaiah, Amos Ezekiel, and Jeremiah, but it is a theme in many of the prophets.

One of the best and clearest examples of this would be in Isaiah 13. In this chapter, Isaiah is given a word about the judgment of Babylon at the hands of the Medes/Persians. In it he declares to Babylon:

Isaiah 13:5-6: 5. They (The Medes) come from a far country, from the end of heaven, _even_ the LORD, (Meaning with the authority of judgment of the Lord going with them) and the weapons of his indignation (As weapons of God's anger), to destroy the whole land. 6. Howl ye; for the day of the LORD _is_ at hand; it shall come as a destruction from the Almighty.

He goes on to declare:

Isaiah 13:10-11: <u>For the stars of heaven and the constellations thereof</u> <u>shall not give their light: the sun shall be darkened in his going forth,</u> <u>and the moon shall not cause her light to shine.</u> 11. And <u>I will punish</u> <u>the world for *their* evil, and the wicked for their iniquity;</u> and I will cause the arrogancy of the proud to cease, and will lay low the haughtiness of the terrible.

We know that this judgment happened around 539 B.C. Obviously, the literal sun, stars, moon, and constellations didn't stop or go away. Rather these were symbolic of the type of judgments that God was declaring. The sun, moon, and stars most likely represented the glory of the nation, its religious or military might, and its civic and religious leaders. We know this from the rest of the chapter, and some following chapters, as God goes on to describe destroying these things. Therefore the above statements about the sun, moon, and stars were a symbolic overview of this act. We will dive more into this in a moment.

Babylonians were obsessed with astronomy and worshiped the stars as gods so when God took away the lights of the constellations it is a reference to the destruction of their gods. We get a glimpse of this in Daniel 2 when God confounds the magicians and astrologers. The whole world is said to be judged when Babylon is judged because it was the first great world empire and all the nations of the known earth were put under it, thus they were all also judged along with Babylon.

God also tells Babylon how he will pass this judgment. This entire prophecy was given about 300 years before Babylon even rose to power:

Isaiah 13:17: Behold, <u>I will stir up the Medes against them,</u> which shall not regard silver; and *as for* gold, they shall not delight in it.

Another way we can understand the prophetic meaning of the sun, moon, and stars comes from a principle in Bible interpretation sometimes called the principle/doctrine of first mention. This principle is the idea that when God introduces a topic, subject, or idea for the first time he usually defines the concept of it in the same passage when kept in context. Then all verses related to said topic will build upon this definition as a foundation. This principle is a very good one and I've found it proves true.

So let us take this same principle and look at the very first time that the sun, moon, and stars are applied to things that are not the actual sun, moon, and stars and we will see with great clarity what they represent prophetically.

Genesis 37:9-10: And he (Joseph) dreamed yet another dream, and told it his brethren, and said, Behold, I have dreamed a dream more; and, behold, <u>the sun and the moon and the eleven stars</u> made obeisance (meaning they bowed down) to me.

10. And he told *it* to his father, and to his brethren: and his father rebuked him, and said unto him, What *is* this dream that thou hast dreamed? <u>Shall I and thy mother and thy brethren indeed come to bow down ourselves to thee to the earth?</u>

This is a really cool passage as we see that the sun, moon, and stars are prophetically symbolizing Joseph's father, mother, and their children (his brothers). When Joeseph tells his father Jacob this dream, Jacob understands what each symbol means. Some may wonder how this helps us in our study. For this let us consider a biblical home.

Biblically the father of the home is the sovereign of the home. God has given him the responsibility to govern, protect, provide, and oversee his house. His wife is the reflection of his glory and strength. She is his helper and co-leader of the home, essentially acting like its heart, but she is not greater than her covering that being her husband just as the moon is not greater than the sun. The children are lesser still than these (when considering an earthly perspective) though they still shine with their light it is much smaller in glory than the sun and moon. This principle is applied in the old and new testament to governments and even to the Church.

We see this in principle all through the bible, but as an example, it is directly spoken about Christ and his kingdom in:

Psalms 89:35-37: 35. Once have I (God the Father) sworn by my holiness that I will not lie unto David. 36. His seed (Jesus) shall endure for ever, and his throne <u>as the sun</u> before me. 37. It shall be established (that being his kingdom for the throne is the seat of power for the kingdom when the throne is established the kingdom is) for ever <u>as the moon</u> (so his kingdom shall be established as the moon), and *as* a faithful witness in heaven. Selah (Selah literally means think about this).

This promise was fulfilled by Christ, something Peter preaches in Acts 2. His throne is like the sun, and the establishment of his throne or kingdom is like the moon. This means that Christ is the sun or source of the Church's light, the Church is the moon. The Church is the seat of his kingdom on the earth that reflects his light into the world, and the stars would then be the children of God produced by their union. This of course can also prophetically be applied to other religious organizations similarly.

The passage in Isaiah 13 that we saw above applies this truth in the same way to the government of Babylon. That being the rulers are the sun, their military or religion would reflect their glory or power as the moon, and the stars would be their people. Once these principles are understood every time they are applied prophetically we can immediately know what they mean. Amazing that God established this very early one in the bible and built upon it.

Let us consider clouds. In the bible, clouds are often associated with God. The Bible claims he is clothed in clouds and he rides the clouds as a chariot (Psalms 104:2-3). That the clouds are like dust beneath his feet (Nahum 1:3) and even proclaimed that he would dwell in thick clouds (1 King's 8:10-12, Job 22:14, etc). All of these are meant to paint a picture of the great sovereignty and majesty of God. When it comes to judgments, clouds are again often associated with God.

Psalm 97:2-3: 2. Clouds and darkness _are_ round about him: righteousness and judgment _are_ the habitation of his throne. 3. A fire goeth before him, and burneth up his enemies round about. 4. His lightnings enlightened the world: the earth saw, and trembled.

Ezekiel 30:3: For the day _is_ near, even the day of the LORD _is_ near, a cloudy day; it shall be the time of the heathen.

Isaiah 19:1: The burden of Egypt. Behold, the LORD rideth upon a swift cloud, and shall come into Egypt: and the idols of Egypt shall be moved at his presence, and the heart of Egypt shall melt in the midst of it.

The above are just some examples of which I could list many others. Let us keep these things all in mind and compare them to something Jesus said. In the following three passages we will see very similar language. These passages are used by modern False-hope teachers who claim they are speaking about the end of the world but compare them to the above passages in Isaiah 13 and the passages of the clouds. These passages come from three gospel accounts of the same discourse given by Jesus but told from three different perspectives:

Matthew 24:29: Immediately after the tribulation of those days <u>shall the sun be darkened, and the moon shall not give her light, and the stars shall fall from heaven, and the powers of the heavens shall be shaken.</u>

Mark 13:24-25: 24. But in those days, after that tribulation, <u>the sun shall be darkened, and the moon shall not give her light, 25. And the stars of heaven shall fall,</u> and the powers that are in heaven shall be shaken.

Luke 21:25-27: 25. And there <u>shall be signs in the sun, and in the moon, and in the stars;</u> and upon the earth distress of nations, with perplexity; the sea and the waves roaring; 26. Men's hearts failing them for fear, and for looking after those things which are coming on the earth: for the powers of heaven shall be shaken. 27. And then shall they see the <u>Son of man coming in a cloud with power and great glory.</u>

All three of these bear a striking similarity to things that Isaiah prophecied about a day of the Lord against Babylon. We will dive at great length into the full context of the above passages in chapter ten of this book, however, I will say that the context of what Jesus is saying related directly to the Destruction of Jerusalem and the temple. This was the Great and Terrible Day of the Lord against Jerusalem.

Most of False-hope's preachers, however, ignore this context and claim that this is the bodily return of Christ. Again compare the same language from the Old Testament prophets to what Jesus is declaring. Jesus is the greatest of all prophets and uses the same language to portray who he is.

Let us consider one other passage to better clarify this. There are many such passages we could turn to and we will look at these in greater detail later in this book:

Matthew 26:63-64: But Jesus held his peace. And the high priest answered and said unto him, I adjure thee by the living God, that thou tell us whether thou be the Christ, the Son of God.

64. Jesus saith unto him, Thou hast said: nevertheless I say unto you, <u>Hereafter shall ye see the Son of man sitting on the right hand of power, and coming in the clouds of heaven.</u>

This passage has confounded many people who do not grasp what Jesus is speaking about. Jesus prophesied a coming judgment against Israel and the religious system often (Matthew 24, Mark 13, Luke 21, and many other passages). When Jesus preached such things he used the same Old Testament symbolism concerning coming in judgment.

This was far more important to the audience he spoke to back in this day as his audience were mainly Jews and they would have been familiar with what he was saying. These types of declarations are one of many examples of when Christ proclaimed himself to be God. He did this by putting himself as the source of the coming judgment that was reserved for God alone in the Old Testament.

Because there is such a misunderstanding of this concept, the entire prophecy concerning this judgment and the related passages in the old and new testaments have been misinterpreted by False-hope's preachers and thus this declaration in Matthew 26 makes little sense. Most people think Jesus was speaking about his bodily return to Caiaphas, yet he would be long dead before Christ would return. So to make this passage work we would have to apply it to the resurrection. This is why many modern teachers say that this statement is true because when Christ returns all the dead are raised and Jesus is talking about that.

However what Jesus is pronouncing to the High Priest is, that when this judgment comes you are going to see me in my glory and power and know that this judgment comes by my hand. Yet he did this using the Old Testament language which the high priest would have known. We will also see in chapter 10 of this book that Jesus pronounced this judgment openly and often before this encounter, so the high priest would have been aware of this teaching, but this is the first time that Jesus directly tells Caiaphas the destruction will come by my hand. By doing so Jesus is claiming to be God judging in the same manner and with the same authority as Jehovah.

This high priest would have known exactly the symbolism that Christ was using. In essence, Jesus was telling Caiaphas, "I am the same

God that destroyed the enemies of Israel and I will likewise come and destroy you." To help prove this notice how Caiaphas responded:

Matthew 26:65: Then the high priest rent his clothes, saying, <u>He hath spoken blasphemy</u> (Why? Because Jesus is equating himself to God by positioning himself as God bringing sovereign judgment and Caiaphas understood that); what further need have we of witnesses? behold, now ye <u>have heard his blasphemy</u>.

When we understand that two such comings of Christ were spoken of, one being a spiritual coming of judgment, and the other physical, it will help shed light on why the Apostles seemed to speak as if Christ would come at any moment, yet at the same time, they spoke as if it would happen in the future. Or why Jesus said it would happen within a generation, yet he has not bodily returned in 2,000 years. All of this we will dive into more as we go deeper into this study.

Pillar Two: Christ can't bodily return at any moment

This is another explosive statement. Let me clarify my point again, Jesus can come suddenly in judgment as has done so throughout history taking people like a thief in the night, and he can come at any moment for your soul, as we are not guaranteed tomorrow, but he cannot return bodily at any moment without violating his father's will.

I would like you to consider again the most quoted Old Testament verse that is quoted in the New Testament and ask yourself what is it saying.

Psalms 110:1: **A Psalm of David.** The LORD (God the Father) said unto my Lord (God the Son), Sit thou at my right hand, <u>until I make thine enemies thy footstool</u>. (this is done through God the Holy Spirit acting through Christ's body, the Church. This whole psalm is a declaration of the son's rule and kingship)

Jesus quoted it:

Matthew 22:43-44: 43. He saith unto them, How then doth David in spirit call him Lord, saying, 44.The LORD said unto my Lord, Sit thou on my right hand, <u>till I make thine enemies thy footstool?</u>

Paul quoted it in Hebrews:

Hebrews 1:8: But unto the Son *he saith,* <u>Thy throne, O God, *is* for ever and ever</u>: a sceptre of righteousness *is* the sceptre of thy kingdom.

Hebrews 1:13: But to which of the angels said he at any time, Sit on my right hand, <u>until I make thine enemies thy footstool?</u>

Lastly, Paul explains this:

1 Corinthians 15:24-28: 24. <u>Then *cometh* the end,</u> when he (Jesus) shall have delivered up the kingdom to God, even the Father; <u>when he shall have put down all rule and all authority and power. 25. For he</u> (Jesus)<u> must reign, till he hath put all enemies under his feet</u>. (Reread these verses a few times and let it sink in. Christ has to reign until all enemies are put under his feet. If the Church is Christ's body where are his feet? Implied in this beautiful passage is the necessity that the Church will play a vital role in fulfilling the Father's declaration to the son. This reign is in/from heaven meaning he will remain there until this is done.)

26. <u>The last enemy *that* shall be destroyed *is* death.</u> (This speaks of the resurrection) 27. For he (the Father) hath put all things under his (Jesus') feet (God already declares this as if it has already happened, yet it is not fully manifested yet on the earth. This is because the declarations of God are certain, he is in absolute control of how everything will turn out). But when he (the Father) saith all things are put under *him* (the Son), *it is* manifest (made clear/revealed) that he (the Father) is excepted (By who? The context is referring to his enemies, meaning his enemies will recognize the Father as God because of the rule of the Son which will put all enemies under Jesus' feet.), which did put all things under him (the Son. Meaning even though the kingdoms and enemies of God are put under Jesus' feet all will know that the Father was the one to do it. This is also seen in the opening declaration in the mind of the Father that this truth is already done and certain, yet for us, it is yet to be fully seen.). 28. And when <u>all things shall be subdued unto him, then shall the Son</u> also himself be subject unto him (God the Father. This shows how the enemies will know that the Father is the one who did this as the Son does not take credit rather he gives the victory to the Father) that put all things under him, that God may be all in all.

If God declares something once it is important when he does so over and over again we should pay attention. So I would ask when the bible says that Christ will—and has to—rule at the right hand of his father until all of his enemies are made His footstool and all powers are made subject to him what does that mean?

I think the only thing it can mean without twisting the clear declarations of truth, is that Christ will not return until all enemies to him and his gospel are put under his feet. I'm not implying that the whole world will be made Christian, rather Christianity will reach a point where it has preeminence (greater authority/influence than all other religions, nations, and peoples of the earth). This is actually a theme all through the old and new testaments about the glorious and victorious reign of Christ, as we will soon see

If we look over the history of the last 2,000 years we can see a progressive move in this direction. In most countries, we went from being burned alive for owning a bible to being able to have as many as we want and openly practice our faith. This trend is growing and the world system is rebelling against it as it has over and over again during the last 2,000 years. Each time it tries to snuff out the growth of the kingdom it only explodes with greater power and beauty.

The reason why False-hope was sent by Satan against the Western Church was to slow down the progress we have made over the last 2,000 years.

Note as well Paul highlights that the last enemy Christ will defeat is Death, which is the resurrection. I want to emphasize this again as False-hope claims that Christ will rapture his Church (resurrect their bodies or change them if they are alive) <u>before</u> all of Christ's enemies are put under his feet. So False-hope claims that Death is the first enemy defeated, not the last. If False-hope is correct then Christ still has to defeat the antichrist, the world systems, all the false religions, and satan at the end of the 1,000-year reign of Christ. Meaning the clear declaration of the most quoted verse in the bible is wrong if this view is correct.

Personally, I have a big issue with that.

False-hope says that Christ's reign mentioned above will not even start in full until Christ physically comes back and sets up his kingdom from Jerusalem after the 7-year tribulation. Yet the verses themselves say this reign is currently at the father's right hand. Thus we have to ignore the fact that Christ is right now ruling at the right hand of the father and the kingdom is not primarily physical it is first spiritual and then manifests itself through the Church in order to believe False-hope. Remember as well that Jesus said the Kingdom cannot be seen for it is inside of us, but False-hope says that it can be seen but it will be in the future.

Meaning False-hope constantly wants to either preach the opposite of what God say's or place it far away in the future. This is a pattern we will see often.

I want to point out that these are not the only verses that declare this truth about Christ's rule and the Church's part in it. It is also spoken of in Psalm 2, Daniel 2:37-45, Daniel 7:13-14, 17-18, Isaiah 2:1-5, and many other Old and New Testament passages. Jesus even declares how this will happen:

Matthew 28:18-20: 18. And Jesus came and spake unto them, saying, <u>All power is given unto me in heaven and in earth. 19. Go ye therefore, and teach all nations,</u> baptizing them in the name of the Father, and of the Son, and of the Holy Ghost: 20. <u>Teaching them to observe all things whatsoever I have commanded you:</u> and, lo, I am with you alway, *even* unto the end of the world. Amen.

By obeying and fulfilling the great commission we are bringing the kingdom of God to earth. By converting the enemies and kingdoms of this world to Christ we place them under his feet. Some enemies like False-hope are sent in retaliation but must be slain by the word of God along the way. The Great Commission is how God will bring his enemies under his feet.

It must be stressed that the Church's role is to bring nations under the kingdom authority of Christ who is the head not to bring them under the authority of the Church. This is one of the errors of Rome. The Church is not the glory of the kingdom, nor its head, she just reflects these. Our role is to teach the world to obey the gospel as a mother teaches her children how to obey the law of God and enforce the rule of her husband in the home. Her husband in this case is Christ he is the focus and source of all not the Church.

As Christians, our role is not to just get people saved or to put them into a Church, but it was also to teach them to obey all things that Christ taught. Jesus doesn't say do this to just individuals, but to nations, and not just some nations, but all nations. This is the concept of discipleship, and Christ's order to the Church is that we do this to all nations. God never orders us to do anything that he doesn't give us the grace to perform through the Holy Spirit.

Peter declares in Acts 2:14-41 that the outpouring of the Holy Spirit was sent as a sign to the world that the Son was sitting down at the right hand of God to begin this reign. His sitting in rule coincided with the empowering of the Church to begin fulfilling the Great Commission.

Unlike what False-hope claims, Jesus is not having to come and sit on David's throne in Jerusalem to begin his rule, as he is already sitting on this throne ruling beside his father on the heavenly Mt. Zion. We will dive much deeper into this whole concept in chapters eleven and twelve.

If these clear verses, of which I have only shown a few, are to be taken at their word, then Christ cannot bodily come at any moment. He must first put all of his enemies under him, he does that through the preaching of the gospel by his Church. The Church is the body of Christ thus his feet are in the Church.

Pillar Three: We have been living in the last days for nearly 2,000 years, and the Antichrist is a Spirit, not a man.

To help clarify this let me ask: "When do the end times start, and what are the events that should take place during this time?"

If you were anything like I was, my mind immediately would conjure up all the chaos around me. I would see the wars and rumors of wars and how wicked my world seemed. I'd see the one-world agenda and technology that might be used as the mark of the beast. I'd think of all the false teachers and false messiahs that I had seen rise, fall, and live in my lifetime.

I'd then consider how so many churches were falling away from the truth of God. Then I would think of what I had been taught about the end times by False-hope and think, "The end days must have started, or soon will. Perhaps the rapture will happen at any moment!" Then my mind would inevitably think of the movie, "Left Behind," the 7-year tribulation, the Antichrist, and the mark of the beast, and I would desperately hope I would not be left behind when God came. I understood the end days or last times as only a reference to the 7-year tribulation.

It is here I want to lay this foundation of truth: That is, we have been living in the end times for 2,000 years. Let me let John prove this.

1 John 2:18-19: Little children, it is the last time: and as ye have heard that antichrist shall come, even now are there many antichrists; whereby (in this way) we know that it is the last time. 19. They went out from us, but they were not of us; for if they had been of us, they would no doubt have continued with us: but they went out, that they might be made manifest that they were not all of us."

This was written by the same John that wrote the book of the Revelation, the books of John, and 1, 2, and 3rd John. This was the apostle that was closest to Jesus. Notice how John said that he and all the believers living when he wrote this book, were living in the last times. Not only that, but there were also antichrists all around them, and that was how he could prove that they were living in the last days.

Then in verse 19, he clarifies who these antichrists were. These were individuals that were once a part of them, meaning they were seemingly Christians at some point. Think about this, they called themselves Christians at one time. This is important because the term Christian means "Christ-like" or "little Christ." Christ means Messiah (John 1:41). Christians were first called Christians because they followed the teachings of Jesus and acted like him. So they were mockingly called, "little Christs" because they were "Christ-like." This was not a compliment when the term was first used.

Presumably, these antichrists made a profession of faith, got baptized, and even attended church, yet they did not continue in the faith. Rather, they went out from the faith, proving that despite their outward appearance or profession, or works that they were never actually a part of the faith. This was God's doing, as John said they went out so that their nature would be manifest (revealed).

Hmm, this sounds an awful lot like Judas to me. Didn't Judas eat with Jesus for 3 ½ years? Didn't he preach and do miracles as the other apostles did? Remember if you will, that none of the other apostles knew that Judas was a betrayer until the very end (except Jesus). Just like these false believers, who John calls antichrists, Judas betrayed Jesus and in the end, all antichrists do.

So what then is antichrist? In the modern English language when we put "anti" in front of a word we know it means, "going against or the opposite of" the object it's attached to. It is true that all antichrists go against the true Christ, and that they are all opposed to and are opposite of him; however, this isn't the only thing that antichrist means. There are two other meanings of this term: first, it means false Christ (false messiah/savior), and second, it means one who stands in the place of Christ (messiah/savior) falsely. All three applications are used in the bible.

Many people think that these concepts are solely reserved for a singular world figure called the "Antichrist," but I hope to show you how this is not the case. John also goes on to describe that antichrist is not a person at all but a spirit, or nature, that manifests itself in individuals:

1 John 4:2-3: 2. Hereby (in this way) know ye the Spirit of God: Every spirit that confesseth that Jesus Christ is come in the flesh is of God: 3. And every spirit that confesseth not that Jesus Christ is come in the flesh is not of God: <u>and this is that *spirit* of antichrist, whereof ye have heard that it should come; and even now already is it in the world.</u>

When I first stumbled onto this verse it captivated me as all my life I was taught that antichrist was a person. John explains that this is not true as we can see in this text antichrist is a spirit. Before we dive a bit deeper into this there are only two other verses in the whole bible that mentions antichirst that I think we should look at them to completely understand what antichrist is. If we can identify it then we can know with confidence, like John, that we are in the end times:

1 John 2:22-23: 22. Who is a liar but he that denieth that <u>Jesus is the Christ? He is antichrist,</u> that denieth the Father and the Son. 23. Whosoever denieth the Son, the same hath not the Father: *(but) he that acknowledgeth the Son hath the Father also.*

Remember Christ means messiah, which means savior; so anyone who denies that Jesus is the messiah this person or group of people is of the spirit of antichrist. Millions of people today think that Jesus either didn't exist or if he did he was just a great teacher or man. When people do this they are denying that Jesus is the Christ, thus they are antichrists.

More than this, however, John says that those who deny the savior also deny the father, which means the modern Jews, Mormons, Jehovah's Witnesses, and the Muslims who all claim to worship the father aren't worshiping him. Meaning their god is no god at all but something else. Each of these groups denies Jesus is the Christ, and God thus these are all manifesting the spirit or nature of antichrist!

2 John 1:7: For many deceivers are entered into the world, who confess not that <u>Jesus Christ is come in the flesh. This is a deceiver and an antichrist.</u>

From these verses, we can begin to see how this spirit of antichrist manifests itself. You see this spirit:

1. If one falls away from the faith (apostasy).
2. If one denies that Jesus was the messiah.
3. If one denies that Jesus was a fleshly being (before or after his resurrection).
4. If one denies that Jesus is God.
5. If one denies that the savior has come.
6. If one denies there is a God
7. If one declares a different god
8. If one denies the son
9. If one takes the place of God or the savior.

Many other truths may be gained by these verses, at the end of the day I would argue that the spirit manifests its ugly head any time someone perverts/changes what the bible says about Jesus, who he was, and what he did.

This means that people can claim to believe in Jesus, or the messiah, or God but if their Jesus does not match the Jesus of the bible then they are teaching another Jesus. Thus they are antichrist. To help confirm this concept let's consider Paul:

2 Corinthians 11:4: For if he that cometh <u>preacheth another Jesus,</u>

whom we have not preached, or *if* ye receive another spirit, which ye have not received, or another gospel, which ye have not accepted, ye might well bear with *him*.

Paul in 2 Corinthians is rebuking the Church in Corinth so that they would not receive these antichrist preachers (bearing with them) when they came representing/preaching a different Jesus and a different gospel and spirit. Meaning even in Paul's day antichrists were doing this very thing, and he was worried about the spiritual state of the Corinthians that they might just get sucked into what the antichrist preachers were saying.

Add to this that Christians are ambassadors of Christ (2 Corinthians 5:20). An ambassador stands in the place of a ruler or king and represents them to a foreign land (Literally they stand in the place of their king and speak with their authority on their behalf). As Christians, our king is Jesus, and we represent Him to this lost world.

Question: What Jesus is your church, teacher, or you representing to the world?

As ambassadors, we stand in the place of Christ and represent (re-present/declare/demonstrate) Christ to this world. If we misrepresent him, pervert him, or change him in any way, we bear a false Christ. Not only do we go against Christ but we then bear the same spirit of antichrist. This should cause all of us who claim the name of Christ to tremble and think carefully about how we live in this world. When we take all of these truths together we have a very clear picture of what antichrist is.

That is why John called those that fell away from the truth, antichrist. This doesn't necessarily mean that they stopped being religious or stopped going to a church or claiming the name of Christ—though I am sure some did—but some left the fellowship of the truth and went out from the sound doctrine of the faith.

Thus all antichrists do not continue in the purity of the faith. Therefore the testimony of their lives and doctrines did great harm to a lost world by leading others into their false teachings. These people exist in great abundance all around us today. I hope going forward that this will help you understand and identify antichrist.

As I hope you can see, the spirit of the antichrist is all around us. Therefore, we can declare boldly with John that these are indeed the last times. They are called such because it is the last period of time before the end of the world. They span from the time of the outpouring of the Holy Spirit when Christ began his rule and will continue until Christ returns on the last day to defeat his final enemy, death, and deliver the fullness of the kingdom to his Father. That also means that the spirit of antichrist will be defeated before then.

Meaning the last days or last times are the days of the reign of Christ. Interestingly, even though they do not think Christ was the messiah, modern Jews teach that the end times, or last days, are the days of the rule of the Messiah. As we already saw the Messiah is right now reigning and we are living under his rule, so their understanding is correct if misplaced.

To further help cement this idea of the last days being the now reign of the Messiah let us consider the following verses:

1 Peter 1:19-21: 19. But with the precious blood of Christ, as of a lamb without blemish and without spot: 20. Who verily was foreordained before the foundation of the world, but <u>was manifest</u> (declared/made known)<u> in these last times for you,</u> 21. Who by him do believe in God, that <u>raised him up from the dead, and gave him glory; that your faith and hope might be in God.</u>

Peter declares that Christ was manifest in the last time, what we often call the last days. Verse 21 links the resurrection of Christ from the dead to this manifestation of Jesus' glory. Meaning Christ was not fully revealed until he was raised and glorified at the right hand of the Father. This highlights the importance of Christ's resurrection as a marker of when these days were fully declared/manifest. Paul declares something similar in:

Hebrews 9:26: For then must he (Jesus) often have suffered since the foundation of the world: but now once in <u>the end of the world hath he appeared</u> to put away sin by the sacrifice of himself.

Christ's appearance and suffering marked the end of the world, or how we would render it the last days of the world. This truth is two-fold: It marked the end of the Old Testament world system which would be destroyed in 70 A.D. and the last period of world history that will end when Christ returns bodily on the last/final day.

I understand that many are taught that antichrist will be a singular figure and may be confused by everything we just went over. However, we need to recognize that the Apostle John identifies antichrist, not as a person but a spirit, and that antichrist can manifest itself in singular individuals as well as whole nations, sects, and religions. In this regard, if a man manifests this spirit it is not wrong to call that man Antichrist, but we must do so by realizing that antichrist is more than just a single man.

Most people are taught that the "Antichrist" will be a world leader that will sit in the rebuilt third Jewish temple in modern Israel and declare himself to be god and that he will rule over the whole earth during the 7-year tribulation and force people to worship him and take a mark. Yet, the above verses about antichrist do not teach this. The above verses are the only verses in the whole bible that talk about antichrist.

Pillar Four: The Church is the third temple and the Man of Sin has already come

I realize this foundation doesn't seem possible, but let's see what the bible says. Let us first start with the main verse concerning the "antichrist" figure that False-hope loves to twist:

2 Thessalonians 2:3-4: 3. Let no man deceive you by any means: for *that day shall not come* (The day of Christ), except there come a falling away first, and that man of sin be revealed, the son of perdition;

4. Who opposeth and exalteth himself above all that is called God, or that is worshipped; so that he as God sitteth in the temple of God, shewing himself that he is God.

I would like to point out that these verses do not say Antichrist will sit in the temple, a teaching many will have heard, but the Son of Perdition. Are these two figures the same? Again, if you look up every mention of antichrist in the bible it is always referring to a spirit that manifests itself in individuals and not solely a singular person. This figure may be of the spirit of antichrist, but it is not Antichrist itself.

Because of this, we should look at these concepts as two different things. Perdition means eternal damnation/destruction. So this figure is the son of damnation and destruction. This implies that not only is he damned but he leads souls to eternal destruction and damnation. The passage also calls him the Man of Sin. I would also like to point out that the Man of Sin, Son of Perdition, and the antichrist are never mentioned by name in Revelation, rather the beast is mentioned.

There is good reason to think that the beast and the Man of Sin are both the same person, but they are never called the antichrists in the bible though they certainly are of that spirit. This passage also says that there will be a falling away, but a falling away of what? False-hope says of the Church, but it doesn't say this, just that there would be a falling away. We will address this more shortly.

This figure exalts himself above God and all things that men worship. He declares himself as God in the temple of God, so it is correct that he is also of the spirit of antichrist.

I want to highlight this again because the spirit of antichrist is one of the devil's perversions of the Holy Spirit. As true believers receive the Holy Spirit, which gives us a new heart and nature from the father by which we become like Christ, the devil's children take on his nature which seeks to kill, steal, pervert, and destroy all things. Above all else, he seeks to destroy how men are saved by perverting the right path of salvation in Christ. All those that hold the spirit of antichrist work together as a singular spirit.

Think of the Man of Sin and the beast, whether they be the same person or not, as heads of which there are many. Even if one is killed the spirit of antichrist has many others to replace it. I could take this further and say some of these heads are governments, world leaders, and religions all declaring the antichrist. As I stated I believe that Christ will put all enemies under his feet. That includes this enemy which I believe will likely be one of the last enemies slain before death.

Because we are not focusing primarily on the Day of the Lord in this book, but more on the Second Coming, we will not be focusing too much on this Man of Sin. If I end up writing the book on Revelation we will look at this and many other passages about the Day of the Lord in far greater detail. To do the Day of the Lord justice, I would need an entire book to properly unravel all the lies of False-hope. To help explain this passage for our needs in this book, however, let us consider the three possible ways we can interpret this passage:

This man existed in the time before Jerusalem fell, and the temple was the one in Jerusalem. Therefore the day of Christ is not speaking about the physical coming of Christ but his coming in judgment against Jerusalem.

This is speaking about a future man in a future third temple.

This is speaking about the spiritual temple in believers, and thus this man can be a past, present, or future person.

To understand this last point we need to know what the New Testament teaches about the final temple of God, which is the temple under the New Covenant:

Act 17:24: God that made the world and all things therein, seeing that he is Lord of heaven and earth, dwelleth not in temples made with hands;

Here in Acts, Paul is making an argument against the idolatry of the pagans in Athens. Like all pagans of that day, they built grand temples and put statues of their god(s) in the temple(s) and they believed their deity would inhabit the statue(s) and temple(s). Paul says that God doesn't dwell in a temple made from human hands. It is important to note that he doesn't say God does not dwell in a temple, just not one made by hands.

This is important because he says in Corinthians:

1 Corinthians 3:16: Know ye not that ye are the temple of God, and that the Spirit of God dwelleth in you? 17. If any man defile the temple of God, him shall God destroy; for the temple of God is holy, which temple ye are.

Twice believers are called the temple of God in this verse. Paul also states that the Holy Spirit (God) dwells (lives) inside of us. This is not the only place he states this:

Ephesians 2:19-22: 19. Now therefore ye are no more strangers and foreigners, but fellowcitizens with the saints, and of the household of God; 20. And are built upon the foundation of the apostles and prophets, Jesus Christ himself being the chief corner *stone; 21.* In whom all the building fitly framed together groweth unto an holy temple in the Lord:

22. <u>In whom ye also are builded together for an habitation of God through the Spirit.</u>

Paul wrote these letters just like he wrote the letters to the Thessalonians. Clearly, when he spoke to churches about the temple of God his doctrine seemed to refer not to a physical temple but a spiritual one. That is not to say that many did not still consider the then standing physical temple the house of God as well. Jesus called it his father's house (Matthew 21:13). Meaning for a brief time in history there were two temples of God, one physical (Old Covenant) and one spiritual (New Covenant).

The question I think everyone needs to consider is if in all of Paul's previous letters he spoke of the temple of God as being the one in believers, why would he suddenly mean the physical temple in 2 Thessalonians? My opinion is that the temple in the 2 Thessalonians passage has nothing at all to do with a physical temple.

Ephesians makes it clear that the spiritual temple was not just made up of modern believers, but the prophets and apostles are also stones that represent all believers even from the Old Testament all coming together in Christ to form this temple. The physical temple was a shadow/type/ pattern of the spiritual. This concept of believers being the temple is all through the New Testament and is a fulfillment of the Old Testament prophecies about the New Covenant.

Not only are believers called the temple of God in the New Testament, but they are called this because of another truth Paul reveals:

1 Corinthians 6:15: Know ye not that your bodies are the <u>members of Christ?</u> shall I then take the members of Christ, and make *them* the members of an harlot? God forbid.

This verse, among many others, is where we get the concept that the Church is the body of Christ. Christ is the head of the New Testament Church and we are his body.

Ephesians 1:22-23: And hath put all *things* under his feet, and gave him *to be* the head over all *things* to <u>the church, 23. Which is his body</u>, the fulness of him that filleth all in all.

Because we are a part of his body we are also a part of the temple. Listen to how Jesus put it:

John 2:19-21: Jesus answered and said unto them (Them being the Jews), <u>Destroy this temple, and in three days I will raise it up.</u> 20. Then said the Jews, Forty and six years was this temple in building, and wilt thou rear it up (rebuild it) in three days? 21. But he (Jesus) spake of the <u>temple of his body</u>.

Jesus puts a distinction between the temple of his body and the physical temple of the Jews. So we see how being a member, or part, of Christ's body, also makes us a part of this temple. Christ is the temple and it is manifest in the world in his Church.

Colossians 1:18: And he (Jesus) <u>is the head of the body, the church: who is the beginning, the firstborn from the dead; that in all *things* he might have the preeminence.</u>

Much of what we just went over is fulfilled in Zechariah's prophecy:

Zechariah 6:12-13: 12. And speak unto him, saying, Thus speaketh the LORD of hosts, saying, Behold the man whose name *is* The BRANCH (This is Jesus); and he shall grow up out of his place, and <u>he shall build the temple of the LORD:</u>

13. <u>Even he shall build the temple of the LORD;</u> and he shall bear the glory, and shall <u>sit and rule upon his throne; and he shall be a priest upon his throne: and the counsel of peace shall be between them both.</u>

Here in verse 13, Zechariah is prophesying Christ's role as the builder, high priest, king, and mediator of this New Covenant and temple. Christ is right now sitting on a throne at the right hand of the father, ever making intercession for us (Romans 8:34). Hence he is also the counsel of peace between God and man! This is all made very clear in the book of Hebrews. The life, death, resurrection, ascension of Christ, and his current rule in heaven perfectly fulfilled Zechariah's prophecy.

So the 2 Thessalonians passage is, in my opinion, speaking about the temple in believers and has nothing to do with the physical temple before it was destroyed in 70 A.D. This concept is one that most of our forefathers knew. As for the idea of a future third physical temple that would be a temple of God, there is not a single verse in the bible that speaks of a third temple beyond the one in believers. Modern teachers claim that the bible talks about the rebuilding of the third temple, but they have no passage in the bible that supports this. Rather they take a passage like the one about the Man of Sin and reason, "Well the temple has been destroyed and this man has not come, therefore a new temple must be built in the future."

This logic is flawed as we will soon see.

All the prophecies about the rebuilding of the temple commonly pointed to by False-hope are having to do with the second temple, which was destroyed in 70 A.D., or the one Christ built (would build) which is the one in believers. These verses are often taken out of context to help support these views. Based on these truths alone, I think this view should be excluded. There is no reason for another temple. Even if one was built, it wouldn't be a temple of God anymore. Christ did away with all the sacrifices and burnt offerings and the rituals of the Levitical Priesthood. Jesus destroyed the temple through the Romans as I will plainly show in chapter 10. Bringing any of these back would be blasphemy to Christ.

That leaves us with only two options, either the Man of Sin existed in the past, or he is coming in the future. In either case, this figure must sit in authority over Christians and declare himself to be god, not just over the Christian God but all gods that are worshipped. So is Paul speaking of some future person or someone that existed when he wrote to the Thessalonians? To help us understand the context let's read the next few verses in the text:

2 Thessalonians 2:5-7: Remember ye not, that, when I was yet with you, I told you these things? 6. And now ye know what withholdeth that he might be revealed in his time.7. For the mystery of iniquity doth already work: only he who now letteth *will let* until he be taken out of the way (Let is an old way of saying hinder, so Paul is saying he that hinders the Man of Sin will hinder until its time for him to come). 8. And then shall that Wicked be revealed, whom the Lord shall consume with the spirit of his mouth (meaning by the preaching of his Word), and shall destroy with the brightness of his coming:

Let us notice a few more details. Paul says he's already told them not only who this Man of Sin was, but he also told them who was preventing this figure from appearing. Both are referred to as a him, meaning these are/were people. So these were figures that the early churches would have known. Paul isn't telling them that this Man of Sin will not be for thousands of years, rather he is saying, "you know who he is and you know who is preventing him from coming I told you that when I saw you last."

The reason why Paul is being vague here will become clear soon, but basically, he was doing this so that if the letter fell into the wrong hands the church wouldn't have been harmed by the Romans for sedition.

False-hope preachers love to say that this is the Holy Spirit or the Church that is holding the Man of Sin back and that this is all speaking about something in the future. They claim that when the Church is raptured, the Holy Spirit's (or Church's depending on your church's view) hindrance on the Man of Sin will be gone and it will allow him to rule during the 7-year tribulation.

There are many issues with this, but one of the main problems is there is nothing of the sort being mentioned in this entire letter. Nowhere in 2 Thessalonians is the Holy Spirit even mentioned let alone linked to preventing this Man of Sin from appearing. Neither is the Church ever linked to this in any way. These are things that False-hope adds to the text by taking this one passage of verses out of context and putting them with others. This should be a huge red flag. Any good student of the bible knows that you must keep things in context to properly understand the bible.

So before we can come to the best conclusion we need to go back in the text to see the full context of what Paul is speaking about. This is found in chapter one of 2 Thessalonians. We must remember when 2 Thessalonians was written it didn't have chapters or verses this was a letter. Like all letters, we need to start at the beginning to understand what the writer is saying.

If you go back and read chapter one, you will find that Paul is addressing this young church that is enduring some hard persecutions. Paul is praising them for their endurance and encouraging them to stand strong because Christ will soon avenge them. Let us focus on these verses:

2 Thessalonians 1:6-8: Seeing *it is* a righteous thing with God to

recompense (repay) tribulation to <u>them that trouble you</u>; 7. And to you who are troubled rest with us, when the Lord Jesus shall be <u>revealed from heaven with his mighty angels</u>, 8. In flaming fire taking <u>vengeance on them that know not God, and that obey not the gospel of our Lord Jesus Christ</u>:

At first glance, this might sound like the Second Coming is described here, but let us notice that Paul is telling these 1st century Christians that Jesus was going to come soon to avenge their suffering on those that were then causing them harm. This promise would mean absolutely nothing to the suffering saints in the 1st century if Paul is speaking about Christ coming thousands of years in the future. However, if Paul is speaking about a soon-coming day of the Lord in Judgement this would be an encouragement to them. This is again why I said it is so important to understand that Christ and the apostles spoke of two different types of comings that when looked at are similar but very different from one another.

Please take a moment and read the first chapter of 2 Thessalonians. You will find nothing that hints that this event is far in the future. Paul is addressing the very real persecution of saints that lived in the 1st century when this letter was written, who were going through things that we cannot even imagine today in our comfy homes. Paul says at the very end that he is praying that the Church in Thessalonica would be faithful and glorified onto the Day of Christ. Again the context focus on this event happening soon. Paul even declares when this event will happen, when Christ is revealed from Heaven. It doesn't say when he returns just when he has been revealed or declared from heaven with his angels.

We have been so conditioned to try and place these events into the future by False-hope that this is hard for many of us to understand. But when we keep in mind that the Apostles all preached about a coming Day of the Lord against Jerusalem, which Christ himself declared would happen within a generation this event would make a lot of sense (we look at this in chapter 10). Christ coming was to cast vengeance on those who were persecuting them (1st century Christians) and who refused to obey the gospel. The context is very clear that these were situations that the church was going through and a promise of their suffering not only coming to an end but being validated. Meaning this event had to have occurred in the 1ˢᵗ century (and it did).

So who was persecuting the Christians in the 1ˢᵗ century that would not obey the gospel? We find Paul explaining this in the first letter to Thessalonica:

1 Thessalonians 2:14: For ye, brethren, became followers of the churches of God which in Judaea are in Christ Jesus: for ye also have <u>suffered</u> like things of your own countrymen, even as they *have* of <u>the Jews: 15. Who both killed the Lord Jesus, and their own prophets, and have persecuted us; and they please not God, and are contrary to all men:</u>

This is a very unpopular truth for many today, but the main persecutors of the early Church was not Rome, but it was the unbelieving Jews. Not only did they not obey the gospel but they killed, persecuted, and made all attempts to destroy Christianity. Simply read the accounts in Acts and you will see this recorded. When Paul is writing to encourage this Church in 2 Thessalonians he is telling them that very soon Christ was going to come and deal with the Jewish persecutors. This indeed happened on the Day of the Lord.

Let's look back at the account in 2 Thessalonians Chapter 1:7. Paul says that this event will be a revealing of Christ from heaven. Christ was revealed as very Lord in this event when he brings judgment. This judgment does something else too:

2 Thessalonians 1:9-10: Who (those persecutors) shall be punished with everlasting destruction from the presence of the Lord, and from the glory of his power; 10. When he (Christ) shall come to be <u>glorified in his saints</u> (So he comes for two reasons, to judge the persecutors, and glorify himself in the saints), and to be admired in all them that believe (Why would Christ be admired by those that believed? Paul answers this in the following line) (<u>because our testimony</u> (their testimony was about the Gospel and Christ)<u> among you was believed</u>) in that day.

So this judgment was not only to punish those Jews who refused to gospel and persecuted the 1ˢᵗ-century Church, but it was to glorify the saints for their faith. This doesn't mean giving the saints a resurrected body, this passage says nothing about that. To glorify something means to acknowledge and reveal the splendor or truth of something. When Jesus came and destroyed the people of God—the Jews—it revealed that they were not in fact the people of God anymore because they had rejected Christ. The glory of the saints is the acknowledgment of Christ that he was their God and they of the Church (the saints) were his people. He defeated their enemies just as he had defeated the enemies of Israel in the Old testament. That is why Christ was admired on this day by those who believed the testimony of the apostles as this affirmed that what they had said was true.

The truth of who the people of God were was declared or glorified when Christ came and glorified the truth of the Gospel, his death, resurrection, and ascension. This declared to the world and the Church that he was very Lord, Christ, and King. John promises something very similar would soon happen to the suffering Church in Philadelphia:

Revelation 3:9: Behold, I will make them of the <u>synagogue of Satan</u>, which say they are <u>Jews</u>, and are not, but do lie; behold, I will make them to come and worship before thy feet, and <u>to know that I have loved thee.</u>

Like John, Paul was encouraging the saints that were being persecuted by the Jews, telling them that their suffering was not in vain, that Christ would soon not only revenge their suffering but vindicate them before the world concerning the truth of the gospel that they believed. I know this is unpopular, but this is something undeniable in the bible. We also need to keep in mind that most of the early churches were made up of Jews who converted to Christianity. They were persecuted by the Jews that would not convert as they saw them as a threat and as blasphemers. This judgment against Judaism was called down upon their own heads:

Matthew 27:25: Then answered all the people, and said, His (Jesus') blood *be* on us, and on our children.

Not only did they call this judgment upon them for Christ's death, but Jesus said:

Matthew 23:34-36: Wherefore, behold, I send unto you prophets, and wise men, and scribes: and *some* of them ye shall kill and crucify; and *some* of them shall ye scourge in your synagogues, and persecute *them* from city to city (describing the events in acts): 35. That upon you may come all the righteous blood shed upon the earth, from the blood of righteous Abel unto the blood of Zacharias son of Barachias, whom ye slew between the temple and the altar. 36. Verily I say unto you, <u>All these things shall come upon this generation</u>.

This event prophecied by Jesus is just one of the many passages about the soon-coming Day of the Lord. It was a Day of the Lord for the enemies of God, but it was the glorious day of Christ for the Christians.

The early church preached repentance to the Jews so that they might repent and avoid the coming judgment and most of them refused instead they persecuted, killed, stoned, whipped, and stirred up war against the Church. All of this is recorded in grave detail in Acts.

This brings us to the main text. Paul says this Day of Christ—the day they are vindicated, glorified, and their enemies are destroyed—shall not come until a falling away happens and the Man of Sin be revealed. Let's put all of the things together to summarize the sequence of events that we are to look for to identify this Man of Sin:

That the Day of Christ was the promised day of the liberation of the persecuted saints at the hand of the Jews in the 1st century.

This day would glorify the truth of the gospel in the saints to the world, especially to the Jews, when Christ was revealed/declared from heaven.

The Man of Sin was a person that Paul identified while he was physically at the Church.

The Man of Sin was being hindered from coming into full power by another man who Paul said would be removed when it was time for the Man of Sin to be revealed.

Once this man is removed a falling away would happen.

After the falling away the Man of Sin would be revealed as the wicked Son of Perdition.

This figure would exalt himself above all the gods that were worshiped, and sit in the temple of God (meaning he stat in authority over Christians as if he were God), and declared himself to be God.

That the day of Christ would come after the above takes place, and Christ would consume this Man of Sin at the brightness of his coming.

If this day of Christ is indeed the Day of the Lord that happened in 70 A.D. against Jerusalem, is there a series of events and a man that matches all these points? The answer is yes with astounding accuracy.

First, let us consider the falling away. Commonly False-hope's preachers like to take you to the Greek and get the word Apostacy from the underlying Greek. Apostacy does mean a falling away from the faith. Nothing wrong with this on the surface, but apostasy doesn't just mean falling away from the faith. It also was used as a term for falling away from civil authority. In the case of the falling away, we see both happen. During the time leading up to the revealing of the Man of Sin, we see a falling away from the faith of the Jews who as a whole utterly rejected Christ the substance of the Old Covenant faith.

The Jews also began to politically rebel against Rome which would eventually lead to the destruction of Jerusalem in 70 A.D. Also during this time, we know that there were Christians that were falling away from the faith as well. This is addressed in many passages, but since we already looked at the ones about antichrist I will just point back to that. John said that many were going out of the Church, "falling away," and were antichrist. So all of this together will more than suffice for the falling away.

Before I unveil the Man of Sin let us look at this verse again:

2 Thessalonians 2:7: For the mystery of <u>iniquity doth already work</u>: only he who now letteth *will let,* until he be taken out of the way.

Paul is once again affirming that this person is already at work in the world. It is believed that Paul wrote this letter around 51 A.D. During this time Emporer Claudius was the Emporer of Rome. He married a wicked woman named Agrippina in 49 A.D. and he adopted her son Nero to be his heir. Agrippina ended up killing Claudius to allow her son to become Emporer in 54 A.D. For a brief time they reigned together, but eventually, Nero would kill his mother and brother who were threats to his power.

I believe that there can be little doubt that Nero is the Man of Sin mentioned in 2 Thessalonians. This is the stance I hold firmly and the more one studies the events of Nero's life and the prophecies around the Man of Sin one will find astounding parallels. Paul did not directly name him in a letter for fear that the Romans might get their hands on it and bring harm to the church.

Nero was being hindered from rising to power by his stepfather and mother. The mystery of iniquity that was at work was the snake of a mother who plotted to put her son on the throne, and Nero's own dark heart. Nero was always a man of gross sin, but he did not appear or be revealed as the Son of Perdition until he took the throne then he slowly became a son of destruction to everyone that stood in his way.

Notice in our text that Paul does not call this figure the Son of Perdition until after the person hindering him is removed. After this, a falling away would reveal him in full. This is important because Nero's reign of terror did not begin immediately but began towards the latter years of his reign. He was the Emporer Caesar that Paul cried out to go before in Acts 25:1-12. Nero's perdition began in earnest after political, civil, and religious unrest (falling away) began to plague Rome as a result of the judgments against Rome by Christ. Judgments that Jesus laid out as natural disasters, pestilences, wars, famines, and civil unrest (We got through each of these in chapter 10). Much of this led to the falling away as we saw earlier. Remember it did not mean just a falling away from the faith.

Nero, to this very day, is remembered as one of the most monstrous Emporers to ever have reigned. He was called a beast by many of his own historians. More importantly, Nero exulted himself above all gods in the Roman empire. He put a statue of himself throughout the empire and instituted Emporer worship across Rome.

He made war against the saints slaughtering hundreds of them for 42 months or 3 ½ years. He declared his sovereignty over the Christians and declared himself to be God. He even decreed war with the God of heaven. He had a coin minted during his rule that showed him as this great god. The coin read, "Savour and Benefactor of the world." He also kicked to death his pregnant wife (meaning he had no respect or love for women). He also murdered another wife and took a male eunuch as his lover because he looked like one of his dead wives.

He famously burned Rome (or more likely ordered it to be burned) and blamed it on the Christians which helped justify his persecution of them and turned the whole world against them. Many modern scholars dispute if Nero did in fact burn Rome, but all the people and historians of his day did believe that Nero had a hand in burning it. Even if he was innocent, the fact that he used it as propaganda and justification for the persecution of Christians is not in dispute.

Regardless, Nero took the land in Rome that burned down and built a massive palace complex which he called his Domus Aurea, or his "Golden House." In the great courtyard of this palace near the area of the Circus Maximus, where tradition says Nero killed many Christians and the Apostles Peter and Paul (this is where the modern Saint Peter's Basilica now stands), Nero built a massive bronze statue of himself that stood 100 feet tall, or more (there is debate on its exact height). It was meant to declare his godhead to the Roman people.

He also loved to dress up in animal skins in the arena and mutilate people's private areas by tearing into their flesh with his mouth. He did the latter to great crowds that he made watch as some sort of sick sport. Citizens that refused to worship him were beheaded or burned on crosses. He was so unpopular by the senate and many military leaders that his own generals and senators eventually forced him to kill himself at the age of 30 a move that wounded the "head" of the Roman beast/ empire that nearly destroyed the empire in civil war as there was no clear heir to the throne.

Because of this, 3 figures quickly took the throne in a single year and each, in turn, lost it being killed. These were the Emperors Galba, Otho, and Vitellius. This began a civil war of sorts that nearly tore the empire apart. Stability wouldn't be restored until the general turned Emporer named Vespasian, whose son Titus destroyed Jerusalem in 70 A.D. took the throne. When the empire didn't collapse, according to historians, the whole world marveled, for the deadly wound to the head of Rome was miraculously healed as if it hadn't been. (If you have read Revelation at all this should sound very familiar to you).

The citizens of Rome outside o the city loved Nero and the cults of Nero rose in prominence even long after his defeat. It was commonly thought that Nero was not dead or if he was he would somehow come back to life. The vast majority of Chrisitan literature for the first several centuries is filled with references to Nero as the Roman antichrist or a beast and terror, so his legacy had far-reaching effects.

As Christ began to pour out judgments upon Rome and Jerusalem in 64 A.D. Nero was revealed as this monster and as the judgments grew brighter he was forced to kill himself in 68 A.D. 31/2 years, or 42 months after his war on heaven and Christians began in earnest. Though he was forced to kill himself, this event was a direct result of the coming brightness of the glory of Christ being revealed from heaven or as Paul states it, at the brightness of Christ's coming.

The brightness of the coming isn't the arrival of Christ in judgment only the headlights, so to speak, of him coming. Paul states in this that just the brightness of his expecting coming, the light being his righteous judgment, was enough to destroy the Man of Sin. Even this plays out as Paul prophecied.

All of these events play out in Revelation as well, for the Revelation is the Revealing of Christ from heaven coming in the clouds of judgment against the harlot (Jerusalem), the beast (Nero), and the beastly system of Rome, as well as the affirmation/declaration/revelation of the bride of Christ.

Take into account what Paul said about this soon revealing of Christ from heaven and compare it to this:

Revelation 1:1: The Revelation (revealing) of Jesus Christ, which God gave unto him (Jesus), to shew unto his servants (Christians) things which must shortly come to pass; and he sent and signified it by his angel unto his servant John:

Revelation 1:7: Behold, he (Jesus) cometh with clouds; and every eye shall see him, and they also which pierced him (Those who pierced him lived in the first century. Both the Jews and the Romans took part in this act): and all kindreds of the earth shall wail because of him (the judgment affected the entire known world under the last great world empire of Rome). Even so, Amen. (They all saw Christ because the whole world saw the judgment he brought upon Jerusalem and Rome, this affirmed his rule, his kingdom, and his bride. This was a judgment prophecied by early Christians for 37 years so those that heard them would have recognized these events as coming from Christ).

To dive into this efficiently we would need to write a separate book, but these two events are speaking of the same thing unlike what False-hope and other two-headed giants try to teach. This will become even clearer as we go on in this study and look at other passages that affirm beyond a shadow of a doubt that the Man of Sin is/was Nero and he had to have been ruler of Rome during the reign of its first 10 kings.

The heart of what I want you to take away from this is the concept of the temple being in believers and the Man of Sin isn't at all what people teach today. Though the direct fulfillment of the Man of Sin has passed, any time a person—be them political or spiritual—sits in authority over the Church and declares themselves greater than all gods and makes themselves equal to God they will take on the nature of the Man of Sin. They always lead people into perdition. Only Christ can sit in that temple greater than any God and declare himself to be God anyone else is a deceiver, an antichrist, and a Man of Sin.

Pillar Five: Christians are Israel

In the last chapter, I claimed that most of our forefathers taught and believed in Replacement Theology which simply says that the Church replaced the Jews as the covenant people of God. However, I think this is a poor explanation. Israel has always been a chosen people of faith made up of Jews and Gentiles even in the Old Covenant. This is why in the Law of Moses there were always provisions added for the sojourner and stranger that dwelt in their land and how they could come into the people of God. We can see a great glimpse of this however when we consider the nation of Israel as it came out of Egypt:

Exodus 12:38: And a <u>mixed multitude</u> went up also with them; and flocks, and herds, *even* very much cattle.

This mixed multitude all came to the mountain of God and all were called the nation of Israel. Meaning it wasn't just the Hebrews that made up this nation but those that came out of Egypt to follow God by faith. These things were but foreshadowings of the fullness of this truth in Christ for in Christ there is no longer Jew or Gentile for he tore down the division between us. Thus the Church is the fulfillment of the promise to Abraham, meaning the Church is what God always intended Israel to be. In the Old Testament, it was only a shadow the fullness of which was revealed in Christ (Colossians 2).

Galatians 3:8-9: And the scripture, <u>foreseeing that God would justify the heathen</u> (Gentiles) <u>through faith,</u> <u>preached before the gospel unto</u>

Abraham, *saying,* In thee shall all nations be blessed. 9. So then they which be of faith are blessed with faithful Abraham.

We are shortly told what this gospel was:

Galatians 3:16: Now to Abraham and his seed (offspring) were the promises made. He saith not, And to seeds, as of many; but as of one, And to thy seed, which is Christ. (Paul is saying that Abraham was told about Christ. The gospel he was preached is the very same gospel that we believe today. The promise of Abraham's seed was for a spiritual nation of believers made up of all nations Jew and Gentile in Christ by faith this is only fulfilled in the Church not in national Israel).

Romans 9:6-8 Not as though the word of God hath taken none effect. For they *are* not all Israel, which are of Israel:

7. Neither, because they are the seed of Abraham (physical decedents), *are they* all children: but, In Isaac shall thy seed be called. (Referring to the fact that Isaac was a son born of a promise through faith because Abraham believed God. We become the children of Abraham by believing in the promise of the savior just as he did. The rest of Romans 9 explains this, and so do Paul's statements in Romans 2:28-29, Galatians 3:8, Galatians 3:16, and Romans 15)

8. That is, They which are the children of the flesh (Those born physically Jews), these *are* not the children of God: but the children of the promise (meaning those of faith) are counted for the seed. (Children of Abraham, meaning you are a Jew/Israel if you are in Christ, outside of Christ you are a Gentile—or unbeliever— even if you are born a physical Jew)

Galatians 3:22: But the scripture hath concluded all under sin, that the promise by faith of Jesus Christ might be given to them that believe.

Romans 11:32: For God hath concluded them all in unbelief, that he might have mercy upon all.

Galatians 3:26-29: For ye are all the children of God by faith in Christ Jesus. 27. For as many of you as have been baptized into Christ have put on Christ. 28.There is neither Jew nor Greek (Greeks were gentiles), there is neither bond nor free, there is neither male nor female: for ye are all one in Christ Jesus. 29. And if ye *be* Christ's, then are ye Abraham's seed (Israel), and heirs according to the promise.

Romans 2:28-29: For he is <u>not a Jew, which is one outwardly;</u> neither *is that* circumcision, which is outward in the flesh: 29. <u>But he *is* a Jew, which is one inwardly;</u> and circumcision *is that* of the heart, in the spirit, *and* not in the letter; whose praise *is* not of men, but of God.

These are but a few verses on this topic. The New Testament firmly teaches that there is no longer any difference between the Jews and the Gentiles. Christ tore down the middle wall of division and made in his body one nation out of both in himself (Ephesians 2:11-22). Those physically born Jews today are not Israel, in the sense of God's chosen people, because they are not the people of faith anymore.

Because they rejected Christ, they are no different than the Gentiles, who in times past did not have the promise of the Messiah as the Jews did. All people no matter race, ethnicity, wealth, poverty, or culture of which one is born are now made equal by the cross and in Christ are made the people of God. This is why John said of Jesus:

John 1:11-13: He (Jesus) came unto his own (the Jews), and his own received him not. 12. But as many as received him, to them gave he power to become the <u>sons of God,</u> *even* to them that <u>believe on his name:</u>

13. Which were born, not of blood, nor of the will of the flesh, nor of the will of man, but of God.

That is not to say there cannot be a great revival among the Jewish nation, but if this happens they would cease being Jews that practice Judaism and would become a part of Christ and his Church. For the last 2,000 years, God has preserved a remnant of Jews among believers. In the Church, there is neither Jew nor Gentile. There will be a revival among national Israel as there will be among all nations for all will be made subject to Christ before the end.

I do not think the bible can be more clear on this issue, however, I understand that this idea will be hard for many to receive. So if you would like to study these concepts more I would recommend reading the entire book of Galatians (Especially chapter 3), Ephesians, 1 Corinthians (Especially chapter 12), Romans (Especially chapters 2, 11, and 15), and the book of Hebrews.

So to end this lengthy chapter here is a list of 8 key principles I hope you were able to grasp from it. Please keep each of these in mind and test them with the scripture as we go along in this book. These truths, which we only touched on briefly, were the pillars of truth or concepts that I had begun to see clearly in the bible. I realized that if what we just went over was true then it directly contradicted some of the things taught by False-hope thus leading me ultimately to this study:

Jesus and the Apostles spoke of two different comings of Christ: the Day of the Lord and the Second Coming.

Christ cannot come back until he makes his enemies his footstool.

We have been living in the end times for almost 2,000 years.

The antichrist is not a man but a spirit.

The Church is the temple of God.

Israel, meaning God's chosen people, is made up of both believing Jews and Gentiles in the Church and is not a nationality/nation in a physical sense.

Prophecy does not revolve around the modern state of Israel or a rebuilt third temple there, but Christ and his Church.

The Man of Sin has already come.

CHAPTER THREE

Who is "Raptured" First?

*"Error indeed is never set forth in its naked deformity, lest, being thus
exposed, it should at once be detected. But it is craftily decked
out in an attractive dress, so as, by its outward form, to make it
appear to the inexperienced more true than truth itself."*

IRENAEUS OF LYONS 130 AD - 202 AD, FROM
HIS BOOK, "AGAINST HERESY BOOK 1."

G rowing up I always assumed that the rapture was something
that every Christian was always taught and believed since
the time of Christ. As I pointed out, in chapter one of this
book, this is simply not the case. I am not one of those that says that
just because a particular articulation of a doctrine is relatively new
that it somehow destroys said doctrine and means we should throw it
away immediately. I believe that so long as what a doctrine teaches is
supported by scripture then said doctrine can and should be embraced
so long as it is consistently in agreement with the Word.

I understand the reality that mankind, due to its fallen state, and
by proxy, the church itself, can at times miss the mark or have less
clarity on things. As redemptive history unfolds and Christ continues to
purify the Church, redeem this fallen world, and the Holy Spirit reveals
more understanding of the truth, the people of God will refine their
understanding of the Word as time goes on. This does not mean we twist

the scripture or change it to match what we want it to say, rather we are changed or conformed more to what the word says.

I am also not saying we just throw out everything that came before as if Christians were completely ignorant of the truth for 2,000 years and only embrace our more modern understandings. In fact, I have found that many of our forefathers had a much better understanding of things than we often do today.

With all of that said, where does the rapture fit into all of this? Just because the term rapture was brought into the Christian community in the last two hundred years that doesn't necessarily mean we should just cast it aside. Rather, we need to ask the question of whether this is a new concept that is supported by the bible, or does it give greater clarity on a consistent truth already affirmed in the bible? If neither is the case then this rapture doctrine is contrary to the word and should then be cast aside. The Word itself is the test by which we measure any doctrine taught by the Church or pastors. To begin answering this we need to ask, what is the rapture and what does it teach?

Without getting super complicated, the basics of the rapture are:

- Christ's Second Coming will happen in two phases. The first is with the secret sudden gathering of his elect (Christians) both of those who had died and those that are still alive when the rapture happens. The second phase happens after the tribulation of the Antichrist approximately 7 years later with the bodily return of Christ and his saints to set up the physical kingdom of Christ on the earth that will last for 1,000 years. Both of these events happen before the general resurrection of all the dead and the final judgment which will happen after the 1,000-year reign of Christ.
- When the elect, or saved, are gathered by Christ, Jesus is in the clouds but does not bodily return or descend to the earth. He will bodily descend after the 7-year tribulation and most teachers believe that there will be another resurrection of tribulation saints. According to this doctrine, most of these tribulation saints got saved during the 7-year tribulation period and most

will be killed because of it. However, some may survive through it. Regardless, there is another resurrection event for just them when Christ returns bodily after the Great Tribulation.

- The unbelieving world will be taken off guard by this rapture. Many proponents of this doctrine have offered many reasons for why this might be so be it due to war, or something as crazy as an alien invasion.

- When the Christians are gathered by Jesus for this rapture, then dead Christians are raised bodily from their graves and then the living Christians shall be transformed to have resurrected bodies like all the other saints and like Christ himself, and together they will all ascend into heaven with Christ to partake in the marriage supper of the lamb. This is separate from the resurrection of the unsaved and the resurrection of those that will be saved during and after the Great Tribulation.

- The rapture of the Church is the glorious hope of the saints that will save them from the final hours of judgment on the earth and the terrible reign and tribulation of the Antichrist. This is our promise because we as the saints are not appointed unto wrath and this time of the Antichrist is the time of God's wrath on the earth.

- People after the rapture can still get saved, die, and have children.

Admittedly there may be more nuance to the way certain people might explain the rapture, but at its core, the above is what most people mean when they use the word.

There are a great many issues with the idea of the rapture and we will deal with most of them in this book. The most glaring of which is that there is not a single clear verse of scripture that teaches anything mentioned above. I realize that modern teachers do use scripture to teach the above, but you will see that they do so by taking the text out of context and merging it with other texts that do not support their argument if those same texts also stayed in their context. We will dive into much of this going forward.

I already stated that when we consider the clarity of Paul's words in

1 Corinthians 15:35-58, we see that Christ will reign until all enemies are put under his feet and the last enemy he will defeat is death, and by this, he meant the resurrection. Meaning, that Paul only speaks of a single resurrection event not several and he claims that it happens at the end. This is also consistent with all the other writings concerning the bodily resurrection. I also claimed that there was a difference between the resurrection and the rapture. So what does the resurrection teach and is it really different?

- Just as before, without getting overly complicated, what does the resurrection teach?
- The resurrection happens when Christ physically returns bodily on the last day and defeats Death. (1 Corinthians 15:12-38, 50-57).
- The resurrection changes Christians to have immortal glorified bodies like Christ's (Philippians 3:21). The unsaved are also resurrected on this same day but rather than being resurrected into life, they are resurrected into damnation (John 5:28-29).
- This is the fullness of the redemption promised in the gospel (Romans 8:23).
- Both the saved and unsaved are resurrected on the same day. (John 5:28-29).
- For Christians, those that have died will be raised first, then those that are alive and remains shall be transformed. (1 Corinthians 15:51 compared to 1 Thessalonians 4:15-18) Yet this resurrection happens on the last day when Christ returns to destroy death and judge the world.
- Both the righteous and the unrighteous will be judged and rewarded for their works. The righteous will be given eternal life and the unrighteous will be cast into the lake of fire. (John 5:29, Revelation 20:13)
- After the defeat of death at the resurrection, there will be no more death for it is destroyed, there will be no more nations for all will be gathered and judged, and there will be no opportunity

to get saved when Christ comes. (Revelation 20:12-14, Matthew 25:31-46)

- Just like with the concept of the rapture there are nuances in how this is taught. Some may have noticed the bible verses I listed after each of the above points and this was something I did not do with the rapture. There is a reason for this as the rapture has no clear biblical scriptures to stand on as I will show in a moment. The scripture verses I gave are not the only ones that teach about the resurrection (the new testament is full of them). Though some of the language that the rapture teachers use are very similar to the resurrection, at times, however, they are not the same event. Simply compare the above lists and you can see that.

The rapture teachers will often use some of the same resurrection passages, but when all are taken together in their context you will not find a single mention of a separate, secret, bodily resurrection of the righteous before the final resurrection on the last day when Christ returns to defeat death, let alone tied to the antichrist, or tribulation.

To help clarify the distinction further let me contrast the two a bit more:

- The rapture teaches Christ's coming in two phases, and multiple bodily resurrection events of the righteous. The resurrection teaches a single victorious return of Christ at the end and a single bodily resurrection event of all.
- The rapture teaches a separate and secret bodily resurrection of just the righteous before the defeat of death. The resurrection says no there is only one bodily resurrection when death is defeated and both the righteous and unrighteous are raised on the last day.
- The rapture happens before the last day, the resurrection happens on the last day.
- The rapture teaches a secret coming of Christ. The resurrection teaches a bodily return of Christ that all will know.

- The resurrection teaches a judgment on the whole earth, the rapture teaches a retreat into heaven for a marriage celebration while the world burns in judgment.
- The rapture says that it is the hope of the faithful of deliverance from the wrath of God and the reign of the Antichrist. While the resurrection says, I am the promise of eternity the reward of the righteous, and the damnation of the ungodly.
- Because death is not defeated by the rapture, people can still die after it. The resurrection defeats death and therefore nothing shall die, and the fullness of redemption shall consume the entire creation.

As I stated in the opening of my book, one can put a clear distinction between a coming of God/Christ in judgment before the bodily return of Christ, but the same cannot be said with the bodily resurrection. If you were to compile all of the scriptures that talked about the bodily resurrection you will find that there is no way a separate bodily resurrection of just the saved takes place before the last day. Notice how I keep saying bodily resurrection. There is a difference between the spiritual resurrection of salvation and the bodily resurrection on the last day. (Ephesians 2:5, John 5:25-29, etc).

As you can see above, the rapture makes a special bodily resurrection for the saved long before the resurrection of the ungodly. So this event is unique and one that you will not find in scripture when it is kept in context. The most common "proof texts" for the rapture come from 1 Thessalonians 4:15-18, Revelation 20:4-6, and all the passages that speak of Christ coming as a thief in the night. The revelation passage will be dealt with in its own chapter so I will not address it now, but in this chapter, I would like to address these other issues.

First I want to point out that the word "rapture" is never said anywhere in the bible. I understand the arguments on what people commonly call the rapture and where it comes from. We will look at that shortly.

Second, I want to state again that if there is no authority from the word to back up a doctrine, then the Church has no authority to teach it. The Church is to be the pillar and ground of the truth (1 Timothy 3:15). This harkens back to the Reformation cry of Sola Scriptura, "the bible alone," shall be our only supreme authority on all matters of faith and practice. It is this heart cry that once rang in the minds of our forefathers, and once united all Protestants, that is what I wish to appeal to and stir back up in our hearts.

So what does the bible teach? Let's begin by looking at the idea of tribulation. Most modern teachers claim that we as believers will not go through tribulation as we are not appointed unto God's wrath. This is the primary reason for the rapture happening before the tribulations of the Antichrist. This often means that wrath and tribulation are commonly equated to one another, and the core concept is flawed in every way. Please carefully read some of the following verses and see if this is something that Jesus or his Apostles ever taught:

John 16:33: "These things I have spoken unto you, that in me ye might have peace. <u>In the world ye shall have tribulation:</u> but be of good cheer; I have overcome the world."

Act 14:21-22: 21. And when they had preached the gospel to that city, and had taught many, they returned again to Lystra, and *to* Iconium, and Antioch, 22. Confirming the souls of the disciples, *and* exhorting them to continue in the faith, and <u>that we must through much tribulation enter into the kingdom of God.</u>

This isn't the only time Jesus or his disciples tell us that we shall be persecuted, killed, and hated for his name, which is what tribulation is. They never promise that God would take us away, or keep us from such things. Jesus even said:

John 17:15: "I pray <u>not</u> that thou shouldest <u>take them </u>(Christians) <u>out of the world</u>, but that thou shouldest <u>keep them from the evil</u>."

Paul also teaches:

Romans 5:3: And not only *so,* but we <u>glory in tribulations</u> also: knowing that <u>tribulation worketh patience;</u>

Romans 8:35: Who shall separate us from the love of Christ? <u>*shall* tribulation,</u> or distress, or persecution, or famine, or nakedness, or peril, or sword?

There are many other examples of this. Tribulation is expected to be a part of the Christian life. What is very interesting however is when we look at this concept in the Old Testament:

Deuteronomy 4:29-31: 29. But if from thence (there) thou shalt seek the LORD thy God, thou shalt find *him,* if thou seek him with all thy heart and with all thy soul. <u>When thou art in tribulation, and all these things are come upon thee, *even* in the latter days,</u> if thou turn to the LORD thy God, and shalt be obedient unto his voice; 31. (For the LORD thy God *is* a merciful God;) he will not forsake thee, neither destroy thee, nor forget the covenant of thy fathers which he sware unto them

Moses is here prophesying about a tribulation that would be unique to the children of Israel (physical Jewish people) in the latter days (last days). This tribulation would come upon them because they abandoned God, and in this text, God says that IF they turn to him and seek him with their whole heart he will be merciful to them. As I already showed, we are in the latter days and this tribulation happened to the Jews as we will look at in chapter 10. In that chapter, I will show how the "Great Tribulation" mentioned in Deuteronomy and by Christ in Matthew 24, Mark 13, and Luke 21 were all referencing the judgment against Israel by Christ in 70 A.D.

False-hope tries to keep Christians bound in fear, helplessness, and powerlessness. He tells the Church not only will you fail, but there will be Great Tribulation for you if you miss the only ticket out of here in the rapture. He also terrorizes them with visions of the Antichrist. Some of these things we have already proven false and soon the rest of it will be likewise exposed.

If you looked up all the references to the bible about tribulation you will never see one verse that even implies that we as believers would not be here for it. Believers are the primary ones going through or promised tribulations. The only exception is the unique tribulation mentioned above concerning the Jews, which already happened, and Christians were indeed spared from it. Or tribulation that God sends against his enemies, which again we are not the enemies of God, and the context would naturally exclude us from this tribulation and wrath.

You will find that all tribulation is allowed to test, try, perfect, and cause the people of God to turn back to God or grow in grace. Even the

Great Tribulation of the Jews was meant to do this. Tribulation, though unpleasant, is not a bad thing in the eyes of the Lord nor should it be in the eyes of Christians.

Christ endured great tribulations and if we are counted worthy to suffer with him so that he might be glorified, we should not run from this but embrace it. We should say with Paul that we rejoice in tribulation. The error comes because many people tie tribulation to the wrath of God. These two can be the same thing when tied to God's chastening of his people, as wrath just means angry/righteous judgment, but it is not the same when the wrath is referencing eternal judgment i.e. Hell. This distinction, however, is often not made, and False-hope links tribulation to the vengeful wrath of God's eternal punishment. The go-to verse for many is:

1 Thessalonians 5:9: For <u>God hath not appointed us to wrath, but to obtain salvation</u> by our Lord Jesus Christ,

Please notice in this verse that the wrath we are not appointed to is the wrath of damnation appointed to unbelievers. That is why Paul linked the reason for not suffering this wrath to salvation. This is important because the bible never claims that we would not suffer the wrath (righteous judgment) of God if we turn from him. That is why Paul said:

Hebrews 10:26-27: 26. For if we sin wilfully after that we have received the knowledge of the truth, there remaineth no more sacrifice for sins, 27. <u>But a certain fearful looking for of judgment and fiery indignation, which shall devour the adversaries.</u>

The fiery indignation is the rightful chastening hand of God. It would be like when you were a child and did something wrong and you knew when your father got home he was going to spank you for what you did. Not because he hated you, but because he loves you and wants to correct a bad habit in your life. This is the same thing with our Father God.

This is clear when we study the scriptures and see God pour out great and sometimes harsh judgment against his people when they turned from him. This was done to correct their sins and turn them back to the truth. In every sense of the word, when God came to judge

Israel in those passages, he poured his wrath on them. The lesson to be learned, however, is God is greatly merciful and if we confess our sins to Him and humble ourselves he is faithful and just to forgive us our sins. We may still suffer the consequences of sin, but we will avoid the just wrath of our sin.

This type of wrath/judgment is different from the wrath that we as saved people are not appointed unto. The eternal wrath of hell is something that no saved person will ever go through. So when it comes to judgment from God we should expect it if we are living ungodly lives. As for tribulation(s), these are honors and trials that we are promised to go through.

1 Corinthians 10:11: Now all these things (referencing Old Testament judgments and events) happened unto them for ensamples (living testimonies of the truth): and they are written for our (the Church's) admonition (warning/reproof), upon whom (the Jews) the ends of the world are come. (This is referencing the end of the Jewish world or Old Covenant again we look at this in chapter 10)

So where does the rapture concept come from anyway? Well if you go to your pastor (assuming they believe in the rapture) and ask them for a verse that teaches the rapture 9 times out of 10 they will take you to:

1Thessalonians 4:15-18: 15. "For this we say unto you by the word of the Lord, that we which are alive *and* remain unto the coming of the Lord shall not prevent them which are asleep (those that have died). 16. For the Lord himself shall descend from heaven with a shout, with the voice of the archangel, and with the trump of God: and the dead in Christ shall rise first: 17. Then we which are alive *and* remain shall be caught up together with them in the clouds, to meet the Lord in the air: and so shall we ever be with the Lord. 18. Wherefore comfort one another with these words."

Question: if this is the passage for the secret rapture, how is it going to be a quiet or secret coming? Paul says that there will be a trumpet, a shout, and an archangel that will all announce this coming. People will undoubtedly hear such a noise and surely notice if millions suddenly exploded out of their graves and float off into the air. According to these verses, that's exactly what will happen for the dead will rise first.

Also, where is there any mention of these people being delivered from the Great Tribulation and Antichrist? Neither are mentioned anywhere near this passage, rather, when kept in its context Paul is encouraging those who were mourning loved ones that had lost Christian family members that they need not mourn but can hope in this promise (read 1 Thessalonians 4:13-14 for the context).

Also, notice it says that Christ shall descend from heaven when this happens. Question if he is descending from heaven where is he going? The only plain reading and meaning of this in my opinion is that he is descending or returning to the earth. The bible doesn't say in this passage or any passage that Christ will only stay up in the air long enough to get his saints and then leave.

Modern teachers will focus on how it says we will meet Christ in the air and ever be with the Lord, but that doesn't mean Christ is returning to heaven after we meet him the text itself says he is descending. There isn't a single verse in the bible that says that after this gathering we go off into heaven and partake in a marriage feast. This is simply added to the text.

Already we can start to see a few issues.

If you reread these verses you can't see the word rapture anywhere. No matter what translation of the bible you use not a single one, that I am aware of, will state rapture anywhere in these verses. So why then is this passage the most turned to when asking about the rapture?

To get this, one has to look back at an old Latin translation of the text. Do you see the phrase "Caught up" in verse 17? In Latin it is the word is often rendered "rapere," sometimes also as "rapturo," or "raptus," (I've heard pastors use all three phrases. These Latin terms are then taken by modern teachers and transliterated (meaning they take the Latin and do not translate it directly into English, rather they make an English word based on the Latin letters) and make the word rapture from it.

On the surface, some people may not think this is a big deal, but we need to keep in mind that the New Testament was originally written in Greek and not Latin, and in the original language the word used here is harpazo not rapere, if you will look those two words up you will find they are very different words. That aside, I will recognize that our culture has been so inundated by False-hope to accept the rapture as a "Christian term" that to argue against it would just be an argument of semantics.

So just for argument's sake, I am going to use the term rapture as most Christians want to use it as it relates to 1 Thessalonians 4:15-18 as a plucking up or gathering of people by God. I have no issue with this term on the surface.

This is not the only issue we have, however. The bible also never says anywhere that only the Church will see him or that this coming will be secretive. The next time someone says this to you politely ask them where the bible says this. They will either turn to the above verses or turn to one that talks about Jesus coming as a "thief in the night." This phrase is the next point we need to look at to show how it is wrong to claim that this concept teaches a secretive coming. This term, "coming as a thief in the night" is very clearly explained by Paul in 1 Thessalonians 5.

1 Thessalonians 5:2-4: For yourselves know perfectly that the <u>day of the Lord</u> (the day of coming judgment) so cometh as <u>a thief in the night.</u> 3. For (Because) when they (those being judged) shall say, Peace and safety; then sudden destruction cometh upon them, as travail upon a woman with child; and they shall not escape. 4. <u>But ye, brethren, are not in darkness, that that day should overtake you as a thief.</u>

This chapter lays out that Christ only comes "as a thief in the night" for those that are not looking for him. They do not look for Christ coming in judgment because they believe that their own security and safety will protect them from God's wrath, or they refuse to acknowledge God at all. This can be people trusting in their government, finances, or other false security to protect them from calamities brought on by God. Paul says that because ye are not in darkness, another word, because you know this day is coming, it will *not* take you as a thief. So it doesn't mean he comes secretively just that people will be taken off guard when he comes because they are not ready or expecting him.

This truth applies to all the days of the Lord mentioned in the bible. Including your day that will come when you die, which can happen like a thief if you are not living for eternity. Remember the phrase, "day of the Lord" just means a day of coming judgment. The above verse is specifically referencing the soon coming judgment of Israel, and nowhere is it speaking about the resurrection event spoken earlier by Paul. The 1 Thessalonians passage doesn't even mention the day of the Lord but the decent or return of Christ for his saints and their resurrection which Christ himself clearly stated happens on the last day.

John 6:40: And this is the will of him that sent me (speaking of God the Father), that every one which seeth the Son, and believeth on him, may have everlasting life: and I will raise him up (referencing those that will believe on the son) at the last day.

We must keep verses in their context to properly understand them. You will find that the only way that the modern views can work is by taking verses from all over the bible out of context and merging them in ways that they were never meant to be. This is not just an empty claim as we go on this will be seen over and over again.

So with all that in mind let's go to the first parable of Jesus concerning his Second Coming, and I ask, who does he say is "raptured" first:

Matthew 13:24-30: 24. Another parable put he (Jesus) forth unto them, saying, The kingdom of heaven is likened unto a man which sowed good seed in his field: 25. But while men slept, his enemy came and sowed tares among the wheat, and went his way. 26. But when the blade was sprung up, and brought forth fruit, then appeared the tares also.

27. So the servants of the householder came and said unto him, Sir, didst not thou sow good seed in thy field? from whence then hath it tares? 28. He said unto them, An enemy hath done this. The servants said unto him, Wilt thou then that we go and gather them up? 29. But he said, Nay; lest while ye gather up the tares, ye root up also the wheat with them. 30. Let both grow together until the harvest: and in the time of harvest I will say to the reapers, Gather ye together first the tares, and bind them in bundles to burn them: but gather the wheat into my barn.

Before I even try and break down the meaning of this parable let's go a few more verses down and let Jesus interpret it.

Matthew 13:36-43: 36. Then Jesus sent the multitude away, and went into the house: and his disciples came unto him, saying, Declare (explain) unto us the parable of the tares of the field. 37. He answered and said unto them, He that soweth the good seed is the Son of man (a title Jesus called himself often);

38. The field is the world; the good seed are the children of the kingdom (Christians); but the tares are the children of the wicked *one* (Unbelievers); 39. The enemy that sowed them is the devil; the harvest is the end of the world; and the reapers are the angels. 40. As therefore the tares are gathered and burned in the fire; so shall it be in the end of this world.

41. The Son of man shall send forth his angels, and they shall gather out of his kingdom all things that offend, and them which do iniquity; 42. And shall cast them into a furnace of fire: there shall be wailing and gnashing of teeth. 43. Then shall the righteous shine forth as the sun in the kingdom of their Father. Who hath ears to hear, let him hear.

Personally, I think this is an extremely damaging declaration to False-hope that claims that the Church is secretly raptured and unsaved people are left behind. Here Jesus clearly states in two different ways that the unsaved are taken (raptured) away first leaving saved people behind. Then the saved are taken. This does not contradict what Paul said in 1 Thessalonians, rather Paul is just giving more details concerning what Christ meant by verse 43. We will look at that in greater detail in chapter 8.

We also see that Jesus said that the saved and unsaved will grow together until the end of the world. This cannot happen if the saved are secretly taken away before the end of the world. We also see that judgment happens immediately when he returns. All that offend and all that are not saved are gathered and burned or sent to hell.

Also, a harvest on that final day implies another truth. A harvest is not going to be one of just tares (weeds) but a harvest has way more wheat than tares. That does not mean there will be no tares, but whenever this harvest happens Jesus is saying there will be more wheat than tares in his field (the world). Remember the foundation of truth concerning Christ ruling until his enemies are made His footstool? This parable teaches this as well not only when considering the harvest but also when considering the state of the field.

When the seed is sown in the field Jesus calls it the world vs. 38, yet when Jesus returns he calls this same field his kingdom vs 41. How is this possible? I believe it beautifully hints at the fact that Jesus will rule in heaven until all enemies are put under him. At this point, the world will not belong to his enemies but will be fully his.

This highlights another issue with False-hope teachers who teach that Christ returns after the 7-year tribulation to set up His 1,000-year kingdom. In this parable, Christ comes from heaven into his kingdom not to set up a kingdom. So either Jesus doesn't know what he is talking about or False-hope and his teachers may be wrong.

I am aware that some believe this parable is more talking about the church and this is speaking about the promise of ungodly antichrists being among the righteous up until the end. Even if you want to take this approach as the focus this still proves the argument I am making. Jesus is still saying that the ungodly are gathered first, and Christ returns on the final day, and both good and bad will grow side by side until the end. The rapture will simply not fit into this parable as the saints cannot be taken before Christ returns and before the wicked are gathered and Christ is saying this separation happens at the very end, not before the end. Also, the idea of a harvest destroys the concept of the apostasy of the church as a harvest will have more good wheat than tares.

Compare this parable to False-hope who says that Jesus comes for his Church—meaning he resurrects and raptures only saved people leaving the ungodly on the earth. Then Christ returns again seven years later to bind Satan and the false prophet and cast only them into hell. When he comes the tribulation saints will be raptured meaning they will get glorified resurrected bodies, but those that followed the Antichrist will remain in regular bodies and will begin to repopulate the earth. The earth will be repopulated by the ungodly that survived the wraths of God during the seven years of tribulation. Then 1,000 years go by and Satan is released to deceive many. There is a great war then Christ wins the battle and then he resurrects all the unsaved people from the dead and then casts them into the lake of fire and takes all the saved into the new heaven and earth.

I don't know about you, but when I read this parable, and Jesus' plain declaration of these events I cannot see even one thing that even hints at anything False-hope teaches.

These views come from a few passages in the Revelation, but if they are accurately interpreting those passages then the Revelation is contradicting what Jesus just plainly laid out. Again I would put forward that the interpretation is wrong not Jesus.

I do not think any honest reader of this parable or Christ's interpretation of the parable can argue that Jesus is not clearly talking about events that will happen right before and after he returns bodily.

If we are honest about what Jesus is saying just in this first parable, we need to rethink some of the things many churches are teaching that are the exact opposite of what Jesus just said. Jesus just said that the unsaved are "raptured" or gathered by God's angels <u>first</u> leaving the saved behind.

Some may argue that this is a parable and we cannot take it that literally, but when Jesus tells us what it means he is no longer speaking in a parable but clearly. In it, he says the wicked will be gathered first and he comes into a world that is his kingdom on the last day v 40. I cannot see any other meaning from any plain reading of this text.

As I said at the very beginning of this book all scripture agrees with itself. Jesus is God, and he is clearly saying something very different than what most people claim will happen. I bet that Jesus is right and those passages of the Revelation are not being accurately understood by disregarding the foundations laid by Christ and the Apostles. This is the hand of False-hope.

Read the parable and its explanation again and ask yourself, what is Jesus saying? Let's take this parable and list out the core principles:

Jesus will return at the end of the world (v 39 & 40).

He will returns escorted by angels.

Saved people and lost people will grow in number side by side until Christ returns at the "harvest." Meaning that saved people cannot be secretly raptured before he returns.

At the time of the harvest, <u>the world</u> in which the seed was sown will be considered Christ's kingdom (verse 41). This cannot be a reference to the 1,000-year physical kingdom on earth as taught by False-hope because they say that during that kingdom, Christ will already be physically ruling on the earth. In this parable, Christ came into this kingdom at the end of the world and is not currently physically ruling on the earth. Therefore a kingdom referenced as <u>his kingdom</u> will have to exist on the earth when he comes.

When Christ comes, he will command his angels to gather all the lost people and all wicked things that offend <u>first</u>.

There will be a judgment on the wicked (they are cast into a furnace of fire—Hell). Notice that this fire doesn't obliterate or consume them, as Jesus said there will be weeping and gnashing of teeth, hard to do if you are burned up right away or if you had no body.

Once the wicked are gathered then the saved people "the righteous" shall shine forth like the sun in the kingdom of the Father. This implies that they are changed in some way as currently, we do not shine like that nor are we in the Father's eternal kingdom, but we are promised this kingdom. This also shows that the kingdom that the earth is considered is different than the kingdom of the Father. Interesting 2 kingdoms? The bible actually speaks of three aspects of this kingdom, which we will dive into later in this book.

It is also equally important to note what we do not see in this passage:

I do not see a secret gathering of the children of God before the gathering of the unsaved.

I do not see any mention of Jesus secretly coming before the end of the world at this harvest.

There is no implication of a literal 1,000-year kingdom before or after Christ returns, or before this gathering of believers and unbelievers, at the judgment. Rather there is a finality to his coming.

Curiously I do not see any hint at a one-world government, antichrist, or any of the other events normally associated with modern eschatology. This to me implies that they are defeated or done away with before he returns, which is what Paul also said, death is the last enemy defeated.

Lastly, we do not see a great army being defeated by Christ when he returns. Rather he simply comes into his kingdom with a grand announcement. A picture of a victorious return

Though I believe this parable is primarily speaking about the literal end of the world, this concept plays out on a small scale when Christ came in the judgment of the Day of the Lord, as he gathered the saved unto him and gathered the damned at Jerusalem for the judgment (we dive into this in chapter 10). The saints then began to shine in the kingdom of the New Covenant, having been glorified by Christ at this coming, while those that remained under the Old Covenant law were cast into fiery judgment with weeping and gnashing of teeth. They were drawn to this judgment before the saints were told to flee. This is the reason why you will find similar language when Jesus prophecies about the destruction of Jerusalem (the Day of the Lord) in Matthew 24, Mark 13, and Luke 21. As I said there are common themes between the two comings of Christ but we will see very different fulfillments.

Before I close this chapter I want to look at one other parable that goes along with this one. Let's see if it agrees:

Matthew 13:47-50: 47. Again, the kingdom of heaven is like unto a net, that was cast into the sea, and gathered of every kind: 48. Which, when it was full, they drew to shore, and sat down, and gathered the good into vessels, but cast the bad away. 49. <u>So shall it be at the end of the world: the angels shall come forth, and sever the wicked from among the just,</u> 50. And shall cast them into the furnace of fire: there shall be wailing and gnashing of teeth.

Jesus does not interpret this parable for us, but I believe we can understand what he is teaching:

* In this parable the sea is the world

* The fish of various kinds are the people both saved and unsaved

* The net is the gathering in by the angels. When it is filled, would be like saying the harvest is ready.

* The good people are gathered/separated into vessels, and the bad are cast away into hell.

This parable is trying to teach the same idea just in a much simpler way as the wheat and the tares. At first glance it may seem to be saying something different; remember the tares were gathered first and in this parable, it seems as if they are gathered at the same time. But notice what Jesus says in verse 49. The angels shall come forth and "sever the wicked from the just" or saved. So Jesus is reaffirming the fact that the angels are coming for the wicked first, you cannot sever something from an object or group of people if that object or group of people is already gone.

So this is not going against the previous parable but is actually giving us a few more details about Christ's Second Coming.

In this parable, we see that not only are the just and the unjust gathered but there is a separation that happens before the judgment.

Remember in the parable of the tares I said that when the righteous are going to shine that this implies that there is a change that happens to them. Well in this parable we are told they are put into vessels. This echoes what Paul and John said about us being transformed at Christ's appearing to have bodies like his (like Christ's glorified body 1 John 3:2, Philippians 3:21) we will look more at that later.

After the wicked are gathered and the righteous are put into vessels there is a judgment passed on the wicked. Again they are thrown into a furnace of fire. I think it is safe to say this furnace is hell. Once again, we see that this punishment lasts more than a few moments.

Let us note what is not said:

I do not see a secret gathering of the children of God before the gathering of the unsaved.

I do not see any mention of Jesus secretly coming before the end of the world.

There is no mention of a 1,000-year reign of Christ before or after this event.

What I hope you've learned in this chapter from Jesus about his Second Coming is:

- Christ will come back at the end of the world
- That the lost and the saved will grow in number side by side until the end of the world. Meaning there can be no secret rapture before the end of the world.
- Jesus comes with his angels

- His coming shall be announced by a shout, a trumpet, and the voice of an archangel.
- At the time of the harvest, the world in which the seed was sown will be considered Christ's Kingdom. This cannot be a reference to the 1,000-year physical kingdom on earth as taught by Falsehope because he says that during this kingdom, Christ will already be physically ruling on the earth, yet in this passage, he is just now physically getting to the earth.
- He will gather first the lost separating them from the saved.
- He will then gather and change the saved.
- There will be a judgment against the lost.
- This judgment is not instant death.
- So far Jesus has not mentioned a secret rapture.
- So far he has not mentioned a physical 1,000-year reign on earth before the final judgment.
- So far no mention of antichrist, one-world government, or any of the main events as taught by modern churches.
- If we take the modern concept of the "rapture" and apply it to what Jesus tells us, the unsaved will be raptured first.

CHAPTER FOUR

Sheep and Goats

"Where the Bible and the Church do not agree, we must obey the Bible, and, where conscience and human authority are in conflict, we must follow conscience."

JOHN WYCLIFFE, THE "MORNING STAR OF THE REFORMATION," 1323-1384

For some, the last chapter will have been enough to point out some major errors. We are far from being done delving into the depths of what Jesus taught on this topic. In the following chapters, we will continue to simply analyze a parable or set of shorter parables to help build our understanding. Then we shall turn from parables to clear sayings from Jesus about the Second Coming. We will then see if the witness of Peter, Paul, John, James, and Jude will agree with the testimony given by Jesus.

By the end of all this, I believe the truth of the bible will be loud and clear concerning the topic of the end times. I will conclude this book with chapters dedicated to The Destruction of Jerusalem, What is the Kingdom, Jacob's Trouble, Daniels 70th Week, the Millenium, and finally how did Darby's teachings become mainstream in churches.

Hopefully, everyone has a clear idea of where we are going, so let's dive into our next parable:

Matthew 25:31-46: <u>When the Son of man shall come in his glory</u> (In the last Chapter we saw the world became his kingdom, here Christ calls it his glory, for it is a work he will do on the earth), and all the holy angels with him, then shall he sit upon the throne of his glory (We can easily call this glory his, dominion, kingdom, and/or sovereignty):

32. And before him shall be gathered all nations: and he shall separate them one from another, as a shepherd divideth *his* sheep from the goats: 33. And he shall set the sheep on his right hand, but the goats on the left.

34. Then shall the King say unto them on his right hand, Come, ye blessed of my Father, inherit the kingdom prepared for you from the foundation of the world: 35. For I was an hungred, and ye gave me meat: I was thirsty, and ye gave me drink: I was a stranger, and ye took me in:

36. Naked, and ye clothed me: I was sick, and ye visited me: I was in prison, and ye came unto me. 37. Then shall the righteous answer him, saying, Lord, when saw we thee an hungred, and fed *thee*? or thirsty, and gave *thee* drink? 38. When saw we thee a stranger, and took *thee* in? or naked, and clothed *thee?*39. Or when saw we thee sick, or in prison, and came unto thee?

40. And the King shall answer and say unto them, Verily I say unto you, Inasmuch as ye have done *it* unto one of the least of these my brethren, ye have done *it* unto me. 41. Then shall he say also unto them on the left hand, Depart from me, ye cursed, into everlasting fire, prepared for the devil and his angels: 42. For I was an hungred, and ye gave me no meat: I was thirsty, and ye gave me no drink: 43.I was a stranger, and ye took me not in: naked, and ye clothed me not: sick, and in prison, and ye visited me not.

44.Then shall they also answer him, saying, Lord, when saw we thee an hungred, or athirst, or a stranger, or naked, or sick, or in prison, and did not minister unto thee? 45. Then shall he answer them, saying, Verily I say unto you, Inasmuch as ye did *it* not to one of the least of these, ye did *it* not to me. 46. And these shall go away into everlasting punishment: but the righteous into life eternal.

Some may disagree with me considering this a parable, but I think it is safe to call it such. Jesus is using this story to give us an idea of what is to come. Jesus uses the metaphor of a shepherd separating his sheep from the goats. Just like the wheat and tares, they can look similar to each other. Then the examples of works that are given by which all are judged or rewarded for I do not think are meant to be literally the only points in which we are judged, rather, they stand as an example of things we are judged by.

If we were to take this parable literally it would seem as if we are saved or lost based strictly on our works, and this of course is not at all what Jesus taught when we take into account the rest of the scripture. Nor is he saying here that the wicked never did any good, rather than the same works that a righteous saved person would do and be rewarded for would be works of sin apart from Christ. Notice Christ is the emphasis behind the works. Apart from Christ, our works of righteousness are as sin (Isaiah 64:6). This is just another reason why we must compare the truths of the bible against the whole bible so that we do not take something out of context.

This parable also adds clarity to what the wheat and tares said about the saints. Before we saw that the saved and unsaved will be gathered out of Christ's kingdom and that the saints would shine in the kingdom of the Father, and now we see that the Father's kingdom is inherited as a reward and is different than Christ's Kingdom.

So these are two different aspects of the kingdom being described in these parables, one is Christ's kingdom on earth when he comes, and then one he gives the saints which is the Father's Kingdom. There is a third aspect described in the bible and that is the kingdom that Christ currently has at the right hand of the Father. These three aspects will become very important and distinct as we go forward, and in them, we see how the Triune God manifests himself in the kingdom. Some may infer here that Christ is speaking of the False-hope view that He will establish a literal kingdom on earth, and that is what he means when he says, "receive ye the kingdom...vs 34"

When we take into account the entire story being presented we find that this cannot be the same kingdom. Let me explain. In False-hope's view of a 1,000-year kingdom of earth, Christ will establish a physical kingdom and rule over the entire world. This world will be made up of those who survived the tribulation and all the judgments of God as well as the glorified saints that return with Christ. In other words, the

False-hope version of the kingdom will have saved and unsaved people in it.

In this and the previous parables, there is no room for this to be as all the unsaved are judged and sent into hell. So either the 1,000-year kingdom is made up of just saved believers, (which brings up the issue of satan deceiving the nations, making war with the saints, and rebuilding the world population after the 1,000 years are up), or Jesus is speaking about a very different kingdom, which seems much more likely. I will assert that it is more likely that the kingdom Christ is referring to is the eternal kingdom of his Father's house.

I'll leave you to decide that.

All that aside what do we learn from this?

Once again we see that Jesus shall come with his holy angels in all his glory.

We learn that he shall sit on a throne when he comes. This may be a literal throne or simply a picture of coming with the authority to judge the earth. This is not the throne he is currently seated on at the right hand of the Father as in this parable he is leaving the throne at his father's side to come and judge the world and destroy death.

Again we see that the lost and saved are both gathered and separated from all the nations of the world.

If all these people are gathered before him for the judgment then everyone will know about it, once again no secret, quiet coming.

We learn that the saved shall be rewarded first before the unsaved are judged. The righteous shall be rewarded and judged according to their good works.

We learn that Christ will then judge the wicked according to their works.

The wicked shall be cast into everlasting fire. Their punishment shall be everlasting verse 46. Notice it's the same phrase as the everlasting life promised to the righteous. If one is not eternal/everlasting neither is the other. I say this because some would say that hell isn't forever and that a person will just burn up and be gone.

We see that the saved are welcomed into the kingdom of their Father.

Again I want to point out what we do not see:

Christ coming secretly to rapture the Church before the end of the world.

I do not see any mention of a literal 1,000-year kingdom established by Jesus when he comes, rather people are separated and judged and are sent to two different eternal places.

I do not see people having children or rebuilding nations.

I do not see Christ coming and defeating the antichrist, or a one-world government, or anything like that.

I understand there will be a lot of people hearing all of this and struggling with it as it seems so opposite to what they have been taught. Many might fear that I am simply making it up or trying to convey a meaning that was never there. To try and put some minds at ease, I would like you to consider the following creed or statement of faith as we might call it today.

For many evangelicals, creeds are archaic and often avoided as if they are irrelevant, but they are no such thing as they hold great historical value and can help us glimpse the fundamental truths that our ancestors believed the bible taught and subsequently what all Christians should profess to believe. These statements of faith were developed at a time long before the printing press or common literacy among peoples. They were meant to teach illiterate people core concepts of Christianity that all Christians needed to believe to be saved and live a doctrinally sound life. They are of course no substitute for the bible, and many would sit under a pastor who could read, and thus they would still hear the word of God. This particular creed was written before 325 AD and in it, you will see that the concept of Christ coming once at the end to judge the righteous and ungodly was very much a foundational truth they taught, all the way back then.

The Apostles Creed

I believe in God the Father Almighty,
maker of heaven and earth;
And in Jesus Christ, his only Son, our Lord,
who was conceived by the Holy Spirit,
born of the Virgin Mary,

suffered under Pontius Pilate,
was crucified, died, and was buried;
he descended into hell.
The third day he rose again;
he ascended into heaven, and
is seated at the right hand of the Father,
from there he will come to judge the living and the dead.
I believe in the Holy Spirit,
the holy catholic (Latin for universal/worldwide) church
the communion of saints,
the forgiveness of sins,
the resurrection of the body
and the life everlasting. Amen.

As you can see this ancient creed also speaks of Christ right now sitting at the right hand of God and will come only once to judge. As our parables confirm, this judgment of all the living and the dead happens on the last day when they are gathered and raised for this judgment. This is a concept that was understood by the very early Church. This truth echoes in nearly every statement of faith and creed from this time until the 1800s when False-hope began to change everything.

Without wanting to overcomplicate things, I would also propose that this parable is not just speaking of the end of the world and the final judgment, but it can also serve as a wonderful picture of the ongoing rule and reign of Christ from heaven. Christ sat down at the right hand of glory on the throne of David. Jesus was then given all authority to rule and judge all the nations of the earth (Psalms 2, 110, Matthew 28:18, Daniel 7:13-14, etc). As history unfolds Christ uses his Church to preach the word, those that embrace the gospel become sheep, and those that do not are shown as goats and judged. By this, I mean that what this parable can also be showing is an ongoing rule of Christ that will continue until the final day. I will not be dogmatic on this point but I find it an interesting thought.

Let's put what we learned from this parable with what we learned from the last chapter:

- Christ will come back at the end of the world.
- The lost and the saved will grow in number side by side until the end of the world. Meaning there can be no secret rapture before the end of the world.
- Jesus comes with his angels.
- His coming shall be announced by a shout, a trumpet, and the voice of an archangel.
- Everyone shall see him, even the dead and unsaved as they are all raised and gathered.
- At the time of the harvest, the world in which the seed was sown will be considered the Kingdom. This cannot be a reference to the 1,000-year physical kingdom on earth as taught by False-hope because he says that during this kingdom Christ will physically be ruling on the earth, yet he is just now physically getting to the earth.
- He will gather first the lost separating them from the saved.
- He will then gather and change the saved.
- Christ will sit upon a throne of judgment over all the world.
- He will judge/reward the saved first based on their good works.
- Then he will then judge the unsaved by their evil works.
- The saints are welcomed into the kingdom of the father. This kingdom is different than the kingdom the earth is now at the time of the harvest. So far we can see 2 distinct kingdoms being mentioned by Christ.
- This judgment of the wicked in hell is not instant death, rather it is everlasting.
- The unsaved are "raptured" first.
- Jesus has not mentioned a secret rapture.
- Jesus has not mentioned a 1,000-year physical reign on earth before or after the final judgment that matches the dispensational view.
- Jesus has not mentioned that he will be coming to destroy antichrist, a one-world government, or a great army.

CHAPTER FIVE

Who's Got a Talent?

"Let us, therefore, forsake the vanity of the crowd and their false teachings, and turn back to the word delivered to us from the beginning."

POLYCARP, 69 AD – 155 AD, BISHOP (PASTOR) OF
SMYRNA, AND DISCIPLE OF THE APOSTLE JOHN.

In the last few chapters, we looked at parables concerning the Second Coming, in this and the next chapter I want to turn to a couple of parables about the Day of the Lord. This will help show a distinction between the two and show how we can still learn things from the Day of the Lord as it relates to the Second Coming. The easiest way to distinguish the two comings is to look at the subject and events surrounding them. The Second Coming always makes mention of the resurrection and the judgment of the entire world, while the Day of the Lord focuses on the soon-coming judgment of Jerusalem and the Old Covenant and the glorification of the saints.

The parable we will look at in this chapter is extremely important. Not only would it be more accurately called a prophecy than a parable, but it also sheds incredible light on both the millennium of Revelation 20 and helps explain the glorifying of the saints that Paul described happening on the Day of the Lord when we looked at the passages about the Man of Sin (2 Thessalonians 2:1-8).

Jesus also told this parable to help correct the error of false doctrine in his disciples:

Luke 19:8-11: 8. And Zacchaeus stood, and said unto the Lord; Behold, Lord, the half of my goods I give to the poor; and if I have taken any thing from any man by false accusation, I restore *him* fourfold.

9. And Jesus said unto him, This day is salvation come to this house, forsomuch as he also is a son of Abraham. 10. <u>For the Son of man is come to seek and to save that which was lost.</u> 11. And as they heard these things (What things? This is answered in a moment I underlined it), he added and spake a parable, <u>because he was nigh to Jerusalem, and because they</u> ("they" is speaking about the disciples and a large portion of Jews that came to see Christ read Luke 19:1-7 to see this.)<u> thought that the kingdom of God should immediately appear.</u>

Once again, we see that the error taught by the Jewish leaders was very prevalent in the minds of Jesus' disciples. Remember I said that the Jewish leaders thought that the Messiah was going to come and make a Jewish kingdom on the earth that would be a golden age, and that his throne would be in Jerusalem? This was something that Jesus' disciples also thought. This is why they often asked him if he would now restore the kingdom to Israel. Israel's kingdom as it was during Christ's time was not a kingdom as in the days of David, and when the prophets spoke about the Messiah's kingdom they assumed it meant that the Messiah would restore the kingdom of David on the earth.

Notice how Jesus told this parable in response to his disciple's false belief about the kingdom and how close they were to Jerusalem. So everything he is about to speak in this parable was to correct their error both of the kingdom and Jerusalem's role in it.

Not only did Jesus reject all attempts of the people from making him king, by which they thought their views of the Messiah would be fulfilled and the kingdom would be built, but at every opportunity, he tried to correct this error in his disciples. They equated the Kingdom to a physical thing and they equated it to Jerusalem as the capital of this kingdom. I find it fascinating that the modern False-hope teachers are teaching the very same thing to Christians today.

False-hope loves to say things like, "The Jews are God's chosen people (meaning the Jews in Palestine/modern Israel). That you have to bless Israel (the nation in Palestine today) or God will not bless you. That Jerusalem is the most important place on earth, one day God will rule and reign from this city. Or that Israel is God's prophetic timepiece, and Christians need to help support efforts for the rebuilding of the third literal temple so that Christ can return."

I'm sure you get the picture. If you understood what we spoke about at length in chapter two, then you will begin to see why I said this way of viewing the bible is misleading. Remember the New Testament clearly says that we are Israel by faith and that we are a Jew by faith, and not by physical descent. Therefore the modern physical descendants of the Jewish people are no longer the people of God until they turn to Jesus.

Consider this for it is written:

1 John 2:22: Who is a liar but he that denieth that Jesus is the Christ? (Christ means messiah) <u>He is antichrist</u>, that denieth the Father and the Son. 23. Whosoever <u>denieth the Son, the same hath not the Father:</u> *(but) he that acknowledgeth the Son hath the Father also.*

The people in modern Israel may call themselves the sons of Abraham, but the bible says that because they rejected the son they also reject the father. I know modern Jews say they still worship the Father, but John says that they are liars, because they rejected Christ! Not only does modern Israel reject Jesus, but they also say he was not the Messiah. That makes them antichrist!

I say boldly that America—especially her Churches—is falling under a curse because the Christians today are blessing antichrist. These False-hope teachers are making modern churches idolize antichrist. Take a moment and ponder that. John warns about this:

2 John 1:9-11: Whosoever transgresseth, and abideth not in the <u>doctrine of Christ</u> (teachings about the Messiah and the gospel), <u>hath not God</u>. He that abideth (remain) in the doctrine of Christ, <u>he hath both the Father and the Son.</u> 10. If there come any unto you, and bring not this doctrine, receive him not into *your* house, neither <u>bid him God speed</u> (God bless you): <u>11. For he that biddeth him God speed is partaker of his evil deeds.</u>

By blessing the workings of antichrist we are partakers of the evils of antichrist. It is my opinion that ignoring this truth was the beginning of the compromise of most Evangelical Churches that brought False-hope in to disarm and oppress the Church. Like cancer, this sin has begun to spread into all facets of the Church. The more we worship and bless antichrist the less like Christ we have become. The modern state of Israel is not the only antichrist we have begun to admire/worship. More and more we take on the image of our affections, and we are in danger of becoming antichrist ourselves.

That does not mean I hate the Jews or that I think we should not minister the truth to them. Just because someone is manifesting the spirit of antichrist doesn't make them beyond salvation, we were all of this spirit once. However, by not recognizing their state or their great need for Christ we do them great harm by blessing their sin and antichrist spirit.

Repentance cannot come until conviction for error and sin comes by the Holy Spirit which happens through the preaching of the word (Romans 10:14). There are a great many pastors that I have heard say that we need not even minister the gospel to the Jews as they have a different covenant with God and that once the Church is raptured then God will bring the Jews to salvation. This is a demonic lie from the very pits of hell!

We reap judgment upon our own heads when we fall into the error of blessing sin. Christ told us to preach repentance to all creatures, through the gospel, and to disciple, all nations baptizing them in the name of the Father, Son, and Holy Spirit (Matthew 28:16-20). That includes the modern state of Israel. I praise God for those that take the gospel to the Jews, but I fear there will never be a national revival among them until the Church repents of their error concerning their spiritual bankruptcy. By supporting their idolatry of the temple, their Babylonian Talmud, their Kabbalah, and their sin of rejecting the Messiah we are only adding to their blindness and our own!

Which makes understanding the truths we have been learning so vitally important. So please note that this parable was in response to this deceived thinking among Jesus' disciples, therefore it was meant to teach them that their entire concept was wrong. May it teach us as well.

Luke 19:12-15: 12. He said therefore, A certain nobleman <u>went into a far country to receive for himself a kingdom,</u> and to return. 13. And he called his ten servants, and delivered them ten pounds, and said unto them, Occupy till I come. 14. But <u>his citizens hated him,</u> and sent a message after him, saying, <u>We will not have this *man* to reign over us.</u> 15. And it came to pass, that when he was <u>returned, having received the kingdom,</u> then he commanded these servants to be called unto him, to whom he had given the money, that he might know how much every man had gained by trading.

Let us notice the symbolism of the parable. Jesus is the nobleman. The far country is heaven. The servants are those of His people that followed him (the early Church). The citizens that hated him were the unbelieving Jews that rejected him. This parable is going to show us the third aspect of the kingdom I mentioned earlier.

There are already servants of the king on the earth because Christ already began to set up the kingdom on the earth before he went into the far country. Remember Jesus said it was inside us. This is the kingdom of Grace that Christ said was in every believer and is sealed by the Holy Spirit in their hearts (Ephesians 1:13). We saw previously that the Father's kingdom is the eternal kingdom of heaven which is the reward of the saints, and now we are seeing Christ receiving his kingdom from the father. This is the kingdom of his rule at the right hand of the Father giving him the right to rule and judge the earth. This has long been termed the Mediatorial Kingdom of Christ, by our forefathers which is something we will look at more as we go on.

I know this will sound odd to most people at first, but I hope this understanding becomes very plain as we go forward. To help clarify consider this, there is only one kingdom just as there is only one God, but we see three aspects of the kingdom as we see a trinity with God. All three work together as one, yet are distinct from one another, yet together they make one. The Holy Spirit dwells in the kingdom on earth, the Son oversees the kingdom as the high priest, mediator, and king, at the Father's right side, and the Father oversees it all from everlasting to everlasting.

This parable, as will soon become very plain, is telling how Christ received the kingdom from the father when he ascended to heaven, and how he brought judgment against the enemies of God, and glorified the saints that were his servants.

The talents/money are portions of truth concerning the word of God, the teaching of this truth, and the ministry of the gospel. The kingdom in which the son goes to get is what most would assume is the Father's Kingdom that he rewards the saints with at his Second Coming.

However, this parable isn't speaking about the Second Coming as we will soon see, it doesn't have a separation of the saints from the wicked, any form of the resurrection, and Christ doesn't come with his angels or anything else. As I stated though this is a parable, these events play out as if they were a prophecy.

To begin to explain I ask, what is a kingdom? A kingdom is usually a nation ruled by a king whose rule and authority are absolute. A king can make laws, pass judgment, and lead his people into combat against other nations and his enemies. So when we look at the bible did Christ receive a throne that gave him the authority to be a king and do these things? Absolutely and if fact the bible lays out this very thing happening as in this parable!

Let's begin when he left to receive this kingdom:

Act 1:9: And when he (Jesus) had spoken these things, while they (the disciples) beheld, he was taken up; and a cloud received him out of their sight.

Daniel saw a vision that tells us what happened next:

Daniel 7:13-14: I saw in the night visions, and, behold, *one* like the Son of man (Jesus) came with the clouds of heaven (This takes place right after Christ ascended in Acts) and came to the Ancient of days (God the Father), and they brought him (Jesus) near before him (the Father). 14. And there was given him (Jesus) <u>dominion</u> (means sovereignty/kingship)<u>, and glory, and a kingdom, that all people, nations, and languages, should serve him</u>: his dominion *is* an everlasting dominion, which shall not pass away, and his kingdom *that* which shall not be destroyed.

So Daniel tells us the kingdom that Christ went to get from his father was the legal rule over all nations, languages, and people. This kingdom was also the legal dominion or sovereignty to judge those who would not serve him. This is when we see the following decrees happen:

Psalms 2:7-9: I will declare the decree: the LORD (God the Father) hath said unto me (Jesus), Thou *art* my Son; this day have I begotten thee (Speaking of Jesus being the first begotten of the dead, see Revelation 1:5). 8. Ask of me, and I <u>shall give *thee* the heathen *for* thine inheritance, and the uttermost parts of the earth *for* thy possession.</u> 9.Thou shalt break them with a rod of iron; thou shalt dash them in pieces like a potter's vessel (this language is symbolic of judgment. Christ will judge the nations by destroying those that rebel. This is something he did, and does and will do until all enemies are put under his feet).

Jesus died for the whole world (1 John 2:2). Of course, when his father says to ask him for all people as an inheritance, Christ would say yes. So God said:

Psalm 110:1-2: 1. The LORD (Father) said unto my Lord (the Son), Sit thou at my right hand, until I make thine enemies thy footstool. 2. The LORD (Father) shall send the rod of thy strength out of Zion: rule thou in the midst of thine enemies.

So this kingship was given to Christ, by the father when he went into heaven. This was the right to rule over all peoples, nations, and authorities of the earth. This is necessary if his rule is to put all enemies under his feet and bring the field of the world in which the seed of the gospel was sown to become the kingdom of the son ripe for the harvest.

So far both our parable and the events following the ascension of Christ play out perfectly. Let us see what else happens:

Luke 19:14: But his citizens hated him, and sent a message after him, saying, <u>We will not have this *man* to reign over us.</u>

So if Christ is away in heaven and his citizens—primarily being the Jews who claim to be a part of the kingdom of God—wanted to send him a message, then that message has to have gone to heaven as well. This might have been done by prayer, but we actually see they sent a messenger with this very message after Christ into heaven. They also told Christ this before he was even killed. While before Pilot, the governor asked the people point blank why he should crucify their kings and they declared that they had no king but Casar (John 19:14-15). Adding to this sin they declared:

Matthew 27:24-25: When Pilate saw that he could prevail nothing, but *that* rather a tumult was made, he took water, and washed *his* hands before the multitude, saying, I am innocent of the blood of this just person: see ye *to it. 25.* Then answered all the people, and said, His blood *be* on us, and on our children.

By these and other statements, we can see how the citizens of the kingdom, the Jews, refused Jesus as their king. After Jesus ascended we see this same message sent through one of the servants of this parable. We see this exact event play out in Acts:

Acts 7:51-58: Ye stiffnecked and uncircumcised in heart and ears, ye do always resist the Holy Ghost: as your fathers *did,* so *do* ye. 52. Which of the prophets have not your fathers persecuted? and they have slain them which shewed before of the coming of the Just One (Jesus); of whom ye have been now the betrayers and murderers: 53. Who have received the law by the disposition of angels, and have not kept *it.*

54. When they heard these things, they were cut to the heart, and they gnashed on him with *their* teeth. 55. But he, being full of the Holy Ghost, looked up stedfastly into heaven, and saw the glory of God, and Jesus standing on the right hand of God, 56. And said, Behold, I see the heavens opened, and the Son of man standing on the right hand of God.

57. Then they cried out with a loud voice, and stopped their ears, and ran upon him with one accord, 58. And cast *him* out of the city, and stoned *him:* and the witnesses laid down their clothes at a young man's feet, whose name was Saul.

In this passage, Stephen is accusing the Jews of rejecting their king and Messiah. So what makes me say that Stephen was the messenger, and his death the message? Let me set the stage. At this point in Acts, the Church has been ministering in Jerusalem for about 3 years. Thousands, we are told, are saved and baptized during this time, and the kingdom began to manifest with great power among the early Christians. These were the original talents given to the servants in the parable

However, the Jews that refused the gospel were the greatest

persecutors of the early believers. All of this is recorded in the early chapters of Acts. In this account, we see the first recorded incident that this persecution resulted in the death of a Christian.

Notice in verse 52, the accusation that Stephen lays at the feet of the Jews. He throws in their faces that they betrayed and killed Christ (referenced to as the Just One) just as they had killed all of the prophets sent unto them. If you read the entire account that Stephen preached to the Jews, (Acts 6:8-15, 7:1-58), you can see how he is pleading with them to repent and turn to Christ their king.

Then in verse 54, we see that the Jews were so angry with what he said that they lost all control of their rage. They rushed upon him and killed him. We see in verse 56 how Christ stood and took notice of this event. Right after this, we see several things begin to happen, first Saul who is later called Paul is mentioned, and then we see Philip begin ministering the Gospel to Gentiles in Samaria (Acts 8:4-8). Saul is then converted (becoming the apostle Paul) and will be given the call to evangelize the Gentiles (Acts 9:4-5). Lastly, Peter is shown a vision to begin ministering to the Gentiles (Acts 10:11).

The death of Stephen was the message to Christ from the Jews that once again declared, "we will not have this man rule over us." I can say this boldly because this is exactly what Stephen was trying to get them to understand, Christ was their Messiah, their king and they betrayed and killed him. These events were all a fulfillment of prophecy and we will look a lot more into it in the chapter titled, "Daniel's 70th Week." False-hope sees this story very differently.

Here is where False-hope loves to say that God added the "Church Age." He will say, "see Jesus was standing when this event happened, he was getting ready to come back then and there to set up his physical kingdom on earth. Because the Jews rejected the gospel and killed Stephen, God decided to put the Jews on a time out and go to the gentiles with the Gospel to try and make them jealous."

Again this ignores the fact that Christ was already ruling in his kingdom as Peter argued earlier in Acts 2:14-47, and as we saw him receive in Daniel's vision (Daniel 7:3-14). In my opinion, the greatest issue with this idea is that it is not found in the bible. We can see no verse that states that Christ intended to come back just before Stephen is killed then changed his mind and instituted a new age because of his death.

Here is the cunningness of False-hope. God indeed brought Gentiles into the Church as a means to try and reach the Jews by provoking them to jealousy. It is, however, wrong to say that God had not intended to do this all along. The salvation of the Gentiles was always a part of God's plan, to call out a people of every tribe, tongue, and nation for His name. This is the exact thing promised first to Abraham:

Genesis 17:4-7: 4. As for me (God), behold, my covenant *is* with thee (Abram), and thou shalt be a father of <u>many nations</u>. 5. Neither shall thy name any more be called Abram, but thy name shall be Abraham; for a father of <u>many nations have I made thee.</u> 6. And I will make thee exceeding fruitful, and I will <u>make nations of thee</u>, and kings shall come out of thee. 7. And I will establish my covenant between me and thee and thy seed after thee in their generations for an everlasting covenant, to be a God unto thee, and to thy seed after thee.

This promise was not that Abraham would be the father of the Jewish nation only, which of course he was, but the father of all peoples and nations of faith. That is why Paul said:

Galatians 3:16: Now to Abraham and his seed were the promises made. He saith not, And to seeds, as of many; but as of one, <u>And to thy seed, which is Christ.</u>

So the fulfillment of this promise to Abraham was fulfilled in Christ, and in Christ, there is neither Jew nor Gentile. So really then what we are seeing with Stephen is not God preparing to come and establish some physical kingdom, as Christ had already received his kingdom at the father's right hand. He had already begun to establish this kingdom by sowing the seeds of grace while on the earth. He then declared it to the Jews by empowering his Church and later to the world when he came on the Day of the Lord. In the death of Stephen, we are seeing a king standing to receive the message from his spiteful citizens by the beloved death of Stephen.

Stephen was the ambassador from Christ, himself a Jew, trying to bring the citizens of the kingdom under the rightful rule of the King, but they killed him instead. Jesus going to the Gentiles was both to fulfill a promise to Abraham, but also to give the Jewish people one final opportunity to turn to him and avoid the judgment of the Day of the Lord. Jesus even said this very thing would happen long before he was crucified:

Matthew 23:29-36: Woe unto you, scribes and Pharisees, hypocrites! because ye build the tombs of the prophets, and garnish the sepulchres (tombs) of the righteous, (outwardly showing great reverence and respect to these, yet despising their message in their hearts and being of the same nature of those who killed them).

30. And say, If we had been in the days of our fathers, we would not have been partakers with them in the blood of the prophets. (meaning when they read how their forefather's killed the prophets they said they would never have done so, yet Christ knows what is in their hearts and how they were no different than their forefathers)

31. Wherefore (because of this) ye be witnesses unto yourselves, that ye are the children of them which killed the prophets. 32. Fill ye up then the measure of your fathers. (A coy way of saying see how you act just like your fathers or see how you measure up to be like them. Because the same things were said by their forefathers, but when it came down to truth they killed and despised the messages of the prophets, just as they were now despising Christ and his Apostles, and eventually killed many of them as well.)

33. *Ye* serpents, *ye* generation of vipers, how can ye escape the damnation of hell? 34. Wherefore (Because of this), behold, I send unto you prophets, and wise men, and scribes: and *some* of them ye shall kill and crucify; and *some* of them shall ye scourge in your synagogues, and persecute *them* from city to city:

35. <u>That upon you may come all the righteous blood shed upon the earth, from the blood of righteous Abel unto the blood of Zacharias son of Barachias, whom ye slew between the temple and the altar. 36. Verily I say unto you, All these things shall come upon this generation.</u>

This declaration of judgment against the Jews did indeed happen, this is the Day of the Lord. Christ further spoke about this in Matthew 24, Mark 13, and Luke 21 (We will unravel this in chapter 10). For nearly 40 years Christ had his Church (Jews and Gentiles) pleading with the rebellious nation of Israel to repent and flee from the wrath to come. This shows the incredible mercy of God. Sadly only a small remnant of the Jewish people heeded the warning.

This truth was also mentioned by Peter in Acts when he referenced the prophet Joel in Acts 2:16 the following verses describe the outpouring of the spirit as a sign of both the kingdom received by Christ and the soon coming Day of the Lord against Jerusalem (Acts 2:16-21).

Act 2:20-21: The sun shall be turned into darkness, and the moon into blood, before that great and notable <u>day of the Lord come</u>: 21. And it shall come to pass, *that* whosoever shall call on the name of the Lord shall be saved.

As we looked at in the foundations, this language is not speaking about the literal sun and moon. Peter is saying that the outpouring of the Spirit was a sign of the imminent coming of this Day of the Lord. This day was against Jerusalem.

So you can see these events play right into the parable we are now looking at. The Jews sent a message to Christ (Stephen) while he was away receiving a kingdom. This kingdom is described as complete dominion and authority over all the earth. This is the Mediatorial Kingdom of Christ at the right hand of the Father. This was an understanding that our forefathers also knew. To help clarify this I would like to quote John Gill who was another Mighty Man of old that lived from 1697 to 1771:

"to receive for himself a kingdom: by this it is intended, not to be speaking of the kingdom of nature and providence; for that he had, and did not receive from another; <u>it was his of right, and by nature;</u> nor <u>the kingdom of grace</u>, set up in the hearts of his people, <u>and which was already within many of them</u>; nor <u>the kingdom of glory, prepared for them from the foundation of the world;</u> though into this he entered at his ascension, and took possession of it for himself and them: but a more visible display of his <u>mediatorial kingdom, he received from his Father; and which, upon his ascension, became more manifest, by the dispossessing of Satan, and casting him out of the Gentile world; by converting large numbers of his people, both among Jews and Gentiles;</u> and by ruling in their hearts, subduing their enemies, and protecting and defending them; and by thus reigning till he has gathered them all in, either in Judea, or in the whole world, and then he will come again:

and return; either to destroy the Jews; the doing of which fully proved he had received his kingdom, was vested with power and authority, and was made, or declared Lord and Christ; or at the end of the world, to judge both quick and dead: and this is said, to show that his personal glorious kingdom on earth, or his kingdom in its greatest glory here, will not be till he comes a second time; and to engage diligence in his servants in the mean while; and to keep up the faith, hope, and expectation of his coming again." From John Gill's commentary on the whole bible, 1763

As you can see, preachers before False-hope came understood the three aspects of the kingdom I described earlier. You can also see that John Gill understood the two comings of Christ, once to judge Jerusalem and another time to judge the entire world. One happened in 70 A.D. and the other will happen on the last day. We can also see how Gill understood the lesson we should take away from this parable.

Let's dig a bit deeper into the parable at hand:

Luke 19:15: And it came to pass, that when he (Christ) was returned, having received the kingdom, (So God gave him the right to rule over all people and judge the earth. Part of this was the declaration that he sit in rule at the father's right hand to bring into subjection all his enemies by dashing them into pieces with a rod of iron) then he commanded these servants to be called unto him, to whom he had given the money (talents), that he might know how much every man had gained by trading.

It must be pointed out that this is speaking of Christ coming on the Day of the Lord, this will become very clear in a moment. Remember when he comes bodily all people are resurrected and judged, yet in this passage, we are seeing he came to judge and reward the saints and in a moment we will see that reward was to rule over cities. We also see he gathers his saints first and then judges this is the opposite of what Christ taught us about his Second Coming further pointing us to the fact that he is speaking of something else. Again if this is speaking of the Second Coming there will be no cities to rule over as they will all be gone.

When we looked at the passage about the Man of Sin we can see that Christ didn't come just to judge Jerusalem but also to glorify the testimony of the saints (2 Thessalonians 1:10). Christ did this by assessing the work of the persecuted saints and then rewarded them accordingly. This is exactly what Jesus is about to describe in this parable.

In a moment, when we look back on Daniel and we will see this very same parable play out. It will also show us what the rule over the cities was meant for and what the glory of the saints means in 2 Thessalonians. Before we do this, let us finish the lesson of this parable.

Luke 19:16-27: 16. Then came the first, saying, Lord, thy pound hath gained ten pounds. 17. And he said unto him, Well, thou good servant: because thou hast been faithful in a very little, have thou <u>authority over ten cities</u>. 18. And the second came, saying, Lord, thy pound hath gained five pounds. 19. And he said likewise to him, Be thou also over five cities. (If this is speaking about the Second Coming this statement about cities would make no sense. As we saw earlier all are raised and gathered and all nations are judged and sentenced. I will clarify what this means in a moment.)

20. And another came, saying, Lord, behold, *here is* thy pound, which I have kept laid up in a napkin: 21. For I feared thee, because thou art an austere (strict) man: thou takest up that thou layedst not down, and reapest that thou didst not sow. 22. And he saith unto him, Out of thine own mouth will I judge thee, *thou* wicked servant. Thou knewest that I was an austere man, taking up that I laid not down, and reaping that I did not sow:

23. Wherefore then gavest not thou my money into the bank, that at my coming I might have required mine own with usury (interest)? (This whole concept of the talents is speaking about the gifts that God gave his servants—Churches—for the spreading of the gospel/kingdom. Christ gathers where he did not sow because the kingdom is to grow if the gospel is faithfully preached. He is taking the reward of this servant away because he did not use what he was given. So what little he had is lost. This is a picture of an apostate or dead church.)

24. And he said unto them that stood by, Take from him the pound, and give *it* to him that hath ten pounds. 25. (And they said unto him,

Lord, he hath ten pounds.) 26. For I say unto you, That unto every one which hath shall be given; and from him that hath not, even that he hath shall be taken away from him. 27. <u>But those mine enemies</u> (the Jews/citizens that sent the message and hated Christ)<u>, which would not that I should reign over them, bring hither, and slay *them* before me.</u> (This is again speaking of the Day of the Lord against Jerusalem)

Let's summarize everything we were taught in this parable to get the best understanding and then let's dig in deeper by looking at Daniel.

Christ went away to receive a kingdom in heaven. This gave him the right to rule over all the nations at the Father's right hand. His Father told him to rule until all enemies are put under his feet and his inheritance over all the earth is come in full.

While he was gone there were citizens on the earth that hated him, and servants that loved him.

Those that hated him sent a message after Christ telling him they will never accept his rule over them. I claimed this was pictured in the stoning of Stephen.

Christ returns having received this kingdom, and first gathers his servants (the saints) to him and rewards them for their service by giving them the right to rule over cities.

He then judges the citizens, whom he now calls his enemies, that hated him by destroying them.

As you can see, this list of truths is very different than the wheat and tares and sheep and goat parables we saw before. That is because this event is speaking about the Day of the Lord. When we go into this event in chapter ten we will see that the gathering of the saints was Christ calling them away from judgment. As we go into that in great detail in that chapter, let us look at some other things we can learn.

When Christ was revealed/came in the full power of his kingdom (or as it is put, having received his kingdom) he rewarded the saints for their service by giving them authority or rule over cities. I will show in the next chapter how metaphorically this can also be called a marriage.

Biblically, when a husband and wife have married the wife receives the authority of her husband's household under the rule of her husband. For example, a queen has great authority to rule and judge as the king, but her authority does not overcome that of the king for he is her head. As we will see in the next chapter the "marriage" of the New Covenant Bride of Christ—the Church—gave the bride the same authority as the husband. This authority was to rule and judge, the same authority that was given to Christ when he went to go get his kingdom.

The whole concept of the servants receiving the authority to rule further proves that this is not speaking about the final bodily coming of Christ as when he comes there are no more cities. As we already saw very clearly all people are gathered before him and judged. Meaning there would be nothing left to rule.

Let's look back in Daniel and see how this same event plays out just as the parable did and we will see with much greater clarity what Christ is speaking about. When you read Daniel 7 you will find several glorious truths, we will not go through the whole chapter verse by verse, but I highly recommend you take a moment and read it. A brief overview is this:

- Daniel sees a vision of four great beasts representing the four great nations of the world empire: Babylon, Medo-Persian, Greece, and Rome. (Verses 1-7) This was a reoccurring theme in Daniel and was explained a few times previously in Daniel. The last beast destroyed all that came before, this is what Rome did when it conquered the ancient world.

- Daniel then sees the last beast has ten horns. It is explained that these ten horns are ten kings. This beast is Rome, these kings are the ten Caesars, the little horn described came before 3 other kings. This was Nero who was the 5th and after which three quickly fell as if plucked up by the roots. This small horn stands out from the others as it is the focus of the events that are about to be described (Verse 8). He is also from the midst or middle of these kings. This narrows our time frame of when these events happened. From this, we know that the Man of Sin figure is a king that rose during the first 10 kings of Rome, as Rome is the 4th beast. In verse 11 we see this horn is also a beast that speaks great things against God this further links him to the Man of Sin and the Beats of Revelation who was Nero.

- Verses 9-12 speak of God the Father sitting in judgment and destroying these kingdoms of world governments described before as beasts.
- Then we back up and see that Christ ascended into heaven before God the Father and received a kingdom verses 13-14.
- Daniel is confused about all of this so God explains it in verses 15-27.
- What we see play out is that the Father decreed the judgment against the beasts and then gave dominion to the Son who comes and judges and then also gives judgment to the saints (over nations and cities) who in turn judge the kingdoms of the earth and takes dominion away from the world empires.
- We learn as well that this little horn came before 3 other kings who fell quickly. And that this little horn exalted himself above God and made war with the saints. This is the exact same language we see about the Man of Sin. Meaning Daniel is seeing that the little horn who was also a king was the Man of Sin that Paul described.
- This further proves that the Man of Sin had to exist when Rome was still an empire. We are given a time frame with the 10 horns that are the 10 kings of this empire. It is further narrowed down that the little horn of the Man of Sin would come before three others who would quickly fall away. Meaning these events took place during the time of the little horn which would have been Nero, he was the fifth Caesar who came before three others who fell quickly. After Nero died three kings rose and fell in one year, they were killed before their rule took root which is the same phrase being used here in Daniel. This again is confirming the identity of Nero being this little horn. This is elaborated in great detail in the Revelation for John saw this same vision but gave us even more details, but for this chapter, we will remain in Daniel.

With this overview in mind let's focus on a few key verses:

Daniel 7:21-22: 21. I beheld, and the same horn made war with the saints (this is the Man of Sin), and prevailed against them; 22. <u>Until</u> the Ancient of days came, <u>and judgment was given to the saints of the most High; and the time came that the saints possessed the kingdom.</u>

So the little horn, the Man of Sin, made war and killed the saints until Christ came. This says Ancient of Days which is a reference to the Father earlier in this same chapter. This speaks both of the unity between the father and the son (there is only one God in three persons) and the fact that Christ came in the same authority as his father when he came to judge something we already saw in the way that Christ proclaimed he came in the clouds.

This too goes along with the parable we are now studying. When Christ came he judged those that refused him and he rewarded the saints with authority over cities. Here in Daniel, it's called judgment which is the same thing you cannot judge if you have no authority. This is also when the saints began to take possession of the kingdom. This is a reference to how the world will become Christ's kingdom at the time of the harvest. Just as the Hebrews had to conquer the promised land for their kingdom, we are to conquer our promised land for ours. We do this through the authority given to us by Christ through the fulfillment of the great commission. Remember the kingdom Christ received from his father was for all nations and people. We receive the same inheritance in Christ.

The fullness of this has yet to happen and even in Daniel it is implied that this will take a long time, listen to this:

Daniel 7:26 But the judgment (of the saints) shall sit (they sit in rule/authority/judgment with Christ), and they shall take away <u>his dominion,</u> (this is speaking about the dominion of the beast of Rome. The Man of Sin or the little horn, was the ruler of Rome so his dominion or kingdom is what the saints will take from him as they sit in judgment) <u>to consume and to destroy</u> <u>*it*</u> <u>unto the end.</u> (When something is consumed it is absorbed into the thing consuming it. In this case, Christianity consumed the Roman empire.)

This did indeed happen. Rome's dominion fell when Rome became a Christian nation. Though I believe that the Roman Church was later judged during the Reformation, the Church has endured and the judgment still sits. I believe God is now judging the Evangelical Church and seeks to bring a purifying Reformation to Christianity again. God desires us to be one as he and Christ are one.

That aside, there can be no denying the fulfillment of this prophecy. This is exactly what will happen to all nations. They shall all be brought under the headship of Christ through the judgment of the saints. The Roman church was judged at the Reformation but the judgment of the saints still stands. This is not how the rule ends however as the saints will continue to sit in judgment until:

Daniel 7:27: And the kingdom and dominion, and the greatness of the kingdom under the whole heaven, shall be given to the people of the saints of the most High, whose kingdom *is* an everlasting kingdom, and all dominions (meaning nations/kingdoms) shall serve and obey him (Christ).

Notice this is the same language Paul used when prophesying about the victorious reign of Christ in (1 Corinthians 15:25) for he must reign until the above is true. Meaning that this concept that was spoken of hundreds of years before by Daniel in the Old Testament is the very same concept that Paul was teaching to Churches about the kingdom reign of Christ at the right hand of the father.

As I stated before, the Church is the body of Christ, and all enemies will be put under Christ's feet before the time of the harvest. This is expressed here. They will do the same to all the kingdoms of the earth as they had done to Rome. This reality is exactly the same reality we have as a theme in the New Testament. For Christ will rule and we rule and reign with him until all enemies are put under his feet. This is what Daniel is being told will happen! This same thing is described in beautiful detail in Chapter 20 of the Revelation, and we will dive into this later in this book in its own chapter. This echoes another promise from earlier in Daniel:

Daniel 2:44: And in the days of these kings (referencing the kings of world empire) shall the God of heaven set up a kingdom (this is the kingdom inside all believers), which shall never be destroyed: and the kingdom shall not be left to other people, *but* it shall break in pieces and consume all these kingdoms (the kingdoms of the world), and it (the kingdom of God) shall stand for ever.

Christ set up the kingdom while he was here on the earth. When he came in the authority of his kingdom on the Day of the Lord he glorified (declared/revealed it through his righteous judgment) and gave authority to his saints to spread this kingdom and overtake all the kingdoms of this earth. The kingdom of Christ consumes the kingdoms of the earth in both passages, Daniel 7 is revealing how and when this begins to take place. Again this is something that happens slowly through the conversion of nations.

This entire concept also disproves the idea of a future one-world government after Rome falls which will belong to the antichrist. The book of Daniel itself lays out the history of the world empire in a vision given to king Nebuchadnezzar. I will not go through the entire chapter in this book, but if you read Daniel chapter two, you will see this vision in full.

In this chapter, Daniel interprets the vision of Nebuchadnezzar's statue to be a vision of all the world empires up to Rome, after which Rome would fall into ten kingdoms, which became the major nations of Europe and Asia Minor that still exist today. These will never again bind to one another under a world empire as they had during the reign of the 4 great world empires: Babylon, Medo-Persian, Greece, and Rome. Because this is so important and goes along with what we are learning in this chapter I feel we should look briefly at this vision. The following is the dream Nebuchadnezzar had:

Daniel 2:32-34: This image's (Nebuchadnezzar saw a great statue) head *was* of fine gold (this is Babylon), his breast and his arms of silver (this is Medo-Persia), his belly and his thighs of brass (this is Greece), 33. His legs of iron (this is Rome), his feet part of iron and part of clay. 34.Thou sawest till that a stone was cut out without hands, which smote the image upon his feet *that were* of iron and clay, and brake them to pieces. (Pay close attention to the stone and where it strikes the image of the statue, it is on its feet)

Daniel goes on to interpret this vision to be symbolic of the four great world empires that started with Babylon. The others were Medo-Persia, Greece, and Rome. Let's pick up with the fall of Rome:

Daniel 2:40-43: And the fourth kingdom (Rome) shall be strong as iron: forasmuch as iron breaketh in pieces and subdueth all *things*: and as iron that breaketh all these (referring to the kingdoms that came before, in Daniel 7 we saw how this beast/kingdom smashed the others just as Daniel is seeing here. Again this is a theme through Daniel), shall it break in pieces and bruise. (In other words, it will have great military might to subdue/conquer the kingdoms of the world. The military might of Rome is still legendary in the ancient world) 41. And whereas thou sawest the feet and toes (This will be what comes after Rome and is the state of the world we now live in), part of potters' clay, and part of iron, the kingdom shall be divided (Rome fell into the ten great nations of Europe/Asia Minor that still stand today); but there shall be in it of the strength of the iron (so these ten nations will remain strong for they were birthed with the strength of Rome), forasmuch as thou sawest the iron mixed with miry clay.

42. And *as* the toes of the feet *were* part of iron, and part of clay, *so* the kingdom (representing the kingdoms of the world) shall be partly strong, and partly broken (this has been true of Europe since Rome fell). 43. And whereas thou sawest iron mixed with miry clay, they shall mingle themselves with the seed of men (The ten kingdoms that Rome fell into, will spread all over the globe, and again this happened): but they shall not cleave one to another (meaning though these ten nations will spread all over the globe and have the strength of Rome they will never cling to one another again, meaning there can be no world empire again), even as iron is not mixed with clay (the iron represents Rome and the clay are the seed of men meaning all the nations of the world. This speaks of the fact that never again will another world empire rise as in the days of Rome for they will not cling one to another).

I find this whole concept amazing. Go back up to what Daniel said in Daniel 2:34. We see that during the time of the divided Roman Empire into ten nations, meaning our time, the stone made without hands strikes the image of the world empire and breaks it into pieces. Daniel also tells us what this stone is:

Daniel 2:44-45 And in the days of these kings (referencing the kings of world empire) shall the God of heaven set up a kingdom (this is the mountain made without hands. This is a reference to the mountain of the New Covenant Galatians 4:23-26), which shall never be destroyed: and the kingdom shall not be left to other people, *but* it shall break in pieces and consume all these kingdoms (the kingdoms of the world), and it (the kingdom of God) shall stand for ever.

45. Forasmuch as thou sawest that the stone was cut out of the mountain (this mountain is the mountain of the New Testament from which God will take a stone, the gospel, and destroy the kingdoms of this world!) without hands, and that it brake in pieces the iron, the brass, the clay, the silver, and the gold; the great God hath made known to the king what shall come to pass hereafter: and the dream *is* certain, and the interpretation thereof sure.

Daniel is literally saying that sometime during the time we are now living in, Christ will use the kingdom he set up here on the earth to destroy the image of the world empire. The only "one-world" order that Daniel foresees is the kingdom of Christ which shall consume the kingdoms of this world! This is the same language we see used in the judgment of the saints in Daniel 7. This is also promised in the victorious reign of the Messiah remember Paul said Christ will reigns until all enemies—including kingdoms—are put under his feet!

God the Father gave the authority to the Son, and Christ gave it to his people. Christ is the head we are the body. When all enemies are put under him the earth will then be Christ's kingdom ripe for the harvest. This is when Jesus comes and defeats death and delivers the fullness of the kingdom up to the Father and is made subject unto him. This truth and reality is the sole purpose of False-hope and all giants of the sort as they do not want the Church to understand any of this.

For those of you who know the Revelation, you will recognize the vision in Daniel 7 as identical to the events in parts of the Revelation. That is because they are speaking of the same event. This is one of the many proofs that Revelation was written before 70 A.D. and was fulfilled long before Rome fell. Unlike what False-hope teaches the bible does not teach a rebirth of the Roman Empire or a one-world-government of the Antichrist.

Some of this is something we touch on more later in this book, but it is the exact opposite of False-hope's lies. I would imagine that very few if any reading this have ever considered these passages in such a way. I pray the truth of these matters is plain for all to see.

Let us look at another short parable that also taught this:

Matthew 13:33: Another parable spake he unto them; The kingdom of heaven is like unto leaven, which a woman took, and hid in three measures of meal, <u>till the whole was leavened.</u>

The leaven is the gospel, the woman is the Church called the bride of Christ, the meal (picture is of a loaf of bread being prepared, leaven is what we would call yeast today) this is the world, the harvest is when the whole loaf is fully leavened. Or as we may put it until all enemies are put under his feet. Just as leaven does not quickly make the loaf rise, so too will the gospel slowly fill up the earth with its glory.

This same truth is prophecied in many places in the Old Testament:

Habakkuk 2:14: For the <u>earth shall be filled</u> with the knowledge of the glory of the LORD, <u>as the waters cover the sea.</u> (75% of the earth is covered by water this implies that at least 75% of the earth will be converted at some point)

This truth was actually declared from the very beginning of the bible:

Isaiah 46:10: <u>Declaring the end from the beginning,</u> and from ancient times *the things* that are not *yet* done, saying, My counsel shall stand, and I will do all my pleasure.

This is something only our God can do. So what did he declare from the beginning that would be manifest in the end?

Genesis 1:26-28: And God said, <u>Let us make man in our image, after our likeness: and let them have dominion over the fish of the sea, and over the fowl of the air, and over the cattle, and over all the earth, and over every creeping thing that creepeth upon the earth.</u>

27. So God created man in his *own* image, in the image of God created he him; male and female created he them.

28. And God blessed them, and God said unto them, <u>Be fruitful, and multiply, and replenish</u> (fill up) <u>the earth,</u> and <u>subdue it</u> (this was

also declared to the Church Matthew 28): and <u>have dominion</u> over the fish of the sea, and over the fowl of the air, and over every living thing that moveth upon the earth.

What is the fullness of the image of God in man?

Colossians 1:15: Who (Speaking about Christ) is the <u>image of the invisible God</u>, the firstborn of every creature:

The fullness of God's declaration of making man in the image of God is only fulfilled in Christ. The entire historical account of the Garden, Adam, and Eve and the declaration of the Lord about the Image of God were all a picture of Christ and the Church, the fruit of which is converted man being indwelt with the Spirit of the Son of God. This will manifest itself in full on that final day:

1 John 3:2: Beloved, now are we the sons of God, and it doth not yet appear what we shall be: but we know that, <u>when he shall appear, we shall be like him; for we shall see him as he is.</u>

Christ will rule upon his throne until all his enemies are put under him. His reign will see the glory and knowledge of God fill the world, and when he returns to conquer death the fullness of what was declared in Genesis will be revealed on the earth and offered up to the Father. The Father declared it, the Son created it, and the Spirit gives it life. The Father's plan or decree to man in the Garden was to take dominion (kingship) over the earth and fill it up with the image of God in man. Our first father Adam rejected this, Christ the Second Adam did not and he will see it accomplished before the final day!

This brings a whole new meaning to the Lord's prayer of praying heaven realities unto the earth. When one grasps and believes the truth about Christ, his kingdom, and our role in it, this prayer will take on a much deeper meaning. The Just shall live by faith and not sight. Though we can't always see the kingdom yet, by faith, we know it's there and we should know what its end goal of it is.

This is the Church's role just as the Children of Israel conquering the promised land, except now the promised land is the whole earth and not just Canaan. This judgment spoken of in Daniel is what I think is the 1,000-year reign mentioned in Revelation, it is the conquest of the Church over the earth and how God will bring the final enemies to heel after the judgment has sat, and then we will see the gospel manifest on the earth in a way not seen except in glimpses. But we will look at that later in its own chapter.

I realize this chapter was a bit long and had a lot in it, but what did we learn:

- Jesus spoke of two distinct comings. One was a coming in judgment to reward the saints by glorifying the truth of the gospel in them and to destroy the Jewish system (which we will look at in far greater detail later), and another distinct and final coming to judge the world. The first was a type of the last.
- The Gospel will slowly grow over the face of the whole earth and fill it with the glory and knowledge of God.
- Christ went and received the power of his kingdom as a reward from the Father after he ascended into heaven. This was authority over all nations, dominions, and powers. In this kingdom, Christ is king, high priest, and mediator between God and man. He rules at the right hand of the Father, and through the Church over all the nations until all his enemies are put under his feet.
- Christ has given authority, which is the ministry and effectiveness of the gospel to people that he expects us to use.
- We are judged by what we did with our gifts. Those that were given the most (Those with a greater calling to the ministry) were judged first.
- When Christ came on the Day of the Lord it was to dismantle the Jewish kingdom/system and affirm the New Covenant kingdom/system. This authority over nations and cities given to faithful churches was manifest in the authority/judgment they were granted in their ministry of the Gospel. In this way, the gospel will go into all the earth spreading the kingdom everywhere they go consuming the kingdoms of this world. We are then told to disciple the nations bringing them under the authority of the Son through the Gospel. At this point, it will become His Kingdom ready for the harvest.

- There will be no other one-world empire after the fall of Rome.
- Those that will abuse their gifts/authority by not using them will be judged by having them taken away and given to another faithful minister. This is something happening in leaps and bounds in the Western Churches.
- Christ rules with a rod of iron over the nations. Meaning he will raise them up and judge them by destroying them as he sees fit. These judgments are days of the Lord the first of these judgments was the Great and terrible Day of the Lord against Jerusalem, but many others have happened since and will still happen in the future. The end will be to ultimately manifest the kingdom of Christ upon the earth. All the while the Church is acting in the world as leaven in a massive lump of dough.
- Those that refuse to accept Christ's authority, accept his gospel, will be judged without mercy when he comes because they have rejected God's mercy which is the Gospel.

Now let us put what we learned in this chapter with those that came before and see what we now know about his Second Coming:

- Christ is now reigning over true Israel, his Church, at the right hand of the father until he makes all of his enemies his footstool.
- Christ has given his people judgment/authority over the nations and areas they are in to spread the kingdom of Christ on the earth through the gospel and discipleship.
- The Gospel will slowly grow over the face of the whole earth and fill it with the glory and knowledge of God. It will consume the nations as Rome had been consumed by the kingdom of Christ.
- There will be no one-world empire again after the fall of Rome which already happened.
- Christ will come back a final time at the end of the world for the harvest. This will take place once the gospel goes into all the world through his Church and has preeminence on the last day. This is another reason why a secret rapture of the Church before the end makes no sense.

- The lost and the saved will grow in number side by side until the time of the harvest. Meaning there can be no secret rapture before this event. It also implies that the saved will outgrow the lost by the time of this harvest.
- Jesus comes with his angels.
- His coming is announced with a trumpet, a shout, and the voice of an archangel. Meaning this cannot be secretive.
- Everyone shall see him, even the dead and unsaved, as they are all raised and gathered before him on the final day.
- Jesus comes to defeat the final enemy, Death, meaning all other enemies have already been defeated before he returns.
- At the time of the harvest, the world in which the seed was sown will be considered the Kingdom. This is because the judgment of the saints through the rule of Christ has been successful. This kingdom is different from Christ's current kingdom at the right hand of the father, and the Father's kingdom which is the reward of the saints. So clearly we can now see 3 aspects of the kingdom of God.
- He will gather first the lost separating them from the saved.
- This means that if we use the modern understanding of the rapture then the unsaved are raptured first.
- He will then gather and change the saved.
- Christ will sit upon a throne of judgment over all the world.
- He will separate the nations one group on his left and another on his right. These are the saved and unsaved.
- He will judge/reward the saved first based on their good works. He will judge those who had the greatest calling first. He will also hold them accountable for the ministry he gave them. He will take away the reward of those that did nothing.
- Then he will judge the unsaved by their evil works. This judgment is final and without mercy, for they have rejected the mercy of God: the gospel.
- The saints are welcomed into the kingdom of the father.
- This judgment of the wicked in hell is not instant death, rather it is everlasting.

- Jesus has not mentioned a secret rapture of the Church.
- Jesus has not mentioned a 1,000-year physical reign on earth before or after the final judgment that matches the False-hope view.
- Jesus has not mentioned that he will be coming to destroy the antichrist, a one-world government, or a great army as all of these will be defeated before his return.

CHAPTER SIX

The Virgins and the Wedding Feast

"Someday, some simple soul is going to pick of the book of God and believe it and put us all to shame. For we have adopted the convenient theory that the bible is a book to be explained, whereas first and foremost it is a book to be believed, and after that obeyed."

LEONARD RAVENHILL, "WHY REVIVAL TARRIES," 1959

I n the last chapter, we saw one of my favorite parables and how it so perfectly fulfilled itself as a prophecy on the Day of the Lord. In this chapter, we will look at one of the clearest parables of the Day of the Lord. As with the last chapter, we can still learn much about the Second Coming by looking at the Day of the Lord.

Matthew 22:2: The kingdom of heaven is like unto a certain king, which made a marriage for his son,

Let us consider the imagery, the King is God the Father, and his son is Jesus. Marriage is a metaphor for the kingdom reality of the New Covenant. The Jews were the first promised the New Covenant which in this parable is called a marriage. The New Covenant is actually an old promise made to Abraham and it is the covenant of Salvation that really goes back to the Garden, but was not manifested on the earth until Christ came.

In this promise, Abraham was told that one of his seed, meaning male heirs/descendants, would be the promised seed of the woman that would crush the head of the serpent (Galatians 3:26-27, Genisis 3:15) by which all nations of the earth would be blessed, and he would be the father of many nations. This is a picture of all nations coming into the covenant promise of Christ by faith. This is all explained by Paul in Galatians 3, Romans 2:28-29, 11:11-24, 15:8-13, and the book of Hebrews along with many other passages in the New Testament.

In the Old Covenant promise, God chose a nation to be stewards of this promise of the Messiah and be a light in the gentile world concerning the truth of God. This was the center focus of the Hebrew religion. When we fast forward to the time of Christ, Jesus came first to offer the kingdom promise of the New Covenant to the Jews who had long known the promise, but they refused Christ. This is the same thing that happens in this parable.

As we will see unfold in this parable, God will destroy those who refused the offer by burning up their city and then turning to others to come into this marriage ceremony. Again this is all a picture of the covenant.

The Church is the New Covenant Bride of Christ it is Israel in the sense of the Covenant people made up of Jew and gentiles by faith in Christ. The marriage is this union reality of the New Covenant being manifested on the earth, during this union the bride is announced to the world as the only true bride or covenant people. This is because those in the church became the Israel of God by faith, and we are the sons of Abraham by our faith and not by our physical birth. Again this is a concept all throughout the New Testament and I would recommend that those struggling with this idea go back and review the fifth pillar of truth I listed in chapter 2.

As we learned in the last chapter when Christ came and gave the judgment to the saints (rewarded them with authority over cities) this was when it was time for the saints to begin to possess the kingdom. This takes place exactly 40 years after the New Covenant was certified in Christ's own blood. The Church was first empowered to begin when the Holy Spirit fell on Pentecost in 30 A.D this was the year of the crucifixion, and resurrection of Christ. 40 years later in 70 A.D Jesus came and destroyed Jerusalem on the Day of the Lord through the Romans.

This 40-year interval is a picture of Israel wandering through the wilderness for 40 years until they were ready to come into the promised land and began possessing their promised kingdom in the Old Testament. Likewise, the Church during these 40 years, was growing and building itself or as Revelation would put it the bride was making herself ready (Revelation 19:7-8). 40 years after Christ ratified the New Covenant the temple and Old Covenant System were utterly destroyed in 70 A.D. and only the Church remained as the people of God who were now the stewards of the New Covenant.

This is why the Day of the Lord marks the marriage. Jesus declared to the world who his people were and were not. He declared to the Church, "Ye shall be my people and I shall be your God," while at the same time he turned to those who forsook their covenant, their marriage vows if you would, "I know ye not, your portion shall be with my enemies." Again this is what we will see play out in this parable as well.

This reward of authority or judgment over cities that we saw in the last chapter is symbolic of when the marriage happened. It was after this marriage, 40 years after the vow was made, that the Church began to shine and grow in the world as the people of God. They received the spiritual authority over cities and nations from their husband who is Christ. Not only is a marriage a covenant, but marriage has always been a picture of Christ and his Church the offspring of which are the children of God.

The marriage feast is a picture of the invitation of the New Covenant by which believers are made a part of the bride of Christ, his Church. The Jews were the first ones invited to leave the apostate system of the Levitical Priesthood which was soon going to be destroyed, and be the first into this covenant marriage. Many are taught that the marriage celebration of the lamb happens in the future during the rapture, but if we step back a moment and consider a few things we know this happened in the past, just as I am trying to show and this parable will teach.

First, let me ask what is the Church called universally by all true believers as she relates to Christ? The answer is that she is his "bride" present tense. Not that she will be his bride, not that we are engaged to him and will one day wed him, but that she is his bride currently. Why is this? I can say that the Holy Spirit is what bears witness to this truth by the word of God. Christ on the wedding day declared to the world that the Church is his bride, that we are his people. He did this when he destroyed the "people of God (the Jews)," on the Day of the Lord which revealed that they were not in fact the people of covenant anymore for they had forsaken the heart of the Old Covenant, which was the Messiah whom they had rejected.

This is prophetically declared in Revelation 21 which speaks of the aftermath of the destruction of the Old Covenant and the bride pictured as "old heaven and old earth passing away" and begins with the establishment of the New Covenant pictured as the new heavens and new earth (we dive into this concept much later in this book). The New Covenant city of the New Jerusalem is descending to earth in Revelation 21, yet Paul tells us in Galatians 4:23 that this city was in heaven.

Again I hold the view that Revelation was focused on the Day of the Lord in 70 A.D. and not the Second Coming. When Paul was writing Galatians, the Day of the Lord had not yet come and the New Jerusalem was not yet brought to the earth. Just like the Hebrews, there was a period of 40 years before they began to take possession of the kingdom. Christ's kingdom was for all nations of the earth, and we are co-inheritors of this promise because we are wed to Christ (Psalms 2, Pslams 110, Daniel 7:13-14, 22-23, Romans 8:17, etc). The way we conquer our promised land of the kingdom is through conversion this is also seen by Christ ruling until all enemies are put under his feet.

Yet the promise of this new world in which the Church would be the sole covenant people of God on the earth was given to the church as a testimony against the old world system (Old verses New Covenants) which was passing away. When the Day of the Lord came there was left only one Covenant people of God who held firm to Christ that is the Church.

The New Jerusalem descending to the earth is the picture of the covenant people of God being manifested on the earth. It is said to come down from heaven for it was a heavenly promise made back to Abraham (See Hebrews 11:10) and the early Church was the first fruit of this promise. Just as Jerusalem was the heart of the Old Covenant where the tabernacle and later temple were housed (symbols of the Old Covenant), the New Jerusalem is where the New Covenant temple is housed which is the Church.

While the Old Covenant system was in place this reality was largely hidden from the world and the Church was allowed to preach in the shadows of the Old Covenant to try and get the Jews to repent. When Jesus finally judged and dismantled the Old Covenant System he established the New Jerusalem (picture of the Church) as the only covenant people on the earth. That is why both the Church and the New Jerusalem are called the bride of Christ as they are one and the same (Compare Revelation 21:2 to Ephesians 5:25-33, 2 Corinthians 11:2, and Revelation 21:9) Just as Israel and Jerusalem are often the same in the Old Covenant. When the New Jerusalem descends on the earth it is a metaphor for the revealing of the Church as the Covenant people of God. We will dive into this more in chapter 15.

I realize the above might be a lot to take in. The easiest way to understand this whole concept is with Covenant. Marriage is the best picture of the Covenant which is why in the Old Covenant, Israel and Jerusalem were sometimes called the bride of God (Jeremiah 3:14, Ezekiel 16:8-21, Jeremiah 3:6-8, and others). In like fashion in the New Covenant, the Church and the New Jerusalem are both called the bride. The first bride (Old Covenant) was put away which is pictured in the Destruction of Jerusalem because she broke the marriage covenant with God by rejecting his son. Now that this has passed, the Church is manifested on the earth as the New Jerusalem which is the steward of the New Covenant and home of the temple of God which is the only place of salvation.

Second, consider the picture of marriage. Paul teaches us that marriage is a symbol of Christ and his church and God instituted it to declare from the beginning the promised reality of Christ and the Church (Ephesians 5:30-33). In this same text, Paul quotes a prophecy that Adam stated all the way back in Genesis about the purpose of marriage (Genesis 2:24 compared to Ephesians 5:31). God instituted marriage because he desired two things, one that Adam would have a helper who was meet (the old way of saying perfectly in shape and design to be what he needed in all things) for him. He needed this help meet so that he could fill the earth with the image of God in man, and take dominion or kingship over the whole earth, which God commanded of him (see Genesis 1:28).

This being a picture of Christ and the Church, according to Paul, teaches us a profound truth that the Church is the helpmeet (bride) of Christ by which we fill the earth with the full image of God in man and take dominion over all the earth by placing all things under Christ's feet through the conversion of the Gospel. When Christ and the Church come together (the church being the steward of the gospel which produces the kingdom inside the lost soul of man) they birth a child of God. Recall the first Adam rejected the will of God causing sin and death to come into the world, but through Christ life and redemption comes (Romans 5:17-21). Jesus will do all that the father commanded man to accomplish on the earth and he uses his helpmeet, the Church, to do this.

Lastly, we should keep in mind that even though all the above is the true and current reality for us, it was yet a future promise to the early Church. The Bride of Christ could not be fully revealed on the earth until Christ came and dismantled the Old Covenant System of the Levitical Priesthood, the temple, and its entire religious system. This was all replaced by the Melchizedek Priesthood which is the priesthood of Christ, the New Covenant, and the Church. That is why the Marriage of Christ coincided with the Day of the Lord.

Let's see how this parable teaches many of these things.

Matthew 22:3: 3. And sent forth his servants to call them that were bidden to the wedding: and they would not come.

The servants in this parable are the men of God, prophets, preachers, teachers, evangelists, and all such like who proclaimed the word of God in the Old Testament. Those that were bidden, meaning those who were first invited and told about the marriage, were the Jews. The concept of the New Covenant promise of Christ was often spoken of in the Old Testament and was not a new reality when Jesus came on the scene. However, when they heard the cry of the prophets they would not come. This is a clear reference to the fact that Jesus was bidding them enter into the Kingdom by faith in him as the Messiah. This is why Jesus came first and preached to the lost house of the sheep of Israel. This was the marriage prepared by the Father not only for his Son but also for all the saints. They refused Jesus as the Messiah and thus they refused to come to the marriage.

Matthew 22:4-7: 4. Again, he sent forth other servants, saying, Tell them which are bidden, Behold, I have prepared my dinner: my oxen and *my* fatlings *are* killed, and all things *are* ready: come unto the marriage.

5. But they made light of *it,* and went their ways, one to his farm, another to his merchandise:

These servants were the disciples and the early Church that followed Christ. The food prepared was the riches of the gospel and the spiritual nourishment that every lost soul so desperately needs. The Church's greatest burden at the beginning was to see Jews saved, but the Jews cared more for their temple and dead religion.

6. And the remnant took his servants, and entreated *them* spitefully, and slew *them.*

As we see play out in the book of Acts not only did the Jews mistreat and persecuted the Church, the servants as they are called in this parable, but they also killed many of them. Remember Stephen was the first.

7. But when the king heard *thereof,* he was wroth: and <u>he sent forth his armies</u>, and destroyed those murderers, <u>and burned up their city.</u>

Here is the Destruction of Jerusalem once again pronounced against the Jews with great clarity for their continued rebellion against God. Notice here how the King came with his armies to pass judgment against their city. This is exactly what Christ said he would do in the accounts of the Day of the Lord in Matthew 24, Mark 13, and Luke 21. Listen again to how Jesus rebuked the rebellious Jews and see how it perfectly matches what is said so far in this parable:

Luke 11:47-51: Woe unto you! for ye build the sepulchres (Tombs) of the prophets, and your fathers killed them.

48. Truly ye bear witness that ye allow the deeds of your fathers: for they indeed killed them, and ye build their sepulchres (Jesus is saying you built grand tombs and honored your forefathers who killed the prophets you also say you honored. Here you see their hypocrisy).

49. Therefore (For this reason, meaning because of their hypocrisy) also said the wisdom of God, I will send them prophets and apostles, and *some* of them they shall slay and persecute: 50. That the blood of all the prophets, which was shed from the foundation of the world, may be required of this generation; 51. From the blood of Abel unto the blood of Zacharias, which perished between the altar and the temple: verily (Truly, without a doubt) I say unto you, It shall be required of this generation.

As I think it is so clear Jesus, again and again, reiterated that judgment was coming upon those living, "that generation" not only because they killed *the* Prophet of God: Jesus, but also because the Jews throughout their history killed the prophets nearly every one of them. Thus this rebellious murderous spirit of the Jews also turned on the apostles and the early Church. For this Christ brought the judgment against their City, Temple, and Religious system all of which had become idols to them. All this was done within a generation. A generation is between 40 and 80 years.

40 years after Jesus declared these judgments, and others we will soon look at, on the 40th anniversary of Christ's crucifixion, on the exact day they crucified him, Rome came down upon Jerusalem. This was the army of the Lord that he sent. Remember as we looked at in the last chapter, Christ is now and always was King of kings. God uses nations all through the bible to fulfill his judgments and mercies. This portion of the parable was perfectly fulfilled to the letter by 70 A.D.

But, this is not where the parable ends let us see now what we can learn about the marriage and lessons for that final coming:

Matthew 22:8-12: 8. Then saith he to his servants, The wedding is ready, but they which were bidden were not worthy. (They were not worthy because of unbelief)

9. Go ye therefore into the highways, and as many as ye shall find, bid to the marriage. (The marriage is the New Covenant)

10. So those servants went out into the highways, and gathered together <u>all as many as they found, both bad and good:</u> and the wedding was furnished with guests.

This is a picture of God turning to the Gentiles and bringing them into the Church. Notice the term in verse ten, both bad and good (saved and unsaved) came into the church. There has always been and always will be antichrist within the Church until the end draws near, as Death and not antichrist is the last enemy slain by Jesus before he delivers the fullness of the kingdom up to the father. It was always the intention of the king to bring in Gentiles but not before the Jews, this was prophesied much in the Old Testament. The above verses also show the spreading out of the gospel into all the world, or as it was stated, "as many as they found."

11. And when the king came in to see the guests, he saw there a man which had not on a wedding garment:

12. And he saith unto him, Friend, how camest thou in hither not having a wedding garment? And he was speechless.

In the last parable, we saw that the wicked servant that did nothing with his talent was being judged by having what little they had taken away, Jesus further builds on this here and says he will also judge them as the unbeliever. This concept is true because true saving faith causes growth, and out of a heart of love good works follow. When we do nothing with what we have been given we show disdain for it and reveal an unconverted heart. God is the perfect judge and if your heart is unconverted, or as this parable puts it, if you have not the wedding clothes on he will know it.

This is pictured here again with the guest without wedding garments. This is also the portion of the parable that best teaches us the truth concerning all the comings of Christ, be them on our final day, the day of judgment to nations, or the final day. At his coming in judgment, it will be revealed who truly is just simply making a profession of faith, and who is truly saved.

The wedding garment here is a picture of the righteousness of God that we are clothed in when we are saved in truth.

Isaiah 61:10: I will greatly rejoice in the LORD, my soul shall be joyful in my God; for he hath <u>clothed me with the garments of salvation</u>, he hath covered me with the <u>robe of righteousness</u>, as a bridegroom decketh *himself* with ornaments, and as a bride <u>adorneth *herself* with her jewels.</u>

Isaiah 45:5-6 I *am* the LORD, and *there is* none else, *there is* no God beside me: <u>I girded</u> (gird means clothe) <u>thee, though thou hast not known me:</u> 6. That they may know from the rising of the sun, and from the west, that *there is* none beside me. I *am* the LORD, and *there is* none else.

When Christ comes during judgment he will cast out the false converts, those antichrists that profess God, but inwardly are lost. This is true now but is also pictured in the separation of the sheep and goats, and wheat and tares. If he had come when I was a young man, though outwardly I looked like a zealous Christian, he would have seen that I wore not the wedding garment, those clothes of the righteousness of salvation. I believe he did this during the Reformation and will do this again for the future Reformation I believe is coming to Christiandom as ultimately Jesus wants his people to be one as he and the father are one (John 17:21-23).

This man in the parable was speechless because there was no defense he could make. The facade of his faith could not hide before the eyes of the King. Once the judgment comes there is no time to repent. This is another truth about all days of the Lord. God is long-suffering but there comes a point where the fullness of the iniquities (sins) and rebellions becomes so great that God passes just judgment on a people. When this happens there is no more opportunity to repent, as the time of grace has passed.

Proverbs 1:24-30: Because I have called, and ye refused; I have stretched out my hand, and no man regarded (meaning God begins to judge to get your attention and you do not see it); 25. But ye have set at nought (ignored) all my counsel, and would none (would not receive) of my reproof: 26. <u>I also will laugh at your calamity; I will mock when your fear cometh</u> (God is speaking!);

27 When your fear cometh as desolation (destruction), and your destruction cometh as a whirlwind; when distress and anguish cometh

upon you. 28. <u>Then shall they call upon me, but I will not answer; they</u> <u>shall seek me early, but they shall not find me</u>: (Why is God being so harsh? He explains) 29 For that they hated knowledge, and did not choose the fear of the LORD: 30. They would none of my counsel: they despised all my reproof.

This is not the only set of verses that teach this truth. God is long-suffering towards man, but there comes a time when mankind has hardened its heart so much against God's mercy, that God gives them the righteous judgment that they deserve. How often does God send natural disasters and other judgments against a wicked land and only then do the people turn to God for a very brief time before returning to their sins? This mocks God as they are ignoring his righteous judgment, that is why he laughs and mocks.

I remember after 9/11 when the twin towers of New York fell every church was full for about a month, for they feared that for the first time the strength of the nation was at risk. They turned to God seeking hope, and then people turned quickly back to their sins once they saw that the nation was not going to be attacked openly. Regardless of why 9/11 happened, did not God allow it? America did not learn so God has sent civil divisions, economic divisions, and natural disasters and still, we have not repented. Will God not judge us more harshly for his own name's sake?

Let us continue in this parable.

Matthew 22:13-14: 13. Then said the king to the servants, Bind him hand and foot, and take him away, and cast *him* into outer darkness; there shall be weeping and gnashing of teeth.

14. For many are called, but few *are* chosen.

Although this individual was in the Church, his portion was with the unsaved. Notice that the other guests did not notice his lack of clothing, otherwise, they would have tried to correct the issue. Rather, it was only when the King came that such lack of clothing was revealed. Judgment always reveals the truth.

Notice as well that there was no opportunity for this man caught without his clothes to get a wedding garment. Why not just get the proper clothes once his lack of clothing was pointed out? That is because once Christ comes there is a finality to it. When he appears you are either saved or you are not. You are clothed with the wedding garments or you are not. This is true about all coming judgments of God be them national, personal, or for the world on the final day

Again because this man had rejected the mercy of God which is the gospel, meaning he never truly believed it, he was cast into hell and judged without mercy something that we all justly deserve. In our concept of what justice is, assuming we understood the reality of sin, God is unjust by giving us grace and mercy. This shows the incredible worth of Christ and shows the unfathomable love of God. More than this it shows our wretched state.

This goes along with what Jesus said:

Matthew 7:21-23: Not every one that saith unto me, <u>Lord, Lord, shall enter into the kingdom of heaven;</u> but <u>he that doeth the will of my Father which is in heaven.</u>

22. <u>Many will say to me in that day, Lord, Lord, have we not</u> prophesied in thy name? and in thy name have cast out devils? and in thy name done many wonderful works?

23. And then will I profess unto them, <u>I never knew you:</u> depart from me, ye that work iniquity.

Just like in the parable, there will be many on the day when Christ returns that think they are saved, hence they will call Jesus Lord, but in reality, they have no wedding clothes. They were never saved. These are those in churches that have a head knowledge of God, but they have never been born again. These can be pastors, Sunday school teachers, worship leaders, and even Christian heroes.

What is the will of the Father mentioned in the above text? This is what clothes us with proper clothing, Jesus answers this directly:

John 6:39-40: And this is the Father's will which hath sent me, that of all which he hath given me I should lose nothing, but should <u>raise it up again at the last day</u>. 40. And this is the will of him that sent me, <u>that every one which seeth the Son, and believeth on him, may have everlasting life:</u> and I will <u>raise him up at the last day.</u>

We will look at this closer in the next chapter, but note that the will of the father is that we believe and look to the Son for our salvation, this gives us eternal life. This is something the Father wants us all to do. This is his will. It is not a work of righteousness that we can do, but it is a work of righteousness that Christ has done, that we trust in for our salvation, righteousness, and security. The last is promised in verse 39. God cannot lie, Jesus says he will not lose a single one that has placed their trust in Him of whom the Father charged the Son with their safety. Thus one cannot lose their salvation if they really have it.

In the rebuke of the false believers in both the parable and the statement of Christ, these people were not trusting in the Son, but in their works and in their religion. That is why Christ said I never knew you, not that he used to and he somehow lost or forgot them, but that he never knew these people. That is why they are speechless when the King comes and finds them without clothing. That clothing is Christ.

Romans 13:14: But put <u>ye on the Lord Jesus Christ</u>, and make not provision for the flesh, to *fulfil* the lusts *thereof.*

We put on Christ, that is his righteousness, by forsaking our own good works, our own righteousness, and resting completely on what he has done for our salvation. This is the Gospel in its purest form, Jesus did all that was necessary for you to get into heaven, look to him and live, trust in him and be clothed in Him, and he will save you. He will raise you up on the last day and you shall never perish but have everlasting life. <u>This is the will of the father for your life.</u> When this happens you will be given a new heart/nature/spirit from which will flow good works and fruits of righteousness. This is all to conform you to the image of his Son (Romans 8:29).

So what all did we learn from this parable about the second physical coming?

That Christ, when he comes, is doing so to bring in the fullness of the kingdom of God. In the parable, the marriage feast was a call to enter the kingdom. The marriage is the kingdom, the fullness of which God will manifest on the earth in its fullness when Christ returns but is already now spreading as the kingdom of God spread over the earth through the Gospel and the power of the Holy Spirit.

His coming(s) will prove the true believers, and expose those that made a profession of faith but never believed. When Christ separates the sheep from the goats, the saved from the unsaved, these antichrists will not be with the saved. This is true at the end when he returns but also true any time Christ comes to judge his people or as this parable says he came to see his guests.

When he comes in judgment there is no more opportunity to get saved as the time of mercy has passed.

We see that all are called (invited) to partake in this feast, but few will come (called the Chosen or the Elect). This also shows how the Church is needed to be the one giving the call (Romans 10:14). Let us now look at a similar parable that had direct application to the day of the Lord and further explains the falling away mentioned in 2 Thessalonians 2:3, the famous Man of Sin passage. Many of these truths taught in this parable could apply to many churches today, but the primary meaning behind this parable took place before 70 A.D. This should highlight why many of the Apostle's writings are filled with both warnings and encouragement to churches going through persecution and the dangers of their time and the fast-approaching Day of the Lord:

Matthew 25:1-13: Then shall the kingdom of heaven be likened unto ten virgins, which took their lamps, and went forth to meet the bridegroom. 2. And five of them were wise, and five *were* foolish. 3. They that *were* foolish took their lamps, and took no oil with them: (They did not expect the wait would be long)

4. But the wise took oil in their vessels with their lamps. (They took the oil because they expected the wait could be long) 5. While the bridegroom tarried, they all slumbered and slept.

Let us see the symbolism in the parable. The ten virgins are representative of the professing believers in the world. The lamp is this profession of faith in the world. The virgins took their profession into the world awaiting the bridegroom which is Christ. Symbolizing that the Church is awaiting the coming of the Lord for the marriage which was declared on the Day of the Lord.

Some felt the wait would be long and others that it would be near at hand. Notice in verse 5, that the bridegroom tarried in his coming, and all the churches fell asleep. I cannot be certain but I propose that this is a reference to the churches becoming more worldly-minded than heavenly-minded.

The oil I do not think is meant, to represent worldly blessings, nor spiritual ones, nor the Gospel, nor the gifts of the Spirit, all of which are sometimes signified by oil. Rather, I think it is the Spirit of God himself, who is the oil of gladness, and the anointing which teaches all things; he is the regenerating and sanctifying grace of the Spirit. Meaning their religion had become dead when the oil ran out or remained vibrant and alive for those that kept their oil. Those that ran out had a form of godliness that professed faith in God, but there was no saving and regeneration of the Spirit. These without oil are the apostate Churches and can equally be symbolic of apostate Judaism. For a time they had both oil and profession, but over time the foolish would lose both.

Matthew 25:6-9: 6. And at midnight there was a cry made, Behold, the bridegroom cometh; go ye out to meet him. 7. Then all those virgins arose, and trimmed their lamps. 8. And the foolish said unto the wise, Give us of your oil; for our lamps are gone out. 9. But the wise answered, saying, *Not so;* lest there be not enough for us and you: but go ye rather to them that sell, and buy for yourselves.

At midnight the cry came. At midnight most everyone is asleep and unprepared. Midnight came for the darkness had enveloped them fully. A call sounds to wake them before he actually comes. This call is one that all the churches hear not just the faithful. This call is the sign that Jesus spoke about in Matthew 24, Mark 13, and Luke 21 and beyond.

It is important to note that even the apostates, these foolish virgins, became aware of the coming at the same time as the wise. This coming is the coming of judgment, as we have seen in the other parables, and just like we saw this judgment was also to reward and glorify his saints. In this parable, this reward is likened to a marriage that is because the saints received from Christ authority and judgment over the nations as he had because we are his Bride.

This announcement of his soon approach made the apostates panic, for their lights had gone out entirely and the night was well dark. Yet the true Churches went out with joy to meet him. Their light did not go out. In contrast, the small glimmer of grace that these apostates had at the beginning was completely burned out here at the end. Their vileness had so extinguished the work of grace that they had become thoroughly unprofitable bound up in false religion and dead works. If half of the Churches fell away into apostasy this would explain the falling away that Paul said must happen before the day of Christ could come.

This is also warned by John in the Revelation he often told the churches that if they did not repent he would come and take their candlestick away (Revelation chapters 2&3).

It says that both the wise and foolish trimmed their lamps, meaning they made sure they were ready to meet the Lord. It was during this process that the apostate churches realized they were not even close to ready for their light had gone out for lack of oil. Remember the light was their profession, meaning at this time even their profession had lost its power over the darkness around them, this is what I believe is meant by their light had gone out. They may still speak as they did before, but what they said meant nothing it had no power or life in it. Now they not only want their profession, meaning the ability to influence a lost world, but the oil as they now saw the true church had.

They looked with envy at the shining light of grace and life now blazing in the true Church of God. Notice when these apostates turned to the wise and asked for their oil, they were denied. This denial did not show a lack of compassion, rather it points out that the state of wretchedness among the apostates was to the point that they thought that this life came from man, meaning they looked to receive the oil from the true church rather than from God. All true grace comes from God, not a church or believers.

By turning to the true Church for their oil, this shows that they had no understanding anymore of were Grace came from. Thus the true Church told the Apostate Church to go and find those that sell the grace and buy from them. This is a reference to the source of grace, the Father, Son, and Spirit through the Gospel. Basically what they are saying is, "don't look to us look to God," It was not found in a religious organization and it could not be bought with money of this world but only by faith.

This reminds me of something that happened in Acts:

Acts 8:18-21: And when Simon saw that through laying on of the apostles' hands the Holy Ghost was given, he offered them money, 19. Saying, Give me also this power, that on whomsoever I lay hands, he may receive the Holy Ghost. 20. But Peter said unto him, Thy money perish with thee, because thou hast thought that the gift of God may be purchased with money. 21. Thou hast neither part nor lot in this matter: for thy heart is not right in the sight of God.

Obviously, this isn't a perfect example, but it seems to be very similar. Simon saw that Peter and the apostles had great power and authority from God. So too did the apostate Church look at the true Church. Just as Peter rebukes Simon for thinking that the Holy Spirit could be bought with money, something that was made by human hands so too does the true Church rebuke the apostate church.

Consider as well, that Christ declared that the day of the Lord will be as in the days of Noah and Lot (Luke 17:28, Matthew 24:37). In the story of Lot, Abraham begged God to spare the city of Sodom for ten righteous men's sake (Genisis 18:16-33). God said if he could find ten he would spare the city. He only found four souls and the city was burned. Lot's story is a parallel to this parable with the virgins. Lot came out from Sodom, and when Christ came the wise virgins left the city that was spiritually Sodom:

Revelation 11:8: And their dead bodies *shall lie* in the street of the great city, <u>which spiritually is called Sodom and Egypt, where also our Lord was crucified.</u>

Jesus was crucified in Jerusalem. It was spiritually like Sodom and Egypt. God declared judgment on this harlot city. When he came to judge it he could not find even 10 righteous churches. The faithful were taken from the city into the mountain refuge of Pella just as Lot was.

Luke 21:2021: 20. And when ye shall see Jerusalem compassed (surrounded) with armies, then know that the desolation thereof is nigh. 21. Then let them which are in Judaea <u>flee to the mountains</u>; and let them which are in the midst of it depart out; and let not them that are in the countries enter thereinto.

When the cry came to go and meet the Bridegroom (Christ) the wise virgins had to leave and go out to him. As we will look at in much greater clarity in a later chapter, the righteous virgin churches all listened to Jesus and fled and were spared the judgment. Those that were apostate remained and were destroyed along with the city.

Let's see how this perfectly plays out in the rest of this parable:

Matthew 25:10-13: 10. And while they went to buy, the bridegroom came; and they that were ready went in with him to the marriage: and the door was shut. 11. Afterward came also the other virgins, saying, Lord, Lord, open to us. 12. But he answered and said, Verily I say unto you, I know you not. 13. Watch therefore, for ye know neither the day nor the hour wherein the Son of man cometh.

We see then that the apostate church went searching for the truth, searching for oil, but notice it doesn't say they found any. Why? Because they searched not by faith, this was blindness as they groped through the darkness of the world searching for oil for their lights. Thus the apostate virgins are revealed to be the Jewish synagogues/church/virgins as well as false Christian churches. When the judgment finally came and the true churches were gathered in safety by Christ, it was too late for those to flee the judgment. During the judgment against Jerusalem the Jews cried out to God to save them as he had done so often in the past, but he declared that he knew them not. The marriage is symbolic of the fullness of the promised kingdom affirmed by Christ's coming on the Day of the Lord.

Because this day was coming, and because Christ warned his Church that it would come within a generation he tells them to watch. This is said often when Jesus directly speaks about the Day of the Lord. Those that do not watch with the expectation of this coming will have that day come upon them as a thief in the night. This was a concept we looked at in chapter 2 and we will dive into it more in chapter 10.

What can we learn from this parable:

That there were two types of churches wise and foolish before the coming of the Lord. These are pictured in the Jewish Churches (synagogues), false Christian Churches, and true Christian Churches all three professed faith in God at the time. This concept is true to this day.

The foolish started out with some oil and light, but as time went on they lost both. This is the falling away mentioned by Paul. The Jews fell away in their apostasy by overall rejecting Jesus and the Church, and many antichrists also existed that did not remain pure in the doctrines of Christ.

This falling away happens during a time of sleeping between when Christ left and when he came in judgment this shows the great mercy of God as he allowed nearly 40 years of ministry to give the Jews one final chance to return to him before the Day of the Lord. This is the primary reason why they mocked the Christians who preached this soon coming day: 2 Peter 3:4: And saying, <u>Where is the promise of his coming?</u> for since the fathers fell asleep (meaning the Jewish fathers/patriarchs), all things continue as *they were* from the beginning of the creation.

There was a cry that warned both the wise and foolish Churches of Christ's coming. The wise went with Christ into safety and the foolish did not.

Let us now put what we have learned from both of these parables with what we have learned from the previous parables:

- The Jews were invited first to come into the kingdom of God but they refused. This was the marriage supper of the lamb to celebrate the soon marriage of Christ and his Church.
- The great falling away has already happened and the Day of the Lord has already come. This event put a clear distinction between the apostates and the true Church.
- Christ is now reigning over true Israel, his church, at the right hand of the father until he makes all of his enemies his footstool.
- The Gospel will slowly grow over the face of the whole earth and fill it with the glory and knowledge of God. It will consume the nations as Rome had been consumed by the kingdom of Christ.
- There will be no one-world empire again after the fall of Rome which already happened.
- Christ has given his people judgment/authority over the nations and areas they are in to spread the kingdom of Christ on the earth through the gospel and discipleship. This was the marriage promised first to the Jews and is the promised heritage of all believers.

- Christ will come back a final time bodily at the end of the world for the harvest. This will take place once the fullness of the kingdom has been manifested on the earth when all enemies are put under Christ. This is another reason why a secret rapture of the Church before the end makes no sense.
- Christ comes to bring in the fullness of the Kingdom and destroy the final enemy which is death.
- The lost and the saved will grow in number side by side until the time of the harvest. Meaning there can be no secret rapture before this event.
- Jesus comes with his angels.
- His coming is announced with a trumpet, a shout, and the voice of an archangel. Meaning this cannot be secretive or silent.
- Everyone shall see him, even the dead and unsaved as they are all raised and gathered.
- At the time of the harvest, the world in which the seed was sown will be considered the Kingdom. This is because the kingdom of Christ's rule through his Church has been successful. This kingdom is different from Christ's current kingdom at the right hand of the father, and the Father's kingdom which is the reward of the saints. So clearly we see 3 aspects of the kingdom of God being spoken of.
- His coming will be final, meaning there will be no opportunity to get saved once he comes. This makes the 1,000-year kingdom taught by False-hope completely in error as they say people will continue to get saved after Christ returns. Clearly, we see that there is no room for this.
- He will gather first the lost separating them from the saved. This includes the false churches and false believers, and anyone found without the wedding dress: which is the righteousness of Christ through the Gospel.
- If we use the modern concept of the rapture then the unsaved are raptured first.
- He will then gather and change the saved.
- Christ will sit upon a throne of judgment over all the world.

- He will separate the people one group on his left and another on his right. These are the saved and unsaved.
- He will judge/reward the saved first based on their good works. He will judge those who had the greatest calling first. He will also hold them accountable for the ministry he gave them. He will take away the reward of those that did nothing.
- Then he will judge the unsaved by their evil works. Many of those of the false churches will try and reason with Christ using their "good works" as proof of their true conversion, but Christ declares he never knew them. They are all cast into hell. This judgment is final and without mercy, for they have rejected the mercy of God: the gospel.
- The saints are welcomed into the kingdom of the father.
- This judgment of the wicked in hell is not instant death, rather it is everlasting.
- Jesus still has not mentioned a secret rapture.
- Jesus has not mentioned a 1,000-year physical reign on earth before or after the final judgment that matches the dispensational view.
- Jesus has not mentioned that he will be coming to destroy antichrist, a one-world government, or a great army when he comes as they will already be defeated.

CHAPTER SEVEN

Jesus said What?

"There is no wisdom save in truth. Truth is everlasting, but our ideas about truth are changeable. Only a little of the first fruits of wisdom, only a few fragments of the boundless heights, breadths, and depths of truth, have I been able to gather."

MARTIN LUTHER 1483-1546, WAS THE MAN
WHO LAUNCHED THE REFORMATION.

There are many other parables we could look at to gain some small grains of truth in which to build our understanding concerning Christ's Second Coming. But I fear at this point that to do so will only be to drive home more of the same points we have already learned, so in the hopes of keeping this work short, let us now turn to what else Jesus said about his coming that was not so hidden as in the parables.

John 14:1-4: Let not your heart be troubled: ye believe in God, believe also in me. 2. In my Father's house are many mansions: if *it were* not *so,* I would have told you. <u>I go to prepare a place for you.</u> 3. And if I go and prepare a place for you, <u>I will come again, and receive you unto myself; that where I am, *there* ye may be also.</u> 4. And whither I go ye know, and the way ye know.

Here is a beautiful passage concerning the coming of our Lord. Jesus is right now preparing our eternal home in the father's kingdom. It is this that Christ told us in past parables will be the inheritance and reward of the saints. From this clear saying we see the promise that when he comes he will gather us to him and we will forever be with him. This is completely consistent with the final coming we have been learning about. As we will learn in chapter 14, those saints that pass on before this final day are in heaven reigning and ruling with us and Christ.

John 5:22-29: For the Father judgeth no man, but hath <u>committed all judgment unto the Son</u>: 23. That all *men* should honour the Son, even as they honour the Father. <u>He that honoureth not the Son honoureth not the Father which hath sent him</u>. (Here is another rebuke to the Jews and Muslims today who say they still worship the Father. Again if they reject and deny the son, they have rejected and denied the Father also).

24. Verily, verily, I say unto you, He that heareth my word, and believeth on him that sent me, hath everlasting life, and shall not come into condemnation; but is passed from death unto life. 25. Verily, verily, I say unto you, The hour is coming, and now is, <u>when the dead shall hear the voice of the Son of God: and they that hear shall live.</u> (This speaks of the first resurrection, the resurrection of the soul of man. This is salvation. This is what it means to be born again. Notice he says that this is happening now. This is important as it ties directly into Revelation 20).

26. For as the Father hath life in himself; so hath he given to the Son to have life in himself; 27. And hath given him authority to execute judgment also, because he is the Son of man. 28. Marvel not at this: <u>for the hour is coming, in the which all that are in the graves shall hear his voice,</u> (Here Christ speaks of that final day, yet coming, notice how he distinguishes this resurrection from the above verse). 29. <u>And shall come forth; they that have done good, unto the resurrection of life; and they that have done evil, unto the resurrection of damnation.</u>

Though Christ did not come bodily the first time to judge the world, for the world was already condemned (John 3:18), it is interesting to point out that in both of the comings of Christ spoken of in the New Testament (that being the Day of the Lord and the Second Coming) he came in judgment. In the previous parables, we saw this judgment unfold as all the world was judged by him. Here we see more clearly that it is not just those that are alive when he comes that are judged, as on the Day of the Lord, but the entire human population that ever lived will be judged because all will be resurrected at the Second Coming.

Until that final day, there will be many days of the Lord against nations that reject him, this is what was meant by:

Psalms 2:9 Thou shalt break them (the nations) with a rod of iron; thou shalt dash them in pieces like a potter's vessel.

The prophets bore witness that Christ was not to just come and save mankind but to also judge. This is prophecied much but here is just one such example:

Isaiah 9:6-7: For unto us a child is born (Jesus), unto us a son is given: and <u>the government shall be upon his shoulder</u>: and his name shall be called Wonderful, Counsellor, The mighty God, The everlasting Father, The Prince of Peace. 7. <u>Of the increase of *his* government and peace *there shall be* no end</u>, upon the throne of David, and upon his kingdom, to order it, and to <u>establish it</u> (to build it) <u>with judgment and with justice</u> (This is why he came in judgment on the Day of the Lord to judge the unfaithful harlot. This was to begin establishing his righteous rule of Christ with great authority and Godly fear. This was the kingdom he went and got, and then he shared it with his bride, and presented her to the world on this same day he came in judgment.) from henceforth even for ever. The zeal of the LORD of hosts will perform this.

We see also that the resurrection of both the righteous and the ungodly <u>happens on the same day</u>. There is a resurrection of the damned as well as the saved. This is how hell is eternal as all are resurrected with bodies that cannot die. Those in hell will die a million deaths but never pass away. Such is the horror of hell. Hell is called the second death because you are eternally separated from the Father the source of all life.

No wonder Jesus spoke about this place more than he did about heaven, no wonder he pleads with his children to preach a gospel to a dying world. No wonder he delays this day for woe unto them at the judgment that who are not prepared to meet him!

This once again proves there can be no secret bodily rapture or resurrection of the saints before the last day, as Christ says that on that last day is when we are all raised both good and bad.

John 11:23-26: Jesus saith unto her, Thy brother shall rise again. 24. Martha saith unto him, <u>I know that he shall rise again in the resurrection at the last day.</u> 25. Jesus said unto her, <u>I am the resurrection, and the life:</u>

he that believeth in me, though he were dead, yet shall he live: 26. And whosoever liveth and believeth in me shall never die. Believest thou this?

Here is the account of Jesus raising Lazarus. We get a picture of the power of the Son of God. But often overshadowed by this great miracle is this brief encounter between Martha and Jesus. Martha is grieving because her brother Lazarus is dead and Jesus could have healed him but had not gotten there in time.

Jesus promises that her brother will live again, notice that her mind immediately goes to the resurrection that will happen on the last day. Either she heard Jesus preach this perhaps as we saw in the last passage in John 5:22-29, or she read of this in the Old Testament as this day is also spoken about there as well.

Regardless, Jesus does not rebuke her for this, rather he tells her that Lazurus can live again now because Jesus is the resurrection. Of course, the story plays out that he calls Lazarus from the grave. We saw in John 5 that Jesus will likewise call all men out of their graves, and we see here that Martha knew about this event and she knew when it would happen. Amazing that so many Christians can't seem to figure out when it will happen... Let's see where else Jesus said this truth.

John 12:47-48: And if any man hear my words, and believe not, I judge him not: for I came not to judge the world, but to save the world. 28. He that rejecteth me, and receiveth not my words, hath one that judgeth him: the word that I have spoken, the same shall judge him in the last day.

Here Jesus states again that the resurrection will happen on the last day. Note that this reference is to the resurrection of the damned on the last day, but we know that they raise on the same day as the righteous as Jesus already stated previously. Notice at well that Jesus said the very word of God will be the testimony against the unbelievers.

John 6:37-40: All that the Father giveth me shall come to me; and him that cometh to me I will in no wise cast out. 38. For I came down from heaven, not to do mine own will, but the will of him that sent me. 39. And this is the Father's will which hath sent me, that of all which he hath given me I should lose nothing, but should raise it up again at the last day. 40. And this is the will of him that sent me, that every one which seeth the Son, and believeth on him, may have everlasting life: <u>and I will raise him up at the last day.</u>

Twice Jesus declares the truth of the resurrection promised to the saved, those that would believe in him, this is the fullness of our salvation. We are saved in part now and the Holy Spirit resides in us as an earnest (down payment) of the promise Jesus is making here (Ephesians 1: 12-14).

It is here I want to remind everyone about the famous rapture passage we looked at earlier 1 Thessalonians 4:14-18. In this passage, Paul is reminding grieving Christians of the hope and promise of the resurrection. The Resurrection that Paul speaks of is the same resurrection that Jesus is now speaking of. The resurrection of the righteous takes place on the last day. Paul just gives us more details on what happens to the saints on this last day. Paul is not contradicting this promise that Jesus is giving at all. We will dive into this more in the next chapter, but the comfort of the saints is the promise of the bodily resurrection.

This is exactly the same promise Jesus has reiterated over and over, but he also clearly said that this day would happen on the last day. Jesus also said that on this same day there would be a resurrection of both the just (saved) and the unjust (damned). This completely destroys the secret rapture doctrine, the 7-year tribulation, and the return of Christ to set up a 1,000-year kingdom. This also shows that Paul and Jesus spoke the same truths.

John 6:44: No man can come to me, except the Father which hath sent me draw him: <u>and I will raise him up at the last day.</u>

John 6:54: Whoso eateth my flesh, and drinketh my blood, <u>hath eternal life</u>; and <u>I will raise him up at the last day.</u>

I do not know how Jesus can be more clear about this. The day we are caught up is the day of the resurrection, it is the day of the judgments, it is the day of the fullness of the Kingdom of God, it is the last and final Day! But Jesus didn't just talk about them rising he also spoke openly about the change that would happen with these raised saints:

Mark 12:24-25: And Jesus answering said unto them, Do ye not therefore err, because ye know not the scriptures, neither the power of

God? 25. For when they <u>shall rise from the dead,</u> they neither marry, nor are given in marriage; but are as the angels which are in heaven.

Please note it doesn't say they will be angels, rather they will be like the angels in the sense that they will not have families and get married anymore. This is also clearly told in Revelation. I know I said that much of Revelation had to be interpreted by what came before. Based on all we have learned so far I can say with absolute certainty that Jesus spoke about this event in the Revelation:

Revelation 20:11-15 And I saw a great white throne, and him that sat on it, from whose face the <u>earth and the heaven fled away;</u> and there was found no place for them. 12. And I saw the dead, small and great, stand before God; and the <u>books</u> were opened: and another <u>book was opened,</u> which is *the book* of life: and the dead were judged out of those things which were written in the books, according to their works.

13. And the sea gave up the dead which were in it; and death and hell delivered up the dead which were in them: and they were judged every man according to their works. 14. And death and hell were cast into the lake of fire. This is the second death. 15. And whosoever was not found written in the book of life was cast into the lake of fire.

As I hope you can see the bodily resurrection and judgment that Revelation teaches is the exact same bodily resurrection that Jesus spoke about. Again this happens on the last day when death is defeated just as Paul expounds in 1 Corinthians 15. For the sake of the length of this book, I would also like to point out that Jesus speaks about the role of the saints in the judgment on the last day.

Jesus describes that on this last day many would rise and accuse the generation that rejected Christ of their evil Matthew 11:20-24. Not all of those that will accuse that generation are fallen. The idea is of a court scene and witnesses will come forth on that day and Christ will render judgment. I only reference this passage to show that Christ spoke in the same language as the Apostles concerning the judgment and the resurrection.

Here we can have absolute certainty about these things, what more do we need of them than Christ's clear word.

What we learn from Jesus:

- Jesus said he would come on the last day.
- He said on that day all men living and dead would hear his voice.
- He said the dead would all rise and stand before him. This is how Death—the last enemy—is defeated.
- He said the saved would be gathered to him to receive the home that he has prepared for them, this is the Father's kingdom.
- He said that all men would be judged by the word of God, and that judgment would be based on what we did with that word. Jesus is the Word made flesh (John 1) In essence Jesus is saying the same truth as he did in the sheep and goats parable. In that parable, they were judged by what they did for/to him.
- He said that when he came he would change the saved to have bodies similar but different to the ones we have now. Not that we would be angels like the cults teach, but we will be like them in the sense we will no longer be given in marriage and have children as we did on the earth.
- We will forever be with Him if you be in Christ.

I ask every honest reader of this book is what Jesus saying consistent with all the parables we have looked at so far? Without a doubt, I say that it is identical to what he said. This may be an obvious statement, but I say it as it proves that we have correctly understood the parables told before. So let's put everything we have learned together:

- The Jews were invited first to come into the kingdom of God but they refused.
- The great falling away has already happened and the Day of the Lord has already come. This event put a clear distinction between the apostate and true Church.
- Christ is now reigning over true Israel, his church, at the right hand of the father until he makes all of his enemies his footstool.
- Christ has given his people judgment/authority over the nations and areas they are in to spread the kingdom of Christ on the earth through the gospel and discipleship. This was the

marriage promised first to the Jews and is the promised heritage of all believers.

- There will be no one-world empire again after the fall of Rome which already happened.
- The Gospel will slowly grow over the face of the whole earth and fill it with the glory and knowledge of God. This kingdom of Christ will consume the kingdoms of the world as it first did with Rome.
- Christ will come back a final time bodily at the end of the world for the harvest on the last day. This will take place once the gospel goes into all the world through his Church. This is another reason why a secret rapture of the Church before the end makes no sense.
- Christ comes to bring in the fullness of the Kingdom. He then offers it up to the father and is made subject to him.
- The lost and the saved will grow in number side by side until the time of the harvest. Meaning there can be no secret rapture before this event.
- Jesus comes with his angels.
- His victorious coming is announced with a trumpet, a shout, and the voice of an archangel. Meaning this cannot be secretive.
- Everyone shall see him, even the dead and unsaved as they are all raised and gathered.
- All the dead saved and lost from the time of Abel (Abel was the first human to die according to the bible) to the very last person to die right before he comes, will explode out of their graves at the shout of the Son of God.
- Death is defeated.
- At the time of the harvest, the world in which the seed was sown will be considered the Kingdom. This is because the reign of Christ has been victorious through his Church. This kingdom is different from Christ's current kingdom at the right hand of the father, and the Father's kingdom which is the reward of the saints. So clearly we see 3 aspects of the kingdom of God.

- His coming will be final, meaning there will be no opportunity to get saved once he comes. This makes the 1,000-year kingdom taught by False-hope completely in error as he says people will continue to get saved after Christ returns. Clearly, we see that there is no room for this.
- He will gather first the lost separating them from the saved. This includes the false churches and false believers, and anyone found in the Church without the wedding dress: which is the righteousness of Christ through the Gospel.
- This means if we take the modern understanding of the rapture then it is unsaved that are raptured first.
- He will then gather and change the saved.
- Christ will sit upon a throne of judgment over all the world.
- He will judge/reward the saved first based on their good works. He will judge those who had the greatest calling first. He will also hold them accountable for the ministry he gave them. He will take away the reward of those that did nothing.
- Then he will judge the unsaved by their evil works. Many of those of the false churches will try and reason with Christ using their "good works" as proof of their true conversion, but Christ declares he never knew them. They are all cast into hell. This judgment is final and without mercy, for they have rejected the mercy of God: the gospel.
- The saints are welcomed into the kingdom of the father. There shall they ever be with the Lord.
- This judgment of the wicked in hell is not instant death, rather it is everlasting. They will have a resurrected body just as the saints, but it is called the second death because the damned will forever be cut off from the father.
- Jesus still has not mentioned a secret rapture.
- Jesus has not mentioned a 1,000-year physical reign on earth before or after the final judgment that matches the False-hope view.
- Jesus has not mentioned that he will be coming to destroy antichrist, a one-world government, or a great army. This is

because they will already be defeated as the last enemy he defeats is death upon his victorious return.

I must ask before we continue, can anyone see anything at all that resembles what False-hope says? Please put your finger in the book on this page and go back and compare it to the list of teachings that False-hope says will happen back in chapter one. Which one do you think has it right? And we still aren't done with this study so hold on tight as we look at the witness of the Apostle Paul.

CHAPTER EIGHT

Paul said What?

"Give me one hundred preachers who fear nothing but sin, and desire nothing but God, and I care not a straw whether they be clergymen or laymen; such alone will shake the gates of hell and set up the kingdom of heaven on Earth."

JOHN WESLEY, 1703-1791, FOUNDER OF THE METHODIST MOVEMENT

We have come on a great journey through many parables and saw Jesus preach of his final coming on the last day, and now we turn to the witness of Paul. Paul claimed to have been taught by Jesus:

Galatians 1:12: For I neither received it of man, neither <u>was I taught it, but by the revelation of Jesus Christ.</u>

Galatians 1:15-19: But when it pleased God, who separated me from my mother's womb, and called *me* by his grace, 16. To reveal his Son in me, that I might preach him among the heathen; immediately <u>I conferred not with flesh and blood:</u> 17. <u>Neither went I up to Jerusalem to them which were apostles before me</u>; but I went into Arabia, and returned again unto Damascus. 18. Then after three years I went up to Jerusalem to see Peter, and abode with him fifteen days. 19. But other of the apostles saw I none, save James the Lord's brother.

Paul was taught by God, he goes out of his way to say that he didn't even go to learn from the apostles. Question: If Paul was taught everything he wrote by Jesus, don't you think he will preach the same things Jesus did? Well according to False-hope, Jesus and Paul preached two different things for two different dispensations/ages. Let's see if this is so.

Please note before we get into this chapter, that Paul wrote much about the Second Coming as well as the Day of the Lord, and we will try and focus only on the ones concerning the Second Coming. Because of how much he wrote, I may have overlooked something, but this should not affect what we will see. I think you will find that Paul taught exactly what Jesus did about this event, just with some specific details about certain events that Jesus did not go into.

Remember I said that men may receive a greater understanding of the truth of God but it will never go against what was already revealed? Well, let's test that theory.

Hebrews 9:28: So Christ was once offered to bear the sins of many; and unto them that look for him shall <u>he appear the second time without sin unto salvation.</u>

Here is the summary of all the promises of Christ to return. His return is to be expected by those that are saved. We should ever be watchful and looking unto the day that he will appear. This is the fullness of our salvation. It is what we hope for, once he returns we will finally be delivered from this world, in which we are strangers and pilgrims. This expectation will spur us on to preach the gospel and disciple the nations which is our rightful duty and necessary for his return. Even though the last day is most likely far into the future, we should still look for the day he will appear to claim our soul either for salvation, or damnation at the end of our lives.

Romans 2:16: In the day when God shall <u>judge the secrets of men by Jesus Christ according to my gospel.</u>

Paul here declares the same thing that Jesus said when he said,

John 12:48: He that rejecteth me, and receiveth not my words, hath one that judgeth him: the word that I have spoken, the same shall judge him in the last day.

Paul's Gospel was the same Gospel truth that Jesus spoke about. Jesus told them point blank if you reject me (he is the very gospel) then my words will accuse you. So when Paul says every man will be judged according to my gospel this is the same thing that the parables said that men would be judged by what they did with Christ (Sheep and Goats). So already we are seeing a consistency of all that came before.

Romans 14:11-12 For it is written, *As* I live, saith the Lord, <u>every knee shall bow to me, and every tongue shall confess to God.</u> 12. <u>So then every one of us shall give account of himself to God.</u>

Jesus said everyone that ever lived will stand before him and get judged. Paul is speaking about the same event, but being more specific about what will happen when you stand before Christ and the books are opened. Here we see that even the unsaved will confess the truth about God, who he is, and what he has done. They will confess that they despised him and that they deserve the judgment. When Christ condemns them every knee shall bow and say, "Amen" agreeing with the just judgment of the King.

This is exactly what the explanation of the rule of Christ was to accomplish:

1 Corinthians 15:27: For he (the Father) hath put all things under his (Jesus') feet. But when he saith all things are put under *him, it is* manifest (revealed/declared) that he (the Father) <u>is excepted</u> (context is speaking about his enemies. So the rule of Christ it to witness to the enemies of God of who God the Father is. Meaning they will recognize their creator), which did put all things under him.

The timing of the resurrection is at the victorious end of Christ's reign. The bodily resurrection promise is the hope of all Christians and the fullness of their salvation.

1 Corinthians 15:50-54: Now this I say, brethren, that flesh and blood cannot inherit the kingdom of God; neither doth corruption inherit incorruption. 51. Behold, <u>I shew you a mystery; We shall not all sleep</u> (die), <u>but we shall all be changed</u>, 52. In a moment, in the twinkling of an eye, at the last trump: for the trumpet shall sound, and <u>the dead shall be raised incorruptible, and we shall be changed.</u> (Again Jesus tells us when this day happens on the very last day)

53. For this corruptible must put on incorruption, and this mortal *must* put on immortality. 54. So when this corruptible shall have put on incorruption, and this mortal shall have put on immortality, then

shall be brought to pass the saying that is written, Death is swallowed up in victory.

Paul is declaring more truth about the resurrection that Christ said would come to all men at the end. Paul is simply saying, that when the end shall come there will be believers on the earth that will not taste death, rather they shall be transformed. This transformation will be almost immediate and those that are alive will have the same bodies like those that were resurrected from the dead. This is a body like Christ's resurrected body.

This goes along perfectly with what Jesus said in the parables of the fish and the net, and the wheat and tares that we looked at in chapter 3. In both accounts, we saw a transformation happen among the saved. Paul is just adding to the understanding of what this change is.

We see this event completely fulfills what God the father told the son, "sit thou at my right hand until I make your enemies your footstool." Paul declares this very truth in:

1 Corinthians 15:24-26: Then *cometh* the end, when he shall have delivered up the kingdom to God, even the Father; when he shall have put down all rule and all authority and power. 25. For he must reign, till he hath put all enemies under his feet. 26. The last enemy *that* shall be destroyed *is* death.

Here Paul declares the same thing that Christ did, this event comes at the end. Here we see as well the fullness of the kingdom being presented to the father. This is when the fullness of the kingdom is manifested, and all three aspects of the kingdom of God will become one. Part of this fullness is the manifestation of the "sons of God," meaning the resurrection of the saints, the fullness of their promise for salvation.

In verse 25 Paul recognizes that Jesus was right now ruling and reigning in heaven and that his spiritual reign would last until this last day at the Resurrection, in which he will return.

This reign will happen until all the enemies of God are put under his feet, and he will return to defeat the final enemy which is death. As we can see Paul is still not teaching anything new, rather he is just clarifying and revealing more understanding about what Jesus had already said. Again the best way of determining which verses are speaking of the Day of the Lord and which are about the Second Coming is that the Second Coming primarily is focused on the resurrection and the fullness of the kingdom, while the Day of the Lord is focused on the judgment of God and the glorification/affirmation of the saints. Paul spoke a lot about the resurrection which is a theme that few in Churches today ever consider.

1 Corinthians 15:42-44: So also *is* the resurrection of the dead. It is sown in corruption; it is raised in incorruption: 43. It is sown in dishonour; it is raised in glory: it is sown in weakness; it is raised in power: 44. It is sown a natural body; it is raised a spiritual body. There is a natural body, and there is a spiritual body.

Paul explains here how the kingdom of grace works in the heart of every believer. It is sown/planted in our corrupt fallen hearts, but when we are raised on that final day the fullness of what grace will produce in us is manifested. That is the image of Christ in man which is the very hope of glory (Colossians 1:27)

2 Corinthians 5:1-5: 1. For we know that if our earthly house of *this* tabernacle (referencing our physical bodies) were dissolved, we have a building of God, an house not made with hands, eternal in the heavens.

2. For in this we groan, earnestly desiring to be clothed upon with our house which is from heaven (This being our resurrected sinless bodies): 3. If so be that being clothed we shall not be found naked. (This alludes to the fact that though we are clothed now in a tabernacle of flesh because it is fallen and sinful our nakedness is not covered. When we receive our sinless bodies, the fullness of our salvation is made plain and we no longer have a body of sin but a body of righteousness, and our nakedness is clothed. All true believers mourn under the burden of their sins and the Spirit in them cries out to make war against the old man.)

4. For we that are in *this* tabernacle do groan, being burdened (by the sin and sorrows of this world): not for that we would be unclothed, but clothed upon (meaning we don't go out of our way to seek death, but we long for the day of our death when we will shed this corrupt body and be clothed in our righteous bodies), that mortality might be swallowed up of life. 5. Now he (God) that hath wrought (Has created) us for the selfsame thing *is* God (meaning God along is the one to be thanked for this desire. Before we were saved we desired not the things

that be of God or that heavenly city, these desires are a gift and a proof of our salvation), who also hath given unto us the earnest (the old way of saying downpayment) of the Spirit.

Paul is expressing that this longing is a work created by God. This is a work of the Spirit that was given to our hearts to cause us to seek out the heavenly home and cry out Abba Father to the God of heaven. This is the downpayment of our salvation and the seal that we are the sons of God. By this we begin to hate our carnal nature and anything that separates us from our Father, thus we take up the cross and begin to mortify or put to death those wicked things.

Philippians 3:20-21: For our conversation (Meaning our manner of life) is in heaven; from whence (there) also we look for the Saviour, the Lord Jesus Christ: 21. Who shall change our vile body, that it may be fashioned like unto his glorious body, according to the working whereby (in this way) he is able even to subdue all things unto himself.

Paul encourages us to have our minds set on the kingdom to come and the reality of the promises of God we have already looked at. Here is a great hope for believers who daily must war against the sins of the flesh, as Christ's final victory in our heart will be to do away with the flesh and subdue it once and for all in his coming. Verse 21 also affirms the defeat of death as the final work that will victoriously have slain and put into subjection all things to God.

Here is even more understanding of the transformation that will happen that Pauls has already spoken about. When Christ raises us he transforms our bodies to be like the one Jesus has now. A body that was familiar to the one he had but was able to do things that a fleshly body as it is now cannot do. This goes along with what Jesus said about how we would be as the angels.

1 Corinthians 3:10-15: According to the grace of God which is given unto me, as a wise masterbuilder, I have laid the foundation, and another buildeth thereon. But let every man take heed how he buildeth thereupon. 11. For other foundation can no man lay than that is laid, which is Jesus Christ. 12. Now if any man build upon this foundation gold, silver, precious stones, wood, hay, stubble;

13. Every man's work shall be made manifest: for the day shall

declare it, because it shall be revealed by fire; and the fire shall try every man's work of what sort it is. 14. If any man's work abide which he hath built thereupon, he shall receive a reward. 15. If any man's work shall be burned, he shall suffer loss: <u>but he himself shall be saved; yet so as by fire.</u>

This statement again reminds us of the parables of Jesus concerning the sheep and goats, as well as the parable of the talents. This also goes along with his statements about the judgment of the saints. This is Paul giving more insight into the judgment of the saints that we have already seen. All of our works will pass through this trying fire and we will be rewarded based on what we have done with the life he has given us. We also see that for Christ's sake even those that did nothing shall still be saved, but they will have nothing but ashes to show for it.

As we have learned from the parables this will be done before the judgment is passed on the unsaved. This shows God's justice. He first holds his children accountable before all they were told to reach with the gospel. This is both a testimony against the saints and the damned showing that all are without excuse. It shows that the same truth that saved sinners was the same truth the ungodly denied.

This is told to encourage saints to live a life of obedience to Jesus. That we would fear the judgment to stand before God and give an account. Do not be the ones that will be saved, yet so by fire!

1 Corinthians 6:3: Know ye not that we shall judge angels? how much more things that pertain to this life?

We are also judged first, and then clearly we are to help Christ in judgment. This is a mystery that is only hinted at in the bible, but it is important to show that after we are judged Christ has another work for us to do in the judgment. That's astounding. This, of course, is also now manifested in part. Recall that judgment was given to the saints when Christ came on the Day of the Lord. He gave the rule over cities and judgment over nations to the Church so that they would consume the dominion of all kingdoms of the earth (Daniel 7) by doing this the enemies of God are put under his feet.

Colossians 3:4: When Christ, *who is* our life, shall appear, then shall ye also appear with him in glory.

We now see an affirmation of Paul for us to keep focused on the day of Christ's coming. When he shall appear we shall be like him. This is another verse that is true for both comings of Christ. When he came on the Day of the Lord Christ was glorified that he was very God, and the persecuted saints were glorified that they were the people of God. Remember to glorify something means to show, manifest, and declare the truth about a thing. On the Second Coming, the fullness of this glory will be revealed when we are transformed to have bodies like Christ's. Again this is exactly what we just saw, and it is consistent with everything that came before. Let us once again look at the famous rapture passage and see how it also agrees.

1 Thessalonians 4:13-18: But I would not have you to be ignorant, brethren, concerning them which are asleep (those that died), that ye sorrow not, even as others which have no hope.

14. For if we believe that Jesus died and rose again, even so, them also which sleep (saints that had died) in Jesus will God bring with him.

15. For this we say unto you by the word of the Lord, that we which are alive *and* remain unto the coming of the Lord shall not prevent (come before) them which are asleep.

16. For the Lord himself shall descend from heaven with a shout, with the voice of the archangel, and with the trump of God: and <u>the dead in Christ shall rise first:</u>

17. Then we which are alive *and* remain shall be caught up together with them in the clouds, to meet the Lord in the air: and so shall we ever be with the Lord.

18. Wherefore comfort one another with these words.

Let us notice how this so perfectly goes along with the passage Paul declared in 1 Corinthians 15:50-54. We see that Paul now adds here more clearly that this transformation in 1 Corinthians happens when the saints are raised. In both passages we see this happens after that final trumpet announcing to the world that Christ our King has come at last. People struggle with the idea of the unjust raising first as we saw in the parable of the wheat and tares, but this does not go against that parable at all.

Paul is simply saying that when it comes to the resurrection of the saints, those saints that had died will be raised first, then those that are alive shall be transformed and taken to meet Christ as he comes to judge the entire world. Paul doesn't mention the raising of the unrighteous first because in this passage, in its context, Paul is addressing grieving Christians who are mourning their Christian family member who had died. To encourage them Paul is reminding them of the promise of the resurrection, and glorifying the truth about departed saints being now present with God.

Paul is not saying that the dead saints are the first being resurrected, just when it comes to the saints the dead raise first. The context of what Paul is saying is not speaking of the general resurrection but is narrowing in on the resurrection of the saints. When Jesus spoke about this event in his parables he was focusing on the general resurrection of all, thus there is no contradiction. We also know from Jesus' own clear words that the resurrection of both the saved and unsaved happen on the very same day, the last day.

I am sure there may be other passages that Paul may have said about the Second Coming, but I think what we have seen is more than sufficient. We can see the same truths that Jesus said would happen when he returns are also declared with greater clarity by Paul. This is a good thing for all truths of God agree with each other. Let us summarise all the things Paul tells us about Christ's coming:

We as believers should ever be looking to the promise of his coming with earnest expectation. This keeps us from falling into the snares of loving this world.

When Christ appears it is to judge the entire world. This judgment will focus on the gospel and the word and our response to it.

Christ's coming will be announced by a trumpet, a shout, and the voice of an archangel.

All the dead are raised and gathered for the judgment

The dead in Christ shall rise and be changed before those that are alive are changed.

When Christ appears we shall be transformed in a moment.

This transformation of all believers will be to have immortal bodies like Christ's glorified body. This is the fullness of our salvation.

That the saints shall have all of their works tried by fire, the works done for Christ will be transformed into rewards, and those done for our selfishness will be burned up. Even though we will suffer loss, we are still saved, if so by fire.

The saints shall judge angels on this day.

That Christ's coming is to defeat the final enemy: death

That Christ's coming is to fulfill the fullness of the gospel

That his appearing is our blessed hope.

Notice what we do not see:

There is no mention of a secret coming before the final day.

There is no coming to take the saints away from Antichrist, or the Man of Sin.

I do not see Christ coming to establish a 1,000-year kingdom on earth.

I do not see any mention of the rebuilding of the temple in Jerusalem.

There is no mention of events that would contradict what Christ has already said about his coming.

Now combine all the things we have learned so far:

- The Jews were invited first to come into the kingdom of God but they refused.
- The great falling away has already happened and the Day of the Lord has already come. This event put a clear distinction between the apostate and true church.
- Christ is now reigning over true Israel, his church, at the right hand of the father until he makes all of his enemies his footstool. The Saints will rule with Christ until all enemies are put under Christ's feet. They shall consume the kingdoms of this world as they did with Rome.
- There will be no one-world empire again after the fall of Rome which already happened.
- Christ has given his people judgment/authority over the nations and areas they are in to spread the kingdom of Christ on the earth through the gospel and discipleship. This was the marriage promised first to the Jews and is the promised heritage

of all believers. Because Christ reigns his bride reigns with him and together the fullness of the image of God in man will be manifested on the earth by Christ.

- The Gospel will slowly grow over the face of the whole earth and fill it with the glory and knowledge of God.
- Christ will come back a final time bodily at the end of the world for the harvest on the last day. This will take place once all enemies are put under Christ's feet. This is another reason why a secret rapture of the Church before the end makes no sense.
- Christ comes to bring in the fullness of the Kingdom. This is the consummation of all things and the fullness of the kingdom, which he will then present to the Father.
- The lost and the saved will grow in number side by side until the time of the harvest. Meaning there can be no secret rapture before this event.
- Jesus comes with his angels.
- His victorious coming is announced with a trumpet, a shout, and the voice of an archangel. Meaning this cannot be secretive.
- Everyone shall see him, even the dead and unsaved as they are all raised and gathered.
- All the dead saved and lost from the time of Abel (Abel was the first human to die according to the bible) to the very last person to die right before he comes, will explode out of their graves at the shout of the Son of God. Death is slain.
- At the time of the harvest, the world in which the seed was sown will be considered the Kingdom. This is because the Gospel has been fully preached. This kingdom is different from Christ's current kingdom at the right hand of the father, and the Father's kingdom which is the reward of the saints. So clearly we see 3 aspects of the kingdom of God.
- His coming will be final, meaning there will be no opportunity to get saved once he comes. This makes the 1,000-year kingdom taught by False-hope completely in error as he says people will continue to get saved after Christ returns. Clearly, we see that there is no room for this.

- He will gather first the lost separating them from the saved. This includes the false churches and false believers, and anyone found without the wedding dress: which is the righteousness of Christ through the Gospel.

Thus if we take the modern idea of the rapture then the unsaved are raptured first.

He will then gather and change the saved. This is the resurrection when our mortality will put on immortality and we become like Christ.

Christ will sit upon a throne of judgment over all the world.

He will judge/reward the saved first based on their good works. He will judge those who had the greatest calling first. He will also hold them accountable for the ministry he gave them. He will take away the reward of those that did nothing. This is done by passing their works through fire.

The saint will judge angels both ministering Spirits and preachers both are called angels.

Christ will judge the unsaved by their evil works. Many of those of the false churches will try and reason with Christ using their "good works" as proof of their true conversion, but Christ declares he never knew them. They are all cast into hell. This judgment is final and without mercy, for they have rejected the mercy of God: the gospel.

The saints are welcomed into the kingdom of the father. This is the home that Christ went away to prepare for us. There shall we ever be with the Lord.

This judgment of the wicked in hell is not instant death, rather it is everlasting. They will have a resurrected body just as the saints, but it is called the second death because the damned will forever be cut off from the father.

Jesus still has not mentioned a secret rapture.

Jesus has not mentioned a 1,000-year physical reign on earth before or after the final judgment that matches the dispensational view.

There is no mention of Jesus destroying armies, antichrist, or a one-world government when he comes. This is because all enemies will have already been defeated when he comes.

CHAPTER NINE

The Apostles said What?

"All truth is given by revelation, either general or special, and it must be received by reason. Reason is the God-given means for discovering the truth that God discloses, whether in his world or his Word. While God wants to reach the heart with truth, he does not bypass the mind."

JONATHAN EDWARDS, 1703-1758, AMERICAN
THEOLOGIAN AND REVIVALIST DURING THE GREAT
AWAKENINGS IN AMERICA (1730-1740)

By now I would hope my readers will see a clear pattern of truth shining through the various paths of the bible. This truth glorifies the words of Christ and exposes the darkness of error. I am sure by now that you would guess that the testimony of the remaining writings and Apostles would all agree with what came before, and you would be correct. Some may wonder why we should proceed if already our points are proven, this is to equip us fully with the biblical testimony of the Second Coming which we can use to test the views and interpret the Revelation.

Just as with Paul, we will look at a great testimony of the various remaining writers of the New Testament, by Luke, Peter, James, John, and Jude. Again I do not intentionally exclude any relevant passages, but I will show all the ones in which I am aware that deal with our topic. Let the truths of God shine as we start with Luke's account:

Act 1:6-11: When they (The disciples) therefore were come together, they asked of him, saying, Lord, wilt thou at this time restore again the kingdom to Israel? (This is the last time that this false understanding of the Pharisees is seen in the apostles and shortly after this the Holy Spirit falls on the Church and the truth about the Kingdom of Israel is made known to them. From this point on, the apostles understood that true Israel is in Christ and the kingdom is the heavenly kingdom of Christ which would be manifested through the Gospel on the earth as we have been learning.)

7. And he (Jesus) said unto them, It is not for you to know the times or the seasons, which the Father hath put in his own power. (If you recall when Paul expounds on the reign of the Messiah in 1 Corinthians 15, Paul said Jesus would reign until all enemies were put under him. He also states that it was the Father who did put all things under him. The kingdom that the earth will be in at the time of the harvest is the Kingdom of True Israel. It is already in heaven and will one day also be manifest on the earth through his Church. Because this is the Father's work it is in his power, and timing to accomplish it.)

8. But ye shall receive power, after that the Holy Ghost is come upon you: and ye shall be witnesses unto me both in Jerusalem, and in all Judaea, and in Samaria, and unto the uttermost part of the earth. (Jesus is redirecting their attention to the Church's call to disciple the nations. It is through this very act that the above kingdom they had been desiring is manifested.)

9. And when he had spoken these things, while they beheld, he was taken up; and a cloud received him out of their sight. 10. And while they looked stedfastly toward heaven as he went up, behold, two men stood by them in white apparel; 11. Which also said, Ye men of Galilee, why stand ye gazing up into heaven? this same Jesus, which is taken up from you into heaven, shall so come in like manner as ye have seen him go into heaven. (Jesus did not leave in war, conquest, or even with a great spectacle. He left while teaching and comforting his friends, having achieved the greatest achievement in all of Creation. Christ had conquered death, crushed the head of the serpent, and redeemed fallen man. Christ will again return in like manner, when the fullness of all has been accomplished.)

Let us notice a few amazing truths about this passage. This account takes place after Christ was raised from the dead and appeared, ate with, and was handled by (touched physically meaning he wasn't a ghost) hundreds of his disciples. First, we see that the blindness of the false teaching of the Jewish leaders concerning a physical kingdom was still upon the disciples even after Jesus was raised from the dead.

The Messiah was to establish the Kingdom of Israel when he came. In their minds, that meant that Christ would eventually overthrow Rome. As we already saw he did both and even overthrew Rome through his Church when the Church consumed it. In like manner, Christ is extending that rule over the world through his people. We reign and do this great work with Christ as our husband for the Church is his bride.

The kingdom was given to true Israel in the days ahead when the Holy Ghost fell on the Christians gathered at Pentecost, and on the Gentiles who came to the faith some years later. This signified the kingdom of both Jew and Gentile being made one in the baptism of faith in the Holy Ghost, but even now there was blindness. The kingdom of Israel in the New Covenant was ratified with his first coming, on the Day of the Lord. This was to be the sign of the Son of Man to all peoples. It is so sad then, that many in the Church today have no understanding of this event.

As the gospel conquers the world, the kingdom is being given to Israel, meaning the New Covenant saints (Christians).

Lastly, let us notice the promise at the very end of this passage, the very same Jesus, the glorified risen savor shall come again physically as he left. He will descend out of heaven in clouds with a trumpet, a shout, and the voice of an archangel announcing to a world that is now His Kingdom, "The king has returned, prepare ye for the judgment!" Peter was there that day and so were many of the men we shall now look to.

Act 24:15: And have hope toward God, which they themselves also allow, that there shall be a resurrection of the dead, both of the just and unjust.

Technically this verse is something Paul declared concerning the Second Coming, but Luke recorded it. Though the second coming is not directly declared in this statement, I show it to reaffirm the fact that

Paul taught the same thing as Jesus did. Previously all the passages we looked at with Paul spoke only of the resurrection of the saved, now we see that this wasn't the only resurrection Paul was familiar with. Here he states that both the unrighteous and righteous will be raised in the resurrection (singular) showing he had no concept that he foresaw two separate physical resurrections. This once again helps us see that there is no concept of the rapture being taught by the apostles.

2 Peter 3:2-4: That ye may be mindful of the words which were spoken before by the holy prophets, and of the commandment of us the apostles of the Lord and Saviour: 3. Knowing this first, that there shall come in the <u>last days scoffers, walking after their own lusts,</u> 4. And saying, <u>Where is the promise of his coming? for since the fathers fell asleep, all things continue as</u> *they were* <u>from the beginning of the creation.</u>

Let us realize some truth in these statements. This declaration is one of many that is true for both the Day of the Lord and the Second Coming. First, we should note its direct significance to the Day of the Lord. We must realize that Jesus and the early church spoke often of the soon-coming destruction of the temple. This is one of the many reasons why the Jews hated the early Church. This mocking originally was directed towards this event essentially they were stating, "Where is the impending destruction you promised."

Second, it is also true of the Second Coming. The last days will continue until Christ returns, so this mocking is something that shall be expected and promised to continue until the very end. We see that because of this men shall mock and scoff at the idea that Christ will actually return. As the years go by, we see a greater and greater rise in this mockery by the unbelieving world. Almost every Christian Church stands on the promise of his coming. This is a promise of a physical return of Christ, and the mocking jeers of the heathen should encourage us.

This does not go against anything we have been learning, as the world begins to be consumed by the kingdom, these mockers will become less in number but louder and more wicked than ever. Remember the saved and unsaved will still be on the earth until the very end, however, we see as well that the saved will outnumber the lost at that harvest.

James 5:7-8 Be patient therefore, brethren, unto the coming of the Lord. <u>Behold, the husbandman waiteth for the precious fruit of the earth,</u> and hath long patience for it, until he receive the early and latter rain. 8. Be ye also patient; stablish your hearts: for the coming of the Lord draweth nigh.

I love how simply James puts it, as he refers to the parable of the wheat and the tares as he does. The husbandman is Christ he waits until the harvest is ripe. Again we see the awareness of His coming being off in the distance. Christ is waiting for the last person that he knows will be saved by the gospel to get saved before he returns. Hence we should expect his coming, which is tempered by patience. This should push us to proclaim the gospel in the world to hasten the day of his coming.

The early and later rain is a picture of the harvest season in the ancient world. These rains would devastate the crops if one failed to come, thus both were needed for the fullness of the harvest. It is my personal opinion that the early rain is a reference to the explosion of the early church which watered the seeds, and the latter will be a large revival near the end of the world.

1 John 2:28: And now, little children, abide in him; that, when he shall appear, we may have confidence, and not be ashamed before him at his coming.

I have long said that some of my favorite portions of scriptures in the whole of the bible are those that are written by John. Here we see the tenderness of his heart. His encouragement to endure and live lives worthy of being able to stand boldly before God. Even if we shall pass before he comes, the reality is we pass and go to stand before him. If you were called before the king today, how would you fare?

John is saying that if we live a godly life we need not fear that day, that we need not be ashamed. I ask again would you be ashamed to stand before him if you were called to him today? We are not guaranteed another breath. May that truth sink into all our hearts.

1 John 3:1-3: Behold, what manner of love the Father hath bestowed upon us, that we should be called the sons of God: therefore the world knoweth us not, because it knew him not. 2. Beloved, now are we the sons of God, and <u>it doth not yet appear what we shall be:</u> but we know

that, <u>when he shall appear, we shall be like him; for we shall see him as he is.</u> 3. <u>And every man that hath this hope in him purifieth himself, even as he is pure.</u>

This is a clear echo of what Paul and Jesus said about the transformation of the saints in the resurrection when Christ returns. Here is another promise of the hope of believers. The hope of Christ coming is to purify our hearts and lives. Why? Because it will cause us to live for the judgment that we know is coming. It will cause us to live holy and acceptable lives sanctified unto God.

Jude 1:14-18: And Enoch also, the seventh from Adam, prophesied of these, saying, Behold, the <u>Lord cometh with ten thousands of his saints,</u> 15. <u>To execute judgment upon all, and to convince all that are ungodly among them of all their ungodly deeds which they have ungodly committed, and of all their hard *speeches* which ungodly sinners have spoken against him.</u>

16. These are murmurers, complainers, walking after their own lusts; and their mouth speaketh great swelling *words,* having men's persons in admiration because of advantage. 17. But, beloved, remember ye the words which were spoken before of the apostles of our Lord Jesus Christ; 18. <u>How that they told you there should be mockers in the last time, who should walk after their own ungodly lusts.</u>

Jude is perhaps the shortest of all the new testament writers, but it packs a lot of truth within its pages. Here is the promise of the coming Christ. Here the last piece of the puzzle is put into place about the Second Coming. The saints shall be gathered to Christ after the unrighteous are gathered, and we shall descend on the world with our savor to judge the world with Christ. This is another reason why we are judged before the unbelievers to show the truth that we are all men saved by the same gospel in the same way that all the unbelievers that will be judged could have been saved. It will be a final testimony against them.

And in the very end, we see the same understanding that this will be a future event. Jude tells the church to remember Peter's, Paul's, and the other apostles' warnings concerning the mocking of the world about Christ's coming. This mocking is an offense to some, and we are told about it time and again so that it may be an encouragement that we are one day closer to His appearing.

These truths also parallel the Day of the Lord. Christ gave judgment to the saints to execute on the earth. There were mockers about the Day of the Lord, and so this is something that was also true concerning that day.

Here then is the end of the main body of scripture that speaks directly to the Second Coming that I have found most insightful. Some might be thinking of other passages that often are associated with Christ's Second Coming, but I will state simply that with careful consideration most if not all that have been excluded dealt with the Day of the Lord and not the Second Coming. Likely, we can still learn things about the Second Coming from those passages as the Day of the Lord is a type of the Second Coming, but I felt as our focus is more on the bodily return of Christ these passages would have just bloated our study.

The parables and saying concerning Christ coming as a thief were primarily focused on the soon-coming judgment of the Day of the Lord. We are still called to be vigilant watchmen looking forward to Christ's return, as John says this hope purifies us, but their primary focus in context was all about the Day of the Lord. As I have stated we all have a day that we do not know the hour and if we are not living for it then it will take us as a thief. That, and Christ can judge our nation (and I think is in the process of doing it) as he has judged others in the past as a day of the Lord if we begin to follow the patterns of judgment and sin in the bible. Thus these passages still have great relevance to us today, however, they are not the focus of this book.

2 Peter 3:8-11 is a passage that I usually get the most questions about as it seems as if Peter is speaking about the end of the world, as he mentions the heavens being burned and a new heaven and earth being made. To this I will say two things, first, Peter himself links this event to the Day of the Lord. We will also see that when Jesus preached on this topic, as we go over in the next chapter, the disciples viewed the Day of the Lord as the end of the world, that being the Jewish world.

The heavens and earth being burned up and a new heaven and earth being established are pictures of the Old Covenant kingdom/system being destroyed (old heaven) and the removal of the old nation of Israel as the covenant people of God (old earth). The New Covenant kingdom/ system is then established (new heaven) and a new covenant people of God is built as a holy nation, the Church (New Earth) also called Israel or New Jerusalem in the bible. We go over this more in upcoming chapters. Christ made all things new, thus the old must pass away. Peter is addressing the Jewish Christians in his letter and highlighting the fact that the temple and all the Jewish ways and places of faith were about to end. This contention between the believing and non-believing Jews is a theme all through the New Testament. Jesus said this very thing to the woman at the well:

John 4:21: Jesus saith unto her, Woman, believe me, the hour cometh, when ye shall neither in this mountain, <u>nor yet at Jerusalem, worship the Father.</u>

This is the same thing pictured in the last few chapters of Revelation which are speaking of the same thing and there are a great many reasons why this cannot be speaking about the literal new heavens and earth (we look at this a lot more in chapter 15). It is possible, but not certain, that there is going to be a literal passing away of the heavens and earth on the last day, and a new heaven and earth created.

With that said there is not a direct verse stating this. I know people will point to some verses that do as the above-mentioned in Peter, Isaiah 65, or even Revelation 21, but I say keep the context. When Jesus comes death and all sinners are gone, yet in nearly every passage where a new heaven and earth are mentioned, death, and sinners are also still mentioned and so are nations, and again we know from this study that these things will all be over when Christ comes.

We do however see a consummation of all things in Christ and his kingdom when he comes. I will not be dogmatic about this but it is entirely possible that just as our bodies will be transformed at Christ's coming, this world may be transformed/restored as it was before the fall or perhaps made even greater than it was before at Christ's coming.

Here are three of many passages that imply this:

Daniel 7:14: And there was given him dominion, and glory, and a kingdom, that all people, nations, and languages, should serve him: <u>his</u>

dominion *is* an everlasting dominion, which shall not pass away, and his kingdom *that* which shall not be destroyed.

As we have already seen in this passage Christ right now has this kingdom and he is ruling it at the right hand of the father and will bring it to its fullness on the earth. The last enemy will be death and then the fullness of this kingdom will be presented to the father. However, when the fullness of the kingdom comes, this promise is that it will never pass away. If Christ brings this kingdom on the earth why does he have to destroy the earth?

Romans 8:18-21: For I reckon that the sufferings of this present time *are* not worthy *to be compared* with the glory which shall be revealed in us. 19. For the earnest (down payment of the) expectation of the creature (animals) waiteth for the manifestation of the sons of God (This is the resurrection of the saints).

20. For the creature was made subject to vanity, not willingly, but by reason of him who hath subjected *the same* in hope, 21. Because the creature itself also shall be delivered from the bondage of corruption into the glorious liberty of the children of God. 22. For we know that the whole creation groaneth and travaileth in pain together until now.

If creation will be delivered from the same bondage that we are in, I would assume that means there will be a time when this liberty under the sons of God will be upon the earth. The beasts and creation were put under man's authority in the garden and were brought into corruption with man's fall. These verses seem to imply that Christ's redemption would include the deliverance of all creation, man included and that this deliverance would coincide with the manifestation of the sons of God i.e. the resurrection on the last day.

Ephesians 3:21: Unto him *be* glory in the church by Christ Jesus throughout all ages, world without end. Amen.

As I said I will not be dogmatic on this point, but I do find it compelling to consider. The very desire of God was to fill the whole earth with the image of God in man and that creation would be subject to that image, the fullness of which will be after Christ returns. Does that mean he has to destroy it to remake it? I am not certain. Perhaps this is a mystery that man will not know until that glorious day.

What do we see from the testimony of the Apostles?

That Christ's coming will be in the future, that his tarrying is for the sake of those that would yet come to Christ.

The same Jesus that went into heaven shall return.

When Jesus returns it will be in judgment against the whole world.

That when Christ comes we shall be transformed to be like him.

That He will bring the saints with him to judge the world.

That mockers and ungodly men would rise more and more mocking his coming as the day of his coming grows ever closer. This can either mean they will grow in number or become more wicked and loud as the day approaches, which is what I think. Remember the wheat and tares there will still be tares on the earth, but they will not be more than the wheat.

Christ endures the mockers for the sake of the harvest that is to come, just as the parable of the tares teaches, Christ will come at the end of the world for the harvest.

Having this hope and understanding will help us live purified and holy lives unto God. In this way, we can have the confidence to stand before him on this day.

Let us see what we do not learn from them:

- We do not see any secret rapture that happens before his final coming. We are told to await the physical coming of Christ for the judgment at the end of the world at this coming he will resurrect the dead. This is the only physical coming of Christ and resurrection that the apostles seemed to know. If they did not know another/separate resurrection why is it that in modern churches we teach a different resurrection of the saints?
- We do not see any room for a 1,000-year physical, literal, reign of Christ on this earth at his coming.
- We do not see the apostles teaching anything different from Paul or Jesus about this topic, rather, they just added greater understanding.
- Let's put everything we have learned together one last time:

- The Jews were invited first to come into the kingdom of God but they refused.
- The great falling away has already happened and the Day of the Lord has already come. This event put a clear distinction between the apostate and true church.
- Christ is now reigning over true Israel, his Church, at the right hand of the father until he makes all of his enemies his footstool.
- Christ has given his people judgment/authority over the nations and areas they are in to spread the kingdom of Christ on the earth through the gospel and discipleship. This was the marriage promised first to the Jews and is the promised heritage of all believers.
- The Gospel will slowly grow over the face of the whole earth and fill it with the glory and knowledge of God. The Church will consume the kingdoms of this world and make them a part of the kingdom of Christ.
- There will be no one-world empire again after the fall of Rome which already happened.
- Christ will come back a final time bodily at the end of the world for the harvest on the last day. This will take place once the gospel goes into all the world through his Church and all enemies are put under his feet. This is another reason why a secret rapture of the Church before the end makes no sense.
- There will be a later rain or worldwide revival that brings in the fullness of the harvest before the Second Coming near the end of the world. This is the stone that dashes the kingdoms as spoken of in Daniel and prophesied by James.
- Christ comes to bring in the fullness of the Kingdom. This is the consummation of all things and the fullness of the marriage.
- The lost and the saved will grow in number side by side until the time of the harvest. Meaning there can be no secret rapture before this event.
- Jesus comes with His angels, and 10,000s of his saints (these are those that have passed before his Second Coming).

- This is the very same Jesus that went into heaven, meaning he bodily went into heaven, and he will bodily return. He ascended in victory and he will likewise return in even greater victory.
- His victorious coming is announced with a trumpet, a shout, and the voice of an archangel. Meaning this cannot be secretive.
- Everyone shall see him, even the dead and unsaved as they are all raised and gathered before him.
- All the dead saved and lost from the time of Abel (Abel was the first human to die according to the bible) to the very last person to die right before he comes, will explode out of their graves at the shout of the Son of God.
- Death is slain.
- At the time of the harvest, the world in which the seed was sown will be considered the Kingdom. This is because the Gospel has been fully preached. This kingdom is different from Christ's current kingdom at the right hand of the father, and the Father's kingdom which is the reward of the saints. So clearly we see 3 aspects of the kingdom of God.
- His coming will be final meaning, there will be no opportunity to get saved once he comes. This makes the 1,000-year kingdom taught by False-hope completely in error as he says people will continue to get saved after Christ returns. Clearly, we see that there is no room for this.
- He will gather first the lost separating them from the saved. This includes the false churches and false believers, and anyone found without the wedding dress: which is the righteousness of Christ through the Gospel.
- If we take the modern understanding of the rapture then the unsaved are raptured first.
- He will then gather and change the saved. When the saints are raised, those that had died will be raised first.
- Christ will sit upon a throne of judgment over all the world. He brings the glorified saints with him to this judgment.
- He will judge/reward the saved first based on their good works. He will judge those who had the greatest calling first. He will

also hold them accountable for the ministry he gave them. He will take away the reward of those that did nothing.

- The saint will judge angels and the nations with Christ. I picture this as Christ being the judge and we being the jury that says Amen.
- Christ will judge the unsaved by their evil works. Many of those of the false churches will try and reason with Christ using their "good works" as proof of their true conversion, but Christ declares he never knew them. They are all cast into hell. This judgment is final and without mercy, for they have rejected the mercy of God: the gospel.
- This coming liberates all of the creation meaning animals and the very earth itself will rejoice.
- The saints are welcomed into the kingdom of the father. There shall they ever be with the Lord. This is the home that Christ is preparing for them. This may be in a glorified/renewed earth where heaven and earth are once again made one as in the Garden, or in an entirely new heaven and earth.
- This judgment of the wicked in hell is not instant death, rather it is everlasting. They will have a resurrected body just as the saints, but it is called the second death because the damned will forever be cut off from the father.
- Jesus nor his disciples still have not mentioned a secret rapture.
- Jesus nor his disciples have still not mentioned a 1,000-year physical reign on earth before or after the final judgment that matches the False-hope view.
- There is no mention of Jesus destroying armies, antichrist, or a one-world government when he comes as they shall all be defeated before he returns.

This concludes the major points concerning the Second Coming. It may be prudent to compare this list with the one we made near the beginning of this book looking at the lies taught by False-hope. Going forward we will not again highlight these points. It should be extremely clear that these two lists are very different. I ask then is False-hope's list of events more biblical or is it the one I presented?

The remaining chapters of this book will be focused on several key passages of scripture that have been misinterpreted to prop up the theology of False-hope. Once they are brought into the proper focus the above truths will shine all the more. By the end of this book, I pray that it is clear in the minds of all pilgrim readers that False-hope has no ground to stand upon and is a liar.

CHAPTER TEN

The Destruction of Jerusalem

*"I consider the prophecy relative to the destruction of the
Jewish nation if there were nothing else to support Christianity,
as absolutely irresistible proof of its divine origin."*

Mr. Erskine's Speech, at the Trial of Williams,
for publishing "Paine's Age of Reason" 1797.

We come at last to one of the most difficult chapters for me
to write about. This subject can and has been the subject
of entire books in and of itself. To do this topic justice in a
single chapter escapes my ability, but I shall do the best I am able if the
Lord helps me. For this reason, I nearly avoided this topic altogether.
Unfortunately due to the gross error of False-hope, this account has
been perverted and the truths of the passage have been lost. So I will
attempt to look at it.

The Destruction of Jerusalem is the most documented incident in
the ancient world. We know more about this event than any other single
event from the same period. There is more documented evidence of this
event than even that of the New Testament. It glorifies the very truth
of the New Testament in a way that nearly all churches once knew and
very few remember today.

This is also one of the most prophesied events in the bible short of
the messiah that I am aware of. Even Moses prophesied about it long

before there even was a city called Jerusalem. Yet, the average churchgoer today has little to no knowledge about it, let alone the profound meaning of its prophetic significance.

I would encourage all my readers to pick up the book, "The Destruction of Jerusalem," by George Peter Holford written in 1805. It is a 68-page book that concisely compiles all the work from Flavius Josephus, the bible, and several other Roman scholars who were eyewitnesses of the events and puts them into a single work. I own both this book and the complete history of the event as recorded by Flavius Josephus who was an eyewitness and survivor of the events, and I can say both works are nothing short of astounding.

There is a misconception among modern Christians that says God's people will not experience the wrath of God. We touched on this concept in the opening chapter of this book, but I feel a need to bring it up again.

I wonder if the people that say such things have ever read the Old Testament? Wrath is righteous anger that results in judgment. If one would read the bible one would see that God often punishes his children when they fall into the sins of the world. Thus it is full of God pouring wrath and judgment against his people when they fell into gross sin as a nation.

This was for their benefit to keep them from falling into even worse sin. Jerusalem itself was destroyed twice. Many of the kings of Judah and Israel were given over to the hands of their enemies due to their sins. Countless times they were enslaved and killed for their wicked ways. Even while Moses led the people, God's anger was kindled against them to the point that he was going to kill them all except Moses interceded on their behalf.

As I have mentioned several times in previous chapters, the prophecy we are about to look at was called the Day of the Lord. This coming was not a physical one, but a coming in sovereign judgment through the Romans. Meaning, that what the Romans did was the just judgment that God had decreed against Jerusalem. Just as a king or judge might call for the death penalty and another carries it out, the judge is the one who bears the responsibility that the action was performed not those who carried out the sentence. Meaning even though Rome did the judgment, the blame is not to be laid on them but on God. That is the heart of what a Day of the Lord is. God is coming in judgment and uses human beings to execute it much like we may use a gun.

Christ came in vengeance through the armies of Rome as he came in vengeance with the Philistines, Assyrians, and Babylonians hundreds of years before. There will be a lot of scriptures in this chapter to help build the understanding of this event, as such, this may be the longest chapter in the book. Please patiently read and consider what is presented.

Let us begin this study with the very last thing Jesus spoke over the temple:

Matthew 23:33-38: *Ye* serpents, *ye* generation of vipers, how can ye escape the damnation of hell? 34. Wherefore (For this cause), behold, I send unto you prophets, and wise men, and scribes: and *some* of them ye shall kill and crucify; and *some* of them shall ye scourge in your synagogues, and persecute *them* from city to city: (This is a description of all the events in Acts)

35. That <u>upon you</u> may come <u>all the righteous blood shed upon the earth, from the blood of righteous Abel unto the blood of Zacharias son of Barachias,</u> whom ye slew between the temple and the altar. 36. Verily I say unto you, <u>All these things shall come upon this generation.</u> 37. O Jerusalem, Jerusalem, *thou* that killest the prophets, and stonest them which are sent unto thee, how often would I have gathered thy children together, even as a hen gathereth her chickens under *her* wings, <u>and ye would not!</u> 38. <u>Behold, your house is left unto you desolate.</u>

This was the very last thing Jesus said as he left the temple for the last time, in other accounts of this discourse it said he wept over the city and said these things. Immediately after this, the prophecy concerning the Destruction of Jerusalem was told in Matthew 24, Mark 13, and Luke 21. All three accounts speak of this judgment from three different points of view. As I stated, many of the Old Testament prophets also spoke of this event, but for the sake that this chapter's length, I would like to just look at Moses as he spoke of this event first. He said this would happen if the people would turn their backs on the Lord. Jesus points this truth out in:

John 5:46-47: For had ye believed Moses, ye would have believed me: for he wrote of me. 47. But if ye believe not his writings, how shall ye believe my words?

This was the accusation Jesus leveled at the Jews who prided themselves on the fact that they had the law of Moses and the writings, but Jesus declared they did not believe them. Had they believed Moses they would have embraced Christ and avoided this judgment:

Deuteronomy 28:49-58: The LORD shall bring a nation against thee from far, from the end of the earth, *as swift* as the eagle flieth; a nation whose tongue thou shalt not understand; (Rome's great banner was the golden eagle. Their armies were swift and deadly upon all that opposed them. Their empire encompassed the earth as it was known in the ancient world. Rome spoke Latin, a language that would not be invented for centuries after this was written.)

50. A nation of fierce countenance, which shall not regard the person of the old, nor shew favour to the young: (Rome was known for destroying rebellion by slaughtering even the children, sick, and elderly of rebels to quell a further rebellion.)

51. And he shall eat the fruit of thy cattle, and the fruit of thy land, until thou be destroyed: which *also* shall not leave thee *either* corn, wine, or oil, *or* the increase of thy kine, or flocks of thy sheep, until he have destroyed thee. (During the siege of Jerusalem a great famine came over the city, but the Roman armies ate in abundance the stores of the lands of Judah. The water wells of Jerusalem dried up, but the wells outside the city, which previously had dried up, began to flow in abundance for the Roman army. This is identical to what happened when Babylon came against Jerusalem some 600 years earlier. Josephus said it was as if God himself wanted the city destroyed (little did he know God did). Josephus was a Jewish soldier who fought against the Romans and was spared to record a record of all he saw. The "he" mentioned in this verse is, in my opinion, speaking about Jesus as he is the one bringing this judgment, but others think it is speaking about Titus the prince and general that led the armies.)

52. And he shall besiege thee in all thy gates, until thy high and fenced walls come down, wherein thou trustedst, throughout all thy land: and he shall besiege thee in all thy gates throughout all thy land, which the

LORD thy God hath given thee. (Jerusalem was thought impenetrable even by the Roman legions, as it was built by King Herod the Great into the 8th wonder of the ancient world. The Jews and the Romans believed the walls would repel all attacks. Titus himself declared that it was only by an act of the almighty that he was able to breach the walls. "*He*" here is either Titus the leader of the Roman armies, not only did he destroy Jerusalem, but many of the cities inhabited by the rebellious Jews, or it is Christ himself. Moses is speaking about this city even before the Hebrews came into the promised land!)

53. And thou shalt eat the fruit of thine own body, the flesh of thy sons and of thy daughters, which the LORD thy God hath given thee, in the siege, and in the straitness, wherewith thine enemies shall distress thee: (The famine in the city was so great during the siege that many slaughtered their children for food.)

54. *So that* the man *that is* tender among you, and very delicate, his eye shall be evil toward his brother, and toward the wife of his bosom, and toward the remnant of his children which he shall leave: (A three-way civil war within the city killed nearly more Jews than the Roman armies did. Titus and Josephus described this as if madness had gone over the city. When the three factions saw the Roman armies surrounding them they quickly tried to band together and fight Rome, but ended up fighting each other as much as the enemy that threatened them. This disorganized bloodbath is what allowed Titus to eventually breach the walls and take the city.)

55. So that he will not give to any of them of the flesh of his children whom he shall eat: because he hath nothing left him in the siege, and in the straitness, wherewith thine enemies shall distress thee in all thy gates. (The siege lasted for 5 months. Rome dug a great trench around all the gates of the city to prevent anything from entering or leaving the city by surrounding it. All those that tried to flee were crucified outside the city walls Josephus describes it as nearly 100,000 such individuals were crucified in the valley of Tophet also known as the valley of the sons of Hinnom which is a fulfillment of Jeremiah's prophecy in Jeremiah 19.)

56. The tender and delicate woman among you, which would not adventure to set the sole of her foot upon the ground for delicateness

and tenderness, her eye shall be evil toward the husband of her bosom, and toward her son, and toward her daughter,

57. And toward her young one that cometh out from between her feet, and toward her children which she shall bear: for she shall eat them for want of all *things* secretly in the siege and straitness, wherewith thine enemy shall distress thee in thy gates. (These verse speaks of noblewomen even eating their children in secret. Even this horrible event was also seen and recorded by survivors of the Destruction of Jerusalem in 70 A.D. Nobles were caught eating their children, the smell of cooking meat drew the starving soldiers exposing this unthinkable act.)

58. If thou wilt not observe to do all the words of this law that are written in this book, that thou mayest fear this glorious and fearful name, THE LORD THY GOD;

This was the decree by Moses against the people of God as a warning to them if they forsook the Lord. This was the covenant that God made to them promising to bless them if they served Him faithfully but also promised bitter judgments if they did not. The crux of all that Moses wrote in the law focused on Christ:

Deuteronomy 18:15-19: The LORD thy God will raise up unto thee a Prophet from the midst of thee (This is Jesus), of thy brethren, like unto me; unto him ye shall hearken; (He explains why God will do this in the following)

16. According to all that thou desiredst of the LORD thy God in Horeb (Mt. Sinia) in the day of the assembly, saying, Let me not hear again the voice of the LORD my God, neither let me see this great fire any more, that I die not. (When God came upon the mountain he intended on meeting with the people, but they were terrified of God. They asked Moses to go up to God for them, Moses did this and received the ten commandments)

17. And the LORD said unto me (Moses), They have well *spoken that* which they have spoken. 18. I will raise them up a Prophet (Jesus) from among their brethren (Meaning he will be a Jew), like unto thee (He will be the bringer of the law, and the covenant like Moses. He will also be the overseer and mediator between God and Man as Moses was.), and will put my words in his mouth; and he shall speak unto them all that I

shall command him. 19. <u>And it shall come to pass, *that* whosoever will not hearken unto my words which he shall speak in my name, I will require *it* of him.</u> (Jesus was going to give to the people all the things God had intended to give them on Mt. Sinai that they could not yet receive then. So the Father sent Christ and gave men his heart and the New Covenant promises of salvation. Contained in this promise was the fact that those who would not receive him would be judged. That is what is meant by, "I will require it of him," what will be required is the wrath of the law against those that do not follow it. All those that refused the Old Covenant Law were cut off from the people and judged, the same is true for the new.)

Incredibly, hundreds of years before Jerusalem was even built, Moses said these things so accurately depicting the destruction we shall soon see, as well as its cause. This destruction came because they hearkened not to the voice of the Prophet and they rejected God from their hearts. It also echoes the same words of Jeremiah in Jeremiah 19 (read the whole chapter 19 if you desire more details). This account also goes well with the events of Babylon's destruction which was a type of the final destruction of Jerusalem. Both were Days of the Lord. There is one other section of the prophecy that Moses said about this event that also should be noted:

Deuteronomy 29:22-28: So that the generation (God is explaining the reason for this judgment it was meant for future generations) to come of your children that shall rise up after you (Jewish descendants), and the stranger that shall come from a far land (Gentile descendants), shall say, when they see the plagues of that land, and the sicknesses which the LORD hath laid upon it;

23. *And that* the whole land thereof *is* brimstone, and salt, *and* burning, *that* it is not sown, nor beareth, nor any grass groweth therein, like the overthrow of Sodom, and Gomorrah, Admah, and Zeboim, which the LORD overthrew in his anger, and in his wrath: (Remember this was the promised land, a land originally flowing with milk and honey a metaphor for how rich and prosperous the land was. Since this destruction, the land has never been what it was it is still mostly a barren waste. God is saying this judgment on the land is something both Jews and gentiles will see and notice and wonder at).

24. Even all nations shall say, Wherefore (why then) hath the LORD done thus unto this land? (Meaning all those that are aware of the land's rich history, will wonder why it suddenly became so barren both spiritually and physically, and why it remains so even after nearly 2,000 years) what *meaneth* the heat of this great anger? (Incredibly this is exactly what people have noted and pondered over the centuries.)

25. Then men shall say, <u>Because they have forsaken the covenant of the LORD God of their fathers, which he made with them when he brought them forth out of the land of Egypt:</u>

<u>26. For they went and served other gods, and worshipped them, gods whom they knew not, and *whom* he had not given unto them:</u> (This used to be the answer of the Church as they understood this truth. Sadly today, the Church has become blind not only to this truth but the lesson it was supposed to warn the world about. This was a sign both physically and spiritually warning people about rejecting the Son and the New Covenant.)

27. And the anger of the LORD was kindled against this land, to bring upon it all the curses that are written in this book: (Moses is referring to the long list of warnings to the Jews that would happen to the land if the people turned from God. When Jerusalem was destroyed in 70 A.D. all of those curses were placed upon her just as God said. These are contained in earlier writings of Moses).

28. And the LORD <u>rooted them out of their land in anger,</u> and in wrath, and in great indignation, and cast them into another land, <u>as *it is* this day.</u> (Moses is writing this before they even came into the land.)

Everything that was spoken by Moses happened. Some understandably will be appalled and horrified by these accounts. They will think this is harsh, but Israel was warned by all the prophets about this event for over a thousand years each one begging the people to turn back to God and avoid this horrible judgment. Nearly every one of the prophets was brutally murdered for their warnings. Jesus spoke about this as we saw earlier in this chapter. Christ himself begged and pleaded with his people to come and escape the coming destruction. Yet, they killed and rejected him.

Then for 40 years, they were warned by the Church. Again many

Christians were killed, stoned, and arrested for doing so. Then God gave them a 3-year window during the Jewish Wars, a brief respite between the great conflicts between Rome and Israel, before Titus' final siege and still they rebelled. They refused to turn back from their rebellion and despite all that God did to try and avoid this day, they hardened their hearts against God and rebelled all the more.

Jesus said that all the judgment for all the righteous blood from all the prophets they killed would be leveled at the city within a generation. Thus the greatest of the prophets to warn the Jews of this Day of the Lord was the very son of God. God cannot be called unjust or unmerciful for what happened in Jerusalem. Not only did Israel reject God and the prophets, but they also slaughtered children to idols, and utterly despised the very one they claimed to worship. Do not think of ourselves above such things, here in America 3,000 children are killed to the gods of "My Choice" and "Convenience" through the alter of abortion every day.

Many in the Church as well as outside are guilty of this slaughter. This is only one of the great sins of the American Churches, I could easily point to fornication, pornography, adultery, idolatry, etc. As America falls into greater sin, the Churches of America follow, and only a small remnant remains faithful. The Destruction of Jerusalem should be a warning to any people that utterly forsake the Lord. The Lord will not be mocked and he will swiftly chasten those that call themselves by His name if they do not repent, for his own name's sake. America's day of the Lord will come if the nation does not turn, and it will not turn until the Church turns.

Jesus lays this truth bare to the Pharisees, the religious leaders of Israel, and their own words condemned them:

Matthew 21:33-46: Hear another parable: There was a certain householder, which planted a vineyard, and hedged it round about, and digged a winepress in it, and built a tower, and let it out to husbandmen, and went into a far country: (This is Jesus painting the picture of the kingdom of the Old Covenant that was given to the Jews by the Father to be a light in the world. The Jews are the husbandmen (caretakers). Similarly, the Church is called to shine in the New Covenant kingdom)

34. And when the time of the fruit drew near, he sent his servants to the husbandmen, that they might receive the fruits of it. (This is a reference to the prophets) 35. And the husbandmen took his servants, and beat one, and killed another, and stoned another. 36. Again, he sent other servants more than the first: and they did unto them likewise. 37. But last of all he sent <u>unto them his son</u>, saying, They will reverence (Respect) my son.

38. But when the husbandmen saw the son, they said among themselves, This is the heir; come, let us kill him, and let us seize on his inheritance. (Jesus is accusing the religious leaders of the fact that they knew exactly who Jesus was. They knew he was the Messiah.) 39. And they caught him, and cast *him* out of the vineyard, and slew *him*. (This is exactly what they did to Jesus) 40. When the lord therefore of the vineyard cometh, what will he do unto those husbandmen?

41. They say unto him ("They" being the Jews Jesus told the parable to), <u>He will miserably destroy those wicked men, and will let out *his* vineyard unto other husbandmen, which shall render him the fruits in their seasons.</u> (Even the Pharisees as blind as they were recognized the judgment that would be passed for such a crime, their pride blinded them at first to the fact that Jesus told this parable about them. Notice they said that they that did such evil should be destroyed and the vineyard (picture of the kingdom) would be taken from them and given to another, is not that exactly what Jesus is about to say in verse 43? Remember this was the Pharisee's response to Jesus.)

42. Jesus saith unto them, Did ye never read in the scriptures, The stone which the builders rejected, the same is become the head of the corner: this is the Lord's doing, and it is marvellous in our eyes? 43. Therefore say I unto you, <u>The kingdom of God shall be taken from you, and given to a nation bringing forth the fruits thereof.</u> (The fullness of this judgment was fulfilled at the destruction of their city, temple, and religious system. This is exactly what we saw in the parable of the talents. Notice Jesus now declares the very same condemnation against them that the Pharisees themselves proclaimed against the people in the parable. Meaning they understood that it would be a just act if God did this thing to them.)

181

44. And whosoever shall fall on this stone shall be broken: but on whomsoever it shall fall, it will grind him to powder. (Speaking of the absolute authority of the gospel, Christ is the stone if you try and come against him, he will destroy you, and if you stand in his way he will "grind you to powder," this just shows that nothing shall stop the earth from becoming the kingdom of God ripe for the harvest.) 45. <u>And when the chief priests and Pharisees had heard his parables, they perceived that he spake of them.</u> 46. But when they sought to lay hands on him, they feared the multitude, because they took him for a prophet.

I think this paints a clear picture of the condemnation of the city. Between Moses and Christ, we should have a clear understanding. Let us now turn to the accounts told so clearly in 3 of the 4 gospels (it is my opinion that John's account of this event was told in the Revelation). I will focus primarily on Matthew's accounts of this as it is the most popular, but I will also look at Luke and Mark's accounts when they give added details.

Remember everything in this chapter that we are going to look at is about the Destruction of Jerusalem: the Day of the Lord, the Day of Christ, and the Great and Terrible Day of the Lord. Nearly every modern teacher of this in Evangelical churches says that the majority of these events are talking about future things, but you will see, as we go on, that this is an impossibility unless Jesus is a liar.

Matthew 24:1: And Jesus went out, and departed from the temple: and his disciples came to *him* for to <u>shew him the buildings of the temple</u>. (Remember Jesus just declared judgment over the temple and his disciples heard him say it, see Matthew 23:27-39)

Mark 13:1 And as he went out of the temple, one of his disciples saith unto him, Master, <u>see what manner of stones and what buildings are here!</u>

Luke 21:5 And as some spake of the <u>temple, how it was adorned with goodly stones and gifts,</u> he said,

As you can see by all three accounts of this, the disciples were concerned about what Jesus had just said about the temple, the Jews, and the city. Christ just moments before declared that all of God's wrath for all the persecution of the prophets and Christian martyrs that were ever killed would shortly come and be leveled at the city, and the people. This is God's chosen people and city in the minds of the disciples so such a declaration would have been horrifying.

We should not marvel that they were so concerned with this, as the Jewish religion focused on the importance of the temple. At this point in history, Herod's temple was described with unmatched beauty and glory to rival that even of Solomon's temple. It was adorned with gold and brass and all manner of precious stones and tapestry.

It would have shone like the sun for miles around atop Mount Zion. The entire complex was made up of massive white marble and alabaster stones that adorned the buildings, porches, columns, and masterful stone carvings that were designed to draw the eye in wonder and majesty. These were plated with fine brass and gold, decorative tapestries, and finely woven silks. It would shine in the sunlight like a pillar of fire, and in the moonlight like a beacon on the horizon.

The Jews prided themselves in the building thinking its outward beauty would please God. But Jesus did not look upon the outward beauty. To him, the temple was filled with dead men, abominations, and all things that offend. This was because the temple had become about man's glory and religion, rather than God. The building and their religion had become an idol. Jerusalem, the once faithful bride of God, had become a harlot (Isaiah 1:21, Ezekiel 23:4, 11-21). How many of our churches today have become just like the temple?

Titus himself wept over the burning of the temple, which he desired greatly to preserve when the Romans attacked, but madness overtook his own men as they ravaged the temple and refused to listen to his orders to preserve it. The accounts given about the burning of the temple said it was as if the very fires of hades erupted from the earth to consume even the stones, and nothing they did could put out the fire until the temple was consumed. Amazing in and of itself considering that it was primarily a stone building!

Peter has the best description of this fiery destruction of the Jewish system:

2 Peter 3:7: But the heavens and the earth, which are now (Old Covenant and Israel), by the same word are kept in store, reserved unto fire against the day of judgment and perdition of ungodly men.

183

2 Peter 3:10: But the day of the Lord will come as a thief in the night; in the which the heavens shall pass away with a great noise, and the elements shall melt with fervent heat, the earth also and the works that are therein shall be burned up. (Speaking of the utter destruction of the Jewish system)

Imagine the pride the Jewish people must have felt when viewing these buildings. This temple was the house of the Lord. They had come through Jacobs Troubles and had managed to gain control of their city again though it was still under Roman rule, they had much freedom of government over their own people, and their own religious liberty. Herod the Great had built the city as a jewel among nations. Imagine then how the disciples felt when Jesus said:

Matthew 24:2: And Jesus said unto them, See ye not all these things? verily I say unto you, There shall not be left here one stone upon another, that shall not be thrown down.

Mark 13:2: And Jesus answering said unto him, Seest thou these great buildings? there shall not be left one stone upon another, that shall not be thrown down.

Imagine if you will for a moment. All your life you were taught by the rabbis, and the Sanhedrin (the ruling religious authorities of Israel) that when the Messiah shall come, he will overthrow all the oppressors of Israel, he will bring in a time of peace and prosperity, the very kingdom of God would be on earth with Christ at its head sitting upon the throne of David in Israel and being a high priest in the temple for all men. These would point to the beauty of the temple and the city and say, "this is prepared for the Messiah, he shall glory in the things we have made by our hands in preparation for his appearing. Messiah will rule from Jerusalem as King of kings."

Perhaps as a child, you would look up upon this beautiful temple, see the great buildings blazing in the rising sun like a beacon of hope for all the world, and imagine what that day of the Messiah would be like. Then the Messiah comes and turns the world upside down with his messages, heals the sick, raises the dead, and then declares everything you held of value in this life will be torn down.

Of course, Jesus as the Messiah did all the things that the rabbis taught, but it did not manifest in a physical way. The oppressors were spiritual, the kingdom was spiritual, and Christ's rule from Jerusalem as high priest and King of kings upon the throne of David was heavenly and spiritual.

Let us see how some of the other prophets said this:

Micah 3:12: Therefore shall Zion (the mountain where Jerusalem and the temple were built) for your sake be plowed as a field, and Jerusalem shall become heaps, and the mountain of the house as the high places of the forest.

Jeremiah 26:18: Micah the Morasthite prophesied in the days of Hezekiah king of Judah, and spake to all the people of Judah, saying, Thus saith the LORD of hosts; Zion shall be plowed like a field, and Jerusalem shall become heaps, and the mountain of the house as the high places of a forest.

I get that Jeremiah is quoting Michah, but I show both because this shows the incredible significance of this prophecy. Indeed Jerusalem was plowed, literally, the very foundation stones were rooted up by the Romans, and only three towers and the wall that connected it were allowed to remain standing as a testimony to Titus' victory. All who saw Jerusalem before 70 A.D. would have seen a grand city that would have thought impossible that it would ever be destroyed. Herod had built it to stand for ages. After these events, people could hardly imagine a city ever existed where Jerusalem stood. What Jesus pronounced over the city would have been inconceivable, yet every word was true.

The modern archeology that is found in Israel of the "old city" was actually the remnants of a Roman garrison and city built centuries after its destruction. Josephus states plainly that nothing was allowed to remain except the towers and the western wall, which was not a part of the temple complex, unlike what modern bible teachers proclaim. It was actually a part of the Roman castle/garrison called Fort Antonia which stood above the temple. We see this written about in Acts when Paul is arrested in the temple and taken up into the garrison above it (Acts 21:27-22:24)

Talk about the Lord derailing your hopes and dreams. Perhaps then the next question will now make more sense:

Matthew 24:3: And as he sat upon the mount of Olives, the disciples came unto him privately, saying, Tell us, when shall these things be? and what *shall be* the sign of thy coming, and of the end of the world?

The significance of where this conversation is about to unfold needs to be understood. The Mount of Olives was a stone's throw away from the walls of the city. From it, the entire city of Jerusalem and the temple would have been seen in all its splendor. I imagine Jesus motioning towards the buildings and the surrounding city as he describes the judgment that would be laid against it. I imagine the disciples looked upon the beauty of it all with horror and sadness reflecting on Jesus' words. They could not fathom that they could be true. If they could somehow be true, surely it would mean the end of the world. I guess that it was Peter who blurted out the question, "When shall this be?"

It would have seemed as if the end of the world must be at hand if the very great city, the beloved city of God, was going to be destroyed in such a profound fashion. Let us compare the question with the other accounts and we will see that they were not meaning the literal end of the world, but rather the end of the world they knew.

Mark 13:3-4: And as he sat upon the mount of Olives over against the temple, <u>Peter and James and John and Andrew</u> asked him privately,

4. Tell us, when shall these things be? <u>and what *shall be* the sign when all these things shall be fulfilled?</u>

As I'm sure you noticed, there was no asking about the end of the world in Mark's account. This is the beauty of comparing the different accounts. From Matthew's perspective as a Jew writing to a Jewish audience, Jesus spoke of the end of the Jewish world, Mark speaking to a Roman audience understood that Jesus spoke of the city's destruction. Mark wrote his gospel based on what Peter told him about Jesus so when we read Mark we can just as easily say we are reading Peter's testimony of these events. Look at Luke's account to a Greek audience and we shall see the same understanding.

Luke 21:7: And they asked him, saying, Master, <u>but when shall these things be? and what sign *will there be* when these things shall come to pass?</u>

It is evident then that they were asking Jesus, "When shall this temple and city be destroyed? And if the temple shall be destroyed what will be the sign that we should look for to know that its destruction is at hand?" Looking back on history we know exactly when these events happened. I say this to point out that the account we are about to read is not speaking of a future event for us, but specifically, Jesus is going to answer this question concerning the judgment he spoke against the city in Matthew 23:28-36, and the prophecy about the very stones of the city being torn down.

Any honest reading of these statements should come to the same conclusion. It is sad then that nearly every modern pastor in America will say everything you are about to read is something that will happen in the future. I'm not sure how they can read what we just read and get that.

Matthew 24:4-5: And Jesus answered and said unto them (Peter, James, John, and Andrew), Take heed that no man deceive you. 5. For many shall come in my name, saying, I am Christ; and shall deceive many.

Right after Jesus ascended into heaven there were dozens of people that came on the scene of the world claiming to be the Messiah. Each of these false prophets gathered tens of thousands to them all promising to overthrow Rome and rebuild the kingdom of the Jews as in the days of Solomon and David. This is exactly who the Jews thought/wanted the Messiah to be and many followed after them. Each time Rome came and disbanded and killed these deserters, as Josephus tells it, nearly daily a new false messiah was coming fourth leading large masses into the deserts to cause insurrection.

Jesus is telling his friends, "don't listen to these liars, and tell my sheep not to listen to them." We need to keep these things in context Jesus is answering their question and telling them things that they would need to watch for and prepare for.

Matthew 24:6-8: And ye shall hear of wars and rumours of wars: see that ye be not troubled: for all *these things* must come to pass, but the end is not yet. 7. For nation shall rise against nation, and kingdom against kingdom: and there shall be famines, and pestilences, and earthquakes, in divers places. 8. <u>All these *are* the beginning of sorrows.</u>

During the times of these false messiahs, a great spirit of rebellion began to stir among the nations of Rome. Not all of these rebellions had anything to do with Jerusalem and the Jews, but many of them did. Peace seemed to flee out of the empire and from 33 A.D. - 70 A.D Josephus, Tacitus, and Tertullian, as well as other historians that lived during these times, speak of a great many wars and rumors of wars throughout the whole empire. 150 pages of Josephus' works (at least in the edition I have) are dedicated to nothing but describing these great many wars and rumors of wars that bathed the empire in blood.

Many great earthquakes also devastated entire regions, mostly focused on Jewish settlements. Josephus sees these as omens from God concerning the destruction soon to come against Jerusalem. One of these earthquakes in Syria was so great that Caesar, to help the region recover, canceled all tribute to Rome for five years. This would have been the tax owed to the capital from Syria. As for famine and pestilences, many of them swept various places in the Roman world.

One such event is even recorded in the book of Acts and some of the Epistles in which Jerusalem was hit with such a terrible famine that Paul asked the Greek churches for a love offering to help buy food and supplies for the city. (1 Corinthians 16:1-4, 2 Corinthians 8:1-9:15, Galatians 2:10, and Romans 15: 25-31)

Matthew 24:9-10 Then shall they <u>deliver you up</u> to be afflicted, and <u>shall kill you</u>: and ye shall be hated of all nations for my name's sake. 10. And then shall many be offended, and shall betray one another, and shall hate one another.

Notice how personal Jesus is making this, he is speaking to Peter, James, John, and Andrew while he is giving this account. He is telling them, "All of you will be afflicted and killed and hated, not just you personally but all that follow me." We see a lot of this played out in the book of Acts. James was killed by Herod because it pleased the Jews, Peter and Andrew would die martyrs deaths, only John would live to see the Destruction of Jerusalem and live for years after the event. Remember Jesus prophesied this about John:

Matthew 16:28: Verily I say unto you, There be some standing here, which shall not taste of death, <u>till they see the Son of man coming in his kingdom.</u>

Jesus declared this statement to the same group now standing in front of him. We know for a fact that John lived to see this. The kingdom is the kingdom received by the father when Christ ascended into heaven, it was poured out on the early Church in the upper room on Pentecost, and it was announced to the world in 70 A.D. The coming was the coming in judgment with the full authority of that kingdom to destroy the unfaithful bride and reveal to the world the bride of Christ.

Jesus also tells Peter and John this:

John 21:22-23: Jesus saith unto him (Peter concerning John's fate), If I will that he (John) tarry till I come (referring to his coming in judgment in the full power of his kingdom), what *is that* to thee? follow thou me. 23. Then went this saying abroad among the brethren, that that disciple should not die: yet Jesus said not unto him, He shall not die; but, If I will that he tarry till I come, what *is that* to thee?

History fills in the time after the New Testament Epistles are finished. History tells us that under the bloody reign of Nero countless hundred if not thousands of Christians would be terrorized and killed. He favored stringing up Christians in Rome and lighting them on fire as streetlights. Or he would gather entire families and feed them to lions at the coliseum for entertainment. Tradition says that Nero beheaded Paul and crucified Peter upside down on a cross.

Nero even burned down Rome and blamed it on Christians turning the entire empire against them.

No wonder Jesus said many of the early Christians would be offended. Imagine seeing your family ripped apart because of your faith. How could most average people not think God was cruel to let such things happen. Luke makes this account even more clear and personal:

Luke 21:12-14: But before all these, they shall lay their hands on <u>you</u>, and persecute <u>you,</u> delivering <u>you</u> up to the synagogues, and into prisons, being brought before kings and rulers for my name's sake. (So clearly what happened in the book of Acts and beyond)

13. And it shall turn to you for a testimony. 14. Settle *it* therefore in your hearts, not to meditate before what ye shall answer: (Notice how

personal each one of these things are. Jesus is telling them what they needed to prepare for. In other places, he says, "These things have I spoken unto you, that ye should not be offended. (John 16:1)"

Luke 21:15-19: 15. For I will give <u>you</u> a mouth and wisdom, which all your adversaries shall not be able to gainsay (Speak evil of) nor resist.

16. And ye (all Christ's disciples) shall be betrayed both by parents, and brethren, and kinsfolks, and friends; and *some* of you shall they cause to be put to death. (There was a great reward for turning in "atheists," which was what early Christians were called because they refused to worship the Roman gods and emperors). 17. And ye shall be hated of all *men* for my name's sake. (Nero accomplished this nationwide hatred by burning Rome and charging Christians with sedition and atheism.) 18. But there shall not an hair of your head perish. (Because even though they would kill the body they would never be able to destroy the soul. For those that did not die a martyr, not a single Christian died in the judgment against Jerusalem for they all fled to Pella and were spared.). 19. In your patience possess ye your souls.

All of these things Jesus is describing and warning his friends of things that would happen to them. This is clearly not speaking of a future event as he makes each of these warnings personal to them in response to their question.

Matthew 24:11-14: And many false prophets shall rise, and shall deceive many. 12. And because iniquity shall abound, the love of many shall wax cold. 13. But he that shall endure unto the end, the same shall be saved. 14. And this gospel of the kingdom shall be preached in all the world for a witness unto all nations; and then shall the end come.

Many of the false Christs that arose after Jesus left had "prophets" that would accompany them and prophecying of their great victories over Rome. This was a mockery by satan of the ministry we saw of John the Baptist preparing the way of the Lord. We see the love of many growing cold in some of the letters written to the churches by Paul, many of the churches struggled with worldliness and some were led away from the faith or stumbled due to the persecutions.

Verse 13 is a reference to the fact that all the believers that were alive during this time of the end, the end being the end of the temple and the city, remember that is what Jesus is talking about here, shall be saved. Saved from the destruction and wrath that will be poured out on the city. What is amazing about this statement is many of the early writings from people that lived through this time, survive to this very day, and they all record that not a single Christian died in the city and the destruction because they fled just as Jesus is about to warn them in the following verses.

Lastly, verse 14, is not speaking about the entire world as we know it today, but rather the entire known world then. America was not known to the Apostles, remember he is telling the apostles that the Gospel shall be preached in all the world, and this would have been to their minds only the world they knew. When they thought of the world they thought of the Roman world and Asia. We know by Roman accounts as well as biblical accounts that this happened before 70 A.D.

For further consideration see how Mark records this statement:

Mark 13:10: And the gospel must first be published (the old way of saying preached) among all nations.

Here we see that Jesus was not referring to the literal whole world, but the nations. In Luke's account, we do not even see this statement. Rather Luke just goes straight from Jesus saying you will all be persecuted as a testimony to talking about the Roman armies surrounding the city. Before we look at that though notice a few things Paul says that show this preaching to the nations/world happened before 70 A.D.

Colossians 1:5-6: For the hope which is laid up for you in heaven, whereof ye heard before in the word of the truth of the gospel; 6. Which is come unto you, as *it is* in all the world; and bringeth forth fruit, as *it doth* also in you, since the day ye heard *of it*, and knew the grace of God in truth:

Paul is clearly saying that the gospel has gone into all the world. Colossians was written about 62 A.D. Paul also says that the gospel was preached to every creature under heaven in:

Colossians 1:23: If ye continue in the faith grounded and settled, and *be* not moved away from the hope of the gospel, which ye have heard, *and* which was preached to every creature which is under heaven; whereof I Paul am made a minister;

Obviously, this isn't speaking in a literal way, rather Paul in both verses is saying that no matter where one could go in the known world the gospel had already been preached in that area. Much of the New Testament follows just the ministry of Paul, but there were tens of thousands of Christians that preached the gospel all over the Roman world and beyond before 70 A.D. It wasn't as if only Paul was preaching and all the rest of the disciples and Christians were just sitting in pews. Rather they were soul winners.

I believe that in a literal sense the gospel will go out into all the world, the literal entire earth, before the end by which the nations are converted and put under Christ. So we see here on a small local scale what must happen on a large global scale before Christ returns at the end for the harvest. That is why I said this was a picture of Christ's Second Coming. This parallel is true for most of this account with the exceptions of the specific portions speaking of the Destruction of Jerusalem. This is what the parables and all the things we have looked at earlier in this book teach as well.

Let's continue:

Matthew 24:15: When ye therefore shall see the abomination of desolation, spoken of by Daniel the prophet, stand in the holy place, (whoso readeth, let him understand:)

Modern churches say this is the antichrist and that this is another proof of why this passage is speaking of a future event. This thinking is flawed when we actually look at Daniel and take in the other accounts. When we do you will realize that the abomination of desolation is a reference to the Roman armies and their flag insignias which bore their pagan gods. It wasn't just the temple that was considered the holy place, but the entire region around Jerusalem, to see these armies encompass the city of God with their idolatry would have been an abomination standing in the holy place. Mark and Luke will give us some added details to fill in what exactly Jesus is speaking about.

Mark 13:14: But when ye shall see the abomination of desolation, spoken of by Daniel the prophet, <u>standing where it ought not</u>, (let him that readeth understand,) then let them that be in Judaea flee to the mountains:

Mark's account adds to this warning that when you see this event happen flee. If this had something to do with a future antichrist how would this make sense, to Peter, James, John, and Andrew who just asked Jesus what they should look for that will bring in the destruction of the city and temple? Think about this, whatever the abomination is, Jesus is saying this is something you all need to look for, and once you see it run.

Let us consider this phrase, the "abomination of desolation." Desolation is an old term that simply means destruction or something that lays waste to something. So whatever this abomination is, it is also a destructive force. Jesus ties this to the immediate destruction of Jerusalem. We know this happened in 70 A.D. Luke is about to tell us clearly what it was, but this thing was the final chance for stragglers to run with all their might and flee the city because once the abomination comes to destroy, there will be no opportunity to flee. This concept is something Jesus will reiterate a few times.

So what is this destroying abomination? Remember I said that not one Christian died in this judgment? That's because they saw this and fled. They fled into the mountains in an area called Pella and not one perished. Luke declares the abomination is:

Luke 21:20 And when ye shall see <u>Jerusalem compassed</u> (surrounded) <u>with armies,</u> then know that the <u>desolation</u> (destruction) <u>thereof is nigh</u>.

Rather than saying the abomination that makes desolate, Luke just says when you see the army surrounding the city then run. So the bible tells us straight out what this abomination that makes desolation is. It is an army that surrounds the city of Jerusalem and destroys it. I've never heard a single modern "prophecy" teacher explain this. Try to recall any of the "prophecy teachers" ever reading Luke's account. My guess is they never did because it would throw their antichrist out the window. Usually, False-hope teachers will only look at Matthew and Mark's accounts when teaching this topic.

These armies were an abomination to the Jews. The Roman armies bore flags bearing symbols of their gods, these banners would have been used as idols. Many soldiers would offer sacrifices and prayers to them in the name of their gods during the battle.

After the city and temple were destroyed alters were made up to the gods on the ruins of the temple to give thanks to the gods for their victory. This too is an abomination.

All of the gospels were written and circulated well before the Destruction of Jerusalem, so Christians took these warnings seriously. The early disciples also preached about this soon-coming destruction of the City. That means they preached about the abomination and looked for it to appear.

Real quick, let's look at Daniel and see how this is not speaking of the antichrist, but the armies. There are three such passages about an antichrist-like figure that False-hope tries to link to the abomination. One was about Antiochus Epiphanes who rose after Alexander the Great and set up pagan sacrifices in the temple and refused to let the Jews offer sacrifices (Daniel 8:8-27) this happened around 175 B.C. The second is the one I believe is the correct one that speaks about Jerusalem being destroyed by Rome which we will look at shortly. The last, in my opinion, is speaking of the Man of Sin, the Beast of Revelation in Daniel 11.

False-hope tries to lump these three accounts into one, but they do not work when taken in context. The only one that fits what Jesus said is also the only passage that is specifically related to the armies surrounding Jerusalem:

Daniel 9:26: And after threescore and two weeks shall Messiah be cut off, but not for himself: and <u>the people of the prince that shall come shall destroy the city and the sanctuary; and the end thereof *shall be* with a flood, and unto the end of the war desolations are determined.</u>

We will look at this prophecy in its fullness in chapter 14. For our study now though, look at how this verse matches what Jesus is saying. The prince that shall come this is Titus, his father was the emperor of Rome making him a prince. He shall come and destroy the city and the sanctuary (temple) the end will be with a flood. This isn't speaking of water, often the bible will call a great army sweeping over a nation a flood. This is exactly what happened. And then notice that at the end of the war that will destroy the city, desolation (destructions) are determined or declared upon it.

This is the abomination of desolation. When we look at Luke's account of this we know he understood that this prophecy in Daniel was what Jesus was referring to. It is what all of our forefathers understood this to be, it was what the Christians living when this happened understood this to be. Why is it today that we can't seem to understand it?

False-hope was the first to propose that the Abomination of Desolation spoken of by Daniel was the Antichrist. Let us continue:

Matthew 24:16-20: Then let them which be in Judaea flee into the mountains: (As I already said, there was a mass exodus of Christians, both Jews and Gentiles into the mountain region known as Pella when they saw the Roman armies, just as Jesus had warned)

17. Let him which is on the housetop not come down to take any thing out of his house: 18. Neither let him which is in the field return back to take his clothes. 19. And woe unto them that are with child, and to them that give suck in those days! 20. But pray ye that your flight be not in the winter, neither on the sabbath day:

Here is Jesus' great warning to any that would heed it. Listen to what Luke said after all these warnings:

Luke 21:22-23: For these be the days of vengeance (that is what the Day of the Lord was all about. This was the vengeance of all the righteous blood slain by the harlot bride being cast upon the city), that all things which are written may be fulfilled (as I said this event was written about all through the Old Testament). 23. But woe unto them that are with child, and to them that give suck, in those days! for there shall be great distress in the land, and wrath upon this people.

Matthew and Mark will put it this way:

Matthew 24: 21: For then shall be great tribulation, such as was not since the beginning of the world to this time, no, nor ever shall be.

Mark 13:19: For in those days shall be affliction, such as was not from the beginning of the creation which God created unto this time, neither shall be.

There are no words to describe the horrors of the destruction and pain that came against Jerusalem. This is the Great Tribulation it isn't some future event. Jesus just said it happened during the judgment of

Jerusalem! All the things Jesus has been speaking about including the Great Tribulation were all the warning signs leading up to the judgment.

Yet, modern teachers try and scare Christians into thinking this event is the reign of the antichrist! Two other verses in Revelation speak of great tribulation, that is because Revelation is also speaking about this event. Jesus is clearly saying this about Jerusalem, and he also said that no other tribulation will ever be greater again in the whole world. Jesus is God, and God can't lie Hebrews 6:18.

Josephus even said that if we took all of the world's histories up to that point we will see not a single greater horror or destruction ever recorded. This statement is still true today. This event was so horrible it even makes the holocaust of the Natzis look like a minor event in comparison. 100,000 men were killed and crucified outside of the city, over 1.1 million Jews were killed during the siege (Considering that the entire population of the Jews in the first century was only a few million this number is astronomical).

Over 2/3 of all the Jewish people were slaughtered by Rome during this event and the 3 ½ years of wars that followed the city's destruction. Blood flowed through the city up to the horse's bridle according to Roman accounts. The bodies of the dead were so massive there was no place left to bury them. All of these things were prophecied and came to pass. This is why Jesus told them to flee. This is why he said it was great tribulation such as was never seen nor never would be seen again.

Only the Christians listened. In reality, Jerusalem was packed when this judgment came as Jews came from all over the Roman world for the Passover, this judgment began on the very anniversary of the crucifixion of Christ! Sad that so many are not listening today to these very same words and understanding them.

This is why Jesus said while he was walking to Calvary, just hours before he died, he once again prophecies of these horrors:

Luke 23:27-30: And there followed him a great company of people, and of women, which also bewailed and lamented him. 28. But Jesus turning unto them said, Daughters of Jerusalem, <u>weep not for me, but weep for yourselves, and for your children</u> 29. For, behold, <u>the days are coming</u>, in the which they shall say, Blessed *are* the barren, and the wombs that never bare, and the paps which never gave suck. (Jesus had uttered these very same words to Peter, James, John, and Andrew in our main text!) 30. Then shall they begin to say to the mountains, Fall on us; and to the hills, Cover us.

Jesus will repeat these very words in the verses ahead, but these things happened. Great famine and pestilence fell over the city. Children were killed for meat. It was so great people hid in the caves under Jerusalem begging to die there rather than be killed by the Romans or their fellow Jews.

Matthew 24:22: And except those days should be shortened, there (where is the there? Jesus has been focusing on Jerusalem he is saying that if the days of wrath were not shortened then) should no flesh (Who's flesh? Again context is speaking of the Jews) be saved: but for the elect's sake those days shall be shortened.

The flesh here is speaking about the Jews as a people. The judgment in contexts of everything Jesus is saying has to do with the Jews. If the day of vengeance was not shortened, then none of the Jews would have survived. For the sake of the elect, it was shortened. This is a reference to Christians both Jews and Gentiles that prayed that the wrath would cease. This is recorded by those watching the events, great prayer was made for mercy upon the Jewish people. It is also a reference to the Jews yet to be born that would yet be saved. As it was, only 95,000 were left alive, Josephus was one of them and they were taken as slaves into Egypt and Rome and from there scattered through the world. Again Moses prophecied this:

Deuteronomy 28:68: And the LORD shall bring thee into Egypt again with ships, by the way whereof I spake unto thee, Thou shalt see it no more again: and there ye shall be sold unto your enemies for bondmen and bondwomen, and no man shall buy you.

The last line of Moses' prophecy was also true. Though the Romans sought to sell the 95,000 captives into slavery, no one would buy them for they were looked upon as a cursed and rebellious people, so Rome gave them away. Luke also says this:

Luke 21:24 And they shall fall by the edge of the sword, and shall be led away captive into all nations: and Jerusalem shall be trodden down of the Gentiles, until the times of the Gentiles be fulfilled.

People think that this last section in Luke speaks about what is happening in Palestine today. Most teachers will say that the time of the gentiles is the same as what Paul means when he says the fullness of the gentiles. This fullness, according to them, is when God has used the gentiles to control Jerusalem as punishment up until now, but now that their time is up, God is restoring it to the Jews. Added to this is the understanding that the gentile Church will soon be raptured so God can return to Israel during the soon coming Tribulation. They view the Jews coming back to Israel as a fulfillment of prophecy, meaning the times of the gentiles have, or soon will pass, and now God is bringing them back to begin the final stages of history.

However, the time of the gentiles is different than the fullness of the gentiles (we dive into this in full in chapter 15). This account by Luke is specifically referencing the protection that God removed from the city of Jerusalem that allowed it to be destroyed by the gentiles, not a period that will pass before the Jews are restored.

The Zionistic movement we see in Palestine is not a fulfillment of prophecy at all. God only ever promised to return the Jews to their land when they repented, so far the Jews as a nation have not received Christ. Even if you want to attribute this to some future prophecy, as the Jews are still unbelievers in Palestine today, then they are still spiritually Gentiles so technically the city is still controlled by gentiles trodding it underfoot further disproving the whole concept of this fulfilling some prophecy.

Matthew 24:23-28: Then if any man shall say unto you, Lo, here *is* Christ, or there; believe *it* not. 24. For there shall arise false Christs, and false prophets, and shall shew great signs and wonders; insomuch that, if *it were* possible, they shall deceive the very elect. 25. Behold, I have told you before.

26. Wherefore if they shall say unto you, Behold, he is in the desert; go not forth: behold, *he is* in the secret chambers; believe *it* not. 27. For as the lightning cometh out of the east, and shineth even unto the west; so shall also the coming of the Son of man be. 28. <u>For wheresoever the carcase is, there will the eagles be gathered together.</u>

Here again, Christ reiterates the events leading up to this day.

He once again references the false Christ that will come. This is also referring to the fact that the Jewish Wars would last for another 3 ½ years after Jerusalem is destroyed and during this time many false Christs once again appeared to lead the Jews against Rome.

He says that as the lightning comes so shall I come. Lightning lights up the entire sky for a moment and then is gone. This is a reference to the fact that the army though it was led by Titus it was brought against them by Jesus. Rome marched on the city from the east to the west. This event lit up the whole known world and astonished all who saw it. Verse 28 is again referencing the fact that Rome was the eagle that brought great carnage against the city.

Compare this language that Jesus is saying about judgment and lightning and compare it to:

Psalms 97:2-4: Clouds and darkness *are* round about him: righteousness and judgment *are* the habitation of his throne. 3. A fire goeth before him, and burneth up his enemies round about. 4. <u>His lightnings enlightened the world: the earth saw, and trembled</u>.

Here in Psalms, the judgments of God are described as lightning that lights up the whole world. Jesus is once again putting himself in the same position as God described in the Old Testament!

Basically what Jesus is doing in this short burst of verses is reiterating everything he had just said before. He wants it to be abundantly clear that what he is saying they need to pay attention to and understand his word. Anyone living at the time would have known what the eagle was a reference to as the golden eagles of Rome flew throughout the empire.

Mark adds a few other details:

Mark 13:21-23 And then if any man shall say to you, Lo, here *is* Christ; or, lo, *he is* there; believe *him* not:

22. For false Christs and false prophets shall rise, and <u>shall shew signs and wonders, to seduce, if *it were* possible, even the elect.</u> 23. But take ye heed: behold, I have foretold you all things.

The false Christs and false messiah did many evils works to try and deceive many. Some of these deceptions were so cunning that the elect, those saved, were in danger of being deceived by them. But Christ said if it were possible, meaning it was not as he held his elect in his hand. These wonders were performed by witchcraft and demonic manifestations of power. Something the bible says is possible. A good New Testament example is with the sorcerer Simon in Acts 8:9-25

The following passages in particular are important to our understanding of Christs' Second Coming as these events foreshadow that coming, but are not that coming. This is where people get so mixed up not understanding the two comings of Christ and the parallel they make with one another.

Matthew 24:29-31: <u>Immediately after the tribulation of those days</u> (the tribulation of the days of judgment we just got done hearing about) shall the sun be darkened, and the moon shall not give her light, and the stars shall fall from heaven, and the powers of the heavens shall be shaken: (remember this, and the following statement is the same language of the Old Testament which describes the sovereign judgment of God against nations (Isaiah 13 and others). The tribulation was the sign leading up to this great judgment. Now that they have passed the judgment begins in full).

30. And then shall appear the <u>sign of the Son of man in heaven</u>: and then shall all the tribes of the earth mourn, and they shall see the Son of man coming in the clouds of heaven with power and great glory. (This entire event of the destruction was the very sign from heaven of God's abolishment of the Levitical priesthood and the kingdom of the Old Covenant. It was declared with great power. Many signs and wonders surrounded the conquest of Jerusalem all of which are recorded and show that Christ himself was with the armies of Rome. The Jews were in every nation in the Roman empire it was for this reason that all the tribes of the earth would morn. Again this is the same language used in the opening of Revelation. Even Jews that were not in the city wept all across the Roman empire and still weep over its loss to this very day. Recall Moses said that the people will look back on the land and this judgment and ask about it and people would say it was because the people turned away, meaning it was to be a sign to all people.)

31. And he shall send his angels with a great sound of a trumpet, and they shall <u>gather together</u> his elect from the four winds, from one end of heaven to the other.

Notice there is no shout, no voice of the archangel in this event. There is no bodily resurrection mentioned or us raising into the clouds with Christ. It just speaks of a trumpet and a gathering together. Remember as well when Christ comes all the nations will be gathered to him and judged we see none of this mentioned in this passage.

Rather, this is a reference to the Old Testament call of the people to gather or march at the blowing of the trumpet (Numbers 10:1-7, Leviticus 23:24-25, etc). This event was to be a signal, a great call if you will, that will send out the angels into the world. Angels are not always angelic beings but pastors and prophets are also called angels. (Revelation 22:9)

It is also the same picture that God taught the Hebrews:

Exodus 19:4: Ye have seen what I did unto the Egyptians, and *how* I bare you on eagles' wings, and brought you unto myself.

God did not literally bear them up on eagles' wings, but he did draw them through the judgment of Egypt. In the same way, we are brought by angels unto Christ at his call when he judged the city that was spiritually Egypt. Revelation 11:8b: great city, which spiritually is called Sodom and Egypt, where also our Lord was crucified. Where was Christ crucified? Jerusalem.

This declaration of Christ affirming his kingdom and Church was also to embolden the pastors to go into the uttermost parts of the earth to gather all the elect, saved, to him. Pastors are also called angels in the bible. Or as we saw previously he gave them authority to sit in judgments and declared that it was now time for the saints to begin to possess the kingdom. This continues to this very day. We bring people into the New Jerusalem, into Christ's kingdom the perfect picture of this spiritually is found in Revelation 21. This gathering is also a reference to the gathering of the true Israel of God to Christ. Up until this point, most thought Christians were just a sect of Judaism. After this event, there was no question they were different.

Though this event seems at first glance to be speaking about Christ's Second Coming, we know it cannot be when we compare it to what Christ and the apostles said about the Second Coming. That is why I saved this chapter until after we had laid those truths bare.

Those facts aside, we can also see that Jesus is not speaking about the Second Coming as he is still answering the disciple's question about the destruction of the city. This is what the entire chapter is doing answering Peter, James, John, and Andrew and their specific question about the judgment of the city. Meaning if we keep this passage in context and just look at it we know that the immediate idea of the end of the world cannot be so as our world has not ended, however, the Jewish world did. Also, the dead have not been raised, and Christ has not bodily returned or done any of the other things we know he must do when he returns.

We can also see from the context that Jesus cannot be speaking of a future thing to his disciples as he links this "coming in the clouds and the darkening of the sun, moon, and stars" to immediately follow the tribulations that he just got done describing against the city and suffered by those that followed Christ. This event happened in 70 A.D. so the gathering and the sun and moon being darkened happened immediately after the days of tribulation in the 1ˢᵗ century. This tribulation led up to the Day of the Lord, and then we see the judgment of the city and the glorification of the saints being prophetically declared in these verses.

Mark declares this a bit differently but he too speaks in the same language:

Mark 13:24-27: But in those days, <u>after that tribulation</u>, the sun shall be darkened, and the moon shall not give her light, 25. And the stars of heaven shall fall, and the powers that are in heaven shall be shaken. (Speaking about the religious, political, and priestly figures falling in the judgment. The heavens are referencing the heavenly covenant of the Old Testament which will no longer exist after this event. 26. And then shall they see the Son of man coming in the clouds with great power and glory. 27. And then shall he send his angels, and shall gather together his elect from the four winds, from the uttermost part of the earth to the uttermost part of heaven.

Luke says it this way:

Luke 21:25-28: And there shall be signs in the sun, and in the moon, and in the stars; and upon the earth <u>distress of nations, with perplexity</u>; the sea and the waves roaring; 26. Men's hearts failing them for fear, and for looking after those things which are coming on the earth: for the powers of heaven shall be shaken. 27. And then shall they see the Son of man coming in a cloud with power and great glory. 28. <u>And when these things begin to come to pass, then look up, and lift up your heads; for your redemption draweth nigh.</u>

As you can see all three accounts are similar. We briefly went over this in the first chapter, but for clarity, I feel we should dig a bit deeper into this now.

First let's start with the sun, moon, and stars, in all of the prophets in the Old Testament would refer to nations, religions, kings, and priests as being the sun, moon, and stars. This happened, for example, when God described the destruction of Egypt in Ezekiel 32:7-8, the fall of Babylon in Isaiah 13:9-10, and in Daniel describing the destruction of the Jews by Antiochus Epiphanes in Daniel 8:10. Even long before this, Joseph in Genesis 37:9 has a dream in which his father, stepmother, and brothers were represented as the sun, moon, and stars in his dream, and all would bow before him.

This is the same type of picture we have to understand that Jesus is using. Jesus is speaking as a prophet anyone who has a grasp on the Old Testament prophets will know that when God speaks of a great judgment upon a nation he will often say the heavens will be shaken and the sun will not give its light. This is often called a Great and terrible Day of the Lord, as God comes in judgment, the judgment is terrible, but God reveals his great power, glory, and authority in the very act of Judgement. This way of prophesying was always to show great destruction that would disrupt both the spiritual and natural world and reshape the world as it was known.

Jesus is also declaring himself as God in this act, as in the Old Testament it was Jehovah that came in the clouds, during this event Christ is coming in the clouds bringing the judgment.

No events shook either in heaven or earth greater than the events in the first century A.D. First Christ was killed, resurrected, and ascended. Then the Church was born and given great power. Then the once-beloved and holy city of God and the entire Jewish religious system were destroyed. When we take in the reality of how much the world changed forever we can see the poetic and apocalyptic, "the heavens shall be shaken," manifest itself. Imagine living through these things, your heart would stop for fear and you would think that the very world is coming to an end.

So what Jesus is saying in this passage when we look at these words with this understanding is: The sun is the city of Jerusalem. The moon is the religious glory of Jerusalem that being the temple and the Levitical Priesthood. The stars are the people who were produced by this union. The heavens being shaken is about the removal of the Old Covenant ordinances/system and the establishment of the New Covenant ordinances/system. This destruction and the affirmation of the saints shook the entire religious world and likened here to the heavens.

Hebrews 8:13 In that he (God) saith, A new *covenant,* he hath made the first old. Now that which decayeth and waxeth old *is* <u>ready to vanish away</u>. (This event is the vanishing away of the Old and the establishment of the New with great signs and wonders. The old was ratified with the judgment of Egypt, the new was ratified with the judgment of the Harlot that Jerusalem had become which was spiritually Egypt Revelation 11:8.)

This event is the casting out of Satan from being able to accuse the people of God as he once had the power to do. It was the binding of the devil from deceiving the Gentile world. It was the stone that would destroy Nebuchadnezzar's image of the empires until the kingdom of Christ filled the whole earth (Daniel 2:44). It was what Jesus claimed when he declared, "Behold I make all things new. Revelation 21:5" This judgment that Jesus speaks about will utterly destroy this system, glory, and power of Judaism, the glory of Israel as it was, and establish a new and better one. This is what Paul quotes Hosea saying:

Romans 9:25 As he saith also in Osee (Greek way of spelling Hosea), I will call them my people, which were not my people; and her beloved, which was not beloved.

This event completely overturned the entire world as it was known, especially the religious world, and eventually led to the downfall of Rome. Just as Jesus said:

Matthew 21:43: Therefore say I unto you, The kingdom of God shall be taken from you, and given to a nation bringing forth the fruits thereof.

Luke adds that there would be signs in the heavens and in the sea. Josephus and many other scholars record that a meteor or some object shaped like a sword hovered over Jerusalem for 15 months just before the judgment. During the siege when the Jews tried to flee by the waters, the very oceans came alive and drowned them according to eyewitness accounts.

After it was done, figuratively a new heaven and earth (speaking of a heavenly kingdom and an earthy kingdom both being in Christ) were made plain upon the earth. The old had passed away: old earthly Israel was replaced by the new heavenly Israel made up of all nations of faith, the old Jerusalem was replaced by the New heavenly Jerusalem, and the Temple was replaced by the Church. Christianity as the bride was revealed, the New Jerusalem, the very bride of Christ was declared from the heavens. It began to grow and continues to grow into the four corners of the earth preparing it for the time of harvest. Preparing it for the return of the Son of God.

As the ages have gone on, Christ is perfecting his Church as he is taking dominion over the earth both are a slow process. It is worldwide sanctification similar to our own personal sanctification. Thus there are times of ups and downs and Christ is quick to purify and cut off parts so his covenant people that have fallen away, just as a vinedresser cuts off dead vines from grapes.

All of these glorious truths are hidden from the eyes of those who fall into False-hope. It is why my heart breaks over this deception and why I hate it with such a perfect hatred. It encourages a defeated Church and spoils the image of the Bride. It makes us worship antichrist and has caused such great harm to the body. It's like cancer and it must be removed. Like cancer, we cannot sugar coat it. We must call this ugly theological system what it is and remove it.

As for the elect being gathered, Judaism was a large stumbling block to people coming into Christianity, now that it was removed the Church began to grow. The angels (ministers of the word of God) were sent out into the four corners of the earth. This is symbolic of North, South, East, and West meaning Christianity would spread over the entire earth drawing people into Christ. When Jesus comes for the harvest at the end of the World the spiritual angels will be gathering the saints from all over the earth. So again what we are seeing is a local scale picture of what will happen on a large scale at the end. This is why I said the Day of the Lord was a type or picture of the Second Coming.

This is important because this is key to knowing what Jesus is speaking about.

When we go back and see that the Day of the Lord also promised to glorify the testimony of the saints as we saw in 2 Thessalonians 1, and elsewhere, we see this gathering take on a different meaning. Remember in Daniel 7 and the parable of the talents, when Christ came he came to judge and then reward his saints with authority over cities. This shows that Christ granted his Church the right of rule that he himself had. The marriage happened, the king rules and the bride rules under the king. So simultaneously you see a gathering and a sending out to gather unto Christ the elect of the world.

Back to our main text. Luke's account of "When you see these things look up..." was always thought of as Christ telling the Jews and all men to look to Him for their salvation. It was as if he was saying, "This wrath is coming upon you, but if you will look to me I will still save you." The redemption is also a reference to the persecuted saints being vindicated. This was to encourage the Church, Jesus is saying when you see this event see me in it, and know your redemption from your oppressors is at hand. This concept of reassurance to the saints is also declared in:

Isaiah 35:4 Say to them *that are* of a fearful heart, Be strong, fear not: behold, your God will come *with* vengeance, *even* God *with* a recompence (to repay); he will come and save you. (This passage was meant for an assurance to those who witnessed judgment that even though God comes to judge the enemies he does so to save his saints. Jesus is saying the same thing, When you shall see this judgment look up and see your redemption...)

All of these things are also what the Church would have been teaching in Jerusalem for 37 years leading up to this event. That is why mockers were saying the day will never come. That is also why the early Church was so hated by the Jews as they were literally telling them of this impending destruction.

Having declared all these things, Jesus is about to give a parable that doubles down on the fact that all of these things were going to happen in the near future (within a generation) including him coming in the clouds with great glory declaring to the world and specifically the Jews, "I am the Christ." This is another section that is twisted by False-hope:

Matthew 24:32-35: Now learn a parable of the fig tree; When his branch is yet tender, and putteth forth leaves, ye know that summer *is* nigh: 33. So likewise ye, when ye shall see all these things, know that it is near, *even* at the doors. 34. Verily I say unto you, <u>This generation shall not pass, till all these things be fulfilled.</u> 35. Heaven and earth shall pass away, but my words shall not pass away.

The fig tree is a reference to Israel, this is something that nearly all bible teachers will agree to, and so would I. The modern teachers will say something very odd when it comes to this passage, however. They will take this parable and say, "Jesus actually isn't speaking about these events happening to the generation then living, but he is speaking of a future generation. The generation that will see Israel become a nation again is actually the generation that will not pass away until all the above things will happen."

Meaning, that they send this whole text into the future and link it to the future reign of the antichrist that will appear in the world after Israel becomes a nation again. So everything that seemed to be talking about the Destruction of Jerusalem in 70 A.D. was really about the reign of the Antichrist in their twisted view.

There is not a single reason to think this at all. Not only is there no scriptural verse to tell them to do this, but by doing this we rip this entire text out of context. Jesus is still answering the question asked by his disciples Peter, James, John, and Andrew. Jesus is using the parable of the fig tree to reaffirm everything he had just mentioned. Stating in essence, "When you see these things begin to happen think of it as the fig tree putting forth its leaves telling you that the summer is upon you. Likewise when these things begin to happen to Jerusalem know that the judgment is near at hand."

He even very clearly states in verse 34 that the generation then living, "<u>this</u> generation" the very one he is now speaking to, would not pass away until all these things (judgments) happened. This is the same thing he has said time and again when speaking about the imminent destruction of the temple in other passages. Again it all happened in 40 years of him saying this! Either Jesus is lying and this is all in the future or he was telling the truth and this all happened in 70 A.D. Jesus is God so he cannot lie, but by saying this all will happen in the future we are calling Jesus a liar or in the very least grossly twisting his words.

There are two other parables of the fig to be considered that will reaffirm this idea. We should look at these as this parable would call the others back to the minds of his disciples, as they all taught the same thing. Jesus used an actual fig tree to represent the fruitlessness of the Jewish religion. This is told in Matthew 21:19, and Mark 11:14.

Matthew 21:19: And when he (Jesus) saw a fig tree in the way, he came to it, and found nothing thereon, but leaves only, and said unto it, <u>Let no fruit grow on thee henceforward for ever.</u> And presently the fig tree withered away.

Mark lets us know when Jesus did this as right after he:

Mark 11:15: And they come to Jerusalem: and Jesus went into the temple, and began to cast out them that sold and bought in the temple, and overthrew the tables of the moneychangers, and the seats of them that sold doves;

This continues through verses 15-19. The fig tree cursed and the overthrowing of the sin in the temple go hand in hand. This is important because Jesus also declared this right before he cleared the temple out:

Luke 19:42-44: 42. Saying (Jesus is speaking this to Jerusalem with tears), If thou hadst known, even thou, at least in this thy day, the things *which belong* unto thy peace! but now they are hid from thine eyes. 43. For the days shall come upon thee, that thine enemies shall <u>cast a trench about thee, and compass thee round, and keep thee in on every side,</u> (Rome did this in 70 A.D.) <u>44. And shall lay thee even with the ground, and thy children within thee; and they shall not leave in thee one stone upon another; because thou knewest not the time of thy visitation.</u>

So after saying this, Jesus cursed the fig tree and then overturned the moneychangers in the temple. In both passages once the disciples notice the fig tree had withered they asked him about it:

Mark 11:20-23: 20. And in the morning, as they passed by, they saw the fig tree dried up from the roots. 21. And Peter calling to remembrance saith unto him, Master, behold, the fig tree which thou cursedst is withered away. 22. And Jesus answering saith unto them, Have faith in God. 23. For verily I say unto you, That whosoever shall say unto this mountain, Be thou removed, and be thou cast into the sea; and shall not doubt in his heart, but shall believe that those things which he saith shall come to pass; he shall have whatsoever he saith.

Jesus now calls the fig tree a mountain. Again when we go back into the Old Testament nations, cities, and religions are often called mountains (a good example is Babylon in Jeremiah 51:25, but there are many other examples). The thing that is both a mountain and a fig tree would be the religious and political system of Jerusalem. Listen to how Matthew records this:

Matthew 21:21: Jesus answered and said unto them, Verily I say unto you, If ye have faith, and doubt not, ye shall not only do this *which is done* to the fig tree, but also if ye shall say unto this mountain, Be thou removed, and be thou cast into the sea; it shall be done.

Notice how Jesus said that they would, if they had faith do the very same thing to the fig tree that he did, and then he says this mountain shall likewise be removed and cast into the sea? The mountain must reference something that the disciples could actually see. I believe when Jesus said this he pointed at the fig tree and said, "ye will likewise do this," and then he motioned to the surrounding temple, buildings, and Jerusalem and said, "Likewise this mountain..."

The sea is not speaking about the literal ocean, most often in the bible, this is a prophetic reference to the gentile nations/world (see Isaiah 17:12, 60:5, Revelation 17:15-18 for some examples). We saw one example of this in the parable of the fish and the nets in chapter 3. Jesus is explaining that the apostles will help bring in the damnation of the religious and political harlot that Jerusalem had become if they had faith.

The casting it into the sea is a reference to its utter destruction at the hand of the gentiles. Luke said this very thing in Luke 21:24. They did this by preaching the gospel which both saved and condemned the world. All of this is exactly what Jesus is also dealing with in the Destruction of Jerusalem. This same event is also declared in Revelation 8:8-9.

Just as the fig tree would never bear fruit again so will the Jewish religious system will never bear the fruits of righteousness again because they have rejected the source of this righteousness, the gospel, and Christ himself.

The second fig tree parable is found in:

Luke 13:6-9: 6. He (Jesus) spake also this parable; A certain *man* had a fig tree planted in his vineyard (this is God the Father and the vineyard is a reference to the world. The fig tree is Israel); and he came and sought fruit thereon, and found none. 7. Then said he unto the dresser of his vineyard (Jesus), Behold, these three years (these are the main years of Christ's ministry) I come seeking fruit on this fig tree, and find none: cut it down; why cumbereth it the ground (He is asking why should he let it take up space that could be used for a fruitful tree)? 8. And he (Jesus) answering said unto him (his Father), Lord, let it alone this year also, till I shall dig about it, and dung *it*: 9. And if it bear fruit, *well*: and if not, *then* after that thou shalt cut it down.

This speaks about the judgment that was withheld for a time against the fig tree (Israel) the dressers in this was Christ the last year of his ministry ended in death sealing the judgment. The judgment was halted while the gospel was preached to see if any fruit would come. Remember John the Baptist warned of this very same judgment:

Matthew 3:7-10: But when he (John the Baptist) saw many of the Pharisees and Sadducees come to his baptism, he said unto them, O generation of vipers, who hath warned you to flee from the wrath to come? 8. Bring forth therefore fruits meet for repentance: 9. And think not to say within yourselves, We have Abraham to *our* father: for I say unto you, that God is able of these stones to raise up children unto Abraham. 10. And now also the axe is laid unto the root of the trees: therefore every tree which bringeth not forth good fruit is hewn down, and cast into the fire.

After receiving and rejecting John the Baptist, Jesus, and his Church the judgment was unavoidable and the saints and martyrs cried out to

God to remove the mountain and fig tree and cast it into the seas. The Destruction of Jerusalem was this very thing happening. That is why Christ wept over the city:

Matthew 23:37-38: 37. O Jerusalem, Jerusalem, *thou* that killest the prophets, and stonest them which are sent unto thee, how often would I have gathered thy children together, even as a hen gathereth her chickens under *her* wings, and ye would not! 38. Behold, <u>your house is left unto you desolate.</u>

The above parables of the fig tree were preached long before the one in Matthew 24. This is important because the disciples would have known what this fig tree was all about. Jesus had already preached its end and showed a visible example of its death.

Because these things would happen while many of those that saw Jesus were still alive he goes on to say:

Matthew 24:36-41: But of that day (the day of judgment against Jerusalem) and hour knoweth no *man,* no, not the angels of heaven, but my Father only. 37. But as the days of Noe (the Greek name for Noah) *were,* so shall also the coming of the Son of man be. 38. For as in the days that were before the flood they were eating and drinking, marrying and giving in marriage, until the day that Noe entered into the ark,

39. And knew not until the flood came, and took them all away; so shall also the coming of the Son of man be. (Speaking in regards to how the flood of soldiers that would overrun the city as the flood of water overran the earth. In both events, the people were living their lives and were taken by surprise. Even though they were warned for all those years of impending judgment, when Rome finally showed up on the feast of Passover, it took the Jews by surprise.) 40. Then shall two be in the field; the one shall be taken, and the other left. 41. Two *women shall be* grinding at the mill; the one shall be taken, and the other left.

This is speaking not of the rapture as is so commonly taught, but of the fact that so many would be slaughtered and taken into slavery and that this would happen suddenly and quickly. The Roman soldiers came on the Passover when Jerusalem was filled to the brim with people. They slaughtered all in their path in the surrounding villages and one would be killed and one would be left as a testimony of the judgment to come. This was a practice Rome often used to terrorize their foes and quell future rebellions.

Even if you want to take this as a picture of the resurrection and harvest that we see shall happen at the end of the world, then we know the one taken is actually the unsaved and the one left behind is the saved according to what Jesus said in the parable of wheat and tares.

Matthew 24:42-51: Watch therefore: for ye know not what hour your Lord doth come. 43. But know this, that if the goodman of the house had known in what watch the thief would come, he would have watched, and would not have suffered his house to be broken up. 44. Therefore be ye also ready: for in such an hour as ye think not the Son of man cometh.

45. Who then is a faithful and wise servant, whom his lord hath made ruler over his household, to give them meat in due season? (This verse and the ones following echo the lessons of the parable of the talents) 46. Blessed *is* that servant, whom his lord when he cometh shall find so doing. 47. Verily I say unto you, That <u>he</u> (Jesus) <u>shall make him ruler over all his goods</u>. (This is exactly what Daniel 7 and the parable of the talents both taught as well. This proves that we were right in our interpretation of that parable and the passage in Daniel)

48. But and if that evil servant shall say in his heart, My lord delayeth his coming; 49. And shall begin to smite *his* fellowservants, and to eat and drink with the drunken; 50. The lord of that servant shall come in a day when he looketh not for *him,* and in an hour that he is not aware of, 51. And shall cut him asunder, and appoint *him* his portion with the hypocrites: there shall be weeping and gnashing of teeth.

This ends everything Jesus was telling Peter, James, John, and Andrew about the destruction to come. In context, everything was something that Jesus said they were all to look for and some would live to see. That is why Jesus also told many parables about the watchmen and told them to be looking for this day. This is also why many of the New Testament writings are filled with warnings and encouragements about this soon-coming Day of the Lord. This day should act as a warning and lesson to us in modern times if the Lord would judge Jerusalem when they forsook him, how much more will he judge us if we turn from him.

It is an astounding fact that everything that was said happened by 70 A.D. That is why the Destruction of Jerusalem was known as great proof that Jesus was indeed a prophet of God in times past. There is much in these verses that were immediately true for those going through this event as well as lessons to learn that can and still do apply to us today. There is so much more that could and perhaps should be said, but this chapter is already longer than I wanted it to be.

What can we learn about the Second Coming based on the Day of the Lord? Remember these two events will foreshadow one another:

- Christ will come in judgment.
- That from that day unto his final coming there will be a rise of false prophets and false Christs. Even unto this very day, some claim to be the son of god and lead cults of thousands after them. They have been in every generation. We should avoid them.
- There may be wars and rumors of wars among and in nations that will grow like birthing pains worse and worse until Christ vanquishes and purifies them. This is true because he rules with a rod of iron. The Judgment against Jerusalem was a warning to all nations that the king has sat in rule over the nations and will judge once that nation's sins have reached their fullness.
- There may be natural disasters on the earth warning of the coming judgment. In general, often natural disasters are judgments by God. We should pay attention to them, as many days of the Lord that are yet to come against nations and peoples as Christ rules this earth with a rod of iron.
- There may be wonders in the heavens that will be signs of these judgments.
- That many of these false prophets will claim to be able to do miracles to deceive many. We see a great rise in this in our culture today with the "faith healers" and prosperity preachers, as well as the new age movements. These are a mockery of the Spirit. We have been given a more sure word of Faith than to be drawn away by such tricks.

- Christians shall be persecuted for Christ's sake. Again this is something Jesus always told his people would happen, that in this life we shall have tribulation. Thank God though for the promise that the Great Tribulation will never happen again. This goes against the heart of the False-hope preachers who say the Great Tribulation is in the future!
- The Gospel will go to the four corners of the earth and gather in all the elect. This is an ongoing metaphor of how the earth becomes the kingdom at the time of the harvest.
- His coming shall be sudden and unexpected upon those that are not looking for him.

CHAPTER ELEVEN

What is the Kingdom (Part 1)

"There are a dozen views about everything until you know the answer. Then there's never more than one. You never know how much you really believe anything until its truth or falsehood becomes a matter of life and death to you."

C.S. LEWIS, 1898-1963, BRITISH THEOLOGIAN AND WRITER

T o properly understand what the kingdom is, I must first try and show what it is not. Today most are taught that the kingdom mentioned in the New Testament is primarily referring to the 1,000-year Kingdom that Christ will establish on earth when he returns. They may say the kingdom is now only in part and is spiritual but it won't be in full until Christ establishes it at his bodily return. Other Christians think it is a reference to the Church.

For those ensnared by False-hope, they believe that during this 1,000-year kingdom Christ will be fulfilling the promises made to national Israel that he never did previously. They also say Christ will physically rule from Jerusalem. This is why modern-day Israel is so important to them as they see it as a major sign that Christ is beginning to fulfill his promises to Israel, and will soon come to take away his bride, the Church, in the rapture.

When Israel became a nation again they thought it was the sign of the fig tree mentioned in Matthew 24 starting to bloom, as in the Old Testament Israel was called a fig tree. They thought it signaled that the time of the Gentiles had come to, or was coming to, an end and God was getting ready to take his Church away so he could return to Israel. In their minds, that meant that within a generation of Israel becoming a nation again God should take the Church away in the rapture.

False-hope will often turn to this passage or others like it in the bible to determine what a generation is:

Psalms 90:10: The days of our years *are* threescore years and ten (70 years); and if by reason of strength *they be* fourscore years (80 years), yet *is* their strength labour and sorrow; for it is soon cut off, and we fly away.

These periods mark what a generation is, the flying away portion is the rapture according to him. False-hope will often say that because Jesus said in Matthew 24:34: Verily I say unto you, This generation shall not pass, till all these things be fulfilled. That the generation that sees Israel restored as a nation will not pass away until the rapture happens.

This whole thinking has led to quite literally hundreds of false prophets predicting when the rapture would come. They often gather large followers around them and say definitively it will happen on such and such a date. Of course, the date rolls around and nothing ever happens. This leads to the faith of many being shaken or destroyed, and God and Christianity being mocked. If you recall from the beginning of this book, Peter said that this was the very purpose of all false teachers.

They are lucky that we do not live under the Levitical Law anymore:

Deuteronomy 18:20-22: 20. But the prophet, which shall presume to speak a word in my name, which I have not commanded him to speak, or that shall speak in the name of other gods, even that prophet shall die.

21. And if thou say in thine heart, How shall we know the word which the LORD hath not spoken? (In other words, how will we know if a prophet speaks on God's behalf?) 22. When a prophet speaketh in the name of the LORD, if the thing follow not, nor come to pass, that *is* the thing which the LORD hath not spoken, *but* the prophet hath spoken it presumptuously: thou shalt not be afraid of him. (Meaning you will know a false prophet when he or she prophesies in God's name and it doesn't come to pass. If this happens they were commanded to kill them vs. 20)

Amazingly some of these so-called modern rapture prophets have managed to do this countless times and still retain a following. Of course, the rapture has not come, and many that believed this have gone from this world leaving a generation questioning their faith. The 80-year mark is fast approaching. I have recently, as of the writing of this book, have heard pastors now desperately trying to add time to their rapture theology and reach for how Jesus said it will be like in the days of Noah and they will pull this verse out:

Genesis 6:3: And the LORD said, My spirit shall not always strive with man, for that he also *is* flesh: yet his days shall be an hundred and twenty years.

So they are now starting to say that a generation can be as long as 120 years. They still say that Jesus can come at any moment and it will either be right before the tribulation starts or right after. Regardless, they say it must happen within the generation of Israel becoming a nation because Israel is God's prophetic timepiece/clock.

If you have grasped anything we have looked at in this book so far, you will already immediately begin to see some red flags in all of this, as the scales of False-hope are starting to fall from your spiritual eyes.

The first issue is that the passage in Matthew 24 about the fig tree was speaking about the Destruction of Jerusalem and not the Lord's Second Coming as we proved in the last chapter. Next, we know that, based on everything we were told by Jesus, Paul, and the Apostles that there is no way a rapture can exist the way they teach it, and there cannot be any physical kingdom after Christ returns. I would encourage everyone to go back to the end of Chapter 9 and review all the points we have learned.

To help us understand all this better, I am going to unravel a few lies that most people have been taught all of their lives in modern churches, me included. In this chapter, I am going to address the promises made to Israel and show from the bible how all of the promises have already been fulfilled. Then I want to address the fact that according to God's own decree Jesus can never rule from a physical throne in Israel ever, as he is not qualified by the Father's own decree.

To finish this chapter, I will show how God divorced national Israel and replaced it with the true Israel that is made up of both believing Jews and Gentiles in Christ. The Destruction of Jerusalem and the Revelation (both speaking of the same thing) in reality was God's divorcement of Israel. We have already seen some of this in earlier sections of this book, but I feel as if we need clarity on all of these issues to correctly understand what the kingdom of God is.

So what are the four promises made to Abraham concerning Israel?

Promise 1: God promised he will make a great nation out of his descendants.

God promised in: Genesis 12:1-2: Now the LORD had said unto Abram, Get thee out of thy country, and from thy kindred, and from thy father's house, unto a land that I will shew thee: 2. And I will make of thee a great nation, and I will bless thee, and make thy name great; and thou shalt be a blessing:

Abraham was told when this would happen: Genesis 15:13-14: And he said unto Abram, Know of a surety that thy seed shall be a stranger in a land that is not theirs, and shall serve them; and they shall afflict them four hundred years; 14. And also that nation, whom they shall serve, will I judge: and afterward shall they come out with great substance.

Even if you have never read the account, most people have seen a movie based on the Exodus and this description should remind you of this right away. This nation did indeed come out of Egypt and it was made up of a great mixed multitude of people (Exodus 12:38) and not just the Hebrews. We see Moses tell of all the great favor that God gave this nation:

Deuteronomy 2:25: This day will I begin to put the dread of thee and the fear of thee upon the nations that are under the whole heaven, who shall hear report of thee, and shall tremble, and be in anguish because of thee.

Later Moses tells us how God also fulfilled his original promise during the time of Moses:

Deuteronomy 4:6-7 Keep therefore and do them (speaking about the Law); for this *is* your wisdom and your understanding in the <u>sight of the nations</u> (The original purpose of Israel was to be a testament to the truth to the heathen nations a small scale picture of the Church), which shall hear all these statutes, and say, <u>Surely this great nation</u> *is* a wise and understanding people. 7. For <u>what nation *is there so* great</u>, who *hath* God *so* nigh unto them, as the LORD our God *is* in all *things that* we call upon him *for?*

Not only does Moses affirm that God did indeed make them into a great nation but King David will bear witness of this as well in:

1 Chronicles 17:21: And what one nation in the earth *is* like thy people Israel, whom God went to redeem *to be* his own people, to make thee a name of greatness and terribleness, by driving out nations from before thy people, whom thou hast redeemed out of Egypt?

These are not the only verses that claim this, but clearly, this promise was fulfilled.

Promise 2: God promised that Abraham will have a great legacy.

This next promise God promised to Abraham on three different occasions in three different ways, let's look at all three times this was promised:

Genesis 13:16: And I will make thy seed as the dust of the earth: so that if a man can number the <u>dust of the earth</u>, *then* shall thy seed also be numbered.

Genesis 15:5: And he brought him forth abroad, and said, Look now toward heaven, and tell the <u>stars, if thou be able to number</u> them: and he said unto him, So shall thy seed be.

Genesis 22:17: That in blessing I will bless thee, and in multiplying I will multiply thy seed as the stars of the heaven, and <u>as the sand which *is* upon the sea shore</u>; and thy seed shall possess the gate of his enemies;

Each one of these verses gave a very specific reference to how many of Abraham's decedents there will be. What's amazing is God declared in three different passages how each of these was fulfilled in the exact manner he promised to Abraham:

Deuteronomy 1:10: The LORD your God hath multiplied you, and, behold, ye *are* this day as the stars of heaven for multitude.

1 Kings 4:20: Judah and Israel *were* many, as the sand which *is* by the sea in multitude, eating and drinking, and making merry.

2 Chronicles 1:9: Now, O LORD God, let thy promise unto David my father be established: for thou hast made me king over a people like the dust of the earth in multitude.

Clearly, God met each one of those promises. Just for good measure, the writers of Hebrews says:

Hebrews 11:12: Therefore sprang there even of one, and him as good as dead (Speaking of Abraham and how he had a son when he was over 100 years old and his wife Sarah in her 90s), *so many* as the stars of the sky in multitude, and as the sand which is by the sea shore innumerable.

Promise 3: Abraham's descendants will own all the land of Canaan.

Just as before God promised this next promise a few times lets look at them:

Genesis 12:7: And the LORD appeared unto Abram, and said, Unto thy seed will I give this land: and there builded he an altar unto the LORD, who appeared unto him.

Genesis 13:14-15: And the LORD said unto Abram, after that Lot was separated from him, Lift up now thine eyes, and look from the place where thou art northward, and southward, and eastward, and westward:

15. For all the land which thou seest, to thee will I give it, and to thy seed for ever.

Genesis 17:8: And I will give unto thee, and to thy seed after thee, the land wherein thou art a stranger, all the land of Canaan, for an everlasting possession; and I will be their God.

Most people will notice that God says this land will be eternally theirs, and they use this to justify the actions of the Zionist state. Here is the issue with that:

Deuteronomy 30:15-18: See, I have set before thee this day life and good, and death and evil;

16. In that I command thee this day to love the LORD thy God, to walk in his ways, and to keep his commandments and his statutes and his judgments, that thou mayest live and multiply: and the LORD thy God shall bless thee in the land whither thou goest to possess it.

17. But if thine heart turn away, so that thou wilt not hear, but shalt be drawn away, and worship other gods, and serve them;

18. I denounce unto you this day, that ye shall surely perish, *and that* ye shall not prolong *your* days upon the land, whither thou passest over Jordan to go to possess it.

This is not the only place God says this, but the land was given to them, but when they rebelled the land would be taken from them. This happened quite often in small instances as God would give their territory over to an enemy for a time. As their rebellion grew, God eventually wiped them out three different times. Once with the northern kingdom of Israel by the Assyrians, and later the southern kingdom with the Babylonians, and lastly by the Romans.

Each time God promised to restore them to the land if they would repent. He also restored them to the land to see the Messiah which most modern preachers do not teach about. Often they actually use prophetic scriptures talking about restoration after Babylon to witness the messiah to help prove a future restoration, which they, in turn, claim the modern state of Israel is a fulfillment. I happen to believe in a great revival among the Jews in the future, but I believe it will happen when they come into the Church.

So far the Jews in modern-day Palestine that call themselves Israel have not come back to God, therefore the "gathering" of the Jews back into the land isn't a true restoration of Israel, but a man-made one. In my opinion, this is the main reason why they have been denied from the whole of the old Israel, the land that they so desperately covet. I do not think the Jews will ever own the entire land again unless they repent and turn to Christ on a national scale.

Only a small remnant of Jews, mostly Zionists, have returned to modern Israel. We do not see all the tribes coming from all the lands back to Israel as all prophecies concerning a return of the Jews to Israel are speaking of. Many orthodox Jews today reject the Zionistic movement in Israel and want no part of it. They believe that the Messiah will be the one to restore them to their lands, they of course do not think he has come yet. I believe they are correct and once they recognize him, I believe God will restore them. Together these points show that without a doubt modern Israel is not a fulfillment of the promise of God concerning the land and the physical descendants of Abraham, rather it is a repeat of something Daniel said:

Daniel 11:14: And in those times there shall many stand up against the king of the south: also <u>the robbers of thy people shall exalt themselves to establish the vision; but they shall fall.</u>

This vision specifically has already been fulfilled around the time of Christ and was a reference to those who were trying to force their own view of prophecy. This was manifested by the rise of many false prophets and messiahs. Even so, the principle it teaches still applies today.

Christians are just as guilty of trying to force prophecy for their own gain, and this promise of their fall is as sure today as it was when Daniel spoke this. God is almighty and sovereign, and so I do not think the nation that calls itself Israel today would exist unless God allowed it to. Perhaps he allows it for an opportunity for the Jews to turn to him once more, or perhaps it has some other purpose that I could only guess at. Despite this, it is wrong for Christians to call it a fulfillment of prophecy and worship antichrist as they do. If they truly want to help Israel return to the land, then they need to preach the gospel to them.

Regardless, False-hope pastors will say that God must restore the whole of the land to them because God never actually gave them the whole land, and so in order for God to fulfill his promise, it must yet be a future thing. Let me show you how this too is a lie either one of ignorance or on purpose for their own goals:

Joshua 21:43-45: And the LORD gave <u>unto Israel all the land which he sware to give unto their fathers; and they possessed it, and dwelt therein.</u> (He did this back with Joshua!)

44. And the LORD gave them rest round about, according to all that he sware unto their fathers: and there stood not a man of all their enemies before them; the LORD delivered all their enemies into their hand.

45. There failed not ought of any good thing which the LORD had spoken unto the house of Israel; all came to pass.

This fulfillment is also declared by Solomon in:

1 Kings 4:21: And Solomon reigned over all kingdoms from the river unto the land of the Philistines, and unto the border of Egypt: they brought presents, and served Solomon all the days of his life.

1 Kings 4:24: For he had dominion over all *the region* on this side the river, from Tiphsah (This is on the river Euphrates) even to Azzah, over all the kings on this side the river: and he had peace on all sides round about him.

Solomon ruled over all the land from the Euphrates River all the way through the entire lands of Jordan and all of Canaan down into Egypt just like God had promised. They did not keep the land for long because of their sin, but God kept all of his promises concerning the land. This means that God does not have to restore Israel to the Jews to keep the promise made to Abraham. This doesn't mean it won't ever happen, but if it does it will be an act of God in response to the Jewish people turning back to him and joining the New Covenant Israel which is made up of Jews and Gentiles in the Church.

Some people will say that God is drawing them back to save them. If this is so, I would not call it a fulfillment until they cast down their symbol of rebellion. If the modern state ever did this, and then turned to Christ, then I would say that God is drawing the Jews back into their land. Let me explain the symbol of their rebellion:

Act 7:43: Yea, ye took up the tabernacle of Moloch, and the star of your god Remphan, figures which ye made to worship them: and I will carry you away beyond Babylon.

Remphan is another name for Molech, who is the same as Baal. The nation of Israel took up the star of their god when they rebelled against the God of Abraham. The only time Israel had the symbol of the star is when they rebelled against God. This star is called the Star of David today, but David never had such a star in the bible. As in the time of Acts, Israel still holds up the star of their rebellion declaring to the world that they do not follow the God of Abraham. Jesus is the God of Abraham. When they reject Christ they reject the Father they are one.

If the modern state of Israel is going to play some sort of role in the restoration of the Jews then the sign we should look for that this is beginning to happen is when they throw down the star of rebellion and come to Christ. However, I state again I do not think the modern state has anything to do with the fulfillment of prophecy.

These same False-hope preachers will also say that the bible promises that God will restore them during the 1,000-year reign of the Messiah, and then be their king. They say that God will rule from Jerusalem and the Law will go out from there to all nations. I do not have enough room in this small book to expose all the errors of this, but I would like to look at one such passage that most will turn to and say this teaches their views:

Isaiah 2:2-4: And it shall come to pass in the <u>last days,</u> *that* the mountain of the LORD'S house shall be established in the top of the mountains, and shall be exalted above the hills; and all nations shall flow unto it. 3. And many people shall go and say, Come ye, and let us go up to the mountain of the LORD, to the house of the God of Jacob; and he will teach us of his ways, and we will walk in his paths: for out of Zion shall go forth the law, and the word of the LORD from Jerusalem. 4. And he shall judge among the nations, and shall rebuke many people: and they shall beat their swords into plowshares, and their spears into pruninghooks: nation shall not lift up sword against nation, neither shall they learn war any more.

This is one of the major passages they will turn to and point to this prophecy and say this is when God reign's on earth and this will happen during the 1,000-year kingdom. In their minds, this prophecy did not happen yet. However, this is not what this prophecy is speaking about. Listen to Jesus :

Luke 24:44: And he said unto them, These *are* the words which I spake unto you, while I was yet with you, <u>that all things must be fulfilled, which were written in the law of Moses, and *in* the prophets, and *in* the psalms, concerning me.</u>

Did Jesus mean he came to fulfill all things? Meaning that he came to accomplish all the prophecies described in the Old Testament about the Messiah. Well, that is what he just said so why would I doubt what he claimed?

I ask this because False-hope seems to think that most things were not fulfilled and will be fulfilled in the future. Seems to me that this is exactly the opposite of what Jesus was saying. In truth, everything that Isaiah and all the prophets spoke about was already fulfilled or is an ongoing fulfillment. Those that are ongoing are all related to the prophecies of the reign of the Messiah, and what it will accomplish. This will take place from the time of his resurrection to his Second Coming.

Isaiah's prophecy is one of many that was and is continuing to be fulfilled. We have already seen that according to 1st John we are living in the last days. These last days take place from the time Jesus received the kingdom and will end when he comes back. So this prophecy has to happen before Jesus returns. Read verse 2 again and see that this must be true.

The writer of Hebrews compares the Old Covenant to Mt. Sinai in Hebrews 12:18-19 in the same passage the writer also compares the heavenly Mt. Zion to the New Covenant. Paul says something very similar in Galatians 4:22-26. Therefore the mountain that the lord's house is built on is the heavenly Mt. Zion. The house of the Lord which is also called his temple is in believers which make up his church (Hebrews 3:6, John 2:19-21, Colossians 1:18, 1 Corinthians 6:16,19, and 2 Corinthians 6:14-18, and many others). Mountains are also symbolic of nations/kingdoms (Jeremiah 51:25, Pslams 2, Daniel 9:16, etc). The kingdom of the lord's house will be established in the last days and be greater than all other houses/kingdoms.

So this portion of the scripture is fulfilled when Christ received the kingdom over all nations (Daniel 7:13-14, Revelation 5). He delivered and established this Kingdom in his church upon the heavenly Mt. Zion. The fullness of this will be manifested more and more as the kingdom of Christ fills the earth and the gospel has more and more preeminence. The bible says he will establish it, which means build it. Daniel describes this same thin in:

Daniel 2:44-45: And in the days of these kings (context the kings of world empire) shall the God of heaven set up a kingdom, which shall never be destroyed: and the kingdom shall not be left to other people, *but* it shall break in pieces and consume all these kingdoms, and it shall stand for ever.

45. Forasmuch as thou sawest that the stone was cut out of the mountain without hands, and that it brake in pieces the iron, the brass, the clay, the silver, and the gold; the great God hath made known to the king what shall come to pass hereafter: and the dream *is* certain, and the interpretation thereof sure.

Now lets back up in this text and see what verse 45 is speaking about and we will see the same mountain as Isaiah is prophesying about:

Daniel 2:35 Then was the iron, the clay, the brass, the silver, and the gold (materials symbolizing the four world empires Babylon, Medeo-Persian, Greece, and Rome), broken to pieces together, and became like the chaff of the summer threshingfloors (Chaff blows away in the wind as if it were nothing); and the wind carried them away, that no place was found for them: and the <u>stone that smote the image became a great mountain, and filled the whole earth</u>.

So Isaiah, like Daniel is saying that in the last days the New Covenant will be established on which his house (temple) shall be built, and all nations shall flow to it. Nations in the bible are always a reference to gentiles. This too is fulfilled in the New Testament Church. Daniel tells us this spiritual mountain will fill the whole earth.

Verse 3 of Isaiah's prophecy is talking about Jesus' ministry while on earth. He often spoke in the temple, atop the physical Mt. Zion. People came and brought many to hear and see him. (John 8:2, Mark 6:54-56, Luke 10:1, John 12:17-21, Luke 22:53, and many others). This ministry was then passed on and fulfilled by the apostles and the Church and is still being fulfilled to this very day. (Matthew 28:18-20, Acts 1). Jesus is also our high priest and left us his word to guide and teach us in the heavenly Mt. Zion the seat of which is in the Church.

Verse 4 of this prophecy speaks about how the born-again life teaches us to love our enemies and pray for those that persecute us. It also speaks of the fact that because we are brothers we no longer have enmity between nations and peoples within the Church. For there is neither male nor female, bond or free, Jew or gentile, we are all one in Christ. The swords that we used to kill each other with are now used to harvest more souls for the kingdom of God. Moreover, it is the picture of God destroying the division between Jews and Gentiles in the New Covenant (Ephesians 2:11-19).

Lastly, I believe this will be literally fulfilled when the earth will no longer learn war anymore. This is a result of the gospel being fully manifested on the earth and united in Christ. Many might scoff and say that I am being unrealistic and that this earth will never be that way, but the Revelation speaks of an event near the end of the messiah's reign that will do this very thing, and so does many prophecies in the Old Testament that refers to the victorious reign of the Messiah. We will dive into that more in chapter 15.

This same breakdown can be done with most of the passages that False-hope tries to say will happen during the physical 1,000-year kingdom of Christ after he bodily returns.

As for God bringing his people back into the land to see Messiah, this happened clearly in the scriptures as great multitudes of Jews came from all over the Roman world, and Jesus also went into many of the lands that they were scattered in. Its fullness however is recorded in Acts:

Act 2:1-12: And when the day of Pentecost was fully come, they were all with one accord in one place. 2. And suddenly there came a sound from heaven as of a rushing mighty wind, and it filled all the house where they were sitting. 3. And there appeared unto them cloven tongues like as of fire, and it sat upon each of them. 4. And they were all filled with the Holy Ghost, and began to speak with other tongues, as the Spirit gave them utterance.

5. And there were dwelling at Jerusalem <u>Jews, devout men, out of every nation under heaven.</u> (Clearly showing a fulfillment of God gathering a remnant of his people to witness the New Covenant. This is a gathering of the dispersed from all nations they were sent into.) 6. Now when this was noised abroad, the multitude came together, and

were confounded, because that every man heard them speak in his own language. 7. And they were all amazed and marvelled, saying one to another, Behold, are not all these which speak Galilaeans?

8. And how hear we every man in our own tongue, wherein we were born? (This shows that the gift of tongues is not vain babbling as some churches teach, rather, people were preaching and everyone understood the preacher as if they were speaking their native tongue. It was a reverse of what happened at the tower of Babel. The following verse name all the various languages of this miracle) 9. Parthians, and Medes, and Elamites, and the dwellers in Mesopotamia, and in Judaea, and Cappadocia, in Pontus, and Asia, 10. Phrygia, and Pamphylia, in Egypt, and in the parts of Libya about Cyrene, and strangers of Rome, Jews and proselytes, 11. Cretes and Arabians, we do hear them speak in our tongues the wonderful works of God.

Once again we see that God has been faithful with all his promises to Israel.

Promise 4: That a messiah will be given and bless all nations/gentiles.

This last promise was promised to Abraham, Isaac, and Jacob. Later it was given to King David. For sake of length let us look at the first promise of this to Abraham.

Genesis 22:18: And in thy seed shall all the nations of the earth be blessed; because thou hast obeyed my voice.

False-hope will say this is speaking about national Israel again. This is also what modern Jews say this passage is referring to. This is why they focus on the need for us to bless Israel. What does the bible say this is referring to:

Galatians 3:16: Now to Abraham and his seed were the promises made. He saith not, And to seeds, as of many; but as of one, And to thy seed, which is Christ.

Romans 9:6-7 Not as though the word of God hath taken none effect. For they are not all Israel, which are of Israel: 7. Neither, because they are the seed of Abraham (Physical descendants), *are they* all children: but, In Isaac shall thy seed be called.

Galatians 3:26-28: <u>For ye are all the children of God by faith in Christ Jesus.</u> 27. For as many of you as have been baptized into Christ have put on Christ. 28. There is neither Jew nor Greek, there is neither bond nor free, there is neither male nor female: for ye are all one in Christ Jesus.

Meaning if you really want to bless Israel then you should be blessing the Church who is Israel. If we are in Christ we are the true Israel of God, we are his temple and his body. I feel like a broken record, but it must be reiterated again. Race, nationality, and social background have nothing to do with you being a child of God, only your faith. The Church is the fulfillment of the promise to Abraham, Isaac, and Jacob that all nations shall be blessed as all nations are now allowed to come and be saved and be a part of the children of God again. The fulfillment of this promise is also an ongoing one as the Church continues to preach the gospel and win souls. Not only were the physical descendants made a great nation, now Christ is making a great nation of all peoples in him.

Hebrews 3:6: But Christ as a son over his own house; <u>whose house are we</u>, if we hold fast the confidence and the rejoicing of the hope firm unto the end.

Colossians 1:18: And he is the <u>head of the body, the church:</u> who is the beginning, the firstborn from the dead; that in all *things* he might have the preeminence.

1 Corinthians 6:19: What? know ye not that your <u>body is the temple of the Holy Ghost</u> *which is* in you, which ye have of God, and ye are not your own?

Pretty clear in my mind that God also fulfilled this promise exactly. God is faithful and he always keeps his promises. The very idea that God needs to restore a physical kingdom on earth in order to fulfill these promises is a lie.

Let us now look at the Throne of David. False-hope will also say that Christ has to return and make a literal physical kingdom to fulfill all the prophecies about Christ ruling on the throne of David. As we saw in an earlier chapter Christ did sit on David's throne and the Holy Spirit falling on the early disciples on Pentecost was the proof of this (Acts 3:14-47) To help clarify this point though, and see why this is so, I will ask the following question. What is the throne of David? It was never an earthly throne, rather it was the throne of God. How can this be?

Will, it surprise you to know that the very fact that Israel asked for a king was an act of apostasy that greatly displeased God? Would it also surprise you if I said that if Jesus had sat on a physical throne in Jerusalem he would have violated his father's will and therefore he couldn't be the Messiah? At first glance, these statements will seem almost blasphemous but let me show you what I mean.

Let's look at how the very act of wanting a king was an abomination to God:

1 Samuel 8:4-7: Then all the elders of Israel gathered themselves together, and came to Samuel unto Ramah, 5. And said unto him, Behold, thou art old, and thy sons walk not in thy ways: now make us a king to judge us like all the nations. 6. But the thing displeased Samuel, when they said, Give us a king to judge us. And Samuel prayed unto the LORD. 7. And the LORD said unto Samuel, Hearken unto the voice of the people in all that they say unto thee: for they have not rejected thee, but they have rejected me, that I should not reign over them.

Most people do not realize that when Israel was first established after the conquest of Joshua over the promised land, God ruled as their king from heaven, and set up judges to lead the people on earth. When Jesus came he came to restore the original plan of God for his people with God as King. God allowed Israel to have a king to show them how man will always be corrupt only God can be a truly righteous king. Because of this, the throne in Israel became a representation of God's throne. God even declares on multiple occasions that the throne in Israel was his throne. We will look at this more in a bit.

Israels' rejection of God as their king is the very same thing the Jews did when Jesus was on earth. They wanted a physical king that would overthrow their enemies, Christ offered them a king that would overthrow the enemy of their soul. They said, "we will not have Jesus rule over us as king." (John 19:14-15) And they said the same thing to God in ancient Israel. Listen to what else God says about this horrible sin:

1 Samuel 12:12-17: And when ye saw that Nahash the king of the children of Ammon came against you, ye said unto me, Nay; but a king shall reign over us: <u>when the LORD your God *was* your king.</u> 13. Now therefore behold the king whom ye have chosen, *and* whom ye have desired! and, behold, the LORD hath set a king over you. (Speaking of Saul) 14. If ye will fear the LORD, and serve him, and obey his voice, and not rebel against the commandment of the LORD, then shall both ye and also the king that reigneth over you continue following the LORD your God:

15. But if ye will not obey the voice of the LORD, but rebel against the commandment of the LORD, then shall the hand of the LORD be against you, as *it was* against your fathers. 16. Now therefore stand and see this great thing, which the LORD will do before your eyes. 17. *Is it* not wheat harvest to day? I will call unto the LORD, and he shall send thunder and rain; that ye may perceive and <u>see that your wickedness *is* great, which ye have done in the sight of the LORD, in asking you a king.</u> (As a punishment for their sin God caused a drought, to show that he was merciful and would still bless them under a king he gave them rain).

It should be clear that the very idea of an earthy king was a sin and God only did it because of the hardness of their heart. Moses also prophesied about this:

Deuteronomy 17:14-20: When thou art come unto the land which the LORD thy God giveth thee, and shalt possess it, and shalt dwell therein, and shalt say, I will set a king over me, like as all the nations that *are* about me (We just read in Samuel when this happened) 15. Thou shalt in any wise set *him* king over thee, whom the LORD thy God shall choose: *one* from among thy brethren shalt thou set king over thee: thou mayest not set a stranger over thee, which *is* not thy brother.

16. But he shall not multiply horses to himself, nor cause the people to return to Egypt, to the end that he should multiply horses: forasmuch as the LORD hath said unto you, Ye shall henceforth return no more that way. 17. <u>Neither shall he multiply wives to himself, that his heart turn not away:</u> neither shall he greatly multiply to himself silver and gold. 18. And it shall be, when he sitteth upon the throne of his kingdom,

that he shall write him a copy of this law in a book out of *that which is* before the priests the Levites:

19. And it shall be with him, and he shall read therein all the days of his life: that he may learn to fear the LORD his God, to keep all the words of this law and these statutes, to do them: 20. That his heart be not lifted up above his brethren, and that he turn not aside from the commandment, *to* the right hand, or *to* the left: to the end that he may prolong *his* days in his kingdom, he, and his children, in the midst of Israel.

If you have read the Old Testament you will notice all the things that Moses said that the king <u>should not</u> do, all the kings started to do. Right away they started taking multiple wives and their hearts were turned away. They also returned and had dealings with Egypt, Solomon even married the pharaoh's daughter. They did not write out a copy of the book of the law, nor kept it faithfully and they turned back to the gods of Egypt. Even David fell into all these errors when he finally became king he tried to move the ark of God on a cart because he didn't read the law that said that the Levites had to carry it and a man died for this sin (1 Chronicle 13). This is what Moses said a king *should* do, and none of them followed this faithfully. This resulted in great judgment coming against Israel and Judah.

God would have known this, and as the king's hearts turned from him, so did the people's hearts. No wonder it displeased God! God ultimately gave true Israel a proper king and that was his son who is King of kings and Lord of lords. Thank God that our King is righteous. He doesn't need to write out a copy of the law to know the will of God as he is the very WORD OF GOD MADE FLESH!

Despite all the above, this physical throne of the king of Israel, became a symbol for God's heavenly throne as we can see this in:

1 Chronicles 28:5: And of all my sons, (for the LORD hath given me many sons,) he hath chosen <u>Solomon my son to sit upon the throne of the kingdom of the LORD over Israel.</u>

1 Chronicles 29:23: Then Solomon <u>sat on the throne of the LORD</u> as king instead of David his father, and prospered; and all Israel obeyed him. 2 Chronicles 9:8: Blessed be the LORD thy God, which delighted in

thee to set thee on his throne, *to be* king for the LORD thy God: because thy God loved Israel, to establish them for ever, therefore made he thee king over them, to do judgment and justice.

2 Chronicles 13:8: And now ye think to withstand the kingdom of the LORD in the hand of the sons of David; and ye *be* a great multitude, and *there are* with you golden calves, which Jeroboam made you for gods.

This means that the throne of David was not a physical throne, rather the physical throne was symbolic of God's throne. Remember God was their king, now the king represented God's will for the people. Israel was always supposed to be a light to a heathen world about the truth of God. The kings became symbolic for God's throne on earth, when we understand this we begin to see the great travesty and horror that happened when the kings and Israel fell into sin. No wonder God so often judged them in the Old Testament. Let us look at an interesting prophecy to David about this throne:

1 Chronicles 17:11-14: And it shall come to pass, when thy days be expired that thou must go *to be* with thy fathers (Meaning when king David died), that I will raise up thy seed after thee, which shall be of thy sons; and I will establish his kingdom. 12. He shall build me an house, and I will stablish his throne for ever.

13. I will be his father, and he shall be my son: and I will not take my mercy away from him, as I took *it* from *him* that was before thee: 14. But I will settle him in mine house and in my kingdom for ever: and his throne shall be established for evermore.

Most people read this and think God is saying this about Solomon, as Solomon famously built the Temple of God. But Solomon's kingdom did not last forever. This prophecy has everything to do with Jesus, of whom Solomon and his temple were just a picture. Read it again and see Jesus is the only son of David who could do what is promised to David. Listen to this verse:

Acts 7:47-49: But Solomon built him an house. 48. Howbeit (How can this be, for) the most High dwelleth not in temples made with hands; as saith the prophet, 49. Heaven *is* my throne, and earth *is* my footstool: what house will ye build me? saith the Lord: or what *is* the place of my rest?

So where is God's house and Kingdom? In the 1 Chronicles 17 passage, we see that whoever this Son is will be set forever on the throne and in the house of God. Remember who Zachariah said this is:

Zechariah 6:12-13: And speak unto him, saying, Thus speaketh the LORD of hosts, saying, Behold the man whose name *is* The BRANCH (This is Jesus); and he shall grow up out of his place, and he shall build the temple of the LORD: 13. Even he shall build the temple of the LORD; and he shall bear the glory, and shall sit and rule upon his throne; and he shall be a priest upon his throne: and the counsel of peace shall be between them both.

So the son that will build the house for the Lord was not Solomon, though he did build a temple that was a picture of this house. The temple that Jesus built, as we have already seen, is in believers. We are the temple, and Jesus was the son of David who built it.

This physical throne of David was born in apostasy and God also took it away in anger and gave it to His Son.

Hosea 13:9-11: O Israel, thou hast destroyed thyself; but in me *is* thine help. 10. I will be thy king: where *is any other* that may save thee in all thy cities? and thy judges of whom thou saidst, Give me a king and princes? 11. I gave thee a king in mine anger, and took *him* away in my wrath. (Here is another clear verse of God's people feeling God's wrath)

God took away this physical throne but then he made a few promises about it:

Luke 1:32-33: He shall be great (Jesus), and shall be called the Son of the Highest: and the Lord God shall give unto him the throne of his father David: 33. And he shall reign over the house of Jacob for ever; and of his kingdom there shall be no end.

Amos 9:11-12 In that day will I raise up the tabernacle of David that is fallen, and close up the breaches thereof; and I will raise up his ruins, and I will build it as in the days of old: 12. That they may possess the remnant of Edom, and of all the heathen, which are called by my name, saith the LORD that doeth this.

Christ did receive this throne. This goes along with the judgment that God declared in Hosea that he would take away the throne and once again be their King. Jesus fulfills both this declaration as he is very God and the promise to David that his son shall sit on the throne forever, that throne being the throne of God. This throne is in heaven now, as it always was, and is one that Christ received from the Father:

Psalms 110:1-2: **A Psalm of David.** The LORD said unto my Lord, Sit thou at my right hand, until I make thine enemies thy footstool. 2. The LORD shall send the rod of thy strength out of Zion: rule thou in the midst of thine enemies.

We know that this throne is in heaven not on earth. It says he shall rule from Zion, this isn't speaking of the mountain in Jerusalem called Zion, but heaven and his rule is on the earth through his people. Jesus had to be high priest, king, and mediator and this was something he could not do here on earth as we will look at shortly. We also know that this rule lasts until all enemies are put under Christ's feet (1 Corinthian 15:25-28)

Isaiah 16:5: And in mercy shall the throne be <u>established</u> (Why would it need to be established if it already had been before Jesus was born? Remember most people make the throne about the kingdom of David which was already long-established, yet God is speaking of Christ's throne now being established. This shows that the kingdom that the throne represented hadn't been established before. This is speaking about the Kingdom that Christ came to establish.): and he (Jesus) shall sit upon it in truth in the <u>tabernacle of David</u> (the Bible often calls the body a tabernacle, meaning that this person that inhabits this throne will be a descendant of David), judging, and seeking judgment, and hasting righteousness. (Where did the bible say Jesus is sitting on this very throne? The above verses say in heaven! This further proves that the throne of David is a heavenly one, not a physical one.)

At the very beginning of this chapter, I made a bold claim that Christ could not sit on a physical throne. We see this clearly in Zechariah 6:12-13. Please read it again. Jesus must be a priest, king, and mediator at the same time or he is not the Messiah. On earth only the Levites could be priests:

Hebrews 8:4-6: For if he (Jesus) were on earth, <u>he should not be a priest</u>, seeing that there are priests that offer gifts according to the law: 5. Who serve unto the example and shadow of heavenly things, as Moses was admonished of God when he was about to make the tabernacle: for, See, saith he, *that* thou make all things according to the pattern shewed to thee in the mount. 6. <u>But now hath he </u>(Jesus)<u> obtained a more excellent ministry</u>, by how much also he is the mediator of a better covenant, which was established upon better promises. (Where? In Heaven)

Jesus is right now our high priest:

Hebrews 4:14-16: Seeing then that we <u>have a great high priest, that is passed into the heavens, Jesus the Son of God</u>, let us hold fast *our* profession. 15. For we have not an high priest which cannot be touched with the feeling of our infirmities; but was in all points tempted like as *we are, yet* without sin. 16. Let us therefore come boldly unto the throne of grace, that we may obtain mercy, and find grace to help in time of need.

Even if you somehow wanted to try and say that Jesus could be a priest on earth because he was God or some other way of explaining how Jesus could somehow get around this, the throne would still not be his by right on earth because God cursed it:

Jeremiah 22:28-30: *Is* this man Coniah (This is the short name of Jeconiah, in Greek his name is Jeconias, he was the last true king of Judah who was overthrown by Babylon) a despised broken idol? *is he* a vessel wherein *is* no pleasure? wherefore are they cast out, he and his seed, and are cast into a land which they know not?

29. O earth, earth, earth, hear the word of the LORD. 30. Thus saith the LORD, Write ye this man childless, a man *that* shall not prosper in his days: for <u>no man of his seed shall prosper, sitting upon the throne of David, and ruling any more in Judah.</u>

This curse was very specific that no man that descended physically from this man could rule from the throne of David in Judah which is where Jerusalem is. Look at the Genealogy of Jesus in:

Matthew 1:12: And after they were brought to Babylon, <u>Jechonias begat Salathiel; and Salathiel begat Zorobabel;</u>

Jesus was a descendant of Jechonias. I've heard pastors excuse this because they say this genealogy is tracing from Abraham down to Joseph who was only Jesus' stepfather. These same pastors claim this is how God planned to get around the curse for Jesus as he wasn't literally descended from this man. However, a lot of them fail to look at this passage in Luke which details Mary's genealogy:

Luke 3:27: Which was *the son* of Joanna, which was *the son* of Rhesa, which was *the son* of <u>Zorobabel, which was *the son* of Salathiel, which was *the son* of Neri,</u>

They ignore this passage because in Luke's account Luke says Salathiel is born from Neri and in Matthew's account it says Jechonias was Seletheil's father. Most people say this must be speaking about two different men who were named Seletheil who also had a son named Zorobabel. However, this isn't the case when we understand the principle of a Levitical marriage:

Deuteronomy 25:5-6: If brethren dwell together, and one of them die, and have no child, the wife of the dead shall not marry without unto a stranger: her husband's brother shall go in unto her, and take her to him to wife, and perform the duty of an husband's brother unto her. 6. And it shall be, *that* the firstborn which she beareth shall succeed in the <u>name of his brother *which is* dead, that his name be not put out of Israel.</u>

What we are seeing is Neri is being honored as the father of Seletheil because of this principle. Many great books have been written on this topic proving this concept far better than I am able to explain. Read this quote from Matthew Henry a renowned preacher and commentator who lived from 1662-1714. He gives a very simple explanation:

"The difference between the two evangelists in the genealogy of Christ has been a stumbling-block to infidels that cavil (meaning trying to raise trivial rejections, or objections) at the word, but such a one as has been removed by the labours of learned men, both in the early ages of the church and in latter times, to which we refer ourselves. Matthew draws the pedigree from Solomon, whose natural line ending in Jechonias, the legal right was transferred to Salathiel, who was of the house of Nathan, another son of David, which line Luke here pursues, and so leaves out all the kings of Judah." – From Matthew Henry's Commentary on the Bible, 1708.

The point I am making is that Jesus was the physical descendant of Jechoniah through his mother and by the right of adoption through his stepfather. The reality is that Marry and Joeseph were most likely first or second cousins which in our modern culture seems wrong, but in the ancient world was not uncommon nor was it against the law of Moses.

This means Jesus had no right to sit on a physical throne of David from Jerusalem, not now, not ever. This means that False-hope's teaching of Jesus needing to sit on a physical throne of David, from the physical Jerusalem is flawed in every way. Jesus is right now sitting on the throne of David which is in heaven, remember the earthly throne represented the one in heaven during the time of the kings.

Peter explains this beautifully in Acts 2:25-35. Peter understood that the throne of David was not here on earth but in heaven. He states boldly that when David was told about a son sitting on his throne, David understood that God was talking about the resurrection of Christ and the establishment of his heavenly rule upon the throne that was in heaven. Read the entire passage again slowly, out loud if you have to, and see the truth. If you thought that Jesus had to sit on an earthly throne you have been lied to. The apostles and prophets knew this throne was in heaven, only in heaven can Jesus fulfill all the prophecies about the Messiah being a priest, king, and mediator.

Lastly, the throne of judgment we see him sit on at his bodily return is never called the throne of David. It simply states that he will sit upon a throne of judgment. So this truth about the throne of David is still perfectly consistent with everything we have already learned up to this point, however, it is completely inconsistent with False-hope.

To end this chapter, I also want to show that God divorced the nation of Israel. This is what the Destruction of Jerusalem represented in full, and it is also what is meant by, "The kingdom shall be taken from you and given to another bearing the fruits thereof. (Matthew 21:43)" This means that God will never have national Israel become the nation that represents his people again. The only way that the nation will be the people of God again is to come into the Church which is the Israel of God in the New Covenant.

Jeremiah 3:8: And I saw, when for all the causes whereby backsliding Israel committed adultery I had put her away, and given her a bill of divorce; yet her treacherous sister Judah feared not, but went and played the harlot also.

Isaiah 50:1: Thus saith the LORD, Where *is* the bill of your mother's divorcement, whom I have put away? or which of my creditors *is it* to whom I have sold you? Behold, <u>for your iniquities have ye sold yourselves, and for your transgressions is your mother put away.</u>

In Isaiah's declaration, he is prophesying about the divorcement of Israel that was declared in Jeremiah. Jeremiah was written about 200 years after Isaiah. In Isaiah's passage, God is calling the Jewish Church, who in the Old Covenant, was the temple and their synagogues, and declaring them as their mother. This is similar to how the New Covenant Church, which is the New Jerusalem, is also called our mother in Galatians 4:26. The Church births us as sons of God through the union of Christ and the Church. This concept was true in the Old Testament as well, however, the Old Testament Church had become a harlot and the children born to her were often times corrupt. I know of no better way to explain this concept then to once again quote Pastor John Gill:

"[Where is the bill of your mother's divorcement, whom I have put away?] These words are directed to the Jews, who stood in the same relation to the Jewish church, or synagogue, as children to a mother; and so "your mother," "your congregation", or synagogue; who were rejected from being a church and people; had a "loammi" (Jewish name and term meaning "not my people." Gill is referring to what Hosea declared over the people in Hosea 1:9) written upon them, which became very <u>manifest when their city and temple were destroyed by the Romans; and this is signified by a divorce, alluding to the law of divorce among the Jews, Deuteronomy 24:1</u>, when a man put away his wife, he gave her a bill of divorce, assigning the causes of his putting her away. Now, the Lord, either as denying that he had put away their mother, the Jewish church, <u>she having departed from him herself,</u> and therefore challenges them to produce any such bill; a bill of divorce being always put into the woman's hands, and so capable of being produced by her; or if there was such an one, see <u>Jeremiah 3:8</u>, he requires it might be looked into, and seen whether the fault was his, or the cause in themselves, which latter would appear:

[or which of my creditors is it to whom I have sold you?] referring to a practice used, that when men were in debt, and could not pay their debts, they sold their children for the payment of them; see Exoduce 21:7, but this could not be the case here; the Lord has no creditors, not any to whom he is indebted, nor could any advantage possibly accrue to him by the sale of them; it is true they were sold to the Romans, or delivered into their hands, which, though a loss to them, was no gain to him; nor was it he that sold them, but they themselves; he was not the cause of it, but their own sins, as follows:

[behold, for your iniquities have ye sold yourselves;] or, "are sold;" they were sold for them, or delivered up into the hands of their enemies on account of them; they had sold themselves to work wickedness, and therefore it was but just that they should be sold, and become slaves:

[and for your transgressions is your mother put away]; and they her children along with her, out of their own land, and from being the church and people of God." --From John Gill's Commentary on the Bible, 1697-1771

To end this chapter with the greatest clarity I know how I would like to look at the promises of the new Covenant as most people do not read the whole thing.

Jeremiah 31:31-34: 31. Behold, the days come, saith the LORD, that I will make a new covenant with the house of Israel, and with the house of Judah: 32 Not according to the covenant that I made with their fathers in the day *that* I took them by the hand to bring them out of the land of Egypt; which my covenant they brake, although I was an husband unto them, saith the LORD: 33. But this *shall be* the covenant that I will make with the house of Israel; After those days, saith the LORD, I will put my law in their inward parts, and write it in their hearts; and will be their God, and they shall be my people.

34. And they shall teach no more every man his neighbour, and every man his brother, saying, Know the LORD: for they shall all know me, from the least of them unto the greatest of them, saith the LORD: for I will forgive their iniquity, and I will remember their sin no more.

All of this was accomplished in Christ. This is the New Covenant that we all recognize. However, there is a part of that covenant that very few ever read:

Jeremiah 31:36-40: If those ordinances depart from before me (these are the sacrifices, ceremonies, and offerings), saith the LORD, *then* the seed of Israel also shall cease from being a nation before me for ever. (We know this happened at Jesus' death, he forever abolished in his flesh the ordinances and the bondage of the law Ephesians 2:15, Hebrews 9:12. Also in a literal way Israel's sacrifices were halted after 70 A.D. Because of this. Israel will no longer be a nation as it was, meaning the only nation that is God's nation. Now all nations can become God's nation in Christ).

37. Thus saith the LORD; If heaven above can be measured, and the foundations of the earth searched out beneath, I will also cast off all the seed of Israel for all that they have done, saith the LORD. (He cast them out and replaced the citizens of Israel with all those of faith) 38. Behold, the days come, saith the LORD, that the city shall be built to the LORD from the tower of Hananeel unto the gate of the corner.

39. And the measuring line shall yet go forth over against it upon the hill Gareb, and shall compass about to Goath. (Verse 38 and 39 speak of the restoration of Israel after the Babylonian captivity) 40. And the whole valley of the dead bodies, and of the ashes, and all the fields unto the brook of Kidron, unto the corner of the horse gate toward the east, *shall be* holy unto the LORD; it (the valley and the city which God called holy) shall not be plucked up, nor thrown down any more for ever.

Verse 40 shows how the rebuilt Jerusalem at the time of Christ was larger than the city had been and all of it was considered holy not just the temple. If you recall from chapter 10 when I told you that the Jews saw not just the temple and city as holy but the whole land around it as well, this verse further proves that point.

The holiness of the area will never be cast down after this point because the destruction was an everlasting sign of a holy God's wrath. Since it had been destroyed (cast down) by God nothing that would be raised on the spot would represent the city as it was before he destroyed it. Meaning that even though there have been many cities built atop and destroyed since the destruction of 70 A.D. the Holy City will never be cast down again because it will never be the holy city again. In the New Covenant, the Holy City is the New Jerusalem a heavenly city.

Revelation 21:9-10: And there came unto me one of the seven angels which had the seven vials full of the seven last plagues, and talked with me, saying, Come hither, I will shew thee <u>the bride, the Lamb's wife</u>. (We know the bride of Christ is his Church and we are also told in a moment it is also the holy city of Jerusalem.) 10. And he carried me away in the spirit to a great and high mountain (This is the mountain of the new covenant that Isaiah and Daniel saw), and shewed me that <u>great city, the holy Jerusalem</u>, descending out of heaven from God, (This is prophetically speaking of God announcing the bride and giving her to the world, not some future mystical world state in the new heavens and earth that most people think these verses speak of. When we take all the other New Testament writings we know who the bride is and we know what the mountain and the holy city are.)

So in summary, part of this New Covenant was that the city would be rebuilt after it was destroyed by Babylon. The sacrifices would begin again in the temple. It is important to remember that even after the temple was destroyed by Babylon the sacrifices were still made by the Jews, therefore, they didn't end yet. The sacrifices had to return to the temple again so that Christ could take them away along with the ordinances of the old covenant (meaning the sacrifices and rituals) by fulfilling them (Matthew 5:17). This was all also prophecied in Daniel 9. Jeremiah says when this happened, Israel would cease being a nation, meaning the nation that physically represents the Kingdom. This speaks of the divorce of Israel, or the taking away of the kingdom from Israel and giving it to a new nation, all this was brought upon themselves by rejecting the offer of the kingdom by rejecting the king.

This is just another truth that proves that the modern state of Israel is not a fulfillment of bible prophecy.

CHAPTER TWELVE

What is the Kingdom (Part 2)

"The kingdom of heaven is like to a grain of mustard seed, which a man took, and sowed in his field: Which indeed is the least of all seeds: but when it is grown, it is the greatest among herbs, and becometh a tree, so that the birds of the air come and lodge in the branches thereof."

JESUS CHRIST, MATTHEW 13:31-32

As we saw in part one, the Kingdom is not the physical kingdom of Christ on earth, but there will be a kingdom of Christ on earth when he comes. As we saw taught in the parable of the wheat and tares the world in which the seed was sworn will be considered His kingdom when he returns. Yet, the Kingdom of God is not something you can point at and say here it is, yet it can impact the entire world around it. It is first spiritual and then physical. Heavenly and heaven manifest on earth. It is the glory, honor, and praise of God.

All of that is easy to say, but what exactly is the kingdom. If it is not physical how can the world become the kingdom at the time of the harvest?

Jesus spoke a lot about this kingdom. Most people today, like those during Jesus' ministry, try to link it to a physical organization that embodies the kingdom, ie the Church, or the supernatural power manifested in Christ, and both interpretations are incorrect. Both may be byproducts of the kingdom, but they are not the kingdom. I will address the most common error of thinking the kingdom is the Church, as I think it has the most far-reaching effects. The kingdom is not the Church, but the Church is in the kingdom.

When we elevate the Church to the kingdom, the kingdom becomes about a religious organization and not a spiritual nation holy unto the Lord under the kingship of Christ. Peter indeed calls the Church a holy nation, for it is, but I think the best understanding as it relates to the kingdom during the harvest would be this: As Jerusalem and the temple was the capital of Israel whose national land spanned Palastine, the Church is the temple and the New Jerusalem is the capital of the Kingdom whose land spans the world. That is why the Church is called Israel, the Temple, and the body, all of which are made up of all nations, tribes, and tongues in Christ.

Re-read the opening parable of Jesus at the top of this chapter. We see that Jesus says the kingdom starts small, like an insignificant mustard seed, but it ends up growing into a great tree. The birds are representative of the people of the earth. A similar picture was shown to King Nebuchadnezzar in Daniel 4:11-12. King Nebuchadnezzar was the first king of the world empire and his kingdom represented the kingdom of the world and which contrasts very well with Christ and his kingdom.

The world empires were conquered with human strength and ingenuity, Jesus conquered by death with a small number of mostly uneducated followers. The world empires started with strength and glory, but with each proceeding, the world empire grew dimmer in glory and ended in weakness and division. In contrast, Jesus went from a little over a hundred on Pentecost which exploded into millions worldwide today. It started out with little glory but will end more powerful and glorious than all world kingdoms combined. It has toppled governments, nations, kingdoms, and built empires and continues to grow and spread over the world even as I write. Meaning his kingdom started small and weak and will become greater than all others.

This is precisely what we have been learning about the reign of Christ with his saints. This kingdom will eventually consume all the kingdoms of the earth. The parable above likens this same idea to the nations roosting as birds in the great tree of the kingdom.

This also tells us that his kingdom is not stagnating or fruitless, it is always growing and it is always producing greater and greater fruit. As we saw in other passages in earlier chapters it will continue to grow to fill the entire earth.

Pair this concept with what Jesus said in Luke 17:20-21 about the kingdom being inside us and the proper understanding of the kingdom can come into focus. The Kingdom of Grace is what Christ most often spoke about when speaking of the kingdom. This kingdom is the manifestation of Salvation in the heart of a man by faith in the Gospel. This is what was taken from Israel. Let me explain.

From its foundation, Israel was given the promises and the prophets of God. All of these from the laws to the ceremonies, to the prophets themselves, pointed them towards the promise of the coming Messiah. This started all the way back in the garden in Genisis 3:15. Therefore salvation was not the Jews themselves but was given first to the Jews as stewards of the truth.

This is why Jesus said, "Salvation is of the Jews," John 4: 22. This was true because they alone of all the peoples/nations of the world were given the promises of salvation that were manifested in the Messiah. They safeguarded the scriptures and they should have been the most willing to receive the promised Messiah when he came.

All people from Adam till the last soul saved on earth were always saved by the same gospel always by faith and not by works. The Gospel was first preached to Adam and Eve in Genesis 3:15, and from that point on all their children that came to faith looked forward to the promised Christ as we look back.

This kingdom was attained by faith in the promises of God, specifically his promise of salvation in the coming Christ. The tragedy was that when the Messiah finally came they didn't want him. Because the Jews rejected this salvation, this Kingdom was taken from them and given to others who would produce the fruits of salvation. This is what the prophets prophesied when they say things like, Israel has been divorced, or the people of God are cast off.

The truth of the matter is that without faith it is impossible to please God. The Jews were and remained cast off because they do not believe, they have no faith in God despite their declarations. Let's look at a few scriptures that teach this:

Mark 1:15: And saying, The time is fulfilled, and the kingdom of God is at hand: repent ye, and believe the gospel.

Here we see the kingdom and the gospel go hand in hand. That is because the gospel produces the kingdom within the dead soul of man that grows up into Christ. This growth begins to produce the fruits of the spirit and results in the salvation and growth of others. The repentance was a turning away of both their sins and the dead religion of the Sadducees and Pharisees, the modern Judaism of that day.

Though this is the starting point of the kingdom it is not it's ending. Think of this as its seed. It starts on an individual level, then it grows to encompass families, villages, towns, cities, nations, and empires all starting back with the tiny seed of faith planted in a single soul. False-hope likes to keep everything on an individual level if he can. He likes to make the Church believe that the world belongs to Satan, but this is not so at all it belongs to Christ and his bride.

For the best understanding of this, we need to look at the end goal of the Kingdom and we need to see what national Israel was a picture of as Paul says:

Hebrews 10:1: For the <u>law having a shadow of good things to come</u>, *and* not the very image of the things, can never with those sacrifices which they offered year by year continually make the comers thereunto perfect.

Israel was fashioned from the patterns of things seen in heaven:

1 Corinthians 10:11: Now all these things happened unto them (referring to Old Testament Israel) for ensamples (An ensample is a living example of something): and they are written (Old Testament scriptures) for our admonition (warning/lesson), upon whom the ends of the world are come (referencing the soon-coming end of the Jewish System on the Day of the Lord).

Israel was not just all about sacrifices and rituals and there is a clear parallel between the new covenant people of God and the Old Covenant people:

1 Peter 2:9: But ye *are* a <u>chosen generation, a royal priesthood, an holy nation, a peculiar people;</u> that ye should <u>shew forth the praises of him who hath called you out of darkness into his marvellous light:</u>

We learn from Peter that God's covenant people are made up of:

Chosen people (often called the elect).

They are a royal priesthood. Meaning we can come before God without the need to go through a priest as our high priest is Christ.

Holy nation. If we are both Jews and Gentiles and spread all over the world how can we be a single nation? This shows as well that this nation is a spiritual one. We are all a part of the kingdom of God and through us, his word goes out to all nations and interacts with the world.

That we are a peculiar people (meaning strange or different to the point we stand apart).

They worship God because they are called out of darkness into his light.

If we take into account some other verses, we also know that believers are:

Baptized into Christ (Galatians 3:27)

Saved by Grace through faith in the gospel apart from works (Ephesians 2:8-10)

Are the sons of God (1 John 3:2)

Are children of Abraham by faith, meaning you are a Jew if you are in faith and a gentile, it doesn't matter who your parents were or their nationality. (Galatians 3:7)

Circumcised in the heart and not the flesh (Romans 2:25-29)

We are his temple (1 Corinthians 3:16-17)

We are a part of Christ's body (Colossians 1:18)

So why am I pointing out all these verses? Well look at what the New Testament said about the Church in the wilderness:

Act 7:38-39: This is he (Jesus), that was in the <u>church in the wilderness</u> with the angel which spake to him (Moses) in the mount Sina, and *with* our fathers: who received the lively oracles to give unto us:

39. To whom our fathers would not <u>obey, but thrust *him*</u> (Christ) <u>from them,</u> and in their hearts turned back again into Egypt,

Stephen under the inspiration of the Holy Spirit called the nation of Israel a Church because they were founded on Christ. When they rejected him they turned back to the land that they were brought out of.

If we take this as a shadow of what we are today, we would see that Egypt represented the world. The Church is taken out of the world into Christ (Colossians 1:13). Listen to what Moses said about Israel and see if it reminds you of what Peter said:

Exodus 19:3-6: And Moses went up unto God, and the LORD called unto him out of the mountain, saying, Thus shalt thou say to the house of Jacob, and tell the children of Israel;

4. Ye have seen what I did unto the Egyptians, and *how* I bare you on eagles' wings, and <u>brought you unto myself</u>. (Very similar language when we compare this to Jesus sending his angels to bring us unto him Matthew 24:31)

5. Now therefore, if ye will <u>obey my voice indeed, and keep my covenant,</u> then ye shall be a <u>peculiar treasure unto me above all people</u>: for all the earth *is* mine:

6. And ye shall be unto me a <u>kingdom of priests, and an holy nation</u>. These *are* the words which thou shalt speak unto the children of Israel.

It is here that we must compare the glory of the New Covenant to the old. The old was based on man's obedience, the new is based on Christ's faithfulness. The old could thrust Christ from their hearts, and the new we receive new hearts (Ezekiel 36:26, John 3:7, etc). The old was promised land for their inheritance, the saints are promised this as well.

If you will recall in Daniel 7 we saw that Jesus was given a kingdom that comprised all the nations of the earth that he was to rule, and when we pair this with Psalms 2 we see that the Father tells the Son to ask for the heathen nations as an inheritance. Christ does this and is then told to sit at his right hand and rule.

Satan once had rule over this world, but Christ crushed the head of the serpent, and now he rules the earth not just as a sovereign God but also as the only pure true unfallen man. This is also why Paul calls him the Second Adam in 1 Corinthians 15:45-49. Not only does Jesus redeem fallen man, but he is also redeeming the purpose of man and creation.

Isaiah 42:1-4: 1. Behold my servant (Jesus), whom I (God the Father) uphold; <u>mine elect</u> (Christians are the elect because they are in Christ), *in whom* my soul delighteth; I have put my spirit upon him: he shall bring forth judgment to the Gentiles. 2. He shall not cry, nor lift up, nor cause his voice to be heard in the street. 3. A bruised reed shall he not break (picture of the poor in spirit), and the smoking flax shall he not quench (speaking of those zealous for God): he shall bring forth judgment unto truth. 4. He shall not fail nor be discouraged, till <u>he have set judgment in the earth: and the isles shall wait for his law.</u>

Isaiah prophecied the promised victory of Christ's rule. This was a common promise by the prophets and is seen in the fact that Christ sits on the throne of David and rules the nations until all enemies are put under him.

All of this repetition has a point. The Church is the Bride of Christ; we saw in chapter 5 how Christ gave judgment or authority to the Church to judge nations and cities because we are his bride. If we picture a kingdom here on earth, the king has ultimate authority, the queen has equal authority under the headship of the king over all of the kingdom. The Church was given authority over the nations as she was subject to the husband to execute his will upon the earth.

Part of the reason for this is we are promised to inherit the earth alongside Christ. Listen to something crazy Paul says:

Ephesians 1:18-23: (Paul is praying that) The eyes of your understanding being enlightened; that ye may know what is the hope of his calling, and what the riches of the glory of his <u>inheritance in the saints,</u> 19. And what *is* the exceeding greatness of his power to us-ward who believe, according to the working of his mighty power, 20. Which he wrought in Christ, when he raised him from the dead, and set *him* at his own right hand in the heavenly *places,* 21. Far above all principality, and power, and might, and dominion, and every name that is named, not only in this world, but also in that which is to come:

22. And hath put all *things* under his feet, and gave him *to be* the head over <u>all *things* to the church,</u> 23. Which is his body, the fulness of him that filleth all in all.

That is not all. Paul also said:

Romans 8:17 And if children, then heirs; heirs of God, and <u>joint-heirs</u>

with Christ; if so be that we suffer with *him*, that we may be also glorified together.

So here is the jest of everything we just went over. The nations and the world and the dominion of it were given to Christ as his inheritance, and likewise, we are joint-heirs with him in these things. This sounds wild but hang on as this all plays into the glorious hope of the future we have as saints and the truth about the kingdom. This is True-hope

Jesus said:

Matthew 5:5: Blessed *are* the meek: for they <u>shall inherit the earth</u>.

We are told that Christ gave the judgment to the saints when it was time to possess the kingdom:

Daniel 7:22: Until the Ancient of days came, and <u>judgment was given to the saints</u> of the most High; and the <u>time came that the saints possessed the kingdom</u>.

So possession and judgment go hand in hand. We know in the context that this judgment was given when Christ judged the beastly system of Rome at his coming on the Day of the Lord, as we looked at previously. This judgment was not to be blind nor without oversight, we are ruling under the headship of Christ:

Psalm 25:9: The meek will he guide in judgment: and the meek will he teach his way.

This is the inheritance of the saints, as it is the inheritance of Christ. Christ was to inherit the earth, and so too are the saints. The kingdom in the parables is one that slowly grows to fill the earth. The reason for this is declared:

Proverbs 20:21: An inheritance *may be* gotten hastily at the beginning; but the end thereof shall not be blessed.

Christ established his kingdom in the hearts of the early Church this was the kingdom of grace. As their tree grew up and produced fruit it spread its seed to others and the Church grew. This is something that was prophecied much in the Old Testament, as we saw very clearly laid out in Daniel 2:44, 7:26-27, etc.

So the kingdom of grace in the hearts of believers will grow outwards into the world. It is a living kingdom, not a dead kingdom. Our kingdom promise is pictured on a small scale with the kingdom promise of the Old Testament Israel. In the New Testament, our conquest of the kingdom is for the whole world, while Abraham's was over the lands of Canaan, yet both were declared as if we already had possession of it. This is because when God declares something it is beyond doubt the truth of what happened.

So when we read that the Father gives Christ the kingdoms of this world that all may serve him (Daniel 7:14) and yet we do not see the nations serve him we know this is a reality in the foreknowledge of God. This is why Jesus was told to rule and it was declared that he must rule until all enemies are put under him. Because we are the helpmeet of Christ and co-heirs of Christ he has given judgment to his faithful bride to help bring about the conquest of the kingdom to the earth. This is conquest through the gospel not through violence or the means of this world.

This is the same thing we see play out with the promised land given to Abraham:

Genesis 13:15: For all the land which thou seest, to thee will I give it, and to thy seed for ever.

This promise was reiterated over and over not only to Abraham but to his descendants. The land of their inheritance was already theirs in the mind of God, yet we know that the land was one they had to take possession of hundreds of years later. It is also important to note that Abraham never lived to see this land, though God declared that it belonged to him.

We see in the book of numbers when the conquest was declared right after the Covenant of the Law was given to the nation of Israel.

Numbers 33:51-53: Speak unto the children of Israel, and say unto them, When ye are passed over Jordan into the land of Canaan; 52. Then ye shall drive out all the inhabitants of the land from before you, and destroy all their pictures, and destroy all their molten images, and quite pluck down all their high places: 53. And ye shall dispossess *the inhabitants* of the land, and dwell therein: for I have given you the land to possess it.

Even though they had to go and take possession of their inheritance it was already theirs by right. We see a similar thing promised to the New Covenant people of God. God declared an everlasting kingdom over the nations to be given to Christ and his saints. Likewise, we are told by Christ to go and possess the land not by warfare but by conversion after the Church received the New Covenant.

Matthew 28:18-20: And Jesus came and spake unto them, saying, <u>All power is given unto me in heaven and in earth.</u> 19. <u>Go ye therefore</u> (because all power and authority have been given unto Christ go), and teach <u>all nations</u>, baptizing them in the name of the Father, and of the Son, and of the Holy Ghost: 20. <u>Teaching them to observe</u> all things whatsoever I have commanded you: and, lo, I am with you alway, *even* unto the end of the world. Amen.

These are the marching orders of the Church. Essentially he is saying go take possession of the kingdom. The nations were already given to him and by proxy, they have been given unto the saints. As the Israel of old had to take possession of their inheritance we are called likewise to take ours. This is not to bring the nations under the Church's headship but under Christ. He is the king. This was one of the main errors of the Roman Church which sought to place the kingdoms under its head and not Christ's. Many seek to bring the world under the Church as if she were the King, but Christ is the one that the world will be made subject to by means declared above in the great commission.

By converting the world through the kingdom of grace and bringing the authority and Law of God into the earth, it becomes Christ's kingdom physically. This was patterned in the original politics of Israel during the time of the judges. God was their king and he ruled the people through judges that represented his rule. The people demanded a King in sin as we saw in the last Chapter. Christ is now bringing the fullness of that pattern on the earth through his Church. This is now seen in the judgment of the saints under Christ the King. We would be akin to the judges which were a picture of Daniel 7 vision of the saints.

All of this is already declared in heaven and the Church was told to pray the heavenly realities and promises of God down to the earth (Matthew 6:10). This is actually a work of faith in the believer who will believe the words of God and pray in faith believing that God is able to accomplish all he declared even when our eyes cannot see how such a thing can be.

We are told over and over in the bible that the just shall live by faith and that applies to this promise. When Israel first went to go and conquer the promised land, the land God already declared was theirs, they faltered because the enemies of the land seemed like giants, and they but grasshoppers before them.

Numbers 13:32-33: 32. And they brought up an evil report of the land which they had searched unto the children of Israel, saying, The land, through which we have gone to search it, *is* a land that eateth up the inhabitants thereof; and all the people that we saw in it *are* men of a great stature. 33. And there we saw the giants, the sons of Anak, *which come* of the giants: and we were in our own sight as grasshoppers, and so we were in their sight.

Because of this report, the people grumbled against God and they were not allowed to enter the promised land until the generation that refused to take possession of the land had died. This is why the children had to wander the desert for 40 years. They did not live by faith but by sight. They did not believe that God could deliver the kingdoms of Canaan to them.

Giants like False-hope have convinced many saints to live by sight and not by faith. By this, they are robbed of their inheritance. How many times did Jesus say, "According to thy faith so shall it be?" Nearly every time he performed a miracle he said something to this effect. I believe the reason why you see declines in the influence of the gospel in the world has everything to do with the faith of those that claim to follow it.

If we believe that the world belongs to the devil and that it is going to spiral out of control into utter darkness, then the world will do just that. But if we believe the promise of God that the world belongs to the Lord and the kingdoms of this world belongs to the inheritance of Christ and his saints we would go out in conquest. But, and this is a big but:

2 Corinthians 10:3-5: For though we walk in the flesh, we do <u>not war after the flesh</u>: 4. (For the weapons of our warfare *are* not carnal, but <u>mighty through God to the pulling down of strong holds;</u>) 5. Casting down imaginations, and every high thing that exalteth itself against the knowledge of God, and <u>bringing into captivity every thought to the obedience of Christ;</u>

Paul fully understood the reality I am speaking about. It is a reality that the Church has been blinded by giants living in the land. That is why he also said:

Ephesians 6:12: For we wrestle not against flesh and blood, but against principalities, against powers, against the rulers of the darkness of this world, against spiritual wickedness in high *places.*

So our weapons and our battles are all spiritual. So when we see giants like Abortion, Social Justice, Pornography, and Political giants that are enemies of God, it is our job to fight them and cast them out of the land through the preaching of the word and the might of God. We are to tear down the high places in society and bring them under the obedience of Christ. In other words, we are charged to put the enemies of Christ under his feet. This is all empowered by the Holy Spirit at the word of God the Father for the glory of the Son.

We are told that this is the Lord's doing and this is another key point. The Holy Spirit dwells within all true believers. The Father declares it, the Son creates it, and the Spirit gives it life. Let us remember that the Lord drove out the enemies from Canaan when the people of God marched in faith:

Deuteronomy 7:22-23: And the LORD thy God will put out those nations before thee by little and little: thou mayest not <u>consume them at once</u> (Just as the kingdom will consume all the nations of the earth, Israel consumed all the nations of Canaan again we see a small scale of what God will do over the earth through us), lest the beasts of the field increase upon thee. 23. But the LORD thy God shall deliver them unto thee, and shall destroy them with a mighty destruction, until they be destroyed.

God is the one that will do these great things man will not glory in it, but he will use men and women who will present themselves by faith before God and step out in faith to conquer giants. Paul said this to the early Churches to encourage them to remain faithful unto the day of Christ. This day came already, but we also have a day of Christ coming and the truths are just as relevant to us today:

Philippians 2:13-16: 13. For it is God which worketh in you both to will and to do of *his* good pleasure.14. Do all things without murmurings and disputings: 15. That ye may be blameless and harmless, the sons of God, without rebuke, in the midst of a crooked and perverse nation, among whom <u>ye shine as lights in the world</u>; 16. Holding forth the word of life; that I may rejoice in the day of Christ, that I have not run in vain, neither laboured in vain.

God never gives us an order that he will not also give us the ability to perform if we step out in faith. The Churches' marching orders are clear: Disciple the nations, preach the gospel and bring all people under the kingdom of Christ. David wrote this psalm in the spirit, and it was one that Christ quoted, and is a profound prophecy about the crucifixion and suffering of Christ, consider this portion of it:

Psalms 22:27: All the ends of the world shall remember and turn unto the LORD: and all the kindreds of the nations shall worship before thee. 28. For the kingdom *is* the LORD'S: and he *is* the governor among the nations.

All of these truths are things that False-hope never wants the Church to know or believe. It was the driving force of the Great Awakenings here in America. It is my conviction that False-hope and other giants all came at once to attack the people of God in response to the fire of truth that was changing the world during this time. Bars closed, crime rates vanished, and the world was being turned upside down. A man of God could walk into a bar and such a great conviction of the spirit fell on people that they began to weep. It was right after this that we saw a rise in Evolution, False religions, and False-hope.

As a child, every Christmas my grandpa would gather the family and read the following prophecy in Isaiah. However, I found that I became so familiar with its promise that I had not realized what exactly it was saying.

Isaiah 9:6-7: For unto us a child is born (Jesus), unto us a son is given: and the <u>government shall be upon his shoulder</u>: and his name shall be called Wonderful, Counsellor, The mighty God, The everlasting Father, The Prince of Peace.

7. <u>Of the increase of *his* government and peace *there shall be* no end</u>, upon the throne of David, and upon his kingdom, to order it, and <u>to establish it with judgment and with justice from henceforth even for ever. The zeal of the LORD of hosts will perform this.</u>

In one of the most popular declarations about Christ, many Christians miss the reality of his coming. Jesus had all power of government placed upon him when he ascended to the Father's right hand. His kingdom spreads on the earth through the preaching of the Gospel and everywhere it goes it does all that is declared above. Christ came not just to save lost sinners but the world, and we have the greatest honor of helping him accomplish this on the earth. How dare we take such an honor for granted.

John 3:16: For God so loved the world, that he gave his only begotten Son, that whosoever believeth in him should not perish, but have everlasting life.

God created all things for his good pleasure, not just man. By redeeming fallen man, God is redeeming his creation of whom mankind was made steward of and corrupted with their fall.

Once the earth is filled with the image of God in man, having taken dominion over all the earth, then the kingdom of the earth has become the kingdom of Christ ripe for the harvest. When Christ comes the fullness of this unity will be manifested in splendor for the carnal will then put on spiritual (1 Corinthians 15:35-49).

In 1 Corinthians 15, we are told that the resurrection of the body is the fullness of redemption. The fullness of the kingdom is the redemption of the earth. Both start in part now and in fullness then.

Ephesians 4:15-16: But speaking the truth in love, may grow up into him in all things, which is the head, even Christ: 16. From whom the whole body fitly joined together and compacted by that which every joint supplieth, according to the effectual working in the measure of every part, maketh increase of the body unto the edifying of itself in love.

All of this is done through the authority of the Godhead. The Father declared it. The Son oversees and directs the fulfillment of this through his body, the Church, and the Spirit enables/empowers it through the hearts of believers.

Christ will use his Church as it manifests itself on the earth, both local and universal, to reach the world until it becomes the kingdom of Christ at the end for the harvest. All of this is done by the Son who directs the Church through the Spirit that dwells within the hearts of all believers, by the will of God the Father for the glory of his Great name. New Jerusalem grows and is built as more and more come into the eternal life promised in the gospel. When Christ returns it is in great glory and victory, His reign has accomplished all that the Father commanded.

This is done by wheels within wheels like cogs on a great machine:

It begins on an individual level who is converted by grace. This infects the family home which brings it into the local assembly, which is a part of the greater whole. The Local Assembly is called to win their town/city/ region for the Lord. I believe this shows a glimpse of the mediational kingdom of Christ at work in every church, as he directs every individual church to achieve his purposes and goals in reaching the lost in every region. In this way, the gospel and the kingdom will grow greater and greater in all parts of the world.

The church physical cannot by its nature be universal. Just as a kingdom has many cities and towns, so too does the kingdom of God. Or as Paul called it as the body has many members (parts) so too are there many members of one body. Each local congregation is a part of the whole, but it is not over the other parts of the body. Meaning churches, though united by their faith, are independent meaning one has no authority over another. Can, the eye say it is greater than the hand? Or does the hand direct the placing of the foot? Are not all a part of the same body whose head is Christ? Does not the head govern the body and not the body the head?

This is best understood by Pauls's declaration of us as ambassadors. Think of every true church, for there are many false churches that these truths do not apply, as an embassy of the Kingdom of God. Each member of this local embassy is an ambassador of Christ to this lost world (2 Corinthians 5:2). Just like in real life, one embassy of a country cannot dictate what goes on in the embassy of the same country in a different region. Only the ruler of the land has authority in it. So too is the local church. Christ is the head of the local assembly which is called to preach the Gospel in their assigned area.

These churches are given greater fruit based on their obedience to the Holy Spirit and the Word of God which is the law of the King. Christ can and will remove the authority/fruit of a church that is being disobedient and may even remove said church. A local assembly as all the Church is called to be a pillar and ground of the truth. They are a light to the Gentile world. Their job is to raise up and train the saints of God and equip them to further the kingdom of God through the preaching of the gospel everywhere they go.

It is my opinion that all the local assemblies within a region have the same order from the king to win that region to the Lord. For example, I live in Kern County California, and all true churches in Kern County are called to take Kern Country for the kingdom. We all join together in fulfilling this in each of our little parts of the county to win our area and each, in turn, wins theirs, and eventually, the whole county will be won. This is brought down even to the personal level as we are all called to preach the gospel everywhere we go not just in the church.

These in turn join all those in the state of California who is called to win California for Christ. This is done by each county winning its portion for the Lord. This is then joined with all true churches in America to win America, this is done by each state church winning their states which in turn were won by winning their counties. Which is then joined by all Churches of the world to win the world, which is done by them winning their nation, which is won by their provinces, which is won by towns and small local assemblies all working together as one. This is a picture of wheels within wheels all working together to turn the kingdom of the gospel into all corners of this world. This whole process is directed by Christ and empowered through the Spirit for the glory of the Father.

Many will say the above is impossible and idealistic, but that is the exact reason why it is. According to our faith so shall it be. Where is the faith of the people of God in the promises of the reign of our king? This promise is the Church's inheritance. Unfortunately, most churches see each other more as enemies than fellow soldiers. This is the great blindness of many today. I blame False-hope and other giants for this.

Just like the giants in Canaan, we must march into the promised land and take it for the Lord.

For now, all of us are called to progress the gospel in the world which extends the kingdom. There may be persecution and trials, but through them, Christ shines all the brighter to a world he died for which belongs to him as his kingdom of inheritance. He desires to claim that kingdom and we have been privileged with helping him do this. We see our world growing darker, for I believe we are about to see another great revival and the enemy is trying everything he can to stop it. Yet take heart my dear brethren, for we are promised the victory for we have the King of kings and Lord of lords guiding us to it!

CHAPTER THIRTEEN

Jacob's Trouble

"If man had his way, the plan of redemption would be an endless and bloody
conflict. In reality, salvation was brought not by Jesus' fist, but by His
nail-pierced hands; not by muscle but by love; not by vengeance but
by forgiveness; not by force but by sacrifice. Jesus Christ our Lord
surrendered in order that he might win; he destroyed his enemies by dying
for them and conquered death by allowing death to conquer him."

A.W. TOZER, 1897-1963, FROM "PREPARING FOR JESUS'
RETURN: DAILY LIVE THE BLESSED HOPE."

When I was about 10 years old I recall a hell fire and brimstone preacher speaking about the sudden coming of Christ. He warned against the great coming antichrist, terrible tribulation, death, and war. I should quickly repent lest I was left behind. The blood shall flow to the horses' bridle and the very souls of man would tremble at the sight of almighty God. In those moments, I could see in my young mind Jesus coming in the clouds angry and vengeful, coming for me.

Rather than seeing a God who loved me and died for me, I saw an angry father who saught to destroy me for the sins I had done, sins I could not hide, and by my very nature I was enslaved to do. I could not understand why he hated me so when I could not help be what I was. I do not believe such thoughts were the goal of the preacher, but it wasn't until many years later that I realized that Jesus was not some angry father whose love and affection I had to earn.

He loved me and died for me while I was yet his enemy, even while I naled the very nails in his hands and drove the crown of thorns into his brow. I mocked him and spat upon him. I killed the savior by the sins I had done. Though he died 2,000 years before I was born, I was just as guilty of his death as the men who lived and killed him. That is the reality of sin, that is the reality of God becoming flesh so he could become the sin of man; so he could become me, become you if you be in Christ. In those moments he was me in the eyes of the father and he took my punishment as I took his life. A clear exchange: his life for mine. Oh, what great love is in his cross! He bore them willingly and offered to forgive me and give me a new life, a new heart. 10,000 times 10,000 years is not enough time to praise him for what he did. Yet:

"...Eye hath not seen, nor ear heard, neither have entered into the heart of man, the things which God hath prepared for them that love him. (1 Corinthians 2:9)

Such things should cause the soul to rejoice! How great is the God of Abraham, Isaac, and Jacob! This truth of the Gospel is the good news of man. I fear that most false conversions we see today were born not by the spirit but by fear and emotional manipulation. This is why so many who start strong in the faith are left shipwrecked and bitter. It is the source of antichrist in many churches. The difference in true conversion is love.

The Spirit produces love towards God and a deep conviction of our sins. He takes the wicked stony heart that is at enmity with God and makes it a fleshy one that cries out Abba Father. Conversions born out of fear or an emotional encounter hardly ever last and few are ever true. In many ways, we in modern churches have forgotten how to preach the gospel in its most simple purity for the sake of shock, horror, and emotional response that filled the alter, but leaves the heart dead after a night passes.

Imagine then the horror of God when he considers our wretched state. Many, even in the Church, turn to idols made by hands, the gods, and the pleasures of this world. Vanities and iniquities. Choosing the flesh rather than the Spirit, walking as dead men, though claiming life. They add sins to their sins hardening their hearts to the truth of God's grace and mercy and putting it to an open shame. Why is this so? We have a heart problem.

The Hebrew nation learned the consequences of this reality many times in the Old Testament. They were at times harshly chastened by God for their rebellion, but I fear their rebellion pales in comparison to the rebellion of the Church. For the Saviour has come, he has shown us his heart, and yet we turn from him. Woe until them, the Lord shall not be mocked. How will a Holy God stand when we pervert the most precious gift ever given to mankind?

What does this have to do with Jacob's Trouble?

That preacher from my youth called the 7-year tribulation of Antichrist, the "Time of Jacob's Trouble." For God was going to deal harshly with the Jews, and the world, as the Church was going to be taken away. Anyone left behind would have to suffer alongside the world.

As a boy, I never questioned that statement. He was not the only preacher to make such a statement, so I did not question it. As I began my journey of study, I decided I wanted to look up the verse(s) speaking about Jacob's Trouble and see if it was speaking about what these preachers claimed it to be. I had already begun to learn all the things I have shared in this book and this was an area I knew I had to understand for the truth to come fully into focus.

What I learned shocked me, as Jacob's Trouble was not only a promise of God's mercy, but it was a profound warning about rebellion in the hearts of God's people. It's a warning we so desperately need to learn in churches today. All around us, even as I write this book, the Christians in America are going into bondage and slavery, because they have not learned the lesson of Jacob's Trouble.

For those who are not aware, the phrase, "Jacob's Trouble," is only found in a single verse in the entire bible. It is in the book of Jeremiah. There is not a single verse in the entire bible that says that Jacob's Trouble has anything to do with Antichrist, 7-years of Tribulation, or even that it is a future event. If your pastor or a preacher you know ever tells you that the 7-year Tribulation is Jacob's Trouble or a future event, lovingly ask them for a clear verse that tells them this. They will not be able to produce one.

They have been deceived and taught a lie. As many readers may guess, this idea of Jacob's Trouble being in the future during the Tribulation was a byproduct of John Nelson Darby the prophet of False-hope.

To fully understand what Jacob's Trouble is, we need to first understand what Jeremiah is speaking about as a whole. I will not be able to present the entire book of Jeremiah in this work, but if this is a topic you are interested in I would encourage you to read the entire book. For the sake of this work, I am going to briefly paraphrase the overall theme of Jeremiah. First, I must set up the scene with a brief history lesson:

The nation of Israel fractured into two kingdoms after the death of Solomon. 10 of the 12 tribes of Israel formed their own kingdom to the north called Israel, while the remaining two tribes stayed in the southern kingdom known as Judah. Both kingdoms had their own king. The kings of Judah were descendants of King David, while the kings of Israel were not. Israel became an abominable nation very quickly that abandoned God and turned to the gods of Egypt and Canaan.

Eventually, Israel became so evil that God brought the nation of Assyria to completely wipe them out. This happened about 732 B.C. The Nation of Judah continued on for a time, but they followed after the sins of Israel. Many prophets were given to both Israel and Judah from God begging them to turn away from their sins or face judgment. Judah's rebellion became worse than Israel's and it is during this time that God calls Jeremiah to plead with the people. Listen to the state of Judah from Jeremiah's own words:

Jeremiah 5:26-31: For among my people are found wicked *men*: they lay wait, as he that setteth snares; they set a trap, they catch men. 27. As a cage is full of birds, so *are* their houses full of deceit: therefore they are become great, and waxen rich. 28. They are waxen fat, they shine: yea, they <u>overpass the deeds of the wicked</u>: they judge not the cause, the cause of the fatherless, yet they prosper; and the right of the needy do they not judge. 29. <u>Shall I not visit for these *things?* saith the LORD: shall not my soul be avenged on such a nation as this?</u> 30. A wonderful (does not mean something good, but something unimaginable) and horrible thing is committed in the land; 31. <u>The prophets prophesy falsely, and</u> <u>the priests bear rule by their means; and my people love *to have it* so</u>: and what will ye do in the end thereof?

Jeremiah 6:10-11: To whom shall I speak, and give warning, that they may hear? behold, their <u>ear *is* uncircumcised, and they cannot hearken:</u> <u>behold, the word of the LORD is unto them a reproach</u> (offensive)<u>; they</u> <u>have no delight in it.</u> 11. Therefore (For this reason) I am full of the fury of the LORD; I am weary with holding in: I will pour it out upon the children abroad, and upon the assembly of young men together: for even the husband with the wife shall be taken, the aged with *him that is* full of days.

Often when I read the prophets I cannot help but see the sorry state of my own people. The Church of America, by and large, has fallen into the same blindness and rebellion. This is why this whole topic is so important. For years Jeremiah preached with tears warning of judgment. For his messages, he was beaten, imprisoned, and eventually killed.

After years of preaching and rejection, the Lord had Jeremiah declare this:

Jeremiah 25:4-12: And the LORD hath sent unto you all his servants the prophets, rising early and sending *them;* <u>but ye have not hearkened,</u> <u>nor inclined your ear to hear.</u> 5. They said, Turn ye again now every one from his evil way, and from the evil of your doings, and dwell in the land that the LORD hath given unto you and to your fathers for ever and ever: 6. And go not after other gods to serve them, and to worship them, and provoke me not to anger with the works of your hands; and I will do you no hurt.

7. <u>Yet ye have not hearkened unto me</u>, saith the LORD; that ye might provoke me to anger with the works of your hands to your own hurt. 8. Therefore thus saith the LORD of hosts; <u>Because ye have not heard my</u> <u>words,</u> 9. Behold, I will send and take all the families of the north, saith the LORD, and Nebuchadrezzar the king of Babylon, my servant, and will bring them against this land, and against the inhabitants thereof, and against all these nations round about, and will utterly destroy them, and make them an astonishment, and an hissing, and perpetual desolations.

10. Moreover I will take from them the voice of mirth, and the voice of gladness, the voice of the bridegroom, and the voice of the bride, the sound of the millstones, and the light of the candle. 11. And this whole land shall be a desolation, *and* an astonishment; and these nations shall serve the king of Babylon seventy years. 12. And it shall come to pass, when seventy years are accomplished, *that* I will punish the king of Babylon, and that nation, saith the LORD, for their iniquity, and the land of the Chaldeans, and will make it perpetual desolations.

No longer could the nation avoid the coming judgment. At this point Jeremiah's message changed not from repenting and avoiding the judgment, but do not resist the judgment lest an even greater judgment come upon the people. When Nebuchadrezzar came, Jeremiah told the king and inhabitants of Jerusalem to surrender unless they would all be slaughtered. Just like they would some 500 years later when Rome came against them, the Jews refused to repent and were utterly destroyed and taken into captivity.

This event is paralleled with Christ as Jeremiah is a type of Christ. Jeremiah stood as a voice crying in the wilderness pleading with tears for the people to turn so that they might avoid the destruction. They in turn rejected and killed him. Just so, Christ came and pleaded and was killed. This is the reason there are so many parallels to the destruction of Jerusalem by Babylon and later by Rome, one was a picture of the other. One was temporary the other permanent.

Jeremiah said that the captivity to Babylon would last 70 years, but this would not be the end of their judgment. After 70 years, Jerusalem and the temple were allowed to be rebuilt, but they would remain under the oppression of the 4 great empires spoken of in Daniel. After Babylon would come the Medo-Persian Empire, the Greek Empire, and finally the Roman Empire. History tells us all of this took place during the 400-year gap between the old and new testaments. Here is where Jacob's Trouble is spoken about:

Jeremiah 30:3-9: For, lo, the days come, saith the LORD, that I will bring again the captivity of my people Israel and Judah, saith the LORD: and I will cause them to return to the land that I gave to their fathers, and they shall possess it. 4. And these *are* the words that the LORD spake concerning Israel and concerning Judah. 5. For thus saith the LORD; We have heard a voice of trembling, of fear, and not of peace.

6. Ask ye now, and see whether a man doth travail with child? wherefore do I see every man with his hands on his loins, as a woman in travail, and all faces are turned into paleness? (Showing that the judgment had caused men to become discouraged and cry out to God). 7. Alas! for that day *is* great, so that none *is* like it: it *is* even the time of Jacob's trouble; but he shall be saved out of it. (Why, is Jacob's trouble referring to a period of time and also as a single day? And who is the he? I'll answer that below).

8. For it shall come to pass in that day, saith the LORD of hosts, *that* I will break his yoke from off thy neck, and will burst thy bonds, and strangers shall no more serve themselves of him: 9. But they shall serve the LORD their God, and David their king, whom I will raise up unto them.

This is the only place Jacob's Trouble is mentioned in the whole bible. In context, God is speaking about the restoration of Israel for the coming of the Messiah. This restoration took place over 500 years, through great trial and tribulation. Focus on and reread verses 7-9. Who is the, "he" that is saved out of these troubles? Some people say the nation of Israel, but I think it's speaking about Christ, more on that in a second.

Next notice verse 8 that God will break the yoke of bondage off the neck of Israel so that they will no longer be the servants of strangers, meaning foreigners as they were taken as slaves by those that were not of their people. What's strange about this is God is clearly talking about the bondage of His people at the hands of strangers these were the four great world empires yet, God also says, "his yoke," and that they don't have to serve "themselves of him." In both cases, we see both plural and singular words used. Who is the him?

Modern scholars say this is speaking about the Antichrist, yet God is promising his people in this chapter that God would restore them and deliver them from their oppressors leading up to the Messiah's coming, we know that Messiah has already come so this had to have already happened.

266

I put forward that the "him" that was their oppressor, is the god of this world: Satan who blinded and oppressed the people through the nations causing them to be in bondage both physically and spiritually. Didn't Christ say:

Luke 4:18-21: The Spirit of the Lord *is* upon me, because he hath anointed me to preach the gospel to the poor; he hath sent me to heal the brokenhearted, to preach deliverance to the captives, and recovering of sight to the blind, to set at liberty them that are bruised, 19. To preach the acceptable year of the Lord.

20. And he closed the book, and he gave *it* again to the minister, and sat down. And the eyes of all them that were in the synagogue were fastened on him. 21. And he began to say unto them, This day is this scripture fulfilled in your ears.

Christ came to set the captives free. The Jews were looking for a physical king to deliver them from their oppressors in these four great empires. Yet Christ came and delivered them from the bondage of their sin and the control of Satan who oppressed them greater than any earthly king. Did Jesus not reconcile God with man?

Look back in the passage of Jeremiah and read verse 9. King David was long dead, this was not a prophecy, as False-hope pastors say. They think this is speaking of God resurrecting King David to rule beside Christ during the 1,000-year reign; rather, many prophecies about Christ often call or refer to him as David, because he was a descendant of David. So this verse is speaking about the coming reign of the Messiah, not David.

When Christ was raised from the dead and ascended into heaven he became the king of Israel, but not all of Israel was Israel but those of faith. Only the true Israel of God Jews and Gentiles came and serve Christ even unto this very day is this true.

Please read verse 7 again. I said I thought the "he" that was saved out of the troubles was a reference to Christ. Listen to something interesting Paul says:

Roman 15:8-13: Now I say that Jesus Christ was a minister of the circumcision (the Jews) for the truth of God, to confirm the promises *made* unto the fathers: (Often God said that for the sake of the fathers, meaning Abraham, Isaac, and Jacob, he did not destroy the rebellious children of Israel, because God made them a promise. Paul is about to talk about this promise in the following verses:)

9. And that the Gentiles might glorify God for *his* mercy; as it is written, For this cause I will confess to thee among the Gentiles, and sing unto thy name. 10. And again he saith, Rejoice, ye Gentiles, with his people. 11. And again, Praise the Lord, all ye Gentiles; and laud him, all ye people.

12. And again, Esaias (Greek way of spelling Isaiah) saith, There shall be a root of Jesse, and he that shall rise to reign over the Gentiles; in him shall the Gentiles trust. 13. Now the God of hope fill you with all joy and peace in believing, that ye may abound in hope, through the power of the Holy Ghost.

Paul is literally saying that the reason God remained faithful to the Jews despite all of their rebellion was for the promise that God would save the Gentiles through the seed of Abraham which was Christ. This is the promise made to all the forefathers of the Jews. Those Gentiles are not just non-Jews by birth, but Jews that by unbelief who are made Gentiles. God preserved the Hebrews for Christs' sake. Please re-read this passage and then read Jeremiah 30:7 again. I believe this is speaking of a remnant being persevered among the people and cuminating in its fullness with Christ. He was the one delivered out of Jacob's Trouble, yet so was the remnant of the Jews.

As for Jacob's Trouble being a reference to a period of oppression, and yet a single day (verse 7), I believe it is referring to the day Jesus was crucified, and the period leading up to it which the Jews had to endure. No other day in the history of man will ever compare to the day that the Son of God was killed for the sins of the world. Christ was delivered from that terrible day, and it was in the resurrection three days after that day that Christ broke the yoke and power of the devil and sin off of the world. It is through Christ that we have peace with God and serve God and have "David" (Jesus) as the king of Israel now and forever!

Even if you do not agree with me about the interpretation of these verses, we can see by its context, that this is talking about a specific period of time in which the Lord was going to bring his people back to Israel out of the hands of their oppressors, and they shall serve God again and Christ. I have already shown you in previous chapters how this happened already during and proceeding the time of Christ and the early church.

To further prove this is not a future event let's read on in this chapter:

Jeremiah 30:9: But they shall serve the LORD their God, and David their king, whom I will raise up unto them. 10. Therefore fear thou not, O my servant Jacob, saith the LORD; neither be dismayed, O Israel: for, lo, I will save thee from afar, and thy seed from the land of their captivity; and Jacob shall return, and shall be in rest, and be quiet, and none shall make *him* afraid. 11. For I *am* with thee, saith the LORD, to save thee: though I make a full end of all nations whither I have scattered thee, yet will I not make a full end of thee: but I will correct thee in measure, and will not leave thee altogether unpunished.

Again we see God making reference to the tribes of Israel being scattered and then regathered. In verse 11 God promises to make an end to all the nations that had oppressed them. When we look at history we see this exact thing happen. Babylon was destroyed by the Medo-Persians, these were destroyed by the Greeks, and the Greeks were destroyed by the Romans, and the Romans fell into the last world state which will eventually be devoured by the kingdom of Christ. That means the modern nation of Israel or a future nation of the Jews would eventually be conquered by the gospel as well.

If you read on in Jeremiah 30, God explains to them why they are suffering.

Jeremiah 30:12-15: For thus saith the LORD, Thy bruise *is* incurable, *and* thy wound *is* grievous. (Didn't the passage we read in Luke mention this bruise? Please go back and reread Luke 4:18-21 before you read further) 13. *There is* none to plead thy cause, that thou mayest be bound up: thou hast no healing medicines. 14. All thy lovers have forgotten thee; they seek thee not; for I have wounded thee with the wound of an enemy, with the chastisement of a cruel one, for the multitude of thine iniquity; *because* thy sins were increased. 15. Why criest thou for thine affliction? thy sorrow *is* incurable for the multitude of thine iniquity: *because* thy sins were increased, I have done these things unto thee.

Just like any good parent who has to punish a disobedient child, God explains to Israel why they must suffer during this time of Jacob's Trouble. Even though they had to suffer for their great sins God promises:

Jeremiah 30:16: Therefore all they that devour thee shall be devoured; and all thine adversaries, every one of them, shall go into captivity; and they that spoil thee shall be a spoil, and all that prey upon thee will I give for a prey.

This is true both in a physical sense, and also spiritual. Jesus took captivity captive by becoming sin and dying he overcame both. Jeremiah will go on to further show how this is speaking of the events leading to the coming of the messiah. Also, the 4 world empires were taken captive by each empire that rose after, the last of which will be taken over by Christ's empire/kingdom. God let Judah and Israel fall captive and become slaves by the nations, and now he is promising to restore them and take those same nations captive again this all happened.

Jeremiah 30:17-22: For I will restore health unto thee, and I will heal thee of thy wounds, saith the LORD; because they called thee an Outcast, *saying*, This *is* Zion, whom no man seeketh after. 18. Thus saith the LORD; Behold, I will bring again the captivity of Jacob's tents, and have mercy on his dwellingplaces; and the city shall be builded upon her own heap, and the palace shall remain after the manner thereof.

19. And out of them shall proceed thanksgiving and the voice of them that make merry: and I will multiply them, and they shall not be few; I will also glorify them, and they shall not be small. 20. Their children also shall be as aforetime, and their congregation shall be established before me, and I will punish all that oppress them. 21. And their nobles shall be of themselves, and their governor shall proceed from the midst of them; and I will cause him to draw near, and he shall approach unto me: for who *is* this that engaged his heart to approach unto me? saith the LORD. 22. And ye shall be my people, and I will be your God.

God did indeed rebuild the city the temple and the Jews were allowed to worship freely. They built synagogues throughout the land and the people multiplied in Jerusalem. Their own people ruled during this time under the reign of the Maccabees until Rome came to power and then the Sanhedrin ruled the people until Christ took the throne.

God also promises to draw many to him vs 21, because none would come on their own. Listen to what Jesus says:

John 6:44: No man can come to me, <u>except the Father which hath sent me draw him</u>: and I will raise him up at the last day.

As we can see, this was fulfilled with Christ all of it. So how is it that modern preachers say this is to happen during the time of Antichrist? Jeremiah continues this message into the next chapter and it is there that God promises a New Covenant and the heavenly Mt. Zion (Jeremiah 31:31-40).

So to summarize everything we see that God declares a desolation to come upon Jerusalem through Babylon that would last for 70 years. Then God would begin to rebuild and restore the people to the land through Jacob's Troubles which was to last about 400-500 years (depends on when you think they started). These troubles were to end when God raised them David their king (Christ) and gives them the New Covenant. I know we just touched on a little bit of all of this if you would like to see the fullness of this read Jeremiah 25-31.

There is no mention of Antichrist in this at all. We see no mention that Jacob's Trouble will happen after the messiah comes. There is no verse in the New Testament, including Revelation, that links Jacob's Trouble to a 7-year tribulation. Rather, it is linked to 70 years of captivity and the 400 years of silence between the old and new testament unto the time of Christ. During that time of Jacob's Trouble, there was no prophet of the land and the people of God suffered, but they were restored just as God promised. God also destroyed their oppressors by bringing them into oppression themselves. And just as he promised he gave them the Messiah.

I will end this chapter by speaking about the lesson that Jacob's Trouble teaches us. God will not suffer his people to live in rebellion and sin. When they do, God always raises up people to oppress them for their own sake so that they might humble themselves and turn back to him. Though Christ has given us liberty, if we use our liberty for lasciviousness (uncontrolled lust), drunkenness, and all manners of the flesh, God will not allow us to tarnish his name long before judgment comes.

Liberty is a God-given gift, liberty can easily be taken away as God will give us the fruits of what we have sown. The captivity, dispersal, and all-around trials and tribulations that Israel went through in the Old Testament should all be warnings that God will first judge his people for his name's sake if we make a mockery of his name in the world by the way we live. That is what is happening in America and the western world today.

The second half of the lesson is about the grace of God, though he is angry for a moment, God will be merciful for the sake of His Son and restore his people. In the New Covenant, all people of faith are Israel as we saw, though he may let us be dispersed and go into captivity we can trust that what he does is for our own good to prevent even worse sins, and he will restore us.

1 Peter 4:17: For the time *is come* that judgment must begin at the house of God: and if *it* first *begin* at us, what shall the end *be* of them that obey not the gospel of God?

Galatians 5:19-21: Now the works of the flesh are manifest, which are *these;* Adultery, fornication (any perversion of sex outside/inside of marriage), uncleanness (living an unholy life), lasciviousness (having uncontrolled lust sexual or otherwise),

20. Idolatry (worshiping or loving something more than God is an idol), witchcraft (rebellion is the spirit of witchcraft), hatred, variance (being double-minded/fence sitter/lukewarm living), emulations (jealousy/covetousness), wrath, strife, seditions (divisions), heresies (any perversion of the truth),

21. Envyings, murders, drunkenness (Anything that puts you out of your right mind), revellings (to celebrate sin), and such like: of the which I tell you before, as I have also told *you* in time past, that they which do such things shall not inherit the kingdom of God.

Check your hearts dear reader. If God would not spare Israel the judgment, which was his people long before we were called his people, what makes you think that we will escape the same judgment for the same sins? If you live in my country—America, ask yourself how long this nation will withstand the fierceness of his wrath when we call evil good and good evil.

The blood of 3,000 innocent children cries out to him every day, slaughtered upon the altar of my choice and convenience called abortion. We pervert marriage and praise homosexuality. We promote wickedness among the children and pervert their minds. Does not the Lord's warning of such things not cause this nation to tremble? If it does not it shows just how sick our hearts have become for when Israel heard of the judgments they didn't tremble either. Just like them, the Lord will come for us and he will judge. Let the lesson of their trials be a profound warning for us!

Luke 17:2: It were better for him that a millstone (a great stone used from crushing wheat) were hanged about his neck, and he cast into the sea, than that he should offend one of these little ones.

My dear brothers and sisters living in this country let us mourn, and pray, and preach righteousness, let us turn our hearts back to God to repent of the dead works and religion that God so despises. Let us break up our fallow ground and return to the Lord for he will bring us into bondage again if we do not.

CHAPTER FOURTEEN

Daniel's 70th Week

"True conversion means turning not only from sin but also from depending on self-righteousness. Those who trust their own righteousness for conversion hide behind their own good works. This is the reason that self-righteous people are so angry with gospel preachers because the gospel does not spare those who will not submit to the righteousness of Jesus Christ!"

GEORGE WHITEFIELD 1714-1770, EVANGELIST AND REVIVALIST.

Here we near the very end of this little book. We have looked and many passages that reveal clear errors being taught in churches concerning many things, not just Eschatology. We have also looked at how many popular passages have been perverted by the lies of False-hope. No single passage has been so perverted as the one we are about to look at in this chapter. This is the key section of scripture that most evangelicals turn to today to "prove" their view of Bible interpretation. Without these verses, there can be no 7-year tribulation or reign of Antichrist the way modern teachers proclaim.

The prophecy of the 70 weeks is found in Daniel chapter 9. Usually, when pastors take people to this prophecy, they will only read and focus on verses 25-27. With proper understanding there is no issue with this, however, due to the lies, we must also understand what comes before these verses to give us a clear context and understanding of the 70 weeks.

Before we go any further, I want to summarize the modern understanding of this passage and compare it to what is being said. I will do this by first explaining what most people teach, and then we will go verse by verse and see how this is more properly understood. No matter who teaches this prophecy of the 70 weeks, everyone understands that the 70 weeks are not 70 weeks of 7 days. It is understood that each day is meant to be a year. Meaning the 70 weeks is a prophetic way of saying 490 years.

Modern teachers will say, that the 70 weeks of Daniel is a prophecy that leads up to the time of Christ, but stops in the 69th week, (meaning it ends after 483 years) with the death of Christ. The final week, or 7 year period, will not take place until the future 7-year tribulation of the Antichrist. Meaning, the antichrist, and the tribulation are only 7 years because it is the 70th week of Daniel.

During this final week, they say that the Antichrist will make a covenant with the modern nation of Israel in Palestine for 7 years, and in the middle of the 7 years, the Antichrist will break this treaty or covenant and at this point stand in the rebuilt Jewish temple and declare himself to be God. They equate this act as the abomination that makes desolate spoken of by Jesus in Matthew 24. This final week will end with the return of Christ and the establishment of the 1,000-year reign of Christ on the earth.

At this point, most readers will probably be questioning the above statements as it doesn't line up with what we have learned in this book. This is a good thing because there is a lot wrong with the above statement.

All of the above will sound familiar to anyone who has gone to a modern church that has taught this subject or heard any teaching about this topic on the radio or in books. Before I go further, I must point out that there is not a single verse in the entire book of Daniel, nor anywhere else in the bible, that says the 70 weeks prophecy stops at 69 weeks and will conclude in the future with Antichrist. There is no mention of Antichrist in the verses about this prophecy. Rather, as you will see, this is a declaration of 490 years that will begin and end in a consecutive period.

To fully understand this I encourage everyone to read the entire 9th chapter of Daniel, but for the sake of this book let's just look at some key passages:

Daniel 9:2: In the first year of his reign (Darius the son of Ahasuerus) I Daniel understood by books the number of the years, whereof the word of the LORD came to Jeremiah the prophet, that he would accomplish <u>seventy years in the desolations of Jerusalem.</u>

This chapter opens up with us seeing how Daniel was a student of the bible. Daniel was reading Jeremiah, and he understood that the captivity, or enslavement, of his people, was only supposed to last 70 years. The captivity began when Daniel was taken as a very young man, Daniel would most likely be in his 80s or 90s when he is seeing this. We find these exact verses in:

Jeremiah 25:12: And it shall come to pass, <u>when seventy years are accomplished</u>, *that* I will punish the king of Babylon, and that nation, saith the LORD, for their iniquity, and the land of the Chaldeans, and will make it perpetual desolations.

Jeremiah 29:10: For thus saith the LORD, That <u>after seventy years be accomplished at Babylon I will visit you</u>, and perform my good word toward you, in causing you to return to this place.

Daniel believed the word spoken by Jeremiah and did some basic math and realized that the 70 years were almost up. This caused Daniel to go into a period of prayer, fasting, and supplication to God. This is recorded in verses 3-19 during which Daniel not only confesses his own sin but the sins of his people. He declares God's righteousness and faithfulness and he greatly seeks to understand how God will accomplish his promise about the 70 years.

Daniel 9:21: Yea, whiles I *was* speaking in prayer, even the man Gabriel, whom I had seen in the vision at the beginning, (This is a reference to earlier visions Daniel had in the book of Daniel not related to this vision beyond Gabriel's appearance) being caused to fly swiftly, touched me about the time of the evening oblation (offering to God).

We see that while Daniel is still seeking God, God sends Gabriel to speak with him. That in itself is amazing, but I must point out that at the heart of Daniel's prayer, he was seeking to understand how God would restore and forgive Israel. Gabriel comes and gives Daniel the 70-week prophecy so that he will understand how God will accomplish these things. Please read Daniel 9:3-19 to get the full picture of this.

Lets now look verse by verse at what Gabriel tells Daniel:

Daniel 9:24: Seventy weeks are determined upon thy people and upon thy holy city, to finish the transgression, and to make an end of sins, and to make reconciliation for iniquity, and to bring in everlasting righteousness, and to seal up the vision and prophecy, and to anoint the most Holy.

This verse here is the key to understanding the entire prophecy of the 70 weeks. Let us note the 6 things these weeks are to accomplish, or in other words, after the 490 years are over these six things shall be done by God:

- God will finish the transgression/sin of Israel
- God will end Sin
- God will cause reconciliation for Iniquity
- God will bring everlasting Righteousness
- God will Seal up the vision of Prophecy
- God will anoint the Most Holy

Read these six points carefully. All six of these are done by Christ, and could only be done by Christ. In the following paragraphs, I will show some verses that show this, but I must point out that the entire purpose of the 70 weeks was focused on the work of Christ, not Antichrist.

Finish the Transgression: This is referring to the transgression of Israel against God. The final transgression of the people was the rejection and crucifixion of His son. This would lead to great judgment over the people in 70 A.D.:

Matthew 27:25: Then answered all the people, and said, <u>His blood be on us, and on our children.</u>

Mark 15:12-13: And Pilate answered and said again unto them, What will ye then that I shall do *unto him* whom ye call the King of the Jews? 13. <u>And they cried out again, Crucify him.</u>

Luke 23:22-23: And he (Pilot) said unto them the third time, Why, what evil hath he done? I have found no cause of death in him: I will therefore chastise (flog) him, and let *him* go. 23. And they were instant with loud voices, <u>requiring that he might be crucified.</u> And the voices of them and of the <u>chief priests prevailed.</u>

John 19:15 But they cried out, Away with *him*, away with *him*, crucify him. Pilate saith unto them, <u>Shall I crucify your King</u>? The chief priests answered, <u>We have no king but Caesar.</u>

To make an end to Sin: Christ is the only means by which sin is dealt with. Christ became sin who knew no sin so that we might become the righteousness of God in him:

John 1:29: The next day John (the Baptist) seeth Jesus coming unto him, and saith, Behold the Lamb of God, <u>which taketh away the sin of the world.</u>

2 Corinthians 5:21: For he hath made <u>him</u> (Jesus) <u>*to be* sin for us,</u> who knew no sin; that we might be made the righteousness of God in him

John 19:30: When Jesus therefore had received the vinegar, he said, <u>It is finished</u>: and he bowed his head, and gave up the ghost.

Made Reconciliation for Iniquity: What does it mean to be reconciled? It means to bring two people that were separated by some cause of offense, back together. The event that separated mankind was their iniquity or sin/rebellion against God. Only Christ can reconcile us with God the Father through his work on the cross:

2 Corinthians 5:18-19: And all things *are* of God, who hath <u>reconciled us</u> to himself by Jesus Christ, and hath given to <u>us the ministry of reconciliation;</u> 19. To wit (Which is), that <u>God was in Christ, reconciling the world unto himself</u>, not imputing (recording) their trespasses unto them; and hath committed unto us the word of reconciliation.

Romans 5:10: For if, when we were enemies, <u>we were reconciled to God by the death of his Son</u>, much more, being reconciled, we shall be saved by his life.

Hebrews 2:17: Wherefore in all things it behoved (was approved by) him (Christ) to be made like unto *his* brethren (Mankind), that he might be a merciful and faithful high priest in things *pertaining* to God, to make <u>reconciliation for the sins of the people.</u>

Bring in Everlasting Righteousness: Christ is our righteousness.

There can be no end to it, for there is no end to Christ. It is everlasting because he is everlasting.

Romans 3:21-23: But now the righteousness of God without the law is manifested (declared made known), being witnessed by the law and the prophets; 22. Even the righteousness of God *which is* by faith of Jesus Christ unto all and upon all them that believe: for there is no difference: 23. For all have sinned, and come short of the glory of God;

Jeremiah 23:6: In his (Christ's) days Judah shall be saved, and Israel shall dwell safely: and this *is* his name whereby he (Jesus) shall be called, THE LORD OUR RIGHTEOUSNESS.

To seal up the Vision and Prophecy: This is a reference to two things, first, a seal is a stamp that showed the official mark of a king or authority declaring the contents within bore the authority of the King. In the context of prophecy, this shows that in Christ all the prophecies concerning him would be understood and manifest that they did indeed come from God. The Old Testament is full of prophecies about Christ. For thousands of years, the prophets spoke about Christ, but the seal that their words were indeed from God was not made manifest until Christ came. This vindicated the prophets whom the Jews killed showing them that indeed they were from God.

Second, this speaks about how there would be no prophets to Israel after Christ. Christ indeed was the last prophet of whom all the prophets were a picture of:

Deuteronomy 18:15: The LORD thy God will raise up unto thee a Prophet from the midst of thee, of thy brethren, like unto me; unto him ye shall hearken; (This prophet was Jesus)

Luke 16:16: The law and the prophets <u>were until John</u> (John the Baptist): since that time the kingdom of God is preached, and every man presseth into it.

Hebrews 1:1-2: God, who at sundry times (ancient times) and in divers manners (different ways) spake in time past unto the <u>fathers by the prophets,</u>

2. Hath in these <u>last days spoken unto us by *his* Son,</u> whom he hath appointed heir of all things, by whom also he made the worlds;

To Anoint the most Holy: In the Old Testament, the prophets would often anoint kings as a picture of the Holy Spirit and favor of God resting on a person. The Most Holy is of course Jesus. So Christ will be declared or anointed by the end of the 70 weeks. This is seen in several different places in the new testament:

Luke 3:22: And the Holy Ghost descended in a bodily shape like a dove upon him, and a voice came from heaven, which said, Thou art my beloved Son; in thee I am well pleased.

Luke 4:17-21: And there was delivered unto him the book of the prophet Esaias (Greek way of spelling Isaiah). And when he had opened the book, he found the place where it was written, 18. The Spirit of the Lord *is* upon me, because he hath anointed me to preach the gospel to the poor; he hath sent me to heal the brokenhearted, to preach deliverance to the captives, and recovering of sight to the blind, to set at liberty them that are bruised,

19. To preach the acceptable year of the Lord. 20. And he closed the book, and he gave *it* again to the minister, and sat down. And the eyes of all them that were in the synagogue were fastened on him. 21. And he began to say unto them, This day is this scripture fulfilled in your ears.

Matthew 26:7-13: There came unto him a woman having an alabaster box of very precious ointment, and poured it on his head, as he sat *at meat*. 8. But when his disciples saw *it*, they had indignation, saying, To what purpose *is* this waste? 9. For this ointment might have been sold for much, and given to the poor. 10. When Jesus understood *it*, he said unto them, Why trouble ye the woman? for she hath wrought a good work upon me.

11. For ye have the poor always with you; but me ye have not always. 12. For in that she hath poured this ointment on my body, she did *it* for my burial. 13. Verily I say unto you, Wheresoever this gospel shall be preached in the whole world, *there* shall also this, that this woman hath done, be told for a memorial of her.

Psalms 2:7 I will declare the decree: the LORD hath said unto me, Thou *art* my Son; this day have I begotten thee. (Speaking of the ascension of Christ and the Resurrection of the dead, Christ was the first begotten of the dead, and on the day he ascended he became the

God-man seated at the right hand of the father fully God and fully man in a glorified state.)

Christ was once again anointed as King in heaven at his ascension which caused the Holy Spirit to fall on the Church.

As we can see from the scriptures, Christ fulfilled all 6 things declared by Gabriel that the 70 weeks would accomplish. More importantly, he fulfilled them all exactly in 490 years just as Gabriel said! I say this again because the focus of the weeks is Christ, not Antichrist. With that in mind let's look at the next verse in Daniel:

Daniel 9:25: Know therefore and understand, *that* from the going forth of the commandment to restore and to build Jerusalem unto the Messiah the Prince *shall be* seven weeks (7 weeks of 7 days each day is a year 7x7=49 years.) and threescore and two weeks (62 weeks each week is 7 days so 7x62=434 years. The reason it is broken down in this way is that Jerusalem and the temple were rebuilt in 49 years and 434 years would pass before the Messiah would be revealed. So 49+434=483 years or 69 weeks. Meaning messiah will come after 69 weeks. This sets up the next set of verses so keep in mind that Gabriel just said that the messiah will come after 69 weeks.): the street shall be built again, and the wall, even in troublous times (These troublous times are to inform Daniel and the Jews that just because the 70 years of captivity are over, there were many trials still left unto the time of the messiah. This is what Jeremiah called Jacob's Trouble as we saw in the last Chapter).

Let us stop here for a moment and re-emphasize something. Gabriel just said that 69 weeks [7+62=69] will pass, during which time the city and walls of Jerusalem will be rebuilt and the Messiah will appear. During the 483 years, Israel would face troublous times, or as Jeremiah called it Jacob's Trouble. So if 69 weeks (483 years) pass before the Messiah comes, doesn't that mean he comes during the 70th week? The answer is yes, the Messiah comes during the 70th week.

Here we have Gabriel telling us exactly when these 70 weeks (490 years) begin. It starts when the decree of a king to restore (rebuild) Jerusalem which had been destroyed by Babylon. We know when this decree happened. This is recorded by Ezra. A lot of people believe that the 70 weeks started by the decree of Cyrus to rebuild the temple, however, this decree was not to rebuild the city, but the temple only. It isn't until the declaration by Artaxerxes in both Ezra and Nehemiah that we see the city also was allowed to be rebuilt. This date was 457 BC in the month of Nisan (March/April) which is also the month of Passover. It took 49 years to complete just as Gabriel said it would.

So what is 490 years after this date? Because B.C. dates count backward and A.D. dates count forward let's figure this out this way: 490-457=33. The date we come to is 33A.D. Meaning the 70 weeks will end in 33 A.D.

What's amazing about this is we know that Jesus also died in the month of Nisan between the years 30 A.D. and 36 A.D., the exact date is not officially known, but with some math, we can figure this out if we trust the 70 weeks prophecy. I believe then that Jesus was crucified in 30 AD as this was exactly 487 years after the decree to rebuild the temple as mentioned above. This is in the middle of the 70th week and this is important.

Daniel will later tell us that Jesus would be cut off, killed, 3 1/2 years after his ministry began during the 70th week of Daniel which puts us exactly at 30 AD for the year Christ died specifically the month of Nisan, the Wednesday or Thursday before the Passover unless you want to go the Good Friday route which I think has some issues, regardless it was around the week of Passover.

We will look at that more in a moment. First I want to show you how amazing the 70 weeks of Daniel are. By using the weeks we can know exactly what year Jesus was born, baptized, and when he was killed

Luke 2:1: And it came to pass in those days, that there went out a decree from Caesar Augustus, that all the world...

Most people think Jesus was born in 0 AD as this was a Catholic tradition that divided the calendar from B.C. (Before Christ) and A.D. (Anno Domini: meaning the year of our Lord). There are several issues with this, first, this decree was made between 8 and 4 B.C. (the exact date is debated), second, we also know Herod the Great was king right before and died shortly after Jesus was born:

Matthew 2:1: Now when Jesus was born in Bethlehem of Judaea in the days of Herod the king, behold, there came wise men from the east to Jerusalem,

Herod died between 4 BC - 1 BC. (Great debate on exactly when Herod died). This means that Jesus had to have been born between 8 and 1 B.C.

Based on all the above I would guess that Jesus was born between 5-4 B.C. just before Herod's death. Most modern scholars feel Herod died in 4 B.C., but there is evidence to support the 1 B.C. date. Regardless, if Jesus was born in 4 BC this would still match the biblical account as Herod died the same year as his birth if he did indeed die in 4 B.C., or a few short years after if he died in 1 B.C. This is important as we go on as we also know when Jesus began his ministry and with some simple math we can confirm this date as the birth year of Christ:

Luke 3:1: Now in the fifteenth year of the reign of Tiberius Caesar, Pontius Pilate being governor of Judaea, and Herod being tetrarch of Galilee, and his brother Philip tetrarch of Ituraea and of the region of Trachonitis, and Lysanias the tetrarch of Abilene,

The above statements are much easier to prove the exact date. The above was true in 26 AD this was the year Jesus was baptized according to this gospel account. His public ministry would not begin until a little after this event as we learn from John's account of Jesus in John 1:29-34, yet his ministry was declared and anointed at his Baptism. In these verses in John, John is describing the event that happened when Jesus was baptized and the Holy Spirit came upon him. After this Jesus goes into the wilderness for 40 days and is tested by satan. Sometime after the end of the 40 days, John the Baptist tells John and Andrew:

John 1:36 And looking upon Jesus as he walked, he saith, Behold the Lamb of God!

We know this happened when Jesus was about 30 years old:

Luke 3:23: And Jesus himself began to be about thirty years of age, being (as was supposed) the son of Joseph, which was *the son* of Heli,

So if Jesus was baptized in 26 A.D. as the above verses claim we can use simple math to prove the 4 B.C. date of his birth (26-30 = -4, which would translate into 4 B.C.) What is amazing, he is baptized in the same year that the 69th week ended and the 70th week began if the weeks started in 457 B.C. Remember that Daniel was told that after 69 weeks the messiah would be revealed? Meaning that he would be revealed at the beginning of the 70th week. As we see, Jesus was indeed declared and baptized at the very beginning of this 70th week. His public ministry did not start for a while after these events, but here he was first made known, we see this in John 2. Listen to what Jesus said to his mother:

John 2:4 Jesus saith unto her, Woman, what have I to do with thee? <u>mine hour is not yet come.</u>

Most people know the story, Mary tells the people to wait on Jesus and Jesus turns the water into wine. Jesus had already begun to gather some disciples to him, but we see here that Jesus is declaring it wasn't yet time for him to be known the context being publicly known. We know from the testimony of the Gospels, he was already known by his early disciples and by the declaration of John the Baptist. So what was he waiting for? When we understand the 70 weeks prophecy this becomes very clear and allows us to confirm all the dates. After this first miracle, the Apostle John goes on to declare:

John 2:11-13: This beginning of miracles did Jesus in Cana of Galilee, and manifested forth his <u>glory; and his disciples believed on him.</u>

12. After this he went down to Capernaum, he, and his mother, and his brethren, and his disciples: and they continued there not many days.

Our next account of Jesus begins after these days. This was the month of Nisan and the Passover is at hand. It is here that we see the beginning of Jesus' public ministry. It started on the Passover and ended 3 years later. I believe though that it started 6 months before when John baptized him and the Holy Spirit fell on him, yet during this time, Jesus was tempted by Satan in the wilderness and called his disciples preparing for the 3 years of ministry ahead.

The 70 weeks when understood properly definitively prove these dates. Remember I said I think Jesus died the month of Nisan/Passover in 30 AD, if we subtract 3 ½ years from that date we would come to 26 AD. About six months before the Passover. This is the same year that Jesus was baptized. This was also exactly 483 years, or 69 weeks, after the decree of Artaxerxes to rebuild the city. Meaning Jesus was baptized at the very beginning of the 70th week of Daniel. He was crucified 3 ½ years later in 30 AD. In 33 AD Stephan was stoned to death and the Gentiles had the gospel preached to them thus concluding the 70 weeks. Keep this in mind as we look at the next verse in Daniel:

Daniel 9:26: And after threescore and two (62) weeks shall Messiah be cut off, but not for himself: and the people of the prince that shall come shall destroy the city and the sanctuary; and the end thereof *shall be* with a flood, and unto the end of the war desolations are determined.

Remember verse 25 says that it was after two periods of time 7 weeks, (49 years) and 62 weeks (434 years, or 69 weeks) that would pass before the Messiah shall come. Now look at verse 26, it is giving us more information about what happens after the 62 weeks (remember the 62 weeks comes after the first 7 weeks meaning this is still saying that after 69 weeks) Messiah will be cut off but not for himself. Meaning Gabriel is saying not only is the Messiah going to come after 69 weeks, but during the final week he is going to be cut off. Obviously, this is a reference to Jesus being killed for the sins of the world. This is happening after the 69 weeks that came before, what comes after 69? Well of course we know 70 comes after 69. So the Messiah is cut off during the 70th week.

Notice the ":" after it says, "not for himself." In English, we put up a colon to connect two sentences that relate to one another. The same is true for verse 26. Meaning one caused the other. Essentially it is saying, "Because Messiah is cut off, the prince that shall come –Titus— and his people—the Roman armies— shall come and destroy the city and the temple with a flood—a great army. We looked at this as the meaning behind the abomination that makes it desolate referenced in chapter ten.

Verse 26 is simply linking the fact that the coming Destruction of Jerusalem was the result of the cutting off of the messiah during the 70th week.

Let's look at the final line of Daniel:

Daniel 9:27: And he shall confirm the covenant with many for one week: and in the midst (middle) of the week (another way of saying, after 3 1/2 years) he shall cause the sacrifice and the oblation (oblation means offerings/ceremonies) to cease, and for the overspreading (covering over/

piling on) of abominations he shall make *it* desolate, even until the consummation (fullness the context is speaking about the fullness of their abominations), and that determined shall be poured upon the desolate.

At this point, most False-hope teachers say that the second half of Daniel 9:26 and the entire portion of 9:27 is a reference to the Antichrist. They say that the prince that shall come is the Antichrist and that this is the antichrist making a covenant with Israel. This is not so.

As I showed previously verse 26 is saying that because Messiah was cut off, Titus shall come and destroy the city. Verse 27 is continuing that theme. This is not talking about Antichrist confirming a covenant, but Christ and the covenant is the New Covenant, which he first made with the Jews. Jesus made a covenant with the people for one week (7 years, this is the 70th week). This is why for the majority of Jesus' ministry he focused on "the lost sheep of the house of Israel (Matthew 15:24)" the New Covenant was first offered to them. This is also why Jesus said in John 10:16 that he had others that he would also bring in, a reference to the gentiles, but to fulfill all that was written in the Law and Prophets concerning Christ, Jesus had to first offer the New Covenant to the Jews.

This act was not an afterthought as False-hope says. Remember False-hope claims that Jesus only went to the Gentiles because the Jews rejected the New Covenant, so the Jews were put on a time out and God went to the Gentiles. This is a lie as the fathers: Abraham, Isaac, Jacob, and David were all promised that the Gentiles would be saved through a descendant of theirs. This means that for Christ to fulfill all that was written of him in the Laws and the Prophets he also had to bring salvation to the Gentiles. This means that the New Covenant was always meant to include the gentiles, but was first offered to the Jews.

This is also why Jesus refused to go to the gentiles during his ministry, and why we do not see the ministry to the gentiles begin until after these 70 weeks were over. Christ was fulfilling a promise to the Jews concerning the New Covenant.

The verses themselves prove that Jesus is the focus of them and not Antichrist. Consider that it is saying that in 3 ½ years or in the midst (middle) of the week, this figure was cut off. To help narrow down this figure consider two things. First, all Christians that I have ever known all understand that Jesus only ministered for 3 ½ years this should be our first clue. Second, His death caused the sacrifices and the offerings (oblations) to cease as he fulfilled them. He abolished in his flesh the ordinances and commands of the Old Covenants:

Jeremiah 31:31-33: Behold, the days come, saith the LORD, that I will make a new covenant with the house of Israel, and with the house of Judah: 32. Not according to the covenant that I made with their fathers in the day *that* I took them by the hand to bring them out of the land of Egypt; which my covenant they brake, although I was an husband unto them, saith the LORD: 33. But this *shall be* the covenant that I will make with the house of Israel; After those days, saith the LORD, I will put my law in their inward parts, and write it in their hearts; and will be their God, and they shall be my people.

Matthew 5:17: Think not that I am come to destroy the law, or the prophets: I am not come to destroy, <u>but to fulfil</u>.

Ephesians 2:15: Having <u>abolished in his flesh the enmity, *even* the law of commandments *contained* in ordinances</u>; for to make in himself of twain (two people) one new man, *so* making peace;

The sacrifices in the temple continued by the Jews because they rejected Jesus who was the lamb of God that all the sacrifices and offerings were a picture of. Yet for the true people of God, those of faith, we all understood that the death of Christ caused an end to the sacrifices and offerings as they were no longer needed. These sacrifices became blasphemous and abomination after Christ's death which is why Daniel says, "for the overspreading (covering over/piling on) of abominations he (Christ) shall make *it* (the Jewish religion/temple) desolate, even until the consummation (fullness, referencing the fullness of their sins) and that determined (judgment) shall be poured upon the desolate (the Jewish religion was spiritually already desolate and dead)."

The "he" in this verse is referring to Christ. He brought Titus the prince against Jerusalem because they rejected God and continued their abominable sacrifices. These covered them in abominations as before the sacrifices that were once a picture of Christ's death covering their sin, and now it was a mockery of Christ's sacrifice. With every animal sacrifice, they were spitting in the face of God saying your son's death was nothing.

Meaning they were declaring each time they sacrificed that Christ was not the Messiah. These abominations were allowed to continue until the consummation or fullness of their sin came in full and they then were poured out upon the desolate in judgment, those desolate were the Jewish people. Remember Jesus declared:

Matthew 23:38: Behold, your house is left unto you <u>desolate.</u>

To summarize all of this, Gabriel gives Daniel a prophetic word declaring the restoration of his city and people unto the time of Christ. These 70 weeks are meant to be consecutive, nowhere does Gabriel say, "well the 70th week will be in the future," rather, we see that the events concerning the Messiah will happen during the 70th week. Let me rewrite the last two verses to try and show the greatest clarity of what these verses teach:

Daniel 9:26-27: And after 69 weeks shall Messiah be cut off, but not for himself: because of this, Titus the Prince and Rome shall come and shall destroy the city and the sanctuary; and the end thereof *shall be* with a great army, and unto the end of the war destructive judgments are determined upon Jerusalem and the people.

27. And Jesus shall confirm the covenant with many for one week: and in 3 ½ years, or in the middle of the week he shall cause the sacrifice and the offerings to cease, and for the piling on of abominations Jesus shall make Jerusalem desolate, even until the fullness of their sins has come, and that determined, which is their judgment, shall be poured upon the desolate.

I did not rewrite the above passage in this way to try and manipulate the scriptures. I did it for teaching purposes only. I think it is also done while remaining faithful to what was being said. I'm going to do the same thing again, this time with the modern way of teaching this passage, and I ask you am I manipulating what is being said, or are the modern preachers manipulating the passage?

Daniel 9:26-27: And after 69 weeks shall Messiah be cut off, but not for himself: and because the Jews rejected Christ, the 70th week shall be in the future after the Church Age ends and the Church is raptured and the Antichrist shall then come and shall destroy the modern state of Israel and the rebuilt Jewish temple; and the end thereof *shall be* with a great army, and unto the end of the war desolations are determined.

27. And Antichrist shall confirm the covenant with many for the 7 years tribulation period: and in 3 ½ years, or halfway through it he shall cause the sacrifice and the offerings to cease, because he will stand in the temple of God and declare himself to be God making the temple desolate even until the fullness of his abominations, and that determined, his judgment, shall be poured upon the desolate.

I hope it is abundantly clear, that the way False-hope teaches this passage is done by grossly manipulating the passage by adding doctrines to it that simply do not exist in the bible.

The reality is, False-hope has taken a clear prophecy about Jesus and the Destruction of Jerusalem and made it about Antichrist and a future tribulation. In my opinion, that is nothing short of blasphemy. Remember the 6 points that Gabriel said that the 70 weeks would bring? All six points were fulfilled perfectly by Christ and in their fullness by his death and resurrection. At the end of the 70th week, Jesus begins to bring in the Gentiles just as he always meant to. This happened exactly 490 years after Artaxerxes ordered Jerusalem to be rebuilt! The end of the weeks was signified by the Gentiles coming into the New Covenant. The close of the weeks was the end of God dealing with national Israel and now dealing with true Israel, the children of faith of all nations in Christ.

Galatians 3:26-28: For ye are all the children of God by faith in Christ Jesus.

27. For as many of you as have been baptized into Christ have put on Christ.

28. There is neither Jew nor Greek, there is neither bond nor free, there is neither male nor female: for ye are all one in Christ Jesus.

Nothing about making this prophecy about the Antichrist makes sense. Antichrist will not fulfill any of the 6 things declared about the weeks. There is no mention of the 70th week being in the future. There is no reason given anywhere in the bible to even hint at the 70 weeks not being consecutive. No one before Darby believed this passage was referring to Antichrist in any way rather, as it so clearly states, it is dealing with the coming messiah and the resulting rejection and judgment by and against the Jewish people.

Meaning the Jews knew the exact date on which the Messiah should appear. Only Jesus fulfills all this and more. It is a great sadness to me that a passage that should be a great proof of who Christ was and the divine origin of the bible, has been so manipulated to cause doubt and division. To take a truth about Christ and make it about Antichrist can have no other origin than Satan, it should make us all wonder where John Nelson Darby got his new doctrines, and who it is that False-hope works for.

May the beauty and truth of God's word shine all the brighter in your hearts as you realize this truth: God's word will never fail and his promises are ever sure. Cast off the lies of antichrist and walk in the light of the Lord.

CHAPTER FIFTEEN

To Millennium and Beyond

"Reformation is a return to the sound doctrine of the bible. Revival is the practice of that sound doctrine under the power of the Holy Spirit"

FRANCIS SCHAEFER 1912-1984, AN AMERICAN THEOLOGIAN

W e now come to the utter end, and perhaps one of the most difficult portions of the bible that I will attempt to expound. As I have already stated before, Revelation is a book that is written in a prophetic language and has been the source of great controversy nearly since it was written. Far greater men than I have attempted to interpret this book, to varying degrees of success. As such, I will not claim to be an authority on what the great mysteries of this book hold, but I will attempt to share what glimmers of truth that I have found. Chapter 20 of the Revelation is the focus of this chapter as it has the only reference to the 1,000-year reign of Christ that many Christians like to argue over. However, I will also dive slightly into chapters 21, and 22 to try and fully grasp what I think John is saying in this portion of the Revelation.

The Revelation is not meant to be a hiding of the truth, but a revealing or unveiling of truth, specifically about Jesus Christ and his kingdom. No matter what point of view one takes on this book, that is what John declares it to be all about:

Revelation 1:1: The <u>Revelation</u> (means revealing/unveiling) of Jesus

Christ, which God gave unto him, to <u>shew</u> unto his servants things which must <u>shortly come to pass</u>; and he sent and signified *it* by his angel unto his servant John:

As this book was not meant to be a focus on the Revelation, I must first lay out a few things before we get into the verses themselves.

First, there have historically been four major views of how to interpret the Revelation throughout Church history they are often called the: Historicist, Preterist, Futurist, and Spiritualist/Idealist views on eschatology. The Historicists say that the Revelation applies to all of Church history beginning in the first century and unraveling slowly throughout history. This view sees historic events in the prophetic visions that will ultimately end with the return of Christ. This was the view most commonly held by the Reformers, and many Protestants and was one I held for a time. The Preterists view Revelation as having to do with the Destruction of Jerusalem and feel that most of the events are already past and now hold spiritual truths that can still apply today, except for Revelation chapter 20 which holds a prophetic view of the future.

The Futurists say that only the first 4 chapters of the Revelation were meant for the 1st century Church, and the rest will all be in the future. This view relates everything from chapter 5 on as a series of events that will quickly unfold over 7 years of tribulation that begins with the rapture of the Church or the appearance of Antichrist. The Spiritualists view the Revelation as not having to apply to history or any event at all, but rather are spiritual allegories that relate to many things, and thus it should not be taken literally. Rather, the Revelation is the ongoing struggle of good and evil and the ultimate promised victory of the good.

These views then diverge into three major camps when they come to Revelation 20. These camps are Premillennial, Postmillennial, and Amillennial. The Premillennial view is that Christ comes back before the 1,000-year millennium. As such they view the 1,000 years as mostly literal during which Christ is physically ruling from a rebuilt Jerusalem with his glorified saints.

The Postmillennial view does not see the 1,000 years as literal, as God often uses this phrase symbolically to speak of a great quantity of time or things (Psalms 50:10, Joshua 23:10, Deuteronomy 7:9, Psalms 90:4, etc). They view the 1,000 years as being a reference to the now current rule of Christ from heaven with the saints that have died and manifested on the earth through the Church and saints that now live. This is almost identical to the Amillennial view with one major difference. The Postmillennial view sees the Gospel going into the world with greater and greater power and authority ultimately having preeminence in the world. After a time of gospel glory, Christ will come back in victory.

The Amillennial view also sees the 1,000 years as not being literal but as a reference to the current reign of Christ in heaven, and also manifested on the earth through the Church. They see the world not getting Christianized, but falling more and more into sin, or that the world will continue as it is being a large majority of the unsaved and a small remnant of saved. Ultimately they believe it ends with the glorious return of Christ. Some in this camp believe that there may be a final antichrist/Man of Sin figure that will also be defeated upon Christ's return. Some of them saw many antichrist figures or a position such as the popes as representing this Man of Sin.

The view I hold is the only one that I feel lines up with all the truths we have already gone over in this book. This point was not at all arrived at all at once, nor was I solidly for any one view. I was raised with a Futurist and a Premillennial view, I moved into a Historicist, and Amilennial view for many years, but after studying and seeing all that I have shared in this book I came to the only clear conclusion that lines up with what Christ and the Apostles said about how we should view such things.

Overall, I now hold a Preterist view of Revelation, and a Postmillennial view of Chapters 20-22 (As I believe that 21, and 22 are just adding meaning to the 1,000-year reign and beyond and not speaking about literal things that happen after the 1,000 years).

However, I do not think that the 1,000 years end with Christ's return—as some Postmillinials do, as we see another event take place after this 1,000 years that I do not think should be overlooked. I also do not think that the 1,000 years is speaking about the entirety of the reign of Christ just a very specific part of it. As far as I know, this take is unique, and I will explain why I feel this way as we go on in this chapter.

So to clarify my view, I think the 1,000 years began with the binding of Satan which happened in 70 A.D. I see the 1,000 years as a reference to the spreading out of the Church all around the world, during which the saints will rule with Christ both on earth and in heaven. This is the judgment of the saints spoken about in Daniel 7 and the parable of the talents.

This phase of the rule of Christ and the saints, I think, is the fullness of the Gentiles mentioned in Romans 11. This specific period is to prepare the world for the final manifestation of the Gospel on the earth. No age of the Church has seen the full promise of the Gospel manifested on the earth as spoken about in the prophets, and even Revelation 21-22. This is a point I will explain in greater detail later in this chapter. This manifestation must happen before Christ comes back, and after the 1,000 years are over.

I say this because this manifestation on the earth speaks of death and sinners still being on the earth which cannot be if Christ has returned. Because this state has never been seen on the earth there must be a time before Christ comes that it will be seen as this is one of the promises of the Gospel. We will dive into this as we go on.

Because I do not focus on the Revelation itself, to convey why I believe the above, I would highly recommend three books: First "When Jerusalem Fell," by Dr. Kenneth L. Gentry Jr. which shows, in my opinion, indisputable proof that Revelation was written before 70 A.D. The next is "When the Man Comes Around," by Douglas Wilson who has written one of the simplest, yet still profound, commentaries on Revelation that I have ever read. The last book is "Revelation/Four View" by Steve Gregg, in this book Steve goes verse by verse through the Revelation showing the interpretation of all four views side by side. These books will differ slightly from the view I will be presenting today, but they are excellent to lay the best foundation possible for understanding Revelation.

So with that out of the way, let's begin to look at this intriguing chapter.

Revelation 20:1-3: And I saw an angel come down from heaven, having the key of the bottomless pit and a great chain in his hand. 2. And he laid hold on the dragon, that old serpent, which is the Devil (meaning this is the same snake from the Garden), and Satan, and bound him a thousand years, 3. And cast him into the bottomless pit, and shut him up, and set a seal upon him, that he should deceive the nations no more, till the thousand years should be fulfilled: and after that he must be loosed a little season.

This chapter takes place after all the events previously described in the Revelation. As I stated I believe that the Revelation is the full revealing of Christ in his kingdom, his judgment against the harlot and the beast, and his declaration to the world about the bride. All of this is describing the significance of the Destruction of Jerusalem that we looked at in a previous chapter. As a result of these events, Satan is seen being bound for 1,000 years. These 1,000 years are the same years that we will be told in a moment that the saints will rule with Christ. This binding must be the first thing we tackle.

The verses do not say Satan is so bound that he cannot influence the world anymore, these chains give him some freedom. We see this in verse 3. So then the binding is specific. It is done to prevent the serpent from deceiving the nations, which is always a reference to the gentile world. This is important because, as I said, I think these 1,000 years are representing the fullness of the Gentiles.

To help build this argument consider that Christ took the kingdom from the Jewish system and gave it to another which is the Church. He did this so that they will bear the fruits of the kingdom (Matthew 21:43) After the Destruction of Jerusalem the Church was mainly made up of Gentiles with a small remnant of Jews. Paul tells us the reasons for this in Romans 11:1-24, but then he says this:

Romans 11:25-27: For I would not, brethren, that ye should be ignorant of this mystery, lest ye should be wise in your own conceits; that blindness in part is happened to Israel, until the fulness of the Gentiles be come in. 26. And so all Israel shall be saved (implying that until the Jews are also saved after the time of the gentiles, then the house is not fully saved yet): as it is written, There shall come out of Sion the Deliverer, and shall turn away ungodliness from Jacob: 27.

For this *is* my covenant unto them (the Jews), when I shall take away their sins.

In my mind, Paul is very clearly telling us that there will be a time when the Gentile Church will fulfill its purpose and then God will remove the blindness of the Jews bringing the full house of God into the covenant thus saving all Israel, Jew, and Gentile. We see this laid out by Jesus in the great commission.

The Church's marching orders were to disciple nations through the preaching of the Gospel. Recall from our study that Christ will rule until his enemies are put under his feet. Jesus is commanding the Church to begin doing just that, by spreading the kingdom on earth through the Gospel. The kingdom was given to the Church to produce the fruits or purpose of this call, which originally was the same call the Jews had in the Old Covenant.

There will come a time when this kingdom will have pre-eminence on the earth. I know this is repetitive, but I really want these promises to sink into our hearts.

Daniel 2:44: And in the days of these kings (the kings of world empire) shall the God of heaven set up a kingdom (Jesus did this), which shall never be destroyed: and the kingdom shall not be left to other people, *but* it shall break in pieces and consume all these kingdoms, and it shall stand for ever.

The end result is that Christ's kingdom will have rule over all the kingdoms of the world shown here by breaking and consuming those kingdoms. This happens by converting the nations. This is a slow process and we are only 2,000 years into it, but we have already made huge progress on a world scale. We went from 12 disciples to millions and entire nations have been birthed as a result of it.

We see this manifest itself with the 1,000-year rule as the saints will reign and rule with Christ the kingdom begins to consume the earth through conversion. Daniel is laying out that these world empires would begin to lose their rule as a result of what God is going to do during this 1,000-year reign both in heaven with his saints and on earth with his saints.

Daniel 7:26-27: But the judgment shall sit (referring to the judgment of the saints), and <u>they shall take away his dominion</u> (Speaking about the dominion of the beastly systems who all belonged to the serpent), to <u>consume and to destroy *it* unto the end.</u>

27. And the kingdom and dominion, and the greatness of the kingdom under the whole heaven, shall be given <u>to the people of the saints of the most High</u>, whose kingdom *is* an everlasting kingdom, and <u>all dominions shall serve and obey him.</u>

We see pretty clearly that the purpose of the saint's rule is to bring about judgment against the worldly beastly system and manifest the kingdom of Christ on this earth. This is done with Christ as our head. The thousand years is the long game of this rule, after which a very short event takes place that will allow the fullness of the gospel kingdom to manifest on the earth. This is when Christ deals the killing blow to Satan and the kingdoms. After this death blow, we will see a manifestation of the kingdom in its purest form that will spread over the earth until a victorious Christ comes to defeat the last enemy which is death.

This is why:

Daniel 7:12: As concerning the rest of the beasts (worldly systems/ kingdoms), they had their dominion taken away (by Christ): <u>yet their lives were prolonged for a season and time.</u> (This was to manifest the kingdom through the joint rule of Christ and his saints on the earth. These kingdoms had to remain so that the kingdom of Christ could consume them.)

This is the overview of what I believe this 1,000-years is speaking about. So let's continue to build our understanding a little better. First, let us look at the process in which Satan was cast out and bound according to Christ and what its purpose was:

John 12:31: Now is the judgment of this world: <u>now shall the prince of this world</u> (Satan) be cast out (Speaking of Satan being cast out of heaven by the death, and resurrection of Christ, see Revelation 12:7-12 to see how this happened). 32. And I, if I be lifted up from the earth (Most people think this is referring to his crucifixion, but it is actually speaking of his ascension into heaven from the earth after the resurrection), <u>will draw all *men* unto me</u> (the Holy Spirit and the preaching of the kingdom through his Church is what draws all men to him).

We see in the Old Testament that the heathen nations were ruled by "gods" (Daniel 10:13) which were not gods but demonic authorities who worked with Satan to bind and blind the nations. Paul also references this hold that Satan had over the gentiles in 2 Corinthians 4:4. We also know that the idols that the heathens prayed to were not gods but devils (1 Corinthians 10:20). All of this speaks to the hold that the devil had over the gentile world. Christ himself speaks about this:

Mark 3:27: No man can enter into a strong man's house (Referencing Satan and his dominion), and spoil his goods (being the heathen and oppressed peoples), except he (Christ) will first bind the strong man (Satan and his devils), and then he will spoil his house (Prophesying of taking the gentiles out of the bondage of Satan).

Satan was cast out of heaven when Christ came into his kingdom. This is prophetically recorded in Revelation 12:7-12 and happened when Christ ascended into heaven and put to shame the powers of the accuser.

Hebrews 9:12: Neither by the blood of goats and calves, but by his own blood he entered in once into the holy place, having obtained eternal redemption *for us.*

Paul speaks of these same concepts in:

Colossians 2:13-15: 13. And you, being dead in your sins and the uncircumcision of your flesh (Speaking about gentiles), hath he quickened (made alive/resurrected spiritually) together with him, having forgiven you all trespasses;

14. Blotting out the handwriting of ordinances that was against us, which was contrary to us, and took it out of the way, nailing it to his cross; 15. *And* having <u>spoiled principalities and powers</u>, he made a shew of them openly, triumphing over them in it.

Christ's victory utterly crushed the head of the serpent and plundered his goods, that being the gentile nations:

Hebrews 2:14: Forasmuch then as the children are partakers of flesh and blood, he (Jesus) also himself likewise took part of the same (Meaning he became a man); that through death he (Jesus) might destroy him (Satan) <u>that had the power of death, that is, the devil;</u>

That is why Christ declared:

Revelation 1:18: *I am* he that liveth, and was dead; and, behold, I am alive for evermore, Amen; and have the keys of hell and of death (These had previously belonged to Satan).

Yet the full binding of Satan did not happen until Jerusalem was destroyed. This plays out as the main theme in Revelation. If you take an overview of it, the Revelation is the revealing of Christ and his kingdom (that kingdom was of all nations, meaning revealed that he had the right to judge them), his judgment of both the Roman world and the Jewish world, the persecution of the saints by the harlot, the beast, and the beastly system, and Christ's ultimate victory over them. It also reveals the harlot, the beast she rides upon, the judgment of the harlot, and ends with the revealing of the bride of Christ (his Church the New Jerusalem) on the earth.

The harlot is the city of Jerusalem (representing the Jewish religious system) which also represented the original bride of God who has played the harlot and called such in many passages (Hosea 2:2-13, Jeremiah 3:1-3, Ezekiel 16:44-48, etc). The beast she rides upon is Rome. She is decked in the priestly garments (Exodus 28:1-12). She is called mystery Babylon because she follows the oral traditions of the Elders rather than the Law, which we know today as the Babylonian Talmud. The veil that separated the holy of holies in the temple was a Babylonian tapestry according to Josephus, which was rendered in two upon the death of Christ (Matthew 27:51). But most importantly she was drunk with the blood of all the saints Jesus lays this at her feet as well:

Matthew 23:35-36: That upon you may come all the righteous blood shed upon the earth, from the blood of righteous Abel unto the blood of Zacharias son of Barachias, whom ye slew between the temple and the altar. 36. Verily I say unto you, All these things shall come upon this generation.

Luke 13:33-34: Nevertheless I must walk to day, and to morrow, and the *day* following: for it cannot be that a prophet perish out of Jerusalem. 34. O Jerusalem, Jerusalem, which killest the prophets, and stonest them that are sent unto thee; how often would I have gathered thy children together, as a hen *doth gather* her brood under *her* wings, and ye would not!

There are many other proofs, but the important issue is the contrast between the harlot and the bride. In many ways, Revelation is the putting away of the harlot from the world and the presentation of the bride to the world. The bride was not able to begin to walk openly as she would until the first wife was put away and the bride could shine in the glory of the bridegroom. Once the bride was revealed, Satan is bound from deceiving the nations, the house of the strong man (gentiles) was plundered and the Church during this time—though it will always be made up of Jews and Gentile—it became primarily one of Gentiles. Thus the gentile Church was bringing in the fruits of repentance that God desired of the kingdom. This too was prophecied:

Matthew 21:43: Therefore say I unto you, The kingdom of God shall be taken from you (The Jews), and given to a nation (the Church) bringing forth the fruits thereof.

Matthew 23:38: Behold, your house (Judaism) is left unto you desolate.

I do not want to paint the Jews unfairly. This was a judgment against long-dead ancestors and a religious system, but it is still important to address. Many today think I am antisemitic because I preach what the bible says about the Jewish religion. I say yet again that I love the Jewish people, but because I love them I will not lie to them. All of us have to see and admit our fault against a Holy God and humble ourselves so that we could be saved by our gracious Savior and Lord. Now that the bride has been revealed, the only way to God and his covenant for salvation is housed in the Church (not as a denomination or organization but as the body of Christ in all true believers). That is why people must enter into the New Jerusalem (described prophetically in revelation 21) and many Jews have and will yet enter in. Paul addresses this very thing:

Romans 11:1: I say then, Hath God cast away his people? God forbid (I say amen). For I also am an Israelite, of the seed of Abraham, *of* the tribe of Benjamin.

The Jews themselves were not cast off, rather their religious system and their place as the covenant people and bride have been removed. Yet God is ever merciful and allows all to come into the heavenly Jerusalem and be born again as sons of God as our father Abraham through faith in the Son. The will of God was to make one of two peoples in

Christ (Ephesians 2:14). This is another very important point that will be relevant to remember in the coming passages, as currently half of this man remains blind, and as we saw there is a promised time coming when this blindness is removed.

None of these things could happen if the serpent had not first been bound. His influence over the heathen was broken so that the kingdom could begin to fill the earth. As such, the prophecies in Daniel began to unfold. The next part of Revelation matches almost exactly with the idea of the saints receiving their rule as mentioned in Daniel 7:22.

Revelation 20:4: And I saw thrones, and they sat upon them, and judgment was given unto them: and I _saw the souls_ of them that were beheaded for the witness of Jesus, and for the word of God, and which had not worshipped the beast, neither his image, neither had received _his_ mark upon their foreheads, or in their hands; and they lived and reigned with Christ a thousand years.

Let us notice that John says he sees thrones and they were given to the souls of them that had been killed. The souls would not be on the earth but in heaven. John never says he sees these thrones on the earth. We see these same souls mentioned several other times in Revelation, here is the first:

Revelation 6:9-10: 9. And when he had opened the fifth seal, I saw under the altar the souls of them that were slain for the word of God, and for the testimony which they held: 10. And they cried with a loud voice, saying, How long, O Lord, holy and true, dost thou not judge and avenge our blood on them that dwell on the earth?

These are the souls of the prophets and early Church that had died. They are told to wait until their fellow martyrs, that were yet to die in the following portions of Revelation, join them. These that would soon join them were the martyrs who died under the Beast (Nero) who refused to take his mark (Emperor worship) which resulted in their gruesome deaths.

This highlights another theme in Revelation. That is: Christ is avenging and vindicating the blood of the persecuted saints and prophets who died at the hand of the harlot (Jerusalem) and the beastly system that she rode on (Rome). That is also why it was declared:

Revelation 14:13: And I heard a voice from heaven saying unto me, Write, Blessed *are* the <u>dead which die in the Lord from henceforth</u>: Yea, saith the Spirit, that they may rest from their labours; and their works do follow them.

Let us return to the main part of our text; we now see that these same souls are being rewarded now that their blood has been avenged. Their reward is that they shall rule with Christ for 1,000 years upon these thrones. It says they lived and reigned. Many people claim this must be a physical resurrection. False-hope will say that this is speaking about the 1,000-year physical reign of Christ on the earth and these saints must therefore have been physically resurrected to rule.

If taken by itself it would seem as if this verse is claiming this, however, we must consider the foundations we learned that Christ taught us about the resurrection. We know that all the dead will be raised on the last day, not just the righteous. Christ, nor his apostles, said that Jesus would resurrect only the saints for 1,000 years (or any length of time) before the unrighteous. What we do see is that when the resurrection happens both are raised together and there would be a judgment that is final upon all. There will be no more death for the last enemy killed when Christ comes is death. There will be no more rule over the unrighteous as they will all be cast into hell.

So whatever these verses are saying it is not speaking of a bodily resurrection. If it were this would be the only time in the entire bible that such a thing is mentioned and it would go against all the foundations laid before. To best understand this we need a bit more information about this reign.

Revelation 20:5-6: 6. But the rest of the <u>dead lived not again until the thousand years were finished</u> (we do not know how long after the 1,000 years this will be, just that it happens afterward). This *is* the <u>first resurrection</u>. 6. Blessed and holy *is* he that hath part in the <u>first resurrection</u>: on such the <u>second death hath no power</u>, but they shall be <u>priests of God and of Christ</u>, and shall reign with him a thousand years.

Let us break down all this. This rule which is the reward of the saint is:

1. The first resurrection.
2. This resurrection protects from the second death.
3. The saints that have a part in it are made priests and kings and shall reign with Christ.
4. The rest of the dead will not be raised until sometime after this reign.

It should be pointed out that all of these points are not reserved only for the saints in heaven, this is also a reality in the born again life. Thus I propose that what we are seeing is a duel reality. We are getting a glimpse into heaven seeing that what is happening in the heavens is also being manifested on the earth in Christ. Let's break each point down to see this a bit better:

Jesus speaks about the first resurrection in:

John 5:24: Verily, verily, I say unto you, He that heareth my word, and believeth on him that sent me, hath everlasting life, and shall not come into condemnation; but is passed from death unto life.

Jesus says you were dead, but I have made you alive. This is a spiritual reality. He explains this a bit more:

John 5:25: Verily, verily, I say unto you, The hour is coming, and now is, when the dead shall hear the voice of the Son of God: and they that hear shall live.

Jesus claims that this resurrection from death into life is something now happening. Yet, he puts a distinction between this first resurrection and a second resurrection:

John 5:28-29: Marvel not at this: for the hour is coming, in the which all that are in the graves shall hear his voice, 29. And shall come forth; they that have done good, unto the resurrection of life; and they that have done evil, unto the resurrection of damnation.

So we see Jesus speaking about a first resurrection referring to the spiritual and a second resurrection referring to the physical just like in Revelation. Paul uses much the same language:

Ephesians 2:1: And you *hath he quickened* (made alive), who were <u>dead in trespasses and sins;</u>

There are many more examples that I could turn to. To have the clearest view of this, however, all we have to do is compare this first resurrection of life to the second death. The second death is declared later in the chapter:

Revelation 20:14: And death and hell were cast into the lake of fire. <u>This is the second death.</u>

So this first resurrection is one that protects us from the final eternal judgment of the lake of fire. Again this is something that happens the moment we are born again. The first resurrection then is the resurrection of Salvation. So what we are seeing is the reality of this truth manifested in heaven and earth. This is made more clear when we realize that the souls in this passage were the souls of the Old Testament saints, and martyred Christians that had been so persecuted and killed. Some had been crying out to God for thousands of years begging that their blood would be avenged against the harlot.

What is being revealed is that these heavenly saints are partakers of the very same reality that we have. We all rule and reign with Christ as well as they do. Their rule coincided with the judgment that was given to the saints on earth as described in Daniel 7 and the parable of the talents. As we saw when we dug into that chapter this rule coincided with the Day of the Lord in 70 A.D. This was often called the communion of saints by our forefathers.

This duel reality is not only found in Revelation we see it in:

Ephesians 2:6 And hath raised *us* up together, and made *us* sit together in heavenly *places* in Christ Jesus:

Hebrews 12:1b Wherefore seeing we also are compassed (surrounded) about with so great a cloud of witnesses (speaking about the Old Testament saints)

In both of these verses, we see two realities. Christians are presently on earth, yet spiritually in heaven at the same time. In heaven, all saints both on the earth and in heaven are assembled together in Christ before God. There are other examples, but I think these will due to prove our point: There can be two things true at the same time. Jesus told us to pray with this reality in mind:

Matthew 6:10: Thy kingdom come. Thy will be done in earth, as it is in heaven.

This concept is laid out in the Old Testament. The tabernacle, temple, and their related relics were made after the pattern of things seen in heaven (Exodus 25:40). The Revelation itself is full of these very same patterns. You see first something happen in heaven and then manifest on the earth. This same principle is true in this text. We are seeing the saints ruling with Christ in heaven and it manifests also in the Church on earth.

This brings us to the next point, "they were made priest and kings..."

This was first declared by the souls when the lamb received the scroll (a picture of his right to rule and judge) from God. This truth became a reality once Christ ascended:

Revelation 5:10: And hast made us unto our God kings and priests: and we shall reign on the earth (this is being declared by the souls in heaven. How do they reign on earth? They do so with the saints in Christ just as we are spiritually assembled right now in heaven in Christ they are still a part of our body and reign with us as we are all one in Christ. This same concept was spoken of by Paul when he said they were a part of the temple which we ourselves are also a part of Ephesians 2:20).

This was declared when Christ received the kingdom authority from the Father in Revelation 5 this is pictured with him receiving the scroll. The souls of the saints go on to praise the truth of this authority in verses 8-14 of the same chapter. This declaration was made manifest after Satan was bound, and then the saints were given rule for these 1,000 years exactly as we also saw prophecied in Daniel being given to the saints on earth. We see this same truth declared over the earthly manifestation of the Church:

1 Peter 2:9-10: But ye are a chosen generation, a royal priesthood, an holy nation, a peculiar people; that ye should shew forth the praises of him who hath called you out of darkness into his marvellous light: 10. Which in time past were not a people, but are now the people of God: which had not obtained mercy, but now have obtained mercy.

Again we see a duel reality. On earth Christians right now are a royal (kingly) priesthood. This is further declared by John before he sees the hotly contested apocalyptic vision:

Revelation 1:5-6: And from Jesus Christ, *who is* the faithful witness, *and* the first begotten of the dead, and the prince of the kings of the earth. Unto him that loved us, and washed us from our sins in his own blood,

6. And <u>hath made us kings and priests unto God and his Father</u>; to him *be* glory and dominion for ever and ever. Amen.

John is writing this to Churches that existed in the first century when he wrote. Meaning this reality is one that all believers are already partaking in through Christ. Yet in Revelation 20, we see this same reality as a reward for the martyred saints, further proving that this 1,000-year reign is not a physical one.

This brings us to the last point, the "rest of the dead lived not again..." If the saints were made alive who were dead (spiritually resurrected) both on earth and heaven, then this is referring to the bodily resurrection of the just and the unjust on the final day. This will happen after the 1,000 years are over, but not immediately afterward as another event is spoken about before even this.

When we go back to the list of points we learned about the Second Coming, we can, with confidence, know exactly when the rest of the dead will live again. That is on the final day when Christ appears in victory with the saints that have gone before us and is announced by trumpet, shout, and archangel at the time of the harvest.

Because of all these truths, we should be able to, see a few points. This 1,000-year reign is both manifested in the saints now on earth as well as in heaven. They rule with Christ, his rule now is at the right hand of the father, and manifested on the earth through his Church. Again this seems to line up exactly with the verses quoted before in Daniel.

We on earth are partakers by being kings, priests, and ambassadors to God on the earth, and our heavenly brothers and sisters do so in heaven. These saints in heaven overcame and Christ was faithful to a promise he also declared to the Churches:

Revelation 3:21: To him that overcometh will I grant to sit with me in my throne, even as I also overcame, and am set down with my Father in his throne.

This is true for both saints living and on earth, and those that had overcome at the cost of their lives in heaven.

All of this is why I propose that the 1,000-year reign is not speaking of a literal 1,000 years, but is speaking about the reign of Christ that began with the binding of Satan, thus it did not begin with Christ's reign as his reign started when he sat down at the right hand of the Father and the Spirit fell on Pentecost some 40 years before Satan was bound. The reign of Christ never ends, but the specific reign of 1,000 years will end once it accomplishes God's purpose on the earth.

Once this time has ended, God will then bring about a time unlike any other the world has ever seen. It is during this time I believe the Jews will be converted to Christianity and the New Covenant and restored to their land, and we will see a manifestation and revival on the earth such as has only been hinted at in the prophets. Again I must state that I do not think what is happening in Palestine today has anything to do with this a point I will further explain shortly.

Remember when Christ does return he defeats death by resurrecting the dead, he transforms the saints, judges the world, and then offers the fullness of the kingdom back to his father (1 Corinthians 15:24). This kingdom will have put all enemies under Christ which includes Satan and the nations of the world and the other religious systems.

I believe that the following event shows how he does this:

Revelation 20: 7-10: 7. And when the thousand years are expired, Satan shall be loosed out of his prison,

8. And shall go out to deceive the nations which are in the four quarters of the earth (Meaning all nations north, south, east, and west) Gog and Magog (Most people think that Gog and Magog are representative of the descendants of Gog and Magog in the bible which causes all sorts of people to try and pin these figures on a specific people group or nation, most popularly on Russia. However, John tells us in the following verses that Gog and Magog are Satan and the last enemies of Christ that will make one final war against the Church, and not a

specific nation. John is referencing a war mentioned in Ezekiel that he wants to draw our attention to so that we can learn from it. Meaning I believe he is mentioning Gog and Magog here as he wants us to look back on that event which we will do shortly), to gather them together to battle: the number of whom *is* as the sand of the sea.

9. And they went up on the <u>breadth of the earth</u> (again we see an allusion to this event being worldwide), and compassed (surrounding) the camp of the saints (the Church) about, and the beloved city (New Jerusalem a picture of the New Covenant) (The saints at this point are worldwide. This is speaking of worldwide persecution of the Church and the New Covenant by Satan and his armies likened to Gog and Magog): and fire came down from God out of heaven, and devoured them (This doesn't say God comes down, it says fire from God comes down. This is a reference to how God always defended the Old Testament saints meaning God will show his great care for the surrounded saints and defeat their enemies which they could not defeat themselves).

10. And the devil that deceived them was cast into the lake of fire and brimstone (A picture showing the final defeat and removal of his influence over/in the earth), where the beast and the false prophet *are*, and shall be tormented day and night for ever and ever.

There are so many different views on these verses, even among those that take the same Postmillennial view as I do. Some think that this passage means that after the Church has been victorious, God allows Satan out of his prison to show that man is still as fallen at heart as ever and is allowed to do this one last time to prove that the Church was not responsible for the victory, but God was. They usually take the fire coming down to devour them to be Christ's Second Coming.

Amillennials see this as the final reign of antichrist, and they too see this fire as the Second Coming. False-hope sees this in many different ways but ultimately he claims this as God's last victory over Satan before the end of the Kingdom Age (remember all ages to them have to end in corruption, and this is the corruption the Kingdom age ends with) and the beginning of the Eternal State. I find it fascinating that many of False-hope's preachers claim that the Gog and Magog war is what kicks off the 7-year tribulation, yet that war originally happened in 175 B.C., and this one is mentioned in Revelation is happening long after their 7-year tribulation would have happened.

I take a slightly unique approach to this. First, I must stress again that the last enemy Christ defeats on his return is not a great army, nor is it Satan, but death itself. If this fire from heaven is Christ's return then it doesn't seem to match with what Jesus already said, he never said he came to defeat an army of Satan, therefore I think this is speaking about something else.

I believe John is referencing Gog and Magog as he wants us to take Ezekiel's Gog and Magog War as a type of the events now being described in Revelation. Meaning the Gog and Magog event that happened in the past foreshadows the event that will happen in the future. This is similar to how the Day of the Lord and the Second Coming have similarities.

The Gog and Magog War described in Ezekiel is describing the war of Antiochus Epiphanes whom Daniel prophesied about in Daniel 8:8-27 and as recorded in the historical book of 2 Maccabees. During this war, Antiochus (Gog) came against Israel with the Syrian army (Magog) and ultimately defiled the temple and the holy place. After which God eventually and miraculously destroyed Antiochus and his army. Most modern preachers say that the war described in Ezekiel is something in our future, however, this is a very modern stance that grossly manipulates the scriptures to fit their teaching. Like many of the errors of modern preaching, I would need a lot longer book to fully unravel the lies and show the truth. If demand is high enough I will gladly write a book delving into the truth of Ezekiel's Gog and Magog War.

For the sake of this book, I will simply say that the Gog and Magog War happened long ago. If you would like more definitive proof of this, I would recommend reading John Gill, Albert Barns, and/or Mathew Henry's commentary on Ezekiel 37-39. These are all available free online and can be found by a simple google search. These commentaries also come free as part of the bible study program called e-sword. I highly recommend and use this program myself and anyone can download it for free at www.esword.com.

These three great men dive verse by verse into the Gog and Magog War and will plainly show how Gog and Magog had to do with Antiochus and his invasion into Israel around 175 B.C. This was the understanding that nearly every church had before the 1900s, and I see no reason to dispute this view. Also, I would recommend reading 2 Maccabees which is an excellent history of the events, and I will state plainly that I think that is all it is. I do not claim it to be scripture.

With all that aside, what can this war teach us that John is trying to bring to mind? In Ezekiel, we see the armies of Antiochus surrounding Israel in Jerusalem and being victorious for a time. God then miraculously defends Jerusalem and destroyed Antiochus and his armies which brings in great peace and stability for the Jews. John tells us in the Revelation that Satan will likewise gather a great final army and comes against the New Jerusalem and the saints meaning Christians. Because Christians are worldwide this is speaking about world persecution of Christians. If we look at the events in the past as a picture I believe we can see what John is seeing just instead of being on a local scale with Israel we will see a global-scale event with the Church.

Part of the Gog and Magog War starts with the prophecy of God bringing back the Jews in Ezekiel 37. This chapter was a picture of the spiritual state of the Jews after Babylon destroyed Jerusalem. Ezekiel sees them as a valley of dead dry bones. God breathes life back into them and unites the two houses of Israel making them one people again. This is a reference to the fact that the Hebrew nation was divided into two kingdoms, ten tribes to the north became Israel, and the two to the south became Judah. The ten of the north were rebellious and cut off for their sin, Jacob was more faithful for a time but ultimately suffered the same fate. In this prophecy, we see the two being made one and brought back to life to serve the Messiah. This happened as God began to draw the Jews back to Israel from every nation they were scattered to.

Modern preachers use these same verses to claim that the modern State of Israel is a fulfillment of this prophecy, but, when we keep this passage in context we do not see this.

This gathering and unity were done to bring the people back into their land for the arrival of the Messiah and make them one people again. This is why you see only one Jewish nation during the time of Christ and not the two kingdom divide you had before with Israel and Judah. This is the same period of Jacob's Trouble we looked at before. Just like in Jeremiah, we see in Ezekiel that God brings them back for the promise of the Messiah from the nations through hardship and trials called by Jerimiah, Jacobs Trouble. The Gog and Magog War is one such great trouble they went through. So once again, we see False-hope take verses out of context and try to place them in the future. All of this did happen and unlike what modern teachers say, Ezekiel is not describing future things, and none of these events were fulfilled by the modern state of Israel.

The Gog and Magog War happened as God was restoring the Jews after Babylon's destruction of Jerusalem. During this, they had a brief time of peace. It was during this time of peace that Antiochus comes and makes war with Israel and is ultimately defeated by God.

All of this I think was meant for us as a picture that John is calling us to look at. When we do so with a New Testament mindset I think these are the 4 major things we can see:

In Ezekiel 37 we see God revealing that Israel had become spiritually dead and cut off as a people because of their sins. Likewise in the New Testament, we see that they had been cut off due to unbelief. In this chapter, God is promising to unite two divided houses and make them one. This is done as blindness is removed after God breathes life back into them. They become united so that they may serve Jesus. In the New Testament Paul says that there will come a time when the blindness of the Jews is removed and they shall come into the New Covenant and all Israel (Jew and gentile) shall be saved). Meaning I think this first picture should be of the Christians and Jews being brought together again in Christ. This can also be a picture of the fragmented Christian cummunities coming back together.

After this union, the people have a time of peace and safety in their own land. This is described in Ezekiel 38. During this time of peace, Gog (Antiochus) sees that the people are in safety and he desires to overcome them as he thinks they are weak. However, it is God who does this so that when he judges Gog and defends the Jews it shows both the gentiles and the Jews that God is a living God. This causes repentance in the land. For us, I believe the picture is that the Gospel will have made great progress over the earth and the Jews have begun to repent and come into the Church, bringing great peace. During this time God allows Gog (Satan) out to gather the final enemies of Christ against the Church. Just as with Antiochus, when God judges Satan it is a testimony to both the Christians and none Christians of who God is. Satan and his army, being the last enemies of Christ and his Church, are all defeated and removed from the earth by this judgment. We see identical language being used of fire coming from heaven when we compare Ezekiel 38:22 to Revelation 20:10.

After this victory, there was a time when the Jews burned their weapons of war and had a time of peace. As I will show shortly, the gospel kingdom also promises a time when there will be no more war anymore.

We see that this war removed many of the barriers and idolatry that Israel had struggled with before. This is why you do not see Baal worship and other such idolatry during Christ's time as you saw with the Israel of old. Their idols eventually became the temple and the doctrines of man. These two points were the largest contentions that Jesus had with the people while he was on earth. We never see him preaching against the idolatry of old. Likewise, I think this would picture a time of great worldwide revival. This judgment of the last enemies is what I believe that the stone mentioned in Daniel two is that destroyed the kingdoms of the world. Satan has been removed and the last enemies and obstacles of the kingdom have been destroyed by Christ allowing a period of great glory on the earth.

Let's dive a bit deeper. Paul says this in Romans:

Romans 11:25-26: For I would not, brethren, that ye should be ignorant of this mystery, lest ye should be wise in your own conceits; that blindness in part is happened to Israel, until the fulness of the Gentiles be come in. 26. And so all Israel (Jew and Gentile) shall be saved: as it is written, There shall come out of Sion the Deliverer, and shall turn away ungodliness from Jacob (referencing the Jews):

Paul goes on to quote the prophets and the promise that God would still remember the Jews and restore them to the New Covenant. This fullness of the gentiles is the pillaging of the heathen world during the time that Satan has been bound and there will come a time when Christ's pillaging of the gentile world is complete. This is pictured as we saw elsewhere as the kingdom of Christ consuming the kingdoms of the earth (most of which are gentile in nature) through the preaching of the Gospel.

Once this happens, I believe there will be a great national revival among the Jews. God then shows the world that he is with these saints Jew and Gentiles by judging Satan and the last enemies of Christ. I believe he waits to do this until the whole house has been reunited so that all the things written about Christ and the reign of the Messiah and the judgment of the saints were all fulfilled. Look again at this verse:

Daniel 2:35: Then was the iron, the clay, the brass, the silver, and the gold, broken to pieces together (symbolic of the world kingdoms), and <u>became like the chaff</u> of the summer threshingfloors; (So far these kingdoms remain and are not yet like chaff, which is weightless outer husks of the good wheat grains that blow off as one tosses them in the air during the summer harvest. I believe this final Gog and Magog event described by John is what will cause the kingdoms to be like this) and <u>the wind carried them away, that no place was found for them</u> (After this final judgment of Satan, we no longer see the kingdoms of the world. All that will be left is Christs's kingdom. There will still be unsaved in this kingdom as we saw with the parable of the wheat and tares, but at this point, the earth will begin to be His kingdom that is why Daniel goes on to say): and the stone (the kingdom of Christ) that smote the image became a <u>great mountain</u> (Symbolic of the mountain of the New Covenant)<u>, and filled the whole earth</u> (I believe this is describing a worldwide revival, Satan and his kingdoms have been destroyed and have vanished as chaff in the wind because of Christ).

A very similar thing is shown again in:

Daniel 7:27: And the kingdom and dominion, and the greatness of the kingdom under the whole heaven, shall be given to the people of the saints of the most High (It is after this Gog and Magog event that I believe we will begin to see the fullness of this promise), whose kingdom *is* an everlasting kingdom, and <u>all dominions shall serve and obey him</u> (Jesus).(So far this has not happened, but I believe it shall happen after Satan is defeated)

Some people think that because the modern state of Israel exists that means the fullness of the gentiles is coming to or has come to an end, but this cannot be.

Paul promised that the blindness would be removed so that they would come into the New Covenant Church after the fullness of the gentiles, not that a small fraction of them will come back into their land. This turning to Christ has not happened. God only ever promised to restore the land to Israel when they repented, which they have not, and this is one of the many reasons they do not have the land or God. We have never seen the Jewish nation do this, and we do not at all see a restoration of the Jews in truth in modern Israel in any case. Only the unbelieving Zionistic Jews, a relatively small sect of religious zionist Jews, and secular Jews have returned and their blindness very much remains. Meaning what we see in modern Israel is not at all related to this prophecy being fulfilled.

Zionism seeks to reestablish old Israel with its political and religious system and temple. They would gladly begin animal sacrifices again if they had a temple an act in itself that is complete blasphemy. The "Christians" that support this antichrist system just want this to happen because they think it will make Jesus come back and rapture them. False-hope has convinced them that a temple has to be rebuilt before the rapture can happen.

When Israel is revived near the end of the world it is not to remain dead but come into the New Covenant, i.e. to be born again and raised from the dead in Christ. The exact opposite of this has happened in modern Israel. Many modern teachers say that the Jews have to be gathered in Israel so that when Christ comes he can save them, but I argue that they must be saved before Christ comes or they will be damned. As we saw in this book, when Christ returns on that final day there is no chance for repentance.

So I think that what we are seeing in Modern Israel is a falsehood orchestrated by the spirit of antichrist to try and deceive the nations and churches. God will still use this for his purpose, but I do not think the end of this time of the Gentiles is close at hand. Entire gentile nations have still been largely unconverted. India, the Middle East, many parts of Asia, Africa, South America, and Israel itself are just now beginning to get touched by the gospel. All of these will still need to have a Christian presence before the fullness of the Gentile world comes in.

Let us dig a bit more into this 1,000-year reign which I propose is the fullness of the gentiles. If we reckon the 1,000 years as the Church conquering the promised land (the gentile world) with the gospel then we would see that as the Israelites had, a time of peace will follow their conquest. When Israel conquered Canaan they did not destroy all their enemies and this became a plague on the Israelites. If we take this to be a picture of how the 1,000-years will play out, then there will come a time when it seems as if the gospel has done its job and the Church becomes complacent. God then allows Satan to unite all the enemies against his people one last time. This had another purpose that we can also see when we look back at the purpose of the Gog and Magog War in Ezekiel I think this is the same reason God allows it in Revelation.

In Ezekiel 38:16 God says he allows the war to happen so: that the heathen (unbelievers) may know me (God), when I shall be sanctified (Set-apart) in thee, O Gog (Satan), before their eyes.

So if we take this reason behind what Christ is doing when he releases Satan it is to declare God to the remaining unbelieving world through the judgment that God will release on him and his followers. Notice that this happens when Gog (satan) comes against God's people Israel at the beginning of this verse. John clarifies this meaning when he says surrounds the saint and the Holy City Revelation 20:9. Listen to the following verses and we will see a perfect picture laid out:

Ezekiel 38:19: For in my jealousy *and* in the <u>fire of my wrath</u> (his judgment of fire from heaven) have I spoken, Surely in that day there shall be a great shaking in the land of Israel (when referring to Revelation Israel will be worldwide in the church so the whole Christian world will be shaken by this final Gog and Magog event);

Remember I think John is saying these events paint us a picture when we look at this with the Revelation in mind. The shaking of the saints of God, pictured as the land of Israel originally, was meant to speak to the heathens and the Saints when God judged them. This caused something to happen in ancient Israel which I believe will happen all over the world:

Ezekiel 38:20-22: So that the fishes of the sea, and the fowls of the heaven, and the beasts of the field, and all creeping things that creep upon the earth, and <u>all the men that *are* upon the face of the earth</u>, shall shake at my presence, and the mountains (Nation/governments/ religious authorities are all representative of mountains. Unsaved people are also called beasts in the bible, and Jesus used a parable calling men fish. I believe this is trying to capture all of creation, not just man.) shall be thrown down, and the steep places shall fall (the remaining stumbling block to the faith), and every wall (defense against the gospel) shall fall to the ground.

21. And I will call for a sword against him (Gog/satan) throughout all my mountains (kingdoms so these will be the nations that have been brought under God's church), saith the Lord GOD: every man's sword shall be against his brother (this last part clarifies that the mountains are kingdoms).

22. And I will plead against him (Gog/satan) with pestilence and with blood, and I will rain upon him (Gog/satan), and upon his bands (Magog), and upon the many people that *are* with him (fence-sitters), an overflowing rain, and <u>great hailstones, fire, and brimstone</u>.

Compare verse 22 to what John says:

Revelation 20:9 And they went up on the breadth of the earth, and compassed the camp of the saints about, and the beloved city: and <u>fire came down from God out of heaven, and devoured them</u>.

As I hope is clear these two events parallel very well with one another. Originally this event in Ezekiel removed the stumbling blocks of the Jews being regathered after Babylon. What John is seeing is the same thing happening on a global scale to the ungodly governments and religious systems, which at this time will be the last of those who stand against Christ. These would be corrupt heathen governments, the spirit of antichrist, and all the other great enemies that must be defeated before death.

So to summarize, we see Satan released, he gathers the remaining enemies of God and begins persecuting both the saints of God and the New Covenant. God will then destroy these enemies miraculously, and Satan's last influence is removed from the earth when he is cast into the lake of fire. This destroys the last mountains of the worldly systems.

This is victoriously declared by God as one of the chief purposes for the ancient Gog and Magog war and I believe it is the same purpose in the final war in the future:

Ezekiel 38:23: Thus will I magnify myself, and sanctify myself; and I will be known in the eyes of many nations, and they shall know that I *am* the LORD.

This is built upon in chapter 39.

Ezekiel 39:7: So will I make my holy name known in the midst of my people Israel; and I will not *let them* pollute my holy name any more: and the heathen shall know that I *am* the LORD, the Holy One in Israel.

Again if these things are a picture that John is wanting us to see I think we can see how this final event with Satan in Revelation will bring a time of great revival on the earth. With Satan's hand fully removed from the earth, Christianity will blossom in purity as it never has before.

I am not certain how long this period will last, but when I read Ezekiel's Gog and Magog War, as John seems to want us to, I cannot see this period ending quickly. So after an unspecified amount of time Christ comes back to defeat death and judge all.

His coming is in great glory and victory having filled the earth with the image of God in man, having taken dominion over the face of the whole earth, and having thrown down all the enemies of God. It is during the period before Christ comes and after the Revelation Gog and Magog event, that I think we will see Isaiah's (and others) prophesied time of the gospel reality being heralded in its fullness; for this is the full manifestation of the gospel once it comes to its glorious fullness on the earth before the appearance of the son of man. Let's look at one such prophecy and see what I mean:

Isaiah 65:17-25: 17. For, behold, I create new heavens and a new earth: and the former shall not be remembered, nor come into mind. (This is a reference not to literal heavens and earth, as we will see in a moment, but the doing away with the Old Covenant and its religious system of Judaism, and the establishment of the New Covenant and the Church. The fullness of this will not, in my opinion, be seen until after the 1,000 years and the Gog and Magog of Revelation are finished, however, it is currently a reality in heaven and we are told to pray it down onto the earth Matthew 6:10.)

18. But be ye glad and rejoice for ever in that which I create: for, behold, I <u>create</u> Jerusalem (referencing New Jerusalem) a rejoicing, and her people a joy.

19. And I will rejoice in Jerusalem (New Jerusalem), and joy in my people: and the voice of weeping shall be no more heard in her, nor the voice of crying.

20. There shall be no more thence an infant of days, nor an old man that hath not filled his days: for the child <u>shall die an hundred years old</u> (This has to happen before Christ returns as once he does there is no more death, and this state has never been since Christ came); but the sinner *being* an hundred years old shall be accursed (again when Christ comes back there will be no more sinners, but even unto the time of the harvest there will still be sinners, so I think this whole event is describing the restoration after the Gog and Magog event after the 1,000 years).

21. And they shall build houses, and inhabit *them;* and they shall plant vineyards, and eat the fruit of them. (Again you see a passage of time while the above-promised longevity is seen on the earth. I believe this will be the state of the world after Satan is removed from the earth)

22. They shall not build, and another inhabit; they shall not plant, and another eat: for as the days of a tree *are* the days of my people, and mine elect shall long enjoy the work of their hands. (Again this has never been fully manifested yet on the earth and yet Isaiah is speaking that it will be, God cannot lie)

23. They shall not labour in vain, nor bring forth for trouble; for they *are* the seed of the blessed of the LORD, and their offspring with them. 24. And it shall come to pass, that before they call, I will answer; and while they are yet speaking, I will hear. 25. The wolf and the lamb shall feed together, and the lion shall eat straw like the bullock: and dust

shall be the serpent's meat. They shall not hurt nor destroy in all my holy mountain, saith the LORD. (Thus we see even the curse lifting from the earth and animals as well. Many other verses claim this same idea).

During this time we will see the fullness of this promise:

Isaiah 2:4: And he shall judge among the nations, and shall rebuke many people: and they shall beat their swords into plowshares, and their spears into pruninghooks: <u>nation shall not lift up sword against nation, neither shall they learn war any more</u>. (I showed how this was a result of the gospel on a personal level in an earlier chapter, but I think this is also meant to be seen on a global level after the Gog and Magog event of Revelation. Now that Satan has been removed from the earth, humanity will not learn war anymore and live in peace under the judgments of the saints as the earth becomes Christ's kingdom ripe for the harvest.)

If this view is correct after the fullness of this time described above comes in, the harvest described in the wheat and the tares is now at hand and so:

Revelation 20:11-15: And I saw a great white throne, and him that sat on it, from whose face the earth and the heaven fled away; and there was found no place for them. (This may not be speaking about the literal heaven and earth passing away as we see Christ gathering the nations on earth and offering them to his father in the parables. We also know Christ's kingdom will never end. I think this is more speaking about the earth being the Church and the heavens being the New Covenant. They are no longer needed for their purpose has been fulfilled and thus there was no place found for them on the earth anymore. At this point, the fullness of the kingdom is at hand and Christ is going to present it to his father after the judgment)

12. And I saw the dead, small and great, stand before God; and the books were opened: and another book was opened, which is *the book* of life: and the dead were judged out of those things which were written in the books, according to their works. (Matches all the parables and sayings of Christ perfectly) 13. And the sea gave up the dead which were in it; and death and hell delivered up the dead which were in them: and they were judged every man according to their works. <u>14. And death and hell were cast into the lake of fire. This is the second death. 15. And</u>

whosoever was not found written in the book of life was cast into the lake of fire.

Notice in verse 14 that it is here that death is judged and defeated, it is the death of death. When did Paul say this event will happen? Well in 1 Corinthians 15 Paul says that this is the last enemy that Christ defeats when he returns. This is also when the resurrection of the just and unjust are raised just as Jesus and all the other resurrection passages the bible teaches. I am highlighting this because this defeat of death comes AFTER the 1,000 years not before, or during. It comes at the end just like it had been told over and over again. This dismantles the concept of Premillennialism as taught by False-hope. Context matters and when scripture is taken out of context we lose the simple meaning.

Here we conclude with the resurrection and the final judgment of all. At this point, Christ offers up the fullness of the kingdom back to the father and welcomes the saints into the kingdom of their Father prepared from the foundation of the earth. The remaining two chapters in Revelation are not speaking about the events that happen next as so many say. The reality is the bible shares precious little about what happens after Christ delivers the kingdom to his Father, but we can know with joy that we should ever be with him.

Before I conclude this chapter, I want to speak briefly on Revelation 21 and part of 22. In these, we see the Holy City is described as coming down to earth and that the spiritual state of people is identical to the spiritual reality of the New Covenant. Keep in mind we saw this same holy city already on earth in Revelation 20 being surrounded by Satan. There is a reason for this.

I believe that Revelation 20 is giving us a prophetic overview of how world history will unfold because of the events described earlier in Revelation. As with the teachings, parables, and sayings of Christ and his apostles we saw that this period ends when Christ comes back, resurrecting the dead and judging the world. Then what we are seeing in Revelations 21 and 22 is John stepping back and filling in some more details about the holy city and the spiritual reality of the New Covenant reign of Christ and the saints.

Many people are taught that Revelations 21 and 22 is describing events that take place after the final judgment that Revelation 20 concluded with, but this is not so. Rather chapters 21 and part of 22, are giving added details to the New Testament state after the harlot was destroyed and how it was being presented or delivered to the earth.

We can know this as John ends up describing the New Jerusalem, as being a great city and uses similar language to descriptions of the Temple of the New Covenant.

Revelation 21:3: And I heard a great voice out of heaven saying, Behold, the tabernacle (dwelling place/temple) of God *is* with men, and he will dwell with them, and they shall be his people, and God himself shall be with them, *and be* their God.

This of course is the exact thing that was prophecied about the temple that would be in believers under the New Covenant see Ezekiel 37:27, Zechariah 6:12-13, and 1 Corinthians 3:16. In the New Testament Paul spoke about this heavenly city being above in heaven (Galatians 4:26) and was a reality we had here on the earth by faith. Revelation is revealing that this heavenly city or temple is now being brought to the earth after the events of Revelation are over. The Revelation was the Day of the Lord against the harlot of Jerusalem in 70 A.D. now that the old had been done away with the new is being presented on the earth.

John goes on to say that this Holy City is also the Lamb's Wife meaning it is the bride of Christ (this is said in Revelation 21:2,9. We know that the Church is the bride and she is already on the earth, but until the harlot was removed she was hidden from the earth. Compare this description of the Holy City to what Paul declares about the temple:

Revelation 21:14: And the wall of the city had twelve foundations, and in them the names of the twelve apostles of the Lamb.

This holy city had the twelve apostles as a foundation, Paul says this same thing about the temple all believers are a part of:

Ephesians 2:20-22: And are built upon the foundation of the apostles and prophets, Jesus Christ himself being the chief corner *stone*; 21. In whom all the building fitly framed together groweth unto an holy temple in the Lord: 22. In whom ye also are builded together for an habitation of God through the Spirit.

We also see the same language used in Revelation 21 as we saw in Isaiah 65. Both speak of a new heaven and new earth and the state of the world under the reign of the Messiah. This is of course not speaking of literal new heaven and earth, though there may be one, but rather the reality of the New Covenant and the fullness of the gospel. We can know this as in both accounts it is described that people will still die and that sinners will be outside of the city. Once Christ comes there will be no more sinners, no more death, or even nations.

We see this reality declared as if it already was in both Isaiah 65 and Revelation 21-22 yet not seen fully on earth yet. Remember the duel reality. In heaven, the fullness of the kingdom is already true, and one day the kingdom will also be true on earth. That is why it was called Christ's kingdom when Jesus returned for the harvest. The goal of Christ's rule is to manifest the fullness of the Gospel on the earth before he returns in victory. Jesus told us this would be a slow process through parables and sayings.

To help clarify some of this further let's step back from Revelation for a moment.

Paul says that all Christians are born from the heavenly Jerusalem now:

Galatians 4:26: But Jerusalem which is above is free, which is the mother of us all.

This is the same city that Abraham and the prophets of old looked forward to:

Hebrews 11:10: For he looked for a city which hath foundations, whose builder and maker *is* God.

This city is a metaphor for the New Covenant:

Galatians 4:24-25: Which things (Agar and Sarah) are an allegory: for these are the two covenants; the one from the mount Sinai, which gendereth to bondage, which is Agar. 25. For this Agar is mount Sinai in Arabia, and answereth to Jerusalem which now is (Physical Jerusalem and the Old Covenant), and is in bondage with her children. 26. But Jerusalem which is above (this being the spiritual New Jerusalem and the New Covenant) is free, which is the mother of us all. (During Paul's time the Old Covenant Jerusalem was still standing so the heavenly promise of the New Covenant Jerusalem was not yet able to manifest in full glory on the earth which is why it was said to be in heaven.)

So these cities Earthly Jerusalem and Heavenly Jerusalem were symbolic of the old and new Covenants. As we all should know, the New Jerusalem or New Covenant has been a part of all Christians from their foundations, but it was hidden from the earth—save in the hearts of the saints, even in the time of the Old Testament as this was the same city Abraham looked for— until the earthly Jerusalem was destroyed then it was presented to the earth as the only city of God. What Revelation 21 is doing is revealing what this New Jerusalem is:

Revelation 21:1-2: 1. And I saw a new heaven (New Covenant) and a new earth (earthy kingdom meaning Christianity): for the first heaven (Old Covenant) and the first earth (earthly Jerusalem) were passed away; and there was no more sea (Sea is a reference to Gentile nations, Isaiah 17:12, 60:5, Revelation 17:12-18, etc show this. This shows that in the New Covenant there are no more divisions of nations as we are all one in Christ.). And I John saw the holy city (this is the same holy city that John said was surrounded by Satan in the last chapter yet here in chapter 21 he speaks as if it is just now coming. This helps to show that this chapter is declaring more truth about the overview of events given in chapter 20. Chapter 21 here is explaining what the holy city is, and chapter 22 adds what the spiritual life in the city will be like this is all symbolic of the New Covenant), new Jerusalem, coming down from God out of heaven, prepared as a bride adorned for her husband (Recall that we saw already how the bride was wed to the husband on the Day of the Lord and pictured in the judgment that was given to the saints. The Revelation was written before the Day of the Lord and is here prophesying that the bride is being presented to the world after the Day of the Lord. That is why all of these events are passed to us, but it was a revelation to the early churches of what will be after the harlot was removed).

To further help understand that these events are just adding details about the holy city, notice how John is shown the bride after the harlot is destroyed as having made herself ready before the 1,000-year reign is shown:

Revelation 19:7 Let us be glad and rejoice, and give honour to him: for the marriage of the Lamb is come, and his wife (the Church) hath made herself ready.

This is declared right after Jerusalem (the harlot, and mystery of Babylon) is judged. This is the exact same thing we saw earlier in our study when looking at the marriage parables, the parable of the talents, and the judgment of the saints. This is the same thing that the 1,000-year reign is all about, that's why these things all go hand in hand. John also calls the New Jerusalem, that holy city, the bride.

Revelation 21:2: And I John saw the holy city, new Jerusalem, coming down from God out of heaven, prepared as a bride adorned for her husband.

This might sound slightly confusing so let me try to explain it better. There is only one bride of Christ which is the Church, it is also called the New Jerusalem which is the New Covenant. They are linked together because just as the old bride (Jerusalem) was the steward of the Old Covenant, the new bride (the Church) is a steward of the New Covenant.

What John is revealing in Chapters 21 and 22 is that God, having done away with the harlot (Jerusalem of old), has taken a new bride (Christianity/the New Jerusalem) and is declaring her to the world. This New Jerusalem was already true in heaven but was made clear upon the earth when Christ announced her after the Day of the Lord. We see this bride manifesting more and more on the earth as the years go by. As long as Satan remains bound and not judged, there will be great opposition to the work of the gospel in the world. This opposition helps us grow and perfect the Church.

This may seem confusing why John would be writing chapters 21 and 22 to add clarity to something he already spoke about, but this is actually a common practice in Jewish writing and is sometimes called Jewish poetry. The best example I can give you of this comes from Genisis.

Think of the creation account in Genesis. In it, God declares an overview of creation in chapter one, then in chapter two he goes back and adds greater detail to what happened on the sixth day with the creation of man. Think of chapter 20 as the account of the events that will happen during the reign of the Messiah after the Bride has been declared to the world, which is our current and future state that will end in the Second Coming. Chapters 21 and 22 are added details of what the spiritual state of the New Jerusalem will be like during that time; the fullness of which will be seen just before Jesus returns.

This is actually revealed in chapter 21 look at this:

Revelation 21:10: And he (the angel giving John the vision) carried me away in the spirit to a great and high mountain (this is the mountain of the New Covenant), and shewed me that great city, the holy Jerusalem, descending out of heaven from God. (Again symbolic of it being presented or declare to the world after the harlot was removed)

Remember Daniel:

Daniel 2:35: Then was the iron, the clay, the brass, the silver, and the gold, broken to pieces together, and became like the chaff of the summer threshingfloors; and the wind carried them away, that no place was found for them: and the stone that smote the image became a great mountain (this is the same great mountain that the New Jerusalem sits on. It purpose is to), and filled the whole earth. (This is exactly what must happen before Christ returns in victory)

I have found it amazing that the view I have just presented has elements of all the major views on Revelation. This was not done intentionally. We see an overview of history as the Historicist, we see a future restoration of the Jews as the Futurist, we see a possible final antichrist (Gog and Magog of Revelation) as some Amillennialists and Futurists, we see the 1,000 years being allegorical and not literal, and we see Christ return at the end of it all as the Postmillenialists in great power and glory as a victorious king. Lastly, some points should be taken spiritually and not literally as the idealist sees them. This should not be shocking. Satan is the father of all lies and divisions in the Church. The best lies have elements of the truth, what better way to divide the Church than to give each a portion of twisted truth with which to beat the others over the head.

I cannot claim to have a perfect understanding of the events we have looked at in this chapter. I am but a man and I will be wrong about many things, but I hope that what I have presented gives all my brothers and sisters hope in a glorious and victorious Savior. I believe that the understanding I presented here is the best view, not because I developed it, but because this is the only view that is also consistent in every point to the foundations laid down before us by Jesus and his Apostles. May we all look to the glorious future of our victorious King as we pray with power and faith, "Father thy kingdom come, thy will be done, in earth as it is in heaven."

For this is the tower of Ture-hope: the promise is of a victorious gospel, king, and Church.

CHAPTER SIXTEEN

The Origin of False-hope

"The idea of preaching the gospel to all nations alike, regardless of nationality, of internal divisions as to rank and color, complexion and religion, constituted the beginning of a new era in history. You cannot preach the gospel in its purity over the world, without proclaiming the doctrine of civil and religious liberty,--without overthrowing the barriers reared between nations and clans and classes of men,--without ultimately undermining the thrones of despots, and breaking off the shackles of slavery,--without making men everywhere free."

ALBERT BARNES 1798-1870, AMERICAN THEOLOGIAN.

I open this closing chapter with a question I asked near the beginning of this book. Having now seen and considered many of the testimonies of Jesus, and his apostles concerning the Second Coming of Christ, and having looked at several passages of scriptures that have been so manipulated by False-hope, was John Nelson Darby correct in his views? I realize this work was not a complete rebuttal of the modern views of eschatology nor was it meant to be. I have no desire to participate in an endless debate that profits nothing and stirs up bitterness and hate. My goal was to combat False-hope and I pray I have been successful in the areas I fought him in. If False-hope is cast down then the modern views will follow.

If I have correctly presented this book, many people will be left with many questions, and I can by no means answer them all in this closing chapter. I hope to write future books that will delve deeper into many of the topics I have only briefly touched on or mentioned in the work. The most critical question that I *do* seek to answer in this chapter, however, is one I hope all of you will have. That is: How did False-hope take the tower of True-hope and deceive so many Evangelical Churches through the false prophet John Nelson Darby?

So how did False-hope become so popular if less than 200 years ago it was mocked and scoffed at as the radical teachings of a fringe cult? This may seem like a straightforward question, but it, unfortunately, does not have a straightforward answer. A great many events came together in a perfect storm that allowed it all to take place. This was by design and we must first take into account the fact that there is a real tangible enemy that is actively making war against the people of God:

Ephesians 6:12: For we wrestle not against flesh and blood, but against principalities, against powers, against the <u>rulers of the darkness of this world</u>, against spiritual wickedness in high *places.*

Many of the modern heresies we see in churches today began around the same time and I do not think this was an accident. If we look at the Church during this time, by and large, it has never been more glorious. We had many great revivals here in America with the first and second Great Awakenings, we had the Welsh Revival sweeping the lands across the sea and many saw the first glimpses of what the kingdom might look like on the earth. Seeing all of this, I think Satan took a council of war from his shackled prison and began assaulting the Church from every angle he could be it political, spiritual, or critical.

Unfortunately, this took the Church mostly by surprise. I could go down a list of examples, but here is one of the best. When Evolution began to become more and more popular, the Church was ill-prepared to combat it. That's because until that point few even questioned the Creation accounts of Genesis.

This was a good thing believe it or not. Until these assaults, Churches were not even aware of such weaknesses and have since begun to go on the offensive. In the case of our example with Evolution, many great men of God today can easily stand toe to toe with evolutionists and put them to shame whereas before it was the opposite. I believe the same will go for all the heresies if we are willing to admit we had faults and address, and correct them.

Satan was/is terrified that the Church was beginning to believe, and step into the fact that it really was the chosen generation, royal priesthood, and ambassadors spreading the kingdom that they truly were. The Church was making great progress destroying his forces, so Satan used his favorite tactics to blur the glory of truth about the kingdom of God.

His favored tactics are deception, imitation, and infiltration. He imitated the religion by causing false religions to rise (Evolution, Mormonism, Jehovah's Witnesses, Freemason, and other such false cults and denominations) he then imitated the kingdom by raising up, (communism, socialism, and marxism), and he infiltrated churches by bringing snakes into the Church's pulpits. This also allowed his third favored tactic of deception. The attacks allowed good godly men to fall into deceptions by playing off their fallen nature and their hopes and fears.

Again, I do not believe anything happens by accident or coincidence. The spiritual world has a great impact on the physical. Our enemies Satan, his devils, and the spirit of antichrist, are working hard in the world. On the flip side so is Christ and his Kingdom. Paul addresses this truth in the above passage. The enemy always seeks to kill, steal, and destroy (John 10:10).

Rarely in this war does Satan appear as the devilish man most make him out to be. Do not get me wrong the wickedness of this world is often fueled by devils, and Satan can accomplish much evil through the unregenerate man. However, he does his greatest evil and harm to the world when he appears as an angel of light and his minions infiltrate the Church of God, and when he builds churches rather than destroys them. Unlike modern movies and myth's about Satan and demons running away when a bible is pulled out, or being unable to step on hollowed/sacred ground—all of which is utter nonsense— the truth is, many of Satan's children are in churches and many demons know the bible far better than most Christians!

2 Corinthians 11:12-14: But what I do, that I will do, (This is a

reference to Paul boasting in Christ and what our Lord has done) that I may cut off occasion from them which desire occasion; that wherein they glory, they may be found even as we. (Paul is attacking the boasting, pride, and hypocrisy of false teachers and prophets. Paul is teaching what he is in this chapter to expose these snakes).

13. For such *are* false apostles, deceitful workers, transforming themselves into the apostles of Christ.

14. And no marvel; for Satan himself is transformed into an angel of light.

This is a pretty clear warning that Satan's greatest attacks are infiltration, imitation, and deception. This truth is not at all new. Listen to what Jesus said to the religious leaders of the Jews these same principles can apply to many of the so-called pastors of certain churches:

John 8:43-44: Why do ye not understand my speech? *even* because ye cannot hear my word.

44. Ye are of *your* father the devil, and the lusts of your father ye will do. He was a murderer from the beginning, and abode not in the truth, because there is no truth in him. When he speaketh a lie, he speaketh of his own: for he is a liar, and the father of it.

If these infiltrators and subverters of the faith will do the works of their father, Satan, then we can learn several things from these passages:

Satan's children infiltrate and appear as children of God.

They are boasters.

They are hypocrites.

They are liars.

They appear good and righteous.

They remain not in the truth, meaning they deny sound doctrine and the truth of the word of God, these are the heretics.

Can be godly men deceived by Satan.

With all this said, to understand how this false teaching came into the Church we have to understand a real enemy is pulling the strings of the events to deceive, pervert, and cripple the Lord's people. He can murder the flock without killing a single one of us in the flesh if he kills the truth and snuffs out the light of the gospel. Meaning we become unsaved sinners with religious clothing on the outside and not saving faith and a born-again soul on the inside. This has always been Satan's greatest perversion of truth and favored tactic.

Not only can the enemy of our soul use unsaved people, both religious and non-religious, he can also use saved people that are not walking by the Spirit. We have many great examples of this, but one of the best is with the Apostle Peter. We have already looked at this passage but let us glean some more truth from it:

Mark 8:31-33: And he (Jesus) began to teach them, that the Son of man must suffer many things, and be rejected of the elders, and *of* the chief priests, and scribes, and be killed, and after three days rise again.

32. And he spake that saying openly. And Peter took him, and began to rebuke him.

33. But when he had turned about and looked on his disciples, he rebuked Peter, saying, Get thee behind me, <u>Satan:</u> for thou savourest (love/delight not in) not the things that be of God, but the things that be of men.

Without trying to be too harsh on Peter, Jesus calls him Satan when Peter rebukes what God is saying. Jesus' rebuke was good, as we should never question the word of God. However, we need to note that Satan took the occasion to take advantage of the emotional state of Peter, who was not in the spirit but in the flesh, and at that moment Satan was able to use Peter for his own evil purposes though Peter was a saved man.

Remember deception begins with not loving the truth and trying to alter it to match our own desires. Peter loved Jesus and didn't want him to suffer. Was this desire good? In itself, it was not evil, but when that love took occasion to challenge the word and attack the savior for his words it became sin. A very similar thing began to happen that fueled the deception of False-hope in the 1800s.

As we saw in the last chapter, the bible is pretty clear that the Jews will one day be restored to Christ and I believe also be given back their land. I would that this day comes sooner than later. Many Christians throughout the centuries have had great burdens and desires to see the Jews come back to the Lord and wanted to see them restored. This is not bad on its own, but Satan developed Zionism that perverted this desire and it became evil. Zionism is both a political and religious agenda that was birthed and is now fueled by False-hope. Rather than see the Jews come back to Christ first, Zionism twisted it around to give the land back first, something God only ever promised to do when the Jews repented. Zionism further made it an effort on man's part to do what God himself said *HE* would do.

This movement began in earnest in Great Britain, the same area where False-hope was born. This eventually resulted in the Balfour Declaration, which was a declaration from the British government that they would support the restoration of national Israel during WW1. This goal was not achieved until after the second world war, but it eventually led to the establishment of the Modern State of Israel not based on the bible, or repentance in Christ, but on Zionism itself.

To this day, it is against the law to openly convert Jews to Christianity in Israel. The religious arm of Zionism wants to rebuild the temple and the levitical priesthood, something that will never happen, while the political arms wants to create a world power. Together both branches of Zionism seek to rebuild greater Israel and bring back the Jews from the nations on their own without a focus on God. This of course does not line up with the biblical promise of what God said he would do.

So how does False-hope play into this? To take full advantage of Zionism, Satan had to twist the view of the Church, about itself, Israel concerning Israel, and the kingdom. Satan needed the Church to stop realizing the Kingdom of Christ was already on the earth inside of them, and that Christ already ruled from David's throne in heaven through his Church. Satan needed the Church to stop believing that they were the covenant people of God (Israel) and believe that the Jews themselves were still a covenant people, and the kingdom and Christ's reign would all be in the future and would be manifested in the Zionist state of modern Israel. So he first had to separate the Church from Israel and the kingdom. He did this through False-hope and the rapture.

When all these twisted doctrines began to first be taught many giants in the faith (like Charles Spurgeon) stood against it. Unfortunately, they did not prepare for the fact that Satan's plan would be so effective. Because the Church was ill-prepared to challenge this deception, like with Evolution, once the voices of the Christian giants died there was no foundation laid to keep the errors from being accepted with their passing.

At this point, after the giants of the faith passed, the second phase of Satan's attack plan began to swing into play, the political systems he established led to the World Wars and the establishment of the modern state of Israel. Satan then used his infiltrated pastors to preach these events, based on False-hope's teachings, as if they were a fulfillment of prophecy. This plan was very effective and eventually led to the near utter deception over the Evangelical Church that remains to this day.

All of this is something God allowed to happen for his own purpose. Just like Evolution, Christ is using this attack to strengthen and purify his Church.

This is the overview of what happened, now let's step back and look at how it came into the Church. As we go forward I will not accuse any of the people mentioned as being Infiltrators or simply Deceived Saints. I believe there is a mixture of both and I am not worthy to condemn any of them. God knows which were which, and in the end, it doesn't matter as the damage has been done. Now is not the time to pass blame it is time for us to recognize it, confess it to God, repent, and begin to fix it.

As I expressed in the first chapter, John Nelson Darby was the first to begin teaching these doctrines. There is a lot of evidence that he got these teachings from the occult practices that his family often partook in. His uncle Admiral Henry D'Esterre Darby owned what is still considered one of the most haunted castles in Leap Ireland. Originally built by the O'Bannon clan in 1250 A.D., this castle eventually passed to the Darby's. John Darby's sister-in-law, Mildred Darby, openly admitted to communing with a goat-like demon during seances that were regularly held in the castle. She originally wrote of their experiences under the pen name of Andrew Merry in a book originally titled, "The House of Horrors." You can still find this book under the modern title, "Leap Castle The House of Horrors: The Most Haunted Castle in Ireland," by Mildred Darby on amazon and other book stores.

In the book, she changed some of the names to protect the family, but she later claimed it was all based on real events. Modern excavations have even found a torture chamber inside the chapel of this castle, which is now called the "Bloody Chapel." The Excavations revealed hundreds of bodies including someone who had been killed in it during the time the Darbys lived there. As far as I know, no accusations of foul play have ever been brought against the Darbys, so I am not accusing them of any. I am simply pointing out that there were many occult and questionable actions taking place in the castle while they lived there.

I cannot definitely prove that this is where John Darby got his teachings from, but he did spend a considerable time there when he was a youth. Years later, he would leave the Anglican Church, of which he had become a pastor, and joined the Plymouth Brethren and started teaching what would become Dispensationalism. Darby's writings themselves are filled with occult references that are not found in the bible but are identical to the New Age, and Freemason movements. Terms like: Heavenly Architect, The Absolute, The Coming One, The Divine Mind, Divine Intelligence, Energy of Faith, Energy of Love, and the Secret Wisdom of God. All these and more fill his writings and printed sermons. There are many more examples, but these terms are New Age, Kaballah, Freemasonry, and not biblical.

That aside, if we look at the fruit that has come from his teachings we can see it had a rotten source.

However, left on its own, Dispensationalism would never have gotten off the ground without the aid of a few men. These were Clarence Larkin, C. I. Scofield, and D.L. Moody. There were a great many others, but these were by far the most famous.

Darby's teachings were extremely complicated, but Clarence Larkin, a follower of Darby, made them less so with elaborate and intricate prophecy charts, illustrations, and maps that are still widely used today. In fact, if you have ever gone to a seminar or read a book and they showed end times charts, drawings, or maps, then most likely, they came from or were based on Larkin's work. Larkin marketed Dispensationalism in his famous book, "Dispensational Truth," written in 1918 which helped the common man understand how all the complicated parts of Dispensationalism worked.

C.I. Scofield took Darby's notes and published them in his famous study bible, the Scofield Reference Bible in 1909 as if they were his own ideas. Scofield was a well-known charlatan and any objective study of his life would show that he was not a godly man, nor was he a doctor as most people claim him to be.

His study bible was handed out by the millions all over the country and for free in seminary schools all around the world and especially in America through organizations like the Moody Bible Institute. This was one of the first real study bibles since perhaps the Geneva Bible, which was published hundreds of years before. Up to this point, most people relied on commentaries to help study the bible or simply just read the bible. The Scofield notes interpreted the bible with a Dispensational view that pointed at every opportunity to False-hope.

The funding for this work was made possible by an openly Zionist lawyer who also worked for the Rothchilds who were instrumental in organizing and funding the Zionist movement at this time. This man's name was Samuel Untermeyer. Scofield and Untermeyer were introduced to each other in the prestigious gentleman's club called the Lotus Club in New York City by Mark Twain of all people.

Satan desired to see the Zionist movement infiltrate the Evangelical Churches. He realized that if he could get the Evangelical Churches to support Zionism, then the power of the United States would follow as the Evangelical movement held great political power over the nation. This seemingly innocent meeting was the very thing that helped to achieve this vision, and soon the Evangelical Church would be the main voice of Zionism in America. This is another tactic that worked, as even to this day, most Evangelical Churches support the most Zionistic candidate. This has led to spiritual blindness in many churches.

D.L. Moody was perhaps the greatest help in propagating the False-hope teachings of Darby. As I stated before, Moody first heard the teachings when he visited England and became fascinated with the concepts of the rapture and Zionism. Both of these he would bring into his own teachings and use them as a foundation for his Moody Bible Institute. Yet in my opinion, the greatest two things Moody did to make False-hope famous was starting the "Prophecy Conferences" that sought to tie all modern events to something in the bible, an act that still is a staple for adherents of False-hope to this very day. The second thing

Moody did was train up an entire generation of new pastors who knew nothing but the Dispensational False-hope view of the bible. Over time, most bible colleges would adopt this view as well.

For many, Moody and Scofield are considered nearly sacred and the very implication that they were not saints is grounds for war in some churches. Do not think I am saying they did this purposefully, they may have, or they may also have just been deceived. I cannot claim to know their hearts nor motives God knows, but it cannot be avoided that without these two men, John Darby's False-hope views would never have become what they are today.

These three men laid the groundwork, but the modern views would still not catch on until after WW2 and the establishment of the modern State of Israel which was the culmination of many plans diverging into one. The enemy had already laid the careful idea through Moody, Scofield, and the teachings of False-hope that when Israel became a nation it would fulfill prophecy, something that both the political and religious arms of Zionism made sure would happen.

WW2 would also change the world's outlook on life. Many began to see the end of the world as a very real possibility. False-hope would take advantage of this and use some of the prophetic apocalyptic languages of Revelation to paint the picture of nuclear wars and other fearful events. The world was ready to receive the idea of a secret rapture that could take them away from this crazy world that was no longer pleasant to live in. They could easily imagine a Hitler-like figure being the antichrist and for the first time since False-hope came around this concept of a one-world government leader no longer seemed far-fetched. But it was in the Cold War Era that this idea began to explode in all-new popularity. The tangible threat of another world war was the perfect environment for False-hope to thrive in.

This started an avalanche of books, movies, radio programs, and television shows all built around Zionism, the rapture, and False-hope which took the entire world by storm. Some of the bigger titles which had the greatest impact would be: "The Late Great Planet Earth," both the film and book originally written by Hal Lindsey in 1970. "A Theif in the Night," a very popular film about the rapture made in 1972. "Left

Behind," both the films and books originally made by Tim LaHaye and Jerry B. Jenkins in 1995. This is not to mention the innumerable books written by authors predicting the rapture and end of the world between 1970-2000.

Rather than the Jews coming to Christ and the Church beginning to flourish for such a thing, the exact opposite began to happen. Rather than having a Christ-centered, Gospel-driven eschatology that focused on Christ and the Church, we began to have a rapture and antichrist-centered eschatology that focused on Israel.

We then saw an immediate downturn in morality, holiness, and overall Church power and authority everywhere this False-hope antichrist system infiltrated both inside and out of the Church. This was of course the exact purpose it was designed by Satan to do. Satan's plan of blinding and bringing spiritual decay and bondage to the Church had worked. This is the result of judgment from God for elevating and worshiping antichrist rather than God. Remember when we love not the truth, God, as a punishment, will give us over to strong delusions so that we will believe a lie. Let us just look at the U.S. as it is the country of my birth as an example.

Israel became a Nation in 1948. America became its strongest ally and supporter. The Evangelical Churches made sure these policies wouldn't change unless the Church repents. They continue to propagate the Zionistic agenda in Churches and politics on both sides of the aisle. They claim that America and the Church are blessed, and our nation is blessed all because we are supporting Israel. If we do not support them, they say, God will curse us. This teaching came from Fale-hope.

I am not saying it's wrong to support a nation politically on its own, specifically, I am referring to the Church supporting, blessing, and encouraging the antichrist system by essentially propagating worship of anything to do with Israel, the temple, and False-hope. Because the Church has become so entwined in the nation's politics when God begins to judge the Church the nation follows. The Church is to be the light shining truth into a nation and acts like its moral compass pointing them to Christ, but now that compass points to antichrist and social agendas. I am not saying Christians should not be involved in government, we need more God-fearing Christians in our government, but it is wrong when the agendas they bring do not support the Kingdom of Christ but the kingdoms of this world and the antichrist systems.

So let's test these modern preachers who claim that the Church and by proxy America is being blessed by God for our support of Israel and False-hope. Let us look at just how blessed we have been:

- The false "Prosperity Gospel" began in 1950.
- In 1954 The U.S. established the 501c3 non-profit status for churches which took the autonomy away from the Churches and put them under the State. As long as churches complied they would be tax-exempt. (Meaning money was more important than the headship and provision of Christ)
- In 1960 Evolution began to be taught in schools.
- In 1963 Bible reading and prayer were banned in schools. Communism, Socialism, and Evolution began to take their place. Immediately there was a 500% increase in drug abuse, bullying, and teenage pregnancies.
- In the 1970s the sexual revolution took place.
- In 1973 Abortion became legalized, the sanctity of life was abolished.
- Also in 1973 pornography became legally available in the U.S. as a form of "art" and legally protected as a "freedom of speech."
- The 1980s saw a generation of sex, drugs, and rock' n' roll.
- The 1990s saw the family home beginning to be broken up.
- The 2000s saw a breakdown of marriage and biblical values. Divorce rates hit an all-time high.
- By 2012 same-sex marriage was legalized. Since then there has been a relentless attack on sexuality, children, and gender through the demonic LGBTQ+ movement. Even Christians are embracing this demonic movement today.
- In 2018, for the first time in U.S. history, more churches were closing in the U.S. than opening.

- Riots, Social Justice, "wokness," and communistic principles have all replaced biblical values and in the last few years they have taken on a demonic power in America.
- 2020 saw a voluntary closing of thousands of churches for a virus that is about as harmful as the flu. The tyranny and corruption of America are nearing their greatest height and our day of the Lord, I fear, is near at hand.
- Today America is in greater debt and in danger of economic and civil collapse more so than at any other time since the Civil War.

Surely America has been blessed these last 7o+ years since we began to listen to these modern preachers!

Matthew 7:15-17: Beware of false prophets (preachers, this warning is also against their teachings), which come to you in sheep's clothing (they appear as innocent, well-meaning Christians), but inwardly they are ravening wolves (they are enemies that seek to destroy and devour you). 16. Ye shall know them by their fruits (by the things their lives and teachings produce in people). Do men gather grapes of thorns, or figs of thistles? 17. Even so every good tree bringeth forth good fruit (if the source is good then what it produces will bring liberty, truth, and life); but a corrupt tree bringeth forth evil fruit (things that come from a corrupt source always produce death, lies, and bondage).

I ask, what type of tree is False-hope? What type of tree is the giant of Zionism, the father of False-hope? What type of tree was John Nelson Darby the prophet of False-hope? You shall know them by their fruits. The above list gives you a glimpse of the fruits these things have produced in our nation. In no way have we benefitted as a society by embracing these things.

I could add an entire list that is focused just on the Church and its wretched state. I will not do so, rather I ask you to look objectively at Christianity and see with your own eyes what has happened to her since we began embracing these rotting trees. Can anyone that does this say, in truth, that in any way we have become <u>more</u> godly, <u>more</u> holy, <u>more</u> spiritual, and <u>more</u> like Christ since we have adopted these trees? I certainly cannot. I pray it grieves your heart, as it surely must grieve our Savour.

A hundred things could be added to this list, but the point should be clear, America, and the Church has been gradually falling further and further away from God as it embraces more and more of the poison of False-hope. If False-hope preachers are correct the exact opposite should be happening. We should be more prosperous now than we have ever been, but we are now more morally, spiritually, economically, and socially bankrupt than ever before. That is because it is an antichrist system that we have bought into. We shall know a false prophet by its fruit.

This same pattern of decline has happened in the entire western world, which used to be an example of Christian values, but since they have begun to embrace this antichrist system the entire west is falling.

Entire denominations are being swept into these false lies embracing immortality and evil in a way not seen since the Dark Ages. Christians are becoming Judaized and falling under a curse, this bleeds into the entire nation. Today it is antiemetic to be an antizionist, but to be a Zionist one must become Antichrist for the Zionist agenda is not of God but Satan.

Let me be clear, I am not promoting hatred towards the Jews, I would denounce anyone who promotes hatred towards any people group/ethnic group regardless of their views. However, the bible tells us to preach the truth and teach the word in season and out of season. Meaning when it is popular and when it is not. That does not mean I wish them harm or violence. I just seek to see their views changed so they may know the glory of Christ

I am simply saying that the Zionistic system that False-hope has created is evil, and the Church cannot support it because it is antichrist. Just as I say False-hope the giant is evil, that does not mean my enemies are those caught in its grip. I want to see liberty from the bondage of falsehood for all people and to do that falsehood has to be exposed so that people can turn to truth in Christ. This should be done in love, not violence.

This is the error I pray this little book will help expose and if the Lord will's, I pray it will be used to help dismantle this beastly antichrist abomination that False-hope, and by extension, most of evangelicalism have helped create. The Church is facing a time where we must learn to stand. Our prosperity brought in complacency that Satan took advantage of. Christ is preparing us to fight with the weapons of faith. A cry is sounding all across this land for those who would stand and fight for the Lord. Jesus seeks a generation who will turn away from the falsehood and turn back to the purity of the faith. If we but stand and march the Lord will drive out the enemies from the land.

Will you answer the call?

Notes

Notes

Notes

Notes

Notes

Notes

Notes